The Legacy of
Martin Luther King, Jr.

The Legacy of

Martin Luther

Lewis V. Baldwin

with

Rufus Burrow, Jr.,

Barbara A. Holmes,

and Susan Holmes Winfield

Foreword by Clayborne Carson

King, Jr.

The Boundaries
of Law,
Politics,
and Religion

University of Notre Dame Press
Notre Dame, Indiana

Manufactured in the United States of America

*A record of the Library of Congress Cataloging-in-Publication Data
is available upon request from the Library of Congress.*

∞ *This book is printed on acid-free paper.*

For Today's
Keepers of the Dream

Contents

Acknowledgments

The discussion that resulted in this volume occurred at the annual meeting of the American Academy of Religion in Orlando, Florida, in November 1998. Roger D. Hatch and I were part of a "Church-State Studies Group" session that addressed the theme "Martin Luther King, Jr.: The Dream Thirty Years After." Inspired by the highly positive responses from the audience, we agreed to make our papers part of a book-length manuscript that explores in great depth the intersection of law, politics, religion, and morality in King's thought and praxis. We are grateful for the encouragement of those who heard our presentations at the AAR meeting, and especially those who suggested that we might consider publishing them in some form.

The Vanderbilt University Research Council provided grants that contributed to the completion of most of the chapters in this work. We express our deepest gratitude to Russell Hamilton, the director of this council, for his support. He has never hesitated to provide grant assistance for research and scholarship on Martin Luther King, Jr., and the modern civil rights movement.

Rufus Burrow, Jr., Professor of Theological Social Ethics at Christian Theological Seminary in Indianapolis, is due a special thanks for reading the chapters and making numerous suggestions for improving the work. In addition to contributing chapter 5, he provided rich ideas and insights that have been incorporated into chapters 1, 2, 3, and 6. Dr. Burrow's careful and critical reading of major portions of the work, and especially his thoughtful editing and helpful suggestions, have contributed enormously to the freshness and the appeal of this volume.

Professor Roger Hatch of Central Michigan University was equally helpful in this regard. The author of an impressive work on the role of the church in the political life of Jesse Jackson, this religion scholar read the entire manuscript, raised hard questions, and made numerous suggestions for improvement. Dr. Hatch also graciously accepted our invitation to write the epilogue.

Dr. Larry J. Griffin, a professor of sociology and political science at Vanderbilt University, read chapter 1 and provided detailed and penetrating criticism while referring us to sources that we had overlooked. A colleague widely known for his scholarship in southern studies, Dr. Griffin offered insights and encouragement that meant more than we, as we look back on that time, can repay.

We are also highly indebted to Jeffrey Gainey, the associate director of the University of Notre Dame Press, for his encouragement and assistance. He remained excited and supportive even in those times when the completion of this project was delayed for one reason or another. More than anyone else, he helped make possible the publication of this manuscript.

We express our deep appreciation to Clayborne Carson, professor of history at Stamford University, for writing the Foreword. Through his outstanding contributions to the King Papers Project and his many publications, Dr. Carson has already earned a unique place among the interpreters of the civil rights movement.

Finally, all the contributors to this volume deserve special recognition and gratitude for their keen and perceptive treatments of Martin Luther King, Jr., in relationship to a range of issues. Representing various disciplines, they made *The Legacy of Martin Luther King, Jr.* an exciting and worthwhile endeavor.

Lewis V. Baldwin

Foreword

Among the unfortunate, unintended consequences of the national holiday honoring Martin Luther King, Jr., has been that he is now widely revered as a historical icon but less fully appreciated for his contributions as a spiritual and intellectual leader. Television and radio news programs often mark the holiday with sound bites from his best-known orations—the "I Have a Dream" address at the 1963 March on Washington or perhaps the "Mountaintop" peroration in Memphis on the night before his assassination—but they rarely play excerpts from speeches and sermons that contain more controversial political content, such as King's antiwar address in April 1967 at New York's Riverside Church. King is mainly honored for his role as an African-American civil rights leader rather than for his broader role as a critic of economic as well as racial injustice and as an influential proponent of world peace. His Gandhian message of nonviolent resistance is usually interpreted as a message intended for oppressed black people rather than for white people in positions of power. Annual celebrations of King tend to look to the past instead of the future, highlighting the remembrances of his contemporaries, rather than drawing attention to the ways in which young people are reinterpreting King's legacy in order to confront the injustices of the present.

One of the virtues of *The Legacy of Martin Luther King, Jr.*—and indeed of all of Lewis V. Baldwin's pioneering scholarly work on King—is that this broad-ranging, interdisciplinary collection of writings does justice to the breadth of King's legacy. The contributors honor King by treating his ideas seriously. No other published volume on King so successfully illuminates the varied implications of King's writings, public statements, and political activism. The essays thereby portray King as one of the twentieth century's seminal social critics. While revealing King's basic affirmation of traditional Christian beliefs and American democratic idealism, the essays also demonstrate that King challenged many of the dominant doctrines of his time. His single most important contribution to the African-American freedom struggles of the 1950s and 1960s was to link those struggles to preexisting and universal traditions of dissent and mass insurgency. He was both a grassroots protest leader working closely with other local activists and a visionary proponent of nonviolence whose influence extended throughout the world. He understood that civil rights campaigns in Montgomery, Birmingham, Selma, and other communities were related to national efforts to combat racial and economic injustice and to worldwide movements against colonialism and imperialism. As King commented during the Montgomery bus boycott, "The great struggle of the twentieth century has been between these exploited masses questing for freedom and the colonial powers seeking to maintain their domination."

The essays included in this volume reveal that King's influence and significance extend not only across national borders but across disciplinary boundaries as well. Baldwin, Rufus Burrow, Jr., Barbara A. Holmes, and Susan Holmes Winfield have made major contributions to the constantly expanding body of King scholarship. Their analyses build upon the previous work of historians, theologians, sociologists, political scientists, legal theorists, and rhetoricians who have produced more than one hundred doctoral dissertations and hundreds of scholarly articles on King's life and ideas. *The Legacy of Martin Luther King, Jr.,* also elaborates the portrait of King that has emerged from the research of my colleagues and myself at the Martin Luther King, Jr., Papers Project. The initial volumes of *The Papers of Martin Luther King, Jr.,* and the project's related publications demonstrate that King's eclectic, dissenting worldview was forged early in his life and was refined through extensive exposure to the ideas of other social critics and political activists. Although some scholars have suggested that late in his life King's concerns became broader and more radical, his worldview was in fact remarkably durable and consistent. Seventeen years before he launched the Poor People's campaign, while still a seminary student, he had acknowledged his "anti-capitalist feelings" in an autobiographical sketch that recalled his childhood questioning of his parents "about the numerous people standing in breadlines" during the Great Depression. While a graduate student at Boston University, he had told his future wife Coretta that a "society based on making all the money you can and ignoring people's needs is wrong." In a 1952 letter to her, he had brashly predicted that capitalism had "out-lived its usefulness," having produced "a system that takes necessities from the masses to give luxuries to the classes."

As the essays in this volume make clear, King's radicalism was firmly rooted in his religious convictions. He dissented from prevailing perspectives of American Christians and even from the views of most other black Baptists in the National Baptist Convention. Throughout the period of his public ministry, King faced strong criticisms from both black and white fundamentalists and evangelists. "In response to Christian conservatives who identified the capitalist ethic with Christian values," Baldwin observes, "King defined capitalism as largely unethical and un-Christian because it encourages unscrupulous competition, selfish ambition, and an excessive profit motive." During a period of Cold War political repression, King took considerable political risks by identifying himself as an advocate of social gospel Christianity. By demonstrating that King derived his distinctive ideas from traditional religious sources, Baldwin and his colleagues remind readers of the radical implications of politically engaged religious faith. "I didn't get my inspiration from Karl Marx," he once explained to his critics. "I got it from a man named Jesus, a Galilean saint who said he was anointed to heal the brokenhearted. He was anointed to deal with the problems of the poor."

By placing King's ideas in the context of modern social thought, the essays in *The Legacy of Martin Luther King, Jr.*, reveal that King's intellectual legacy is at once simple and complex. It is rooted in traditional Christian beliefs, yet it is also heretical. An advocate of older traditions of social justice activism, and a symbol of mass struggles initiated and sustained by others, King was also an enormously influential leader whose legacy continues to inspire contemporary movements for social change. His writings, speeches, and sermons reward sophisticated scholarly analysis of the kind presented in this book, but his essential message can be understood by people from all walks of life. A Nobel Peace laureate who accepted his award on behalf of the "unknown soldiers in the second great American Revolution," the epitaph that King suggested for himself was aptly down-to-earth: "Say I was a drum major for peace. I was a drum major for justice, and all the other shallow things will not matter."

CLAYBORNE CARSON

Introduction

This book is part of a broader effort by scholars in various fields to examine unexplored areas in the life, thought, and activism of Martin Luther King, Jr. More specifically, the book treats the range of ways in which law, politics, religion, and morality intersected in King's thinking and in his efforts to create a more democratic America and a more inclusive world.

King was the very embodiment of what Frederick L. Downing terms "the praxis tradition"—that tradition which refuses to separate religious faith and moral considerations from politics, legal matters, and social reformism.[1] Variously called "a religious genius," "a moving exemplar of American democratic religion," "a public theologian," "a moral leader," "a political liberal," and "a practitioner of creative civil disobedience," King represented an alliance between religion, morality, law, and politics that transcended church-state boundaries, and that permeated every facet of American life.[2] Moreover, the civil rights leader became a prophetic critic of those clergy and churches which chose to remain aloof from political struggle, and which insisted that an *apolitical* stance is more consistent with the biblical faith and Judeo-Christian traditions.

Serious studies of how King united moral-religious convictions and political activity are very rare. Prior to this publication, no major book-length manuscript had been written on the subject. This is unacceptable in view of King's own treatment of the subject in his books and essays.[3] Frank L. Morris's essay on the political policies and agenda of King, and Douglas Strum's essay on the political and legal significance of King's "Letter from the Birmingham City Jail" (1963), stand as important and insightful sources, but they fail to go beyond the usual, often cursory and obvious, discussions of how the civil rights leader articulated and embodied the role of religion and morality in democratic politics and lawmaking.

The Legacy of Martin Luther King, Jr. is designed to correct this glaring pattern of neglect or omission in King scholarship. Indeed, it is the first in-depth, interdisciplinary study of King's views on the roles that religion and morality ought to play not only in public debate concerning political choices and law, but also in efforts to create political and legal structures that are just and in line with the best traditions of participatory democracy.

Chapter 1 treats King as an advocate and promoter of the New South as a sociopolitical and economic ideal. Lewis V. Baldwin, an American church historian and a leading authority on King, places the civil rights leader in dialogue with generations of New South journalists, writers, and idealists, from Henry W. Grady, Atticus G. Haygood, Francis W. Dawson, and others in the late nineteenth century, to Booker T. Washington, W. J. Cash, and others in the early twentieth century, and to Lillian Smith, Ralph McGill, Harry Golden, and others in the 1950s and 1960s. King's views concerning the importance of increased industrial-urban development, advanced educational and economic opportunities, and transformed legal and political structures as necessary avenues to a New South are compared and contrasted with those of the other New South advocates. Some attention is also given to King's importance for New South idealists from the 1970s to the present.

This chapter ends with a discussion of King in relationship to what Charles R. Wilson calls "southern civil religion." In contrast to Wilson's image of King as one who stood in the tradition of a southern civil religion, Baldwin argues that the civil rights leader, while understanding the South's struggle with the politics of race in religious and theological terms, is best understood as a prophet of "American civil religion."[4] On this issue, Baldwin agrees with Robert N. Bellah, John D. Elder, and other scholars who have focused on King's application of biblical terminology and Christian rhetoric to the American national experience.[5] Baldwin concludes that King emerges more as a critic than a promoter of southern civil religion. The discussion here is essential to any clear understanding of how King united moral-religious principles with political activity in both the "southern" and "American" contexts.

Chapter 2 discusses King in conjunction with church-state issues. Special attention is devoted by Baldwin to King's developing attitude toward law and government, and to his clashes with black and white fundamentalists and evangelicals over the question of the moral responsibility of the Christian in an unjust state. King's view of the church as "the conscience of the state" is highlighted and contrasted with the perspectives of Bob Jones, Joseph H. Jackson, Billy Graham, and other conservative clergymen, who subscribed to the Apostle Paul's statements on obeying duly constituted authorities, and who insisted that King's political activities and civil disobedience could not be reconciled with biblical teachings and Christian morality.[6] The chapter closes with reflections on the various ways in which elements of the so-called Christian and political right have distorted and misrepresented King's legacy of ideas and struggle since his death.

Chapter 3 explores King's interest in and appeal to America's political traditions. Baldwin underscores King's often uncritical use of and appeal to founding documents such as the Declaration of Independence and the Constitution in his pursuit of the "American dream." Baldwin claims that for King the principles of freedom and the sacredness of human personality embodied in these documents were consistent with Judeo-Christian teachings, the cherished values of the black church, the Enlightenment ideals of Tolerance, Reason, and Natural Law, and the personal idealism of theologians and ethicists such as Edgar S. Brightman and L. Harold DeWolf.

The discussion shifts in the third chapter from King's appreciation for America's great documents of freedom to the question of his involvements with presidential politics and the nation's major political parties. King's struggles with Dwight D. Eisenhower, John F. Kennedy, and Lyndon B. Johnson over the question of the proper role of the federal government in the crusade for civil rights is examined in some detail. Baldwin also captures King's uneasiness with and distrust for the Democratic and Republican Parties, both of which had, in his estimation, long betrayed African Americans. The last part of the chapter treats King as "a political liberal" and "a consummate politician."[7] The contention is that the apostle of nonviolence put forth major political proposals and recommendations that are still relevant for contemporary America, and that he left a political legacy that remains meaningful for those who regard serious involvement in coalition and electoral politics as vital and necessary bridges to freedom.

Chapter 4 assesses King's role in reshaping American society and its system of jurisprudence. Written by Barbara A. Holmes, an accomplished attorney and a scholar in the field of ethics, and her sister, Judge Susan Holmes Winfield, who was appointed to the federal bench by President Ronald Reagan, this chapter focuses specifically on the effects of King's nonviolent strategy on the nation's judicial system. The various ways in which King applied the ethics of agape and nonviolence to societal structures and systemic injustice are emphasized. The civil rights leader's engagement with the American judiciary is set against the historical background of constitutional amendments and Supreme Court opinions in the *Dred Scott* case (1857), *Plessy v. Ferguson* (1896), and *Brown v. Board of Education* (1954). This chapter has broader significance for understanding America's historic use of law to define the citizenship status of its peoples.

In chapter 5, Rufus Burrow, Jr., a seminary professor with a broad knowledge of the intersection between ethics and law in King's thought, explains the civil rights leader's practice of judging just and unjust civil law and political policies by the more basic standards of objective moral law. The impact of the philosophy of personalism on King's thought at this level is carefully considered. Burrow shows how King's strong belief in the moral foundations of the universe and in objective moral law informed his prophetic critique of America's legal structures and the society as a whole.

King's attitude toward the United Nations (U.N.) as a peacemaking and peacekeeping force in the arena of international law and global politics is the focus of the final chapter. Lewis V. Baldwin analyzes the communitarian ideals of King and the U.N., noting the points at which they intersected. King's pursuit of the *beloved community* or the totally integrated society at home and abroad is compared and contrasted with the U.N.'s efforts to translate its human rights agenda and communitarian ideal into practical reality since its founding in 1945. Baldwin shows that King's refusal to actively seek the U.N.'s support on behalf of the African American struggle not only revealed his break with a tradition that stems from W. E. B. DuBois and Paul Robeson up to Malcolm X, but it was also inconsistent with his oft-repeated call for an international alliance against racism, poverty, and economic injustice. The chapter ends with a discussion of U.N. recognition of King since his death in April 1968.

The content of this volume proves that King refused to view law, politics, religion, and morality as polar opposites. For King the Hegelian, these phenomena at their best formed a creative union that, when properly understood, could lead the United States beyond the glaring and tragic ambivalence in her soul. This is the central idea coursing through *The Legacy of Martin Luther King, Jr.*

King was not afraid to affirm the political, legal, and moral scope of the biblical revelation and the Christian faith. The manner in which he addressed the role of religion and the church in revolutionary settings has helped stimulate the development of moral and political theologies over the last four decades. King provided us with religious and moral ways of thinking about law, politics, government, and the common good. As a nation in the midst of the greatest spiritual, moral, legal, and political crisis in its history, we would do well to revisit and honor his legacy.

NOTES

1. Frederick L. Downing, "A Review" of David J. Garrow, *Bearing the Cross: Martin Luther King, Jr. and the Southern Christian Leadership Conference* (1986), in *Theology Today*, vol. 44, no. 3 (October 1987): p. 391.

2. Preston N. Williams, "A Review" of Frederick L. Downing, *To See the Promised Land: The Faith Pilgrimage of Martin Luther King, Jr.* (1986), in *Theology Today*, vol. 44, no. 5 (April 1988): p. 127; Coleman B. Brown, "Grounds for American Loyalty in a Prophetic Christian Social Ethic—with Special Attention to Martin Luther King, Jr.," Ph.D. diss., Union Theological Seminary, New York (April 1979), pp. 194 and 254; Cushing Strout, *The New Heavens and the New Earth: Political Religion in America* (New York: Harper & Row, 1974), pp. 320–321; Obery M. Hendricks, Jr., "The Domestication of Martin Luther King, Jr.," *The A.M.E. Church Review* (April–June 1988): p. 54; Frederick L. Downing, "Martin Luther King, Jr. as Public Theologian," in David J. Garrow, ed., *Martin Luther King, Jr. and the Civil Rights Movement* (Brooklyn, N.Y.: Carlson Publishing, 1989), pp. 269–285; and John J. Ansbro, *Martin Luther King, Jr.: The Making of a Mind* (Maryknoll, N.Y.: Orbis Books, 1982), p. xiii.

3. For examples, see Martin Luther King, Jr., "Love, Law, and Civil Disobedience" (1961), in James M. Washington, ed., *The Essential Writings and Speeches of Martin Luther King, Jr.* (San Francisco: HarperCollins, 1986),

pp. 43–53; Martin Luther King, Jr., *Why We Can't Wait* (New York: New American Library, 1964), pp. 76–95; and Martin Luther King, Jr., *Where Do We Go from Here: Chaos or Community?* (Boston: Beacon Press, 1968), pp. 146–157.

4. Charles R. Wilson, *Judgment & Grace in Dixie: Southern Faiths from Faulkner to Elvis* (Athens: University of Georgia Press, 1995), pp. 31–32 and 162–163.

5. See Robert N. Bellah and Phillip E. Hammond, *Varieties of Civil Religion* (San Francisco: Harper & Row, Publishers, 1980), p. 194; and John D. Elder, "Martin Luther King and American Civil Religion," *Harvard Divinity Bulletin*, New Series, vol. 1, no. 3 (Spring 1968): pp. 17–18. Brief but perceptive treatments of King in relationship to American civil religion are also provided in Brown, "Grounds for American Loyalty," pp. 63–375; and Strout, *The New Heavens and the New Earth*, pp. 320–321.

6. "Hugh Downs's Interview with Martin Luther King, Jr.," NBC "Today" Show (18 April 1966), Archives of the Martin Luther King, Jr. Center for Nonviolent Social Change, Atlanta, Georgia, p. 2.

7. These labels are used in reference to King by Hendricks, "The Domestication of Martin Luther King, Jr.," p. 54; and Brown, "Grounds for American Loyalty," pp. 194–195.

To Witness in Dixie

King, the New South, and Southern Civil Religion

LEWIS V. BALDWIN

I think it is of the utmost importance to realize that King loves the South; many Negroes do. The ministry seems to afford him the best possible vehicle for the expression of that love. At that time in his life, he was discovering "the beauty of the South"; he sensed in the people "a new determination"; and he felt that there was a need for "a new, courageous witness."

—James Baldwin[1]

Martin Luther King, Jr., was by far the most important black leader in the American South since Booker T. Washington.[2] Born and raised in Atlanta, Georgia, the so-called "gateway to the South," King, in ways untypical of Washington, developed a sense of regional identity and regional responsibility that was not confined by the cultural norms and the sociopolitical realities of the region.[3] Although King's world of hope and possibility began in the South, the civil rights leader's persistent and trenchant critique of the region's institutions, values, and customs put him at odds with the vast majority of white southerners in his time, many of whom had long attached political and moral-religious significance to the so-called "southern way of life."[4] In King's critique of the region, the white South's system of Jim Crow and legalized segregation (unfreedom) was at odds with the ideals and the goal of America (freedom), opposites he created for rhetorical, moral, and political purposes.

Whether or not King wielded as much political influence in the South as Booker T. Washington is open to serious debate. In his own way, each articulated and struggled for the realization of a New South, challenging white and black southerners to transcend racial barriers while working together for the social, economic, and political advancement of the region.[5] But Washington's call for southern blacks to abandon the quest for civil rights and political power, while concentrating on the agricultural and mechanical arts as "the prerequisite to economic independence," a position embraced widely by black clergymen in the late nineteenth and early twentieth centuries, contrasted sharply with King's efforts to secure basic constitutional rights and political and economic empowerment for African Americans through a reliance on the very best in liberal arts education, religion, legislation and court action, and creative nonviolent dissent and protest.[6] Clearly, King stood much more in the intellectual and political tradition of W. E. B. DuBois than that of Washington.

The Gospel of Southern Progress:
King and Earlier Advocates of "a New South"

The New South movement originated soon after the Confederate defeat, almost a century before the rise of the modern phase of the civil rights crusade. The movement, which had blossomed by the 1880s, was led not by politicians, but by white southern journalists, who argued that increased industrialization and urbanization, enlightened agricultural practices, improved educational opportunities, harmonious race relations, and national reconciliation afforded the best avenues to a triumphant South.[7] Henry W. Grady of the *Atlanta Constitution*, Francis W. Dawson of the Charleston *News and Courier*, Richard H. Edmonds of Baltimore's *Manufacturers' Record*, Henry Watterson of the Louisville *Courier-Journal*, and Daniel A. Tompkins of the Charleston *Observer* became the "prime movers" and the "chief advocates" of the New South movement, but strong support also came from white businessmen, white southern ministers like the Methodist Bishop Atticus G. Haygood, and southern black leaders such as Booker T. Washington.[8] Martin Luther King, Jr., shared some of the views of these men as he set forth his own vision of the New South in the 1950s and 1960s, but perhaps more important are the ways in which the civil rights leader differed from these earlier advocates in his articulation and pursuit of that vision, especially with respect to racial equality.[9]

In a Thanksgiving sermon called "The New South," delivered in Oxford, Georgia, in 1880, Atticus Haygood urged white southerners to break with the worst aspects of their past while preparing for a bright and prosperous future that would include African Americans.[10] Henry Grady echoed this challenge in a speech on "The New South" in New York in December 1886, attracting far more attention nationwide than Haygood.[11] From that point, "New South" became a term of wide usage and enormous symbolic power. King stood prominently among the generations of southern-born idealists who, from the time of Haygood and Grady, employed images of the Old South and the New South in conveying their sense of the history and features of the region. The images of both have long embodied the hopes, values, and ideals of white and black southerners.[12] In the minds of King and of New South theorists before and after him, the Old South is uniformly associated with a rampant and antiquated agrarianism, slavery, secession, and the Confederacy. However, pictures of the New South vary from Haygood and Grady to King and more contemporary idealists. Paul M. Gaston highlights the difficulties involved in assigning a single image or definition to "New South":

> Almost from the beginning of its popularity, the term "New South" has had a blurred and ambiguous meaning. Historians have not had much success with their efforts to bring it into sharp focus. For one thing, they have never agreed on the central characteristics of Southern history itself, so that different interpretations of the region's past necessarily lead to conflicting accounts of what is new in the New South. Other factors have similarly complicated the historians' job of clarifying the image. For some, New South signifies a doctrine or point of view, not always clearly defined, that has been characteristic of certain groups of Southerners. For others, it has been used to delimit a period of time, with little agreement on beginning or terminal dates. It may mean the South since 1865; since 1877; from 1877 to 1913; since 1900; or simply the South of the present. And some compound the ambiguity by using it to designate both a doctrine and a period of time.[13]

Gaston is right in saying that "the concept of a New South, unlike the picture of the Old South, has always been a contemporary one, useful as a propaganda device to influence the direction and control of Southern development." New South advocates in the late nineteenth century championed causes ranging from industrialism to high tariffs and Social Darwinism, and those in the twentieth century supported movements extending from communism to tax reform to racial justice and equality. "Used in these and other ways," continues Gaston, "'New South' may stand for whatever kind of society adopters of the term believe will serve the region's interests best or promote their own ambitions most effectively."[14] This was most certainly the case with many New South theorists who lived before and during King's time, and it applies also to many who have emerged since the civil rights leader's death. Clearly, King's use of the term "New South" reflected his desire for a society ripe for what he called "a moral, political, and economic boom."[15]

The earliest New South advocates were virtually forced to confront the issue of race at a time when memories of slavery were still strong and vivid—at a time when black southerners, to the disgust of many whites, were exercising their newly achieved right to vote and hold public office. Less than three decades after the adoption of the Emancipation Proclamation, Atticus Haygood, Henry Grady, and Henry Watterson publicly thanked God that slavery existed no more, but they, like all New South idealists, had to consistently address the whole question of the continuing significance of race.[16] Haygood, as would be the case with King almost a century later, saw race as both a southern and national problem that could be eliminated only through the collective efforts of whites and blacks nationwide.[17] Haygood, Grady, Watterson, Francis W. Dawson, Richard H. Edmonds, and Daniel A. Tompkins encouraged the races to work together, and even embraced the idea of the South as a biracial society and culture, but their writings and speeches never seriously critiqued or questioned the ways in which whites and blacks commonly related to each other, socially, economically, politically, religiously, and otherwise, in the decades prior to the emergence of King.[18] Furthermore, their image of a biracial society, shaped and nurtured in white southern culture, was not as inclusive and interdependent in nature as the one King later envisioned.

Even as the spokesmen for the New South called for racial harmony and goodwill, they found it virtually impossible to break with many of the racist values and practices of the Old South. They "regarded the Negro as an alien, a menial, and a reprobate," and they often sanctioned southern racial policies based on the assumed superiority of whites.[19] When it came to the question of black advancement, they opted for Booker T. Washington's program of vocational education, hard work, frugality, and economic self-uplift, while opposing W. E. B. DuBois's call for African Americans to work through the courts, lobbying strategies, boycotts, and other methods of protest to secure political power and full civil and human rights. Although Bishop Haygood urged whites to respect black rights, including the right to vote, and to educate newly freed persons, his "vision of a South free of strife and prejudice was not based on black and white equality, but on a mutual respect for the place of blacks and whites in the society."[20] The same and more could be said of Grady, Dawson, Watterson, Edmonds, and Tompkins, all of whom supported the overturning of the civil rights legislation of Reconstruction, vigorously defended the disfranchisement of blacks, and uncritically embraced segregation as a custom, a sociopolitical order, and a legal system.[21]

Thus, it was only natural for Watterson, Edmonds, and Tompkins to accept the Supreme Court's decision in *Plessy v. Ferguson* (1896), which established "separate but equal" as law, and which constituted a major legal barrier to equal rights for African Americans for more than half a century. Grady, Haygood, and Dawson were deceased when *Plessy v. Ferguson* was rendered, but there is no reason to believe that they would have rejected the decision. In contrast, King, speaking decades later, denounced "the infamous 'separate but equal' philosophy" for compromising "not only the liberty of the Negro but the integrity of America."[22] Referring to the tragic outcome of this philosophy, King wrote:

> But we all know what happened as a result of that doctrine; there was always a strict enforcement of the separate without the slightest intention to abide by the equal. And so as a result of the old *Plessy* doctrine, we ended up being plunged across the abyss of exploitation, where we experienced the bleakness of nagging injustice.[23]

Strangely, the New South proponents justified segregation and white rule largely on the basis of religion, morality, and political expediency. "Behind the laws of man . . . stands the laws of God," declared Henry Grady, and "what God has separated let no man join together."[24] Daniel Tompkins insisted that each southern state should remain under "Anglo-Saxon control," and Richard Edmonds held that Anglo-Saxonism would always be "a tremendous factor in the development of . . . the South's interests and in safeguarding its political affairs."[25] For these and other white journalists in the New South movement, Booker T. Washington's portrait of a South in which blacks and whites could be "as separate as the fingers" in "all things that are purely social," and yet "one as the hand in all things essential to mutual progress," became the ideal. King would denounce this ideal on moral and pragmatic grounds, in part because it promoted biracialism within the larger framework of a system of continued white dominance. Thus, it contradicted his ideal of the beloved community—of a society based on mutual acceptance, authentic interpersonal and intergroup living, and shared power.[26]

The New South enthusiasts who preceded King did not properly analyze the problem of race as a barrier to the social, cultural, political, and economic development of the region. Often consumed by a misguided optimism mixed with racist understandings, they pictured African Americans sharing freely in the South's vast resources and mounting prosperity, and, consequently, were not prepared to confront forthrightly the centrality of race in the life of the region. Although Atticus Haygood and Henry Watterson occasionally criticized the racial attitudes of their fellow white southerners, their preference for *de jure* segregation indicated that they did not see the problem in its wholeness.[27] Henry Grady's limited perspective was equally evident, as he constantly stated that the South's racial problems had been eliminated, despite the increasing efforts, throughout the late nineteenth century, to disenfranchise, segregate, exploit, and subjugate blacks by violence and tyranny. In any case, Grady's claim, which amounted to *the politics of denial and deceit*, was echoed in more subtle ways by W. J. Cash, Hodding Carter, and other New South newspapermen in the 1930s and 1940s. Indeed, this tendency to minimize the South's struggle with race persisted until the mid-1950s, when King and other civil rights activists began to focus national and international attention "on the rigid biracialism that seemed most inconsistent with the goal of a modernized, progressive industrial society."[28] Clearly, King came to see that much of the New South myth and romanticism of the previous generations was undermined by a general failure to come to terms with race as the region's most serious problem.

Grady, Watterson, Francis Dawson, Richard Edmonds, and Daniel Tompkins joined white businessmen in claiming that economic regeneration through industrialization and laissez-faire capitalism was the South's most pressing need. To solicit the northern capital and technology necessary for such regeneration, they felt the need to stress the best aspects of race relations in the South. This strategy continued with Watterson, Edmonds, W. J. Cash, John Temple Graves, and other New South writers into the first half of the twentieth century, a strategy that seemed unnecessary since northern investors and industries that either supported or moved South, even up to the time of King, generally "accommodated themselves to the" region's "racial hierarchy."[29] Even so, New South optimists apparently saw some connection between the region's handling of the race issue and its efforts for industrial expansion and reconciliation with the North.[30] This connection was probably more evident in the 1950s and 1960s, as King and his followers, in Birmingham and other southern cities, sought to exploit it for civil rights gains. "As civil rights concerns mounted," writes James C. Cobb, "it seemed reasonable to conclude that most image-conscious, nationally known firms would shy away from an area whose racial policies were becoming so offensive to mass society values."[31]

The earliest New South enthusiasts seemed surprisingly naive in thinking that the region could sustain significant industrial growth, urbanization, and economic prosperity over time without the elimination of all racial barriers. At times, Grady, Dawson, Edmonds, Tompkins, and Watterson spoke of a South which, due to enlightened agricultural practices and advancing industrialization and urbanization, basked in the rays of material prosperity, without even considering the extent to which white power arrested the economic development of blacks, denied them the basic liberties necessary for success in a competitive economy, and retarded the entire southern economy. Their claim that all southerners were sharing liberally in the region's growing material riches had lost all credibility by the time of the first wave of the Great Migration, when hundreds of thousands of blacks moved North in search of new opportunities for industrial employment, and it had become perhaps the most disturbing aspect of the New South myth by the time of the Great Depression, when the region was still being labeled "the nation's primary economic problem."[32] Although signs of a vigorous industrialization, with a concomitant urbanization and considerable economic growth, were quite evident in the South when King emerged a few decades later, the region, due to the prominence of the color bar, remained the poorest in the country.

It was during the twentieth century that New South idealists first gave sufficient consideration to the relationship between racial injustice and economic injustice, and to the highly negative impact this had on the quality of life for black and white southerners. Henry Watterson became increasingly sensitive to the problem. In a 1908 editorial on "The Negro and His Vote," printed in his *Courier-Journal*, Watterson insisted that blacks be given "a white man's chance," for, as he put it, "the prosperity and happiness of the black people are indispensable to the prosperity and happiness of the white people."[33] Other well-known New South thinkers expressed the same sentiment in different ways. In a 1912 speech on "The Negro and the New South," Willis D. Weatherford, the noted churchman, author, and educator from Texas, declared that while the region had improved economically and intellectually, a lack of genuine respect for black humanity and citizenship rights still kept it from attaining "the essence of greatness." Like King decades later, Weatherford drew on Immanuel Kant's ideas, maintaining that from an economic standpoint, blacks were being treated not as ends-in-themselves, but as mere means to an end for the white power structure.[34] This perspective reached new heights of clarity and power during the 1930s and 1940s with writers like Lillian Smith and newspapermen such as W. J. Cash and Virginus Dabney, all of whom were outspoken in the areas of racial and economic discrimination.[35] King's earliest intellectual contact with this New South thinking most likely occurred at Atlanta's Morehouse College in the 1940s, when he, as a student, heard Lillian Smith lecture on the tragic effects of segregation laws.[36] In some ways, Smith's ideas anticipated King's profound reflections on the economic roots of southern racism and black inequality.

Having studied the economic determinism of Karl Marx, the Christian socialism of Walter Rauschenbusch, and the ethics of George Kelsey and the Boston Personalists, King always maintained that the only sure path to a New South required not only the elimination of injustice and patterns of exclusion based on race and economics, but also the extension of educational opportunities to blacks and whites on a nonsegregated basis.[37] While echoing Henry Grady's and Richard Edmonds's earlier claims regarding the many positive features of the South, King, in terms remarkably similar to Lillian Smith's, asserted nevertheless that the region's health and vitality were stunted by a lack of *equal* and *shared* opportunity under the law:

> Even the most casual observer can see that the South has marvelous possibilities. It is rich in natural resources, blessed with the beauties of nature, and endowed with a native warmth of spirit. Yet, in spite of these assets, it is retarded by a blight that debilitates not only the Negro but also the white man. Poor white men, women, and children, bearing the scars of ignorance, deprivation, and poverty, are evidence of the fact that harm to one is injury to all. Segregation has placed the whole South socially, educationally, and economically behind the rest of the nation.[38]

The earliest spokesmen for the New South movement agreed that the social, moral, economic, and political advancement of the region could occur only with greater educational opportunities for blacks and whites.[39] This message, initially expressed on a serious note in the speeches and writings of Atticus Haygood and Henry Grady, extended into the first half of the twentieth century with W. J. Cash in Charlotte, Mark Ethridge in Louisville, John Temple Graves in Birmingham, Hodding Carter in Greenville, Mississippi, Harry Ashmore in Little Rock, Virginus Dabney in Richmond, and other influential newspapermen who, beginning in the 1930s, "helped revive the idea of a New South of economic, educational, and racial progress."[40] Thus, the message had long been a vital part of the New South movement when King gave powerful expression to it. But the earlier New South idealists typically had in mind a dual system of education based on race, the very kind that Lillian Smith and King later denounced as part of the South's greatest problem. The idea of a segregated educational system came naturally for most white New South spokesmen up to World War II, especially since they viewed African Americans as intellectually inferior to themselves and doubted the capability of southern blacks for the highest moral, economic, and political achievement. Categorically rejecting such thinking, and the paternalism which undergirded it, King stood among the very first New South advocates to argue consistently that the best educational opportunities for southerners could only come through a fully integrated school system and a careful program of reeducation—one which prepared people for genuine patriotic cooperation and participation in a democratic system.[41]

Much of the foregoing discussion indicates that politics was actually at the heart of the program put forth by most New South advocates who predated King.[42] In other words, the emphasis was essentially on maintaining, often in subtle and sophisticated ways, the structures of Jim Crowism—of white power and black subordination. Across the spectrum, from strong conservatives like Grady to moderates such as Haygood, Watterson, and Graves, New South idealists boasted of a redeemed, transformed, and triumphant South, even as they, much in the tradition of southern apologists, justified and often romanticized some of the ways of the Old South. They supported enlightened agricultural practices, the use of the latest farming technology, and the proper compensation of labor, without seriously addressing the neglect and exploitation of black farmers. They accepted black access to the ballot, but felt that whites should control the elections, the local governments, and the statehouses and legislatures. They called for racial harmony, while failing to flatly condemn much of the psychological and physical torture of African Americans by the Ku Klux Klan and other white bigots. While promoting national reconciliation, they embraced white politicians who symbolized segregation and raised the banner of states' rights. Moreover, they invited northern businessmen and industries into the South, but harbored an extreme neurotic sensitivity to interference from so-called *outsiders*. This strange ambivalence, lurking in the spirits of Grady, Haygood, Watterson, Graves, and others, was never characteristic of King.[43]

Significantly, Haygood, Grady, Dawson, Edmonds, Watterson, Tompkins, Weatherford, Graves, Cash, and others did not go as far as King subsequently went in pursuing the ideal of a New South. These earlier New South advocates wrote and spoke extensively, and expressed an incurable optimism, but they, due in part to limited perspectives on race, were, unlike King decades later, not able to divorce themselves from the myth of white supremacy and the structures of a monopoly and racialized capitalism. Moreover, they, in further contrast to King, were not prepared to engage in the type of organized mass protest needed to significantly change the social, economic, and political condition of the region they claimed to love so much. In King's case, "New South" was not merely a concept to write and talk about, or something to simply hope for, but a racially inclusive ideal for which all moral and rational persons had to struggle and die collectively. With King, the New South principle actually organized itself into a nonviolent movement for the basic constitutional rights, the political enfranchisement, and the economic empowerment of all southerners, irrespective of race.[44]

Most of King's predecessors in the New South movement would not have supported his civil disobedience, especially his breaking of segregation laws and his defiance of court injunctions. Their belief in the sacredness of the southern way of life, despite all of its moral deficiencies, was simply too strong. King, in exceedingly profound ways, redefined and gave fresh meaning to the New South creed that was passed down from Haygood and Grady to Weatherford, Dabney, Lillian Smith, and others. "Even more significant," says Louis D. Rubin, Jr., "was the collapse of the New South racial program in the face of the modern civil rights movement and the Second Reconstruction."[45] In more precise terms, King and his followers offered a different set of prescriptions for the range of racial, economic, and political problems in the South in the 1950s and 1960s. Even so, their ideas and activities were a fair reminder that the legacy of the "New South" movement has been an enduring one, and so have the many efforts to cope with its mythology.[46]

New South Idealism and the Civil Rights Movement: King and Southern Writers in the 1950s and 1960s

The civil rights movement of the 1950s and 1960s contributed to the public emergence of yet another generation of New South advocates. Unlike the figures just discussed, this new generation consistently expressed the conviction that white supremacy and segregation had to be strongly opposed, even eliminated, before the New South could become a reality. King figured prominently in this new generation, one which, interestingly enough, was also led by southern white journalists and writers. Almost from the beginning of his practical quest for a New South in Montgomery in the mid-1950s, King sensed that these journalists and writers would become a vital part of his whole effort to create what he often termed "a coalition of conscience." He saw great leadership potential in Buford Boone, the award-winning editor of *The Tuscaloosa News*, Tuscaloosa, Alabama, who had become known in some circles for his "moral courage and profound dignity" in addressing the South's racial dilemma. Early in 1957, King wrote Boone, noting that

> I have just read that you received the 1957 Pulitzer Award for outstanding editorials. May I extend my congratulations to you for such a noble achievement. It is my hope that many other persons in the white South will rise up and courageously give the type of leadership that you have given. I share with you your conviction that our difficult problems can be solved only by attitudes founded upon patience, tolerance and loving understanding of the frailties and imperfections of man. That you have been able to follow and promote such an attitude speaks most highly of you and, in my judgment, accounts for the success with which your efforts have met.[47]

Less than a decade later, King pointed to several white journalists and writers who were providing powerful and provocative critiques of the politics of race in the South. In his celebrated "Letter from the Birmingham City Jail" (1963), the civil rights leader penned these words, clearly demonstrating that he did not view the white South as monolithic when it came to the civil rights cause:

> I am thankful, however, that some of our white brothers in the South have grasped the meaning of this social revolution and committed themselves to it. They are still too few in quantity, but they are big in quality. Some—such as Ralph McGill, Lillian Smith, Harry Golden, James McBride Dabbs, Anne Braden and

Sarah P. Boyle—have written about our struggle in eloquent and prophetic terms.[48]

King saw in these writers tremendous resources of hope and possibility as far as the quest for a New South was concerned. He called McGill, the editor of the *Atlanta Constitution* and successor to Henry W. Grady, "one of the South's social prophets," and noted that his "candor and keen analysis of our region of the nation" have "strengthened my hope for the South."[49] King referred to Lillian Smith of Georgia, who coedited with Paula Snelling a literary magazine called *South Today* (1936–1945), and who regularly reviewed books and wrote articles for the *Chicago Tribune, Saturday Review,* and other publications, as one who represented "the true and basic sentiments of millions of southerners, whose voices are yet unheard, whose course is yet unclear, and whose courageous acts are yet unseen."[50] Harry Golden, an editor for *The Carolina Israelite* in Charlotte, North Carolina, was for King one of an impressive number of Jewish thinkers and political activists who gave unselfishly to the freedom cause. James Dabbs of South Carolina, a farmer, poet, and essayist who addressed issues ranging from agrarianism and industrialism to social, economic, and political change in the South, impressed King as an amazing blend of the realist and the idealist. Anne Braden, who served as a reporter for the *Louisville Times* and for newspapers in Anniston and Birmingham, Alabama, struck King as one of the most courageous young white females in the human struggle, especially since she identified proudly and unapologetically with the political left. King called Sarah Boyle "one of the great Christians and humanitarians of our day," and declared that "your witness and . . . unswerving commitment to the ideals of freedom and human dignity will be an inspiration to generations yet unborn."[51]

Interestingly enough, King found in all of these writers a source of moral, physical, intellectual, and financial support that he never got from the vast majority of white ministers and churches in the South. Also, he discovered in them a respect for law and a devotion to participatory democracy and human rights that he did not find in the vast majority of white southern politicians, judges, and law enforcement officers he encountered. In King's own estimation, Boone, McGill, Smith, Golden, Dabbs, Braden, and Boyle afforded proof that the white South was not completely devoid of a conscience, all the more because these figures were willing to sacrifice their good names, reputations, and even their lives to make their society more just and inclusive.[52] In noting this, King complicated the notion of "white South." For him, the white South was racist to the core, but some white southerners also sympathized with and supported the black freedom movement. The South, then, was never as simple as the images that most people had.

The New South idealists of the 1950s and 1960s provided keen and penetrating critiques of the social, economic, and political structures of the Old South, thus distinguishing themselves from Henry Grady, Francis Dawson, Henry Watterson, and others who preceded them.[53] Perhaps the most searching critiques came from Smith and Braden, who, much like Virginia Durr, Ella Baker, and other white and black and female activists, recognized the interrelationship between class issues, racial oppression, and the subordination of women.[54] In this regard, they showed a depth of insight that was not so typical of King, McGill, Dabbs, Golden, Harry Ashmore, and other male activists and critics, who attacked racism and economic exploitation while largely ignoring sexism. Lillian Smith's persistent assault on the patriarchal structure that perpetuated racism and sexism, encouraged rigid and repressive attitudes toward sexuality, and upheld the intertwining myths of race and sex in southern culture, vividly revealed the breadth of her vision of the New South. She had little patience for southern writers "who were not in the New South tradition" as she defined it.[55] The same could be said of Braden and Boyle, both of whom ultimately concluded that white women should refuse to comply with white men in perpetuating the laws, institutions, and practices of a racist and sexist society.[56]

Virtually no disagreement surfaced among the new New South thinkers when it came to the southern system of Jim Crow. King's view of *de jure* and *de facto* segregation as the most visible, painful, and enduring symbol of the Old South was generally accepted. In King's thinking, segregation in all forms constituted a blatant denial of the universal parenthood of God, the inherent sacredness of all humanity, and the interrelated and interdependent structure of reality.[57] Disagreeing with his famous predecessor, Henry Grady, on the subject, Ralph McGill gave equal weight to religious and moral considerations, denouncing segregationists who invoked the name of God in their cause as "false prophets of prejudice."[58] Viewing herself as "a missionary whose evangelistic zeal caused her to focus on the 'evil' of caste," Lillian Smith, a coeditor of "the first antisegregation publication below the Mason-Dixon line," is said to have fought "Jim Crow" or "enforced segregation"

> with the fervor of a fundamentalist preacher attacking sin. She believed that somewhere, deep inside the souls of white Southern Christians, there surely must have lurked the recognition that Jim Crow was a sin. This Nonsegregated South of the spirit was the Silent South that Lillian Smith spoke for and appealed to.[59]

The same could be said of the early King, whose confidence in white southern Christians, as he noted in the "Letter from the Birmingham City Jail," was clearly misplaced.[60] Like King, McGill, and Smith, Harry Golden, James Dabbs, Anne Braden, and Sarah Boyle also used religious and moral arguments against both *de jure* and *de facto* segregation. Golden labeled Jim Crow "an evil" which "corrupts everything it touches."[61] Dabbs echoed McGill's concern for segregationists who used the name of God to support "a supposed instinctive sympathy for" their "own race as against all others."[62] Braden termed Jim Crow "an evil" and "a curse" which "winds itself around your soul like the arms of an octopus."[63] Boyle's decision to challenge Jim Crow—"to take my stand with Negroes against the white South"—grew out of a deep need to "defend a Christian ideal and a democratic principle."[64] Like King and the other promoters of the New South ideal, she denounced the separation of the races by law and custom as not only outrageous, but also undemocratic, un-American, and un-Christian. Moreover, Boyle joined King, McGill, Smith, Golden, Dabbs, and Braden in criticizing white churches for sanctioning segregation, and for contributing, often unconsciously, to the evolvement of race into a sacred myth.

Clearly, legalized segregation crippled the South at all levels while putting it at odds with the best in the American dream. It erected physical, spiritual, and psychological barriers that hurt both races, and it kept African Americans politically disfranchised and economically dependent. Its impact on both black and white children was especially painful for King and Lillian Smith, both of whom treated the subject at some length in their writings and speeches.[65] Equally disturbing for them, and for other New South advocates, was what King described as the "blighted pattern of segregated justice," which put blacks at even more of a disadvantage. King remained fixated on this problem, or on what he saw as the southern dilemma. "Many Americans are aware of the fact that, on the crooked scales of 'Southern justice,'" said King in 1966, "the life, liberty and human worth of a black man weigh precious little." Fully aware of the complicated past of the South, a past that violated many of the very religious precepts that southerners had long preached, he elaborated further:

> The segregated character that pervades southern justice runs all the way through the judicial system, extending from the lowest municipal courts all the way up to the federal bench. The South- ern Regional Council Report on Justice states: "The clerks and the 109 jury commissioners attached to the federal courts of the 11 states of the Old Confederacy are all white—all appointed by the 65 white district judges." Through these appointments, the judges build higher the walls of segregated justice.[66]

Lamenting "our failure to give the Negro equal justice in our courts," Ralph McGill pleaded with white southerners "to demon- strate that we are people who believe in supremacy of law." As long as the South failed to grant "equal protection for the Negro before the law," he held, "the federal government had no alternative but to step in."[67] Although McGill and other white New South idealists shared King's concern regarding the double standard of southern justice, they, with the possible exception of the socialist writer Anne Braden, seem to have had more faith than the civil rights leader in the lawyers, judges, and courts of the South. Even Lillian Smith, regarded in some circles as "the most liberal and outspoken of white southern writers," was ill-prepared to support King or any other civil rights leader who lost complete confidence in the legal and judicial systems of the South.[68] This was to be expected because even the most enlightened white southerners, unable to totally transcend the cultural condition- ing of the white racist society in which they were raised and nurtured, brought to their efforts for social change a strong and abiding attachment to most of the South's institutions. Thus, they, unlike King, never quite comprehended the depth and breadth of racism in the region.[69]

The civil rights movement became the embodiment of the social vision of King and others who spoke of a New South. For King, the movement was the greatest hope for a genuinely New South because it, by its very nature, gave "practical lessons of democracy's defaults and shortcomings."[70] White New South advocates who, like King, brought to the movement a sense of the region and of southern history as a whole, agreed, though most were not always in favor of King's strategies and tactics. Often moved to "feelings of both anxiety and compassion" by King-led civil rights campaigns, Ralph McGill ultimately concluded that the movement was a necessary step in the maturation of both black and white southerners.[71] Lillian Smith, who followed the struggle from the time of the Montgomery bus boycott, and who was particularly interested in the roles played by the young people, identified the quest for civil rights as "a spontaneous religio-social movement" with "tremendous moral and political significance."[72] In a similar vein, Harry Golden maintained that the movement "made the Constitution of the United States a living document," convincing all Americans that it "means just what it says."[73] James Dabbs also spoke of a struggle designed to make real "the great charters of the Declaration of Independence and the Constitution."[74] Referring to King's Southern Christian Leadership Conference (SCLC) as an organization "with a soul," Anne Braden praised the movement for helping southerners to understand the dream of freedom and the civil liberties embodied in the Bill of Rights.[75] Sarah Boyle saw it as part of a long struggle to translate moral and democratic principles into practical reality.[76]

The personal qualities and the leadership style King brought to the civil rights crusade impressed and even fascinated other New South advocates. Although never completely comfortable with King's activities, McGill came to see him as "the essence of moral power in the movement"—as the one whose "superb courage and moral force . . . stirred Congress to action on the rights bills."[77] Smith, whose correspondence with King and other activists afford significant evidence for exploring the relationships between intellectual, political, and literary history, regarded the civil rights leader as "the most powerful

Negro from the symbolic viewpoint down here"—as one "known in every corner of the world as a symbol of freedom for the dark races."[78] This controversial female writer insisted that "we are indeed lucky to have Dr. Martin Luther King, Jr. leading this movement instead of a southern Adam Clayton Powell" or a "Malcolm X and 'his hate-filled followers.'"[79] Golden labeled King the preeminent "religious leader of the protest movement of the Southern Negro."[80] Dabbs considered King "almost certainly the best known, probably the most important, man in the South today"—"the South's one contemporary world figure."[81] Braden viewed King as "the best equipped person in the whole movement to provide the long range vision on this question" of integration.[82] Boyle wholeheartedly agreed, calling King "the symbol of all that is highest in our nation."[83] Such views of King's role were rarely expressed publicly in the white South, where attitudes toward the civil rights leader covered the spectrum, from admiration and respect to hostility, suspicion, contempt, and cynicism.

Of particular significance to the New South idealists were the ways in which King translated religious and moral convictions and fervor into social and political activity. The ethical, religious, and philosophical principles that King embraced, articulated, and applied within the context of the struggle reinforced their belief that the beloved community would ultimately be realized for all southerners. They were persuaded by King's powerful claim that love and nonviolence—as revealed through mass protest, civil disobedience, redemptive suffering, forgiveness, and reconciliation—was "not an expression of impractical idealism," but the only moral and practical route to the full realization of the New South.[84] Ralph McGill, sometimes called "the conscience of the South," held that it was King's "advocacy of the Gandhi-like passive resistance," not the "rhetoric of revolution," that "won him and his followers early success and attention."[85] Viewing King's nonviolent ethic as "the essence of what religion ought to be," as "a compound of Christian-pacifist and Gandhian principles," Lillian Smith favored his methods "as being more expeditious than the wearying and costly legal battles waged by the NAACP":

> The effectiveness of nonviolence and passive resistance as a means of abolishing segregation became the second new emphasis in her thinking. . . . She responded positively to King's nonvio-

lent protest methods partly because they were an outgrowth of the Gandhian philosophy she had long admired, but also because they now seemed to her the most effective means of solving the race problem in the South.[86]

As was the case with McGill and Smith, Harry Golden deemed the nonviolent protests of King and others a challenge to those white southerners who denied any relationship between religion and politics, and who had long counseled blacks to forget "the here and now" in favor of some "future rewards" in the afterlife. "Little did the Southerner suspect that one day the descendants of slaves would wield Christianity as a finely tooled political weapon," Golden declared, "asking jobs, schools, wages, and hospitals in its name." "The Negroes have used Christianity to contain their revolution and though the Negro is in the streets," he continued, "he is in the streets with prayer and humility, not with rifle and incendiary grenades."[87] James Dabbs, who occasionally wrote for *The Christian Century*, commented similarly, concluding that King and his followers were acting "in the spirit of love" as symbolized supremely by Jesus Christ.[88] While prone to be more critical of the Christian ethic as understood and practiced by her fellow southerners, Anne Braden found in King's advocacy of love and effective employment of nonviolent means support for her claim that it would "require resources of the mind and spirit" to defeat the forces of racism and segregation in the South.[89] Sarah Boyle, a bit more religiously conservative than Braden, praised King for striving so hard to create the kind of racial harmony and intergroup understanding that "can only come through Christian love."[90]

But the New South idealists never thought of the civil rights movement merely in terms of King. Despite their many expressions of praise and support for King's philosophy, methods, and leadership style, they knew that he was a product of the movement, not the movement itself. King himself often said that he was not the only actor in the drama that played out in the movement. The civil rights leader spoke of the struggle in the South as involving many who were just as courageous, persistent, and unselfish as himself, and he pointed specifically to what he called "the New Negro," who, due to "a new sense of dignity and destiny," and to "a determination to struggle and sacrifice until the walls of injustice crumble," figured prominently in his vision of the New South:

> The most important thing in this whole movement is what has happened to the Negro. For the first time, the Negro is on his own side. This has not always been true. But today the Negro is with himself. He has gained a new respect for himself. He believes in himself. World opinion is on his side. The law is on his side and, as one columnist said, all the stars of heaven are on his side. It seems to be historically true that once an oppressed people rise up there is no stopping them short of complete freedom. The Negro is eternally through with segregation; he will never accept it again, in Mississippi, Georgia, or anywhere else.[91]

In proclaiming the rise of a New Negro, King stood in a long tradition of intellectuals and New South optimists. Booker T. Washington had used the term as early as 1895, when he urged his people to help transform the South through their contributions in agriculture, mechanics, commerce, domestic service, and other professions.[92] In 1900, this New South enthusiast collaborated with N. B. Wood and Fannie B. Williams on a work entitled *A New Negro for a New Century*. In 1905, black leaders and a few liberal whites "hailed the advent of a 'New Negro'" as they organized the Niagara Movement, an effort aimed at gaining full human rights for African Americans, and one that resulted in the NAACP in 1909. In 1916, William Pickens wrote *The New Negro: His Political, Civil and Mental Status, and Related Essays*, and Eric Walrond issued an essay, "The New Negro Faces America," in 1923. Images of the New Negro became fixed in the American mind in 1925, when Alain Locke, E. Franklin Frazier, Charles S. Johnson, and others, inspired by the so-called Harlem Renaissance, published *The New Negro: An Interpretation*.[93] By this time, as George B. Tindall has indicated, "New Negro" carried meanings as varied as those of "New South":

> The growing spirit of protest was but one among a cluster of tendencies in the Negro world that received their generic name in 1925 when a special "Harlem" issue of *Survey Graphic* reappeared in revised book form as *The New Negro*. The capital of the

movement was in upper Manhattan, where Negro immigrants had created a new black belt in Harlem. Definitions of the New Negro varied; some emphasized achievement in literature and the arts; others the rise of a group economy in the ghettoes, together with the development of middle-class standards of education and refinement; still others the proud, self-assertive Negro, fretful at discrimination and injustice. But out of their very separation it was apparent that American Negroes were evolving a sense of race pride, solidarity, and self-realization that would give a formidable support to future demands for recognition.[94]

The vigorous and determined leadership provided by the New Negro in the South in the 1950s and 1960s reinforced King's belief in the black messianic vocation. In other words, it strengthened his conviction that African Americans have a special redemptive role to play in American and world civilization. In a real sense, King could not have been more perceptive, especially since African Americans, through their folklore, art, and spiritual values, and through the movement itself, were already having perhaps a greater impact on the world than any other single group of people in Western society.[95]

King's emphasis on the meaning and significance of the New Negro in the struggle was generally shared by other New South advocates in his time. Ralph McGill saw in the New Negro much hope for the South, despite his differences with young black militants.[96] Much like King, Lillian Smith underscored the prominence of the New Negro in shattering "the stereotypes whites had made of themselves and of Negroes." In her estimation, "the ideas of equality before God and before the law," which sprouted full-blown from the heart of the New Negro, were essential for the complete development of the human being. "There is, today, a revolution going on in the Negro's mind," Smith maintained. "He is discovering his powers; moral, economic, psychological, political. . . ."[97] Referring to the New Negro as "a unique revolutionary," as one who "infused Christianity with a new vigor," and as one who reactivated "all the old American traditions, including civil disobedience," Harry Golden, with some exaggeration, remarked:

In his earliest campaigns for simple justice, the Negro, perhaps mistakenly, relied upon the leadership of whites who were sympathetic, who tried to help him by telling him to wait. But it was when he himself—the black man—began to fight that the limits of legal racial segregation narrowed, access to the franchise and education widened, and he began to realize that he will get what is his because he and he alone will finally force communication and recognition.[98]

Drawing on King's discussion of the New Negro in *Stride toward Freedom: The Montgomery Story* (1958), James Dabbs concluded that the "growing demand for justice on the part" of African Americans proved that they understood the Bible's "greatest lessons" better than southern whites. Noting the contribution that the New Negro could possibly make to eliminating the structures of white supremacy in the South, Dabbs declared, in words that clearly recall King's, that "it's partly your job to save us from this idolatry."[99] Anne Braden argued in similar terms, contending that the Negro's demand for "a new kind of freedom" was "forcing this question to the conscious level of the minds of white people everywhere."[100] Using the term "New Negro" in her book, *The Desegregated Heart: A Virginian's Stand in Time of Transition* (1962), Sarah Boyle marveled at the determination of African Americans to lead their struggle free of the paternalistic oversight and timetables of the white South.[101]

These promoters of the New South ideal constantly struggled with questions about their own place in a movement that obviously needed support from well-meaning and socially active whites in order to succeed. They never shared a crowded jail cell with freedom riders or lunch-counter demonstrators, nor did they experience the shock of a sheriff's cattle prod, the bite of police dogs, or the paralyzing effects of tear gas and powerful water hoses. But they contributed to the struggle in other ways. They supported it through their writings and speeches, and through their many appeals to local, state, and national governmental officials in favor of civil rights legislation. They made personal sacrifices to help keep the major civil rights organizations functioning. While avoiding street demonstrations, Ralph McGill and his wife reported that they supported King and his SCLC "with our pocketbook to a degree that was sometimes a real charge against our limited resources."[102] Like McGill, Harry Golden and James Dabbs supported the movement morally and financially, while choosing not to assume major, visible roles in the freedom marches. Golden proposed a number of integration plans and challenged fellow Jews who were either silent or noncommittal when it came to civil rights concerns.[103] Dabbs advanced his vision for an integrated South through organizations such as the South Carolina Council on Human Relations (SCCHR) and the Southern Regional Council (SRC), "which employed educational methods to achieve its purpose." King himself apparently had some involvement with the SRC.[104]

The white female writers in the New South crusade were involved in the movement on several fronts, sometimes extending their activities beyond those of McGill, Golden, and Dabbs. Due to a constant bout with cancer, Lillian Smith, who considered herself an "interpreter and clarifier for the movement," was unable to march and to honor some of King's requests for speeches before civil rights groups, but she contributed financially to the SCLC, the Congress of Racial Equality (CORE), the NAACP, and the Student Nonviolent Coordinating Committee (SNCC), and she held memberships in some of these civil rights organizations. Pointing to a close relationship between "art and politics," and refusing "to separate the seemingly conflicting roles of artist and activist," Smith saw students and other young people in the movement, many of whom communicated its values through song, as the brightest hope for a genuinely New South.[105] She became a kind of mentor for these youngsters, especially since she stood among that sacrificial few in the white South who appeared ready to risk all for the immediate and total elimination of the region's racial hierarchy. Thus, when King wrote his essay "Who Speaks for the South?" (1958), a title later chosen for a book by James Dabbs, the civil rights leader highlighted the name of Smith along with that of Harry Ashmore. Moreover, King's oft-repeated statement, "Now is the time," which became his rallying cry during the Selma campaign in 1965, was taken from the title of a book published by Smith a decade earlier.[106]

Anne Braden and Sarah Boyle agreed wholeheartedly with King's and Smith's insistence that New South idealists and activists not limit their energy and resources too narrowly in the struggle. Braden was active in the NAACP, the Negro Labor Council, and other interracial and peace organizations, and she also worked with committees to end segregation in hospitals and bus stations, the Department of Christian

Social Relations of the Episcopal Church, and groups devoted to ending discrimination in housing. Braden also tried to forge a strong working relationship between her Southern Conference Educational Fund (SCEF) and groups such as the SCLC and SNCC.[107] Equally supportive of civil rights organizations, and of coalition politics as an avenue to racial justice, Boyle, in a letter to King, declared that "I am willing, even eager, to make this witness total by going to jail and refusing bail—*if it would help.*" King graciously accepted Boyle's suggestion, noting that "your active participation in demonstrations would be a most significant gesture of support and encouragement," but he instructed her to "follow the judgment of our staff at this point."[108] By taking to the streets with King and his followers, Boyle hoped to make a powerful appeal for winning more white southerners to a cause that all too few seemed to really understand.

King was always somewhat ambivalent about the moral and spiritual capacity of the white South for radical and much-needed social and political change, despite the contributions of McGill, Smith, Golden, Dabbs, Braden, Boyle, and others. In December 1956, toward the end of the Montgomery bus protest, King spoke of "the great resources of goodwill in the Southern white man that we must somehow tap," and one year later he remarked:

> We are convinced that the great majority of white southerners are prepared to accept and abide by the Supreme Law of the land. They, like us, want to be law-abiding citizens. Yet a small but determined minority resorts to threats, bodily assaults, cross-burnings, bombings, shooting and open defiance of the law in an attempt to force us to retreat.[109]

At the same time, King expressed disappointment with the lack of strong leadership from white southern moderates, especially religious moderates, a problem that later became more frustrating as he challenged economic injustice and America's misguided foreign policy:

> It is unfortunate indeed that at this time the leadership of the white South stems from the closeminded reactionaries. These persons gain prominence and power by the dissemination of false

ideas, and by deliberately appealing to the deepest hate responses within the human mind. It is my firm belief that this close-minded, reactionary, recalcitrant group constitutes a numerical minority. There are in the white South more openminded moderates than appears on the surface. These persons are silent today because of fear of social, political, and economic reprisals. God grant that the white moderates of the South will rise up courageously, without fear, and take up the leadership in this tense period of transition.[110]

For much of his public life, King shared with Lillian Smith and other white southern moderates the belief that the South would discover interracial community before the rest of the nation. Indeed, such a discovery would be merely a matter of course, they thought, once white southerners "recognized that being Southern was more important to all" people in the region "than the fact that some were white and others black."[111] For King, the signs clearly pointed in this direction. Thus, in 1963, quoting a statement from the *Atlanta Constitution* on the changing attitudes of blacks and whites toward race, he could speak of "a Declaration of Independence of a new South."[112]

But King doubted that the white South could solve its race problem alone, or without the assistance of liberal white northerners and the federal government, a position that set him apart from New South advocates such as Ralph McGill and Lillian Smith. Although McGill denounced much of the white southerner's preoccupation with "outside interference" as "harmful and stupid," he was at times as concerned as Henry Grady and other earlier New South thinkers about too much northern involvement in the South's racial situation.[113] While sharing King's frustration over the appalling silence of most open-minded white moderates in the South, Smith urged the prophet of nonviolent resistance to "keep the northern do-gooders out." Reflecting, perhaps unconsciously, a paternalism that was all too typical of white southerners generally when advising African Americans, she constantly reminded the civil rights leader not to "let outsiders come in and ruin your movement." Smith was convinced that black and white southerners could transform their own society without outside help, especially considering the "religious symbols" they shared, or "the deep ties of common songs, common prayer, common symbols that bind our two races together on a religio-mystical level, even as another brutally mythic idea, the concept of White Supremacy, tears our people apart."[114] James Dabbs and Sarah Boyle were equally mindful of the biracial elements in the South's religious culture, and they, too, felt that what blacks and whites shared in those terms afforded a possible foundation on which to develop strong, collective action in the interest of the democratization of the South.[115]

The forces of resistance and retrogression in the white South constantly reminded King of the tactics to which members of the oppressor race are willing to resort in order to maintain power and domination over the oppressed.[116] Of particular concern for King and the other New South advocates were the political enemies of the civil rights cause, from local politicians like Eugene "Bull" Connor to state officials like George C. Wallace to the many southerners in the U.S. Congress, all of whom engaged in race-baiting politics while using their power to halt the forces of progress. King made numerous references to Connor, one of the city commissioners in Birmingham, who "displayed as much contempt for the rights of the Negro as he did defiance for the authority of the federal government."[117] King called Alabama's Governor Wallace "a demagogue with a capital D," a "merchant of racism, peddling hate under the guise of states' rights," and one "who symbolizes in this country many of the evils that were alive in Hitler's Germany." The civil rights leader was equally critical of Mississippi's Governor Ross Barnett, whose lips "dripped with words of interposition and nullification," and of Georgia's Governor Lester Maddox, whose "credentials as" a racist "are impeccable." King also spoke boldly of "the power and moral corruption of" Senators James Eastland of Mississippi, Richard Russell of Georgia, and Herman Talmadge of Georgia. In King's view, all of these men, who were a part of the South's "racist power structure," promoted the time-honored myth that "the Negro prefers segregation," while categorically refusing to distinguish between "southern justice" and "substantive justice" when confronting the issues of black protest and civil rights legislation.[118]

Whites in the New South movement eagerly joined King in denouncing southern officials who exploited the race problem out of mean-spiritedness and for personal political gain. Ralph McGill constantly attacked "the states'-rights dogmatists" and "the more blatant and racially demagogic of the southern governors, senators, congressmen and local officials" who stubbornly refused to accept the Supreme Court's ruling in *Brown v. the Board of Education* (1954). With Governors Wallace and Maddox among his most active foes, McGill argued that "one of the saddest aspects of the southern race problem has been that governors have, by plan, had lawyers join with them in statements which deliberately deceived the people by distorting, and falsifying, the facts of the Constitution." "All too often," he continued, "this alliance has been assisted by lawyer-members of the Congress."[119] Echoing McGill, Lillian Smith spoke disparagingly of Governors Barnett and Maddox, Senators Talmadge and Eastland, and "other racial demagogues" and "opportunists" who reduced racial integration to sex and mongrelization, who defied the federal courts, and who exploited the fear and anxiety of the white South "to their political and economic advantage."[120] Like King, Smith compared the political situation in the South to that of Nazi Germany, and she mentioned several groups, aside from southern white politicians, who sought to benefit from the nation's racial climate:

> The five major groups are the politicians; the mentally unstabled who use "the Negro" as an object on which to pour their hate and anxieties; real estate owners and businessmen who make money from city ghettoes and "restricted areas"; a group of industrialists who use race prejudice to divide and weaken unions; and a few owners of large farms. As for the rest of us, we pay the heavy costs, economic and spiritual, of maintaining this system which profits so few and injures so many.[121]

Harry Golden, James Dabbs, Anne Braden, and Sarah Boyle joined in the assault on white southern politicians, viewing many of them as extremists and as instigators of mob violence against legitimate social protest. Unlike the earliest generation of New South enthusiasts, who defended *Plessy v. Ferguson,* these writers vigorously defended King, the NAACP, and other civil rights forces who, in opposition to white southern politicians, struggled to implement the Supreme Court's decision against segregation in public schools. Referring to Eastland's claim that African Americans in Mississippi were happy with apartheid, Golden suggested that the senator "was not only blind in the way segregationists are blind, but deaf too." Golden added: "He must never have heard the songs these 'happy' people sing: 'Nobody Knows the Trouble I've Seen,' 'Father, Let Me Be Rid of This World,' and 'Let My People Go!'"[122] Dabbs repeated these sentiments, and expressed the hope that the South would one day vote all the racist politicians out of office.[123] Braden shared this hope, and she clearly felt that the presence of the Wallaces, the Eastlands, and others, who undermined civil liberties and the freedom of the individual, merely heightened the significance of King and the movement he was leading.[124] Armed with the same conviction, Boyle suggested that the South's politicians were among those who had missed the opportunity to provide "white leadership" in the civil rights struggle.[125]

These writers provided strong moral support for King as he faced southern politicians who accused him of being a communist. Constantly confronted by those who used McCarthyite tactics to discredit the movement, King vowed that "we will not allow Eastland, Barnett, or the George Wallaces to use the 'Red' issue to block our efforts, to split our ranks, or to confuse our supporters."[126] Equally disturbed by this tendency to identify King and others in the movement with the radical left, Ralph McGill declared that "they are not Communistic and are not un-American" because they operate "from a base of law and of court decisions."[127] Lillian Smith, as vehement in her anticommunism as McGill, maintained that King's struggle was rooted not in the godless system of communism, but, rather, in Christian and Gandhian principles, an assessment with which James Dabbs and Sarah Boyle would have wholeheartedly agreed.[128] Harry Golden asserted that King "was as vigilant against Communists as Mr. J. Edgar Hoover."[129] Quite aware of powerful politicians in the white South who dismissed King's movement as communist-inspired and financed, Anne Braden, known for her ties with the radical left, simply suggested that such charges were rooted in desperate attempts to preserve a social and political order that could no longer be sustained on pragmatic and moral grounds.[130]

There were more obvious, violent culprits in the white South who posed a greater threat than King to the peace and well-being of the region. No one knew this better than King himself. The violence visited upon black and white civil rights workers by the Ku Klux Klan, the States' Rights and Nazi parties, mobs, and even law enforcement officials blatantly exposed the demonic side of southern life, and reminded King of the extent to which "the unresolved question of race" remained "a pathological infection in our social and political anatomy."[131] McGill, Smith, Braden, and other New South proponents shared King's concern regarding this violently racist element, and some favored antilynch laws and other protective measures for blacks, but the common view was that the lynchings, beatings, shootings, and maimings would, in the long run, advance the very cause that the enemies of true democracy sought to defeat.

Much more pressing for King was the "planned and institutionalized tokenism" which existed as "a carefully constructed roadblock" to southern progress. He complained:

> Many areas of the South are retreating to a position which will permit a handful of Negroes to attend all-white schools or the employment in lily-white factories of one Negro to a thousand white employees. Thus we have advanced in some areas from all-out, unrestrained resistance to a sophisticated form of delay embodied in tokenism. In a sense, this is one of the most difficult problems our movement confronts. But I am confident that this tactic will prove to be as vain a hope as the earlier quest to utilize massive resistance to inhibit even a scintilla of change.[132]

King came to see tokenism "not only as a useless goal, but as a genuine menace," especially since many southern white moderates had come "to accept token victories as indicative of genuine and satisfactory progress." Addressing the problem at greater length, King commented: "It is a palliative which relieves emotional distress, but leaves the disease and its ravages unaffected. It tends to demobilize and relax the militant spirit which alone drives us forward to real change."[133] Anne Braden was probably the only white New South writer to speak as strongly and freely as King on the subject. She essentially equated tokenism with "gradualism," which promoted the "ideal of steady, if slow, progress into the future," insisting that it would ultimately fail because it was advocated "by many of the same people who are actively seeking to perpetuate segregation forever."[134]

King and whites in the New South crusade could not have been more unified in their conviction that the goal should be the creation of a totally integrated society. This perspective was informed as much by economic and political considerations as by Christian compassion, reasonableness, and goodwill. For King, as for other New South advocates, the developing alliance between the New Negro and "enlightened whites" in the South constituted a significant step in the direction of an integrated existence. Indeed, King "viewed the composition of the civil rights movement"—with its coalition of professional leaders and common laborers of different racial, ethnic, and economic backgrounds—"as a microcosm of the Beloved Community."[135] He believed, as he stated in 1962, that economic and industrial growth in the South would ultimately lead to the breakdown of many of the barriers that separated the races:

> If the South is to grow economically it must continue to industrialize. We see signs of this vigorous industrialization, with a concomitant urbanization, throughout every Southern state. Day after day, the South is receiving new multi-million dollar industries. With the growth of industry the folkways of white supremacy will gradually pass away. . . . This growth of industry will also increase the purchasing power of the Negro, and this augmented purchasing power will result in improved medical care, greater educational opportunities, and more adequate housing.[136]

In King's estimation, an integrated South was unthinkable apart from a sharing of material resources across race boundaries. Expressing his thoughts on the matter, Coretta Scott King has written: "We must have the same quality and quantity of power that other ethnic groups possess, so that blacks, as a group, can hold their own in a society where, instead of a melting pot, separate peoples function beside each other, exchanging the power they control for the power the other fellow has."[137] In other words, King spoke of black economic power intersecting with white economic power. This idea of mutual power sharing registered well with white New South thinkers, some of whom sought to persuade department stores, banks, and other business communities to break the color line and employ African Americans. James Dabbs emphatically noted the need to overcome "economic discrimination," and so did Harry Golden, who observed in 1967 that "the hotels, restaurants, and theaters are open to the

Negro but he does not have the price of admission."[138] Economic empowerment as an avenue to interrracial cooperation and community in the South could not have been more important for Anne Braden, who, due to her socialist leanings, agreed with much of King's critique of capitalism in the late 1960s.[139]

The integrated society in the southern context would also require what King termed "new social and political attitudes." In 1963, he explained how the growing alliance between blacks and white moderates was not only changing the social outlook of people in the South, but also "registering momentous gains in the electoral arena." King pointed specifically to the "Negro-white *de facto* alliance" in Georgia which, in 1962, "elected a moderate Governor, a moderate Mayor in Atlanta, a moderate Congressman from the most populous county, and sent a Negro to the State Senate for the first time in nearly a hundred years."[140] As King always said, duplicating this trend across the South required greater accessibility on the part of blacks to the ballot. He contended that "the effort of Negroes to vote" extended beyond the "matter of exercising rights guaranteed by the United States Constitution" to the issue of "duty" or "moral obligation."[141] The same message coursed through the writings of the white New South advocates, all of whom joined King in opposing the poll tax, "the white primary," white political machines, and other obstacles to black voting rights. According to one of his biographers, Ralph McGill made "the right to vote" the "heart of" his "vision of a 'New South.'"[142] This was also the case with James Dabbs, who consistently reminded southern blacks that "your registering and your voting are necessary if this democratic structure is to function healthily."[143] Although not as well-respected in some circles for her ideas on the subject as McGill, Anne Braden saw the voting booth as one powerful arena in which southern blacks and whites could express their collective will in the interest of authentic, participatory democracy.[144]

The vital role of education in this maturation process was not ignored. King, McGill, Lillian Smith, and others longed for the day when a culture of learning would replace the culture of resistance in the South. They felt that education, much like religion, was needed to transform the types of racist attitudes and behavior that prevented southerners from enjoying a communal and prosperous existence. They hoped that black students, who had for generations been hampered by a shortage of textbooks, laboratory equipment, and other resources, could find their place in integrated classrooms, where they could, along with white students, develop a healthy sense of diversity and of themselves as social beings who find authentic existence through relations with each other. For King and the white New South idealists, replacing a vicious and crippling system of miseducation with a powerful program of reeducation afforded the best route to a more just economic order, a more participatory political structure, and a reformed legal system. They also realized that such changes necessitated some level of involvement on the part of the federal government.[145]

Clearly, few models of genuine interracial community existed in the South for King and the other New South optimists. Myles Horton's Highlander Folk School and Clarence Jordan's Koinonia Farm were rare examples of southern-based interracial communities. Strangely, white churches supported racial segregation as an article of faith, despite the prophetic preaching and activism of Robert Graetz, Will Campbell, and a few other southern white preachers who embraced King. The Highlander Folk School, a unique embodiment of unionism, democracy, and Christian socialism, had been established by Horton in Monteagle, Tennessee, in 1932, and it became "an interracial training center for labor, socialist, and religiously oriented community organizers in the South."[146] The Koinonia Farm, a racially integrated expression of Christian community, had been started by Jordan in Americus, Georgia, in 1942. King saw in both Horton's and Jordan's movements the embodiment of his vision of the New South. Speaking at the twenty-fifth anniversary observance of the Highlander Folk School in 1957, in the presence of Horton and other activists, King stated that "I have long admired the noble purpose and creative work of this institution," and he expressed delight that "you have given the South some of its most responsible leaders in this great period of transition."[147] Writing Jordan at a time when the Koinonia Farm endured brutal attacks from segregationists, King gave voice to his hope that "you will gain consolation from the fact that in your struggle for freedom and a true Christian community you have cosmic companionship."[148]

King's assessment of the communitarian ethics of the Highlander Folk School and the Koinonia Farm was undoubtedly shared in some measure by the white writers in the New South movement. Ralph

McGill, Lillian Smith, James Dabbs, and Sarah Boyle had every reason to respect these institutions' devotion to interracial community, but their uneasiness with the radical left probably explains why they never became strong and vocal supporters of the Highlander Folk School. The activities of Harry Golden, and especially of Anne Braden, seem to have been more in line with the politics and mission of both institutions. Braden corresponded regularly with the Koinonia Farm, and she asked Clarence Jordan "to be a petitioner for clemency for her husband after his conviction for contempt of the House Un-American Activities Committee." Even Boyle, who strongly promoted school integration in Virginia, admitted that Jordan's "unconscious witnessing" had done much for her "inner being."[149]

It became increasingly evident to King that only a tiny minority of white southerners were willing to go as far as Horton and Jordan to promote community and the peaceful coexistence of the races. As the civil rights leader became more militant, his optimism concerning the possibility of radical change in the South waned. Coleman B. Brown is right in saying that King experienced "a growing sobriety,"

> a sobriety that emerged especially after 1965—not as a judgment that earlier southern victories had been dismantled, or rendered meaningless. There simply is no evidence of that in King. Rather, there seems in him a growing grief that the New South—which he was confident had somehow arrived—had, despite everything, so much resistance to itself. Moreover, he seems to have been grieving that the New Negro—for whom the sense of inferiority and even the experience of overt segregation were increasingly dead things—would nonetheless have to bear, even as a new people, continued injustice and struggle in the South.[150]

King's declining optimism regarding the South was not always shared on the same level by McGill, Smith, Golden, Dabbs, Braden, and Boyle, all of whom seemed wedded to the conviction that white southerners had deep within the kind of moral and spiritual capacity needed for radical self-transformation and social change. They were perhaps too preoccupied with defending the dignity of white goodwill to see the true depths of racism in the South. Unable to fully identify with King's struggle, pain, and frustration, these writers assumed that strong appeals to reason, religion, and democratic principles, especially as embodied in the civil rights movement, would ultimately lead to the total elimination of racial inequality and injustice. By 1966, and perhaps even before this time, King had come to see that this simply was not the case. Indeed, he faced the painful realization that the white South was determined, even in unconscious ways, to maintain the structures of white power and supremacy.[151]

King's determination to develop more radical ways of challenging white racism and domination in America helps explain why he was criticized by some of the New South thinkers in the late 1960s. Congratulated by all of the major white New South writers for receiving the Nobel Peace Prize in 1964, King, less than two years later, found himself and young militants in the movement heavily criticized by Lillian Smith and Ralph McGill. In early 1966, Smith, lamenting the gradual abandonment of nonviolence and the rise of black power and nationalism in certain circles of the movement, seemed to place some of the blame for these developments on King's "lack of tough-mindedness."[152] She referred to black power advocates as "new killers of the dream," denounced black nationalism as "a new kind of slavery for the Negro," referred to critics of nonviolence in SNCC and CORE as "the Intruders," and insisted that "King isn't too bright as a politician."[153] On her deathbed in 1966, Smith resigned from CORE, feeling that she no longer had a place in the increasingly radical civil rights movement.[154] Moreover, she had concluded, and rightly so, that the young militants were beginning to greatly influence King, a development that was far more meaningful and productive than she was prepared to admit. Had Smith lived to hear King's controversial anti–Vietnam War speech in 1967, she, given her opposition to the antiwar movement and loyalty to President Lyndon Johnson, would have responded in disbelief, and probably would have broken completely with the civil rights leader.[155]

Ralph McGill repeated many of Smith's criticisms of King and young militants in the movement. By 1967, McGill felt that King was no longer a strong and respected leader, in part because the prophet of nonviolence was slowly losing ground to Stokely Carmichael and other young militants in SNCC. McGill denounced SNCC as "a hate group" or "the new Klan in reverse," and pointed to what he saw as the need for new and responsible leadership in the movement. Concerning this shift in McGill's thinking, one of his biographers has written:

> Over the years he had been preaching that the Negro was the most patient and gentle of men, who had endured with superhuman stoicism the generations of insult and discrimination that had been his lot. Now he discovered that the modern young black was neither patient nor gentle but angrily, militantly aggressive, demanding his rights instantly, and sometimes was rashly irresponsible and unreasoning in his pursuit of them. This disturbed McGill. In a letter to McGeorge Bundy, congratulating the Ford Foundation on making a grant to CORE, one of the more conservative of the Negro organizations, he outlined what he believed to be the dilemma of Martin Luther King, Jr.—who, he said, was being forced to go part of the way with the violent wing, the Black Panthers, while at the same time opposing their methods. . . . After a visit to a little Negro church, once the haven and refuge of the gentlest and meekest of the blacks, he had come away convinced that King's days as a leader of his people were coming to an end. King, he felt, was rapidly losing the following of the Negroes under thirty-five. What was needed, he believed, was a responsible Negro leader, younger than King, who could stand off the challenge of the violent men, Stokely Carmichael and Rap Brown.[156]

King's strong attack on the Johnson administration's role in the Vietnam War, leveled in a speech at New York's Riverside Church on April 4, 1967, angered McGill, leading him to cease financial support for the SCLC. Especially troubling for McGill was King's call for young men who "find this war objectionable and abominable" to file as "conscientious objectors." "We are certain that, until a few weeks ago," said McGill in a letter to King a month later, "you had the full confidence and unbounded admiration of virtually *all* of the right-minded people, black and white alike, in the United States." Disturbed by King's "attempts to link the civil rights movement to your crusade for peace in Vietnam," McGill not only publicly joined Carl Rowan, Whitney Young, Ralph Bunche, and other black leaders in scolding King, but declared that "we are obliged to part company with you."[157] McGill's bitterness toward King lingered, as the civil rights leader fused attacks on America's foreign policy with calls for a total restructuring of the capitalistic system. That bitterness subsided only when King was brutally assassinated in 1968, as McGill joined other New South idealists in expressing deep anger and outrage over the tragedy. For McGill, as for the others, the death of King signaled the need for black and white southerners to struggle together with an even greater sense of urgency.[158]

King, Smith, McGill, and the other New South writers prepared the ground for the South's gradual evolution around the issues of race. They all had what James Dabbs called a "southern sense of place," and their love for the region accounted for their persistent calls for blacks and whites to learn how to relate in new, fresh, and creative ways.[159] Otherwise, they would never attain the level of social and political maturity worthy of a democratic people. By pressing their claims with words and deeds, the New South prophets of the 1950s and 1960s etched their names and faces in the region's social, cultural, literary, and political history.[160]

A Transformed Society or an Old Order?
Images of the New South since King

It is commonly believed that a New South had come into being by the time of King's death in April 1968. The battle for basic civil or constitutional rights had been won, and many of the customs of the Old South had faded. The quasi-legal barriers to the right to vote had been struck down, full access to restaurants, hotels, and other public facilities had been achieved, barriers to black advancement in elite universities and law firms were beginning to crumble, efforts to place black and white children together in schools were increasing, and the stage had been set for black elected officials to take charge as mayors, sheriffs, councilpersons, judges, state officials, and legislators. Schools, libraries, churches, parks, community centers, and many other institutions which are named for King and other civil rights activists extend across the South. These gains, materially and symbolically, are often measured by different standards, but they unarguably attest to King's effectiveness, and to the influences of "ordinary" African Americans, in taking a diffuse sense of a New South proposed by a wide variety of southerners, mainly white, giving it clarity and focus, and then showing how—through the civil rights movement—this more focused vision could be translated into a New South reality that embraced racial justice.[161]

The South has consciously taken steps over the past four decades to purge itself of the old image, or to render absurd the notion that it is the most intransigent and rugged region in the country in the area of race relations. In some cases, well-known racists have acknowledged the error of their ways and have stated publicly that segregation is morally and legally wrong. Among the most notable examples are the televangelist Jerry Falwell of Virginia and the recently deceased Alabama Governor George C. Wallace. In the early 1980s, Wallace, whom King included among the South's most vicious racists, appeared at black churches and political gatherings, embraced African Americans of all ages, and included several blacks on his staff.[162]

The white South's gradual shift away from the racism of its past is much more evident in the work of Morris Dees, an Alabama-born lawyer, Attorney General Michael Moore of Mississippi, Attorney General Bill Baxley of Alabama, former president Jimmy Carter of Georgia, and former president Bill Clinton, who hails from Arkansas. Dees has emerged as perhaps the foremost enemy of the Ku Klux Klan and other white supremacist organizations, and since 1971 has monitored hate groups through his Southern Poverty Law Center in Montgomery.[163] Moore has been a force behind the prosecution and conviction of Byron De La Beckwith, Samuel H. Bowers, and other bigots responsible for civil rights violations and crimes in Mississippi in the 1960s. Baxley has made similar contributions in Alabama. Carter made human rights the rallying cry of his administration from 1976 to 1980, and has continued in that vein up to the present. He and Clinton appointed more African Americans than any other U.S. presidents to their campaigns and White House staffs, to cabinet- and subcabinet-level positions, and, perhaps more important, to the various levels of the federal court system. Clinton also sought, unsuccessfully, to initiate a national dialogue on race in the late 1990s. These and other white southerners of goodwill have been heavily inspired by the rich and powerful legacy of King and the movement he led.[164]

Strangely enough, however, white churches in the South have done virtually nothing since King's death to advance this movement toward a genuinely New South. Donald E. Collins has documented the failure of white United Methodist Churches in the Alabama–West Florida Conference to minister to the needs of black and increasingly mixed neighborhoods since the 1970s, noting that they have chosen instead to follow their fleeing members to the surburbs.[165] White southern churches and their leaders are still silent and noncommittal when confronted with the question of race relations. Although the Southern Baptists and a few congregations and church conferences in other denominations apologized for slavery and racism in the 1990s, they oppose affirmative action and reparations, and have done little or nothing along practical lines to compensate African Americans for their sufferings.[166] This is not only an affront to King's legacy, but it is ironic since the civil rights leader has been a major influence in the *politicization* of white churches and clergypersons in recent years.[167]

Be that as it may, the strides made since the Supreme Court's *Brown v. Board of Education* decision (1954) are being cited as evidence that the Old South is dead. This much and more is claimed today by southerners in all stations of life—from politicians and lawmakers to clergypersons to newspaper commentators, poets, and artists in various fields. Undoubtedly, this perception, held by most whites and even a surprising number of blacks, helps explain the lingering inability of the South to live out the full meaning of King's dream. King's blueprint for a New South remains clear and eminently worthy of serious consideration and pursuit, but it is being distorted under the power of those who seek material and psychic benefits from the continuing racial divide in this country.[168]

The past four decades have witnessed a deep conflict between a complex, stubborn southern past that will not die and a new, more creative South that is determined to live. In describing this conflict or tension, some have spoken of "a new South with old problems," giving special attention to the region's inability to match its rapid rate of industrial-urban development with a strong, persistent, and meaningful assault on the economic roots of racism.[169] James C. Cobb has addressed this problem as it stood by the late 1970s, providing more evidence that, contrary to what King had envisioned, increased industrialization does not necessarily result in a genuinely and thoroughly integrated southern society:

Though less victimized by conscious discrimination after the Civil Rights Movement, the Sunbelt South's blacks still found it difficult to share in the region's growth. Developers seemed unable to steer industries into impoverished rural areas with high concentrations of blacks, whom employers spurned as poorly trained and union prone. Many blacks left these enduring pockets of poverty for southern cities where opportunities for unskilled workers often failed to meet expectations and where overcrowding and dramatic contrasts in standards of living contributed to tensions that manifested themselves in rising crime rates, expanding ghettoes, and a white exodus to the suburbs.[170]

The situation remained largely the same for low-skilled black laborers in the South in the 1980s and 1990s. The massive movement of industry, technology, and capital into the increasingly urbanized South, the advanced educational and employment opportunities resulting from federal legislation and information technology, and the increase in black elected officials made African Americans a more vital part of the labor force, but these developments hardly placed the masses on a more solid economic foundation. Black southerners in the so-called middle class are enjoying greater purchasing power, improved medical care, and better housing, but they are still dominated by the structures of white power. Thus, King's belief that advanced industrial-urban development in the South would necessarily result in the demise of "the folkways of white supremacy" still stands in need of vindication.[171]

While even some interracial couples were enjoying life in the New South in the early 1970s, this alone said little about the true nature of race relations as they would unfold in the region in the three decades that followed. Antiquated miscegenation laws, which banned sex and marriage between the races, would remain as a vestige of the Old South.[172] Reminders of racially motivated violence against African Americans would surface from time to time, becoming painfully real with the lynching of Michael Donald in Mobile, Alabama, in 1981, the dragging death of James Byrd, Jr., in Jasper, Texas, in 1998, and the random acts of violence against blacks and other minorities in various sectors of contemporary southern society.[173] The threat of heightened racial tensions still looms, as Asians, Mexicans, and other immigrants move into the region to compete for jobs and space, and as blacks and whites bitterly disagree over the meaning and significance of the Confederate flag, state songs that contain racist lyrics, and other symbols of the Old South.[174] Such disturbing trends seem to render dubious, and perhaps untenable, King's prediction, made in the late 1950s, that "the idea of freedom" would be born "in the Southland."[175]

For some in the current world of academia, the term "New South" suggests that there is no longer anything unique or strikingly distinctive about relations between black and white southerners. A growing contention is that southern race relations have become *nationalized*, or that race relations across the country have become *southernized*.[176] This view is accepted by Angela McCoy, the daughter of the murdered civil rights activist James Chaney, who has concluded that "racism in modern Mississippi has taken on the subtler hue of racism in the North."[177] This may well be said of the South as a whole. However, there have been indications in recent years that race relations are generally better in the South than in the North. To a much greater extent than the northern part of the United States, the South was forced to face forthrightly her racial dilemma during the King years, and she has tried much harder to change her old image and to ease old racial tensions. Thus, it is not surprising that, in recent years, the North has become the center of so many racial incidents on college and university campuses, of the fastest growing and the most evangelistic-minded hate groups, and of the most brutal physical attacks on blacks by law enforcement officers.[178] These interesting developments could substantiate King's claim, set forth in 1968, that "the South is going to get ahead of the North" in the field of race relations.[179]

This is not meant to minimize the struggle that lies ahead for the New South. The region is still confronted with the challenge of creating the type of integrated educational system that tears down racial stereotypes and creates new racial alliances. Black and white children along with the children of more recent immigrant groups must have more opportunities to study together, to exchange ideas about the contributions of different peoples to world civilization, and to learn together in an atmosphere that fosters acceptance, understanding, self-worth, and tolerance for human differences. Opportunities of this nature are consistent with King's view that education for critical consciousness provides one significant avenue to real freedom, community, and social democracy.[180] Moreover, any viable system of education in the South must address several pressing realities. First, it is necessary to reframe the dialogue on race because immigration patterns show that the problem is no longer merely one of black versus white. King had come to see this before his death, and this helps explain his efforts to bring peoples of various racial and ethnic groups together in the Poor People's Campaign. Second, southerners, especially whites, must become more open to issues of diversity and multiculturalism, spiritually and intellectually. Finally, the South must embrace the fact that its future progress hinges on its ability to transcend the racist past, with all of its mythology and symbolism, while devoting itself to a cooperative model of human advancement.

The New South must establish the type of atmosphere that leads to economic empowerment for all its citizens. This is what King had in mind when he opted for democratic socialism and called for the intersection of black power and white power. This was the motivation behind the civil rights leader's planning of the Poor People's Campaign. The South that King once called "new" is still facing the need to eliminate the black-white wage gap and to integrate its economic resources across race, ethnic, and class boundaries.[181]

The New South is also faced with the responsibility of making more drastic changes in a legal system that has long been dominated by racist police and court officials. King consistently spoke of the wise use of law enforcement and court action, which together with proper legislation and education could considerably reduce the kind of racist practices commonly associated with the Old South. Although the number of black judges, lawyers, jurors, prosecutors, constables, police officers, sheriffs, and legislators has increased significantly in the South since King's death, too many African Americans, Hispanics, and other minorities remain the victims of racial profiling, police brutality, and hate crimes, and surprising numbers still doubt that their grievances and cases can be handled fairly through the legal system.[182]

Moreover, the New South must bring more integrity to its political structures in order to sustain itself. Currently, Mississippi, Alabama, and the other southern states claim hundreds of elected black officials, but the question of fairness in the political processes still looms large. It is still rare for black politicians to be elected on a

statewide basis, Douglas Wilder's becoming governor of Virginia in
the 1990s notwithstanding. Even today, votes from predominantly
black precincts in the rural South are destroyed, ignored, or thrown
into rivers, redistricting processes and other means are employed to
limit black voting power, and black politicians suffer unwarranted harassment and are occasionally forced out of office without justification.[183] The general dissatisfaction of black Floridians with the 2000
presidential election process highlights some of these problems. Hundreds of black registered voters in Florida were harassed at the polls,
denied entrance to voting places, and deprived of the ballot based on
distorted or erroneous information. This vindicated some of the fears
that King had about the extremes to which those in power would go
in order to disfranchise African Americans. The idea that the South
will go back to the dark days of the late nineteenth century, when
black Reconstruction politicians and voters were disenfranchised, is
not likely to materialize, but African Americans, given their experiences in the past, and especially during the 2000 election, cannot
afford to become complacent. King consistently made this point as he
challenged his people to make greater use of their "untapped political
power."[184]

The road to a newer New South will require a greater sense of
where the region is today, and of where it must go in order to actualize
King's vision. King gave southerners hope for a new, just, and moral society. That hope must be continuously revived or rekindled if the South
is to reach its fullest potential in terms of social and political democracy.

The Religious Dimensions of Dixie: King, Southern Civil Religion, and Regional Identity

The foregoing discussion suggests that King and the white New South
advocates of his time refused to separate religious values from public
life. In this regard, they broke with that Old South tradition which
tended to reduce religion to the private sphere, and which separated
piety from politics. The ways in which King fused religion and politics
in his articulation of and quest for the beloved community ideal have
led some to label him a proponent of a civil religion. Civil religion is
commonly defined as "the general faith of a state or nation that fo-

cuses on widely held beliefs about the history and destiny of that state or nation." Variously referred to as public, political, civil, or societal religion, it is "a religio-political phenomenon" or "a religious way of thinking about politics which provides a society with ultimate meaning."[185] Viewing this faith as one shared by all Americans, black and white, the sociologist Robert N. Bellah, whose 1967 essay triggered debate on the subject, has described King as

> a person seemingly destined to go down in history as a true interpreter and prophet of the American civil religion. The nonviolent character of King's protests, his readiness to accept penalties imposed by the very system he was challenging, reflect precisely civility elevated to civil religion.[186]

John Dixon Elder offers a more thorough and compelling analysis of King as both a civil theologian and an embodiment of American civil religion. Elder contends that King, by blending biblical references and the values of the Judeo-Christian tradition with American democratic ideals, made American civil religion a much more positive, inclusive, and relevant phenomenon than what usually and superficially involves the merging of the themes of country, flag, and God:

> In a remarkable way, Martin Luther King served both as preacher to the people of his own Baptist tradition and as spokesman for an enlarged American civil religion. His sermons are filled with the biblical terminology that from the beginning was applied to the American national experience—the exodus, the wilderness, and the promised land. But King revived this terminology, making a fresh and profoundly meaningful application to our present national situation. Though he was speaking to black Americans of "going up on the mountain" and "looking over Jordan," his words rescued an inheritance of religious terminology for white Americans as well. In a day when the usefulness of "God talk" is widely questioned, King used the biblical symbols that are at the heart of American civil religion and gave them fresh meaning. "Freedom," for instance, is a hallowed word in the American vocabulary, but it is amazing how many whites who have marched with King, been in jail with him, or even merely heard

him preach claim to have experienced a new sense of freedom in his presence. For the authentic meaning of freedom we turn now to a Negro who gave his life trying to achieve for his fellows the freedom proclaimed in the fundamental documents of the nation.[187]

Elder makes several other points in establishing the uniqueness of King's contribution to American civil religion. In words that merit extended quotation, he writes:

American civil religion was revivified by King; it was also extended. The subtle and not-so-subtle identification of "the American dream" with the white race is pervasive in our society. Yet it was a black man who gave "the American dream" contemporary content in the soaring "I have a dream" speech before the Lincoln Memorial. Though criticized and even condemned by both blacks and whites, he, as no other, verbalized their common "dream." It is likely then that King, a Negro preacher who never held public office, has joined Kennedy, Lincoln, and other white statesmen as a source of definitive statements of national self-understanding and divine, transcending judgment. King has thus enabled black Americans to shape the substance of a civil religion from which, ironically, they have been heretofore excluded. . . . Furthermore, King introduced new elements that may endure in American civil religion. "Love" and "nonviolence" have been two of these. The reconciling character of King's theology, demonstrated in his life as well as in his words, has only begun to affect our national religion.[188]

Denying that King's civil religion was merely regional or even national in character, Elder goes on to support Andrew M. Manis's claim that the civil rights leader "often becomes the virtual personification of a prophetic manifestation of the American civil religion":

In the line of the Hebrew prophets that Lincoln joined when he emphasized the gap between national achievement and divine will, King proclaimed that a nation that disregards human needs and rights abroad or at home is subject to divine judgment. . . . The awarding of the Nobel Peace Prize indicates his success in moving toward a universally meaningful "civil religion." King was often introduced as a "Moses" of our time, and the title is not inappropriate for one who has led the way to unity and freedom for the diverse tribes of men now facing the choice between "chaos or community." Like Presidents Kennedy and Lincoln, he has contributed profoundly to a more genuine apprehension of that universal and transcendent religious reality by which all nations are judged.[189]

While it is quite easy to see that King used the rhetoric of American civil religion, the extent to which he employed the language and symbols of what Charles R. Wilson calls "a southern civil religion" is open to serious debate. Wilson brilliantly explains the difference between "Southern civil religion" and the "American civil religion" that Robert Bellah, Sidney E. Mead, Will Herberg, and other scholars have treated in their works:

> In the Post-Civil War and twentieth century South, a set of values existed which could be designated a Southern Way of Life. Those values constituted the basis for a Southern civil religion which differed from the American civil religion. Dixie's value system varied from the one Herberg discussed—Southerners undoubtedly were less optimistic, less liberal, less democratic, less tolerant, and more homogeneously Protestant. In their religion Southerners stressed "democracy" less than the conservative concept of "virtue." The Enlightenment tradition played no role in shaping the religion of the Lost Cause, while the emotionally intense, dynamic Revivalist tradition was at its center. The secularized legacy of idealistic, moralistic Puritanism also helped form its character. While the whole course of Southern history provided the background, the Southern civil religion actually emerged from Dixie's Civil War experience. . . . Without the Lost Cause, no civil religion would have existed.[190]

Wilson goes on to say that "King used the language of the late nineteenth century Lost Cause, speaking of suffering, tragedy, honor, the need for virtuous behavior, the need of a defeated people to achieve dignity, and the search for group identity and destiny." The same could be said of Ralph McGill, Lillian Smith, and other white New South visionaries. The suggestion here is that many of the "traditional southern white values," which stood at the core of "a southern civil religion," were embraced by King and his people as they struggled to redeem and transform the South—socially, politically, morally, spiritually, and otherwise.[191]

Unquestionably, King's analysis of the South's struggle with race relations carried religious and theological dimensions. Like Sarah P. Boyle, Harry Golden, and James M. Dabbs, he prayed consistently for God's guidance in the South, and he saw the civil rights movement as proof that the Supreme Being was at work in the region.[192] Displaying a strong tendency to make a connection between the South and God, between region and religion, King said, as the movement gained momentum in the late 1950s, that

> God still has a mysterious way to perform His wonders. It seems that God decided to use Montgomery as the proving ground for the struggle and triumph of freedom and justice in America. It is one of the ironies of our day that Montgomery, the cradle of the Confederacy, is being transformed into Montgomery, the cradle of freedom and justice.[193]

Thus, it is not surprising that throughout the 1960s, King constantly noted how God had used the worst areas of the South "to bring some of the most creative advances for the black man in the United States of America."[194] The belief that "the future of America" would possibly be determined in the Southland, where "democracy faces its most serious challenge," formed much of the basis of King's Christian optimism and hope. Indeed, his view of the South as the focal point of God's liberating activity for the nation was echoed in James M. Dabbs's description of the South as "God's project." "Perhaps the mystery," Dabbs asserted, "lies in the fact that God is working here, and, as men have long recognized, he works in mysterious ways." He and King shared the idea that religion is essential to understanding the meaning and significance of the South.[195] Moreover, the religious language of the two men contained biblical terminology and imagery that related to the southern experience. Dabbs wrote poignantly of how the Negro in the South had been "shoved aside through segregation, into a sort of Babylonian Captivity."[196] Echoing themes that coursed through the songs and tales of his slave forebears, which clearly carried political overtones, King often alluded to "Pharaoh" in characterizing white oppressors in the South, and he used the biblical story of Jesus and terms like "bearing the cross," "Egyptland," "wilderness," and "the promised land" in assessing the unfolding history and destiny of black southerners and the region as a whole. Indeed, King marveled at the thought that God "is leading us out of a bewildering Egypt, through a bleak and desolate wilderness, toward a bright and glittering promised land."[197]

While having a deep spiritual and physical attachment to the South, King did not embrace uncritically its range of institutions, values, myths, and rituals. Much of the white South's tendency to identify the southern way of life with the will of God and the highest ethical ideal disturbed him greatly. He criticized the white South's segregated churches, its racist theology, and the various ways in which it used scripture and Christian rhetoric to justify and even sanction the existing social, political, and economic order. Furthermore, King never embraced the white South's sanitized version of the Confederate tradition, its reverence for Confederate heroes, its respect for the Confederate flag and other symbols of the Old South, and the sacredness it commonly attached to the singing of "Dixie."[198] He remembered the Confederacy as a feeble attempt to create a separate political nation on the basis of a "master race" ethos.[199] Thus, the civil rights leader emerged as more of a critic than a proponent of southern civil religion. Unlike the public faith embraced by most white southerners, King's civil religion was unequivocally and unapologetically prophetic, and geared toward a communitarian ethic that knew no racial or regional boundaries. Andrew Manis is quite right in identifying "two sharply divergent" civil religions in the South, one black and the other white, with one often in conflict with the other.[200]

Also in contrast to southern civil religion, King's civil religion was a product of both a dynamic revivalist tradition and the Enlightenment tradition. Edward Lee Moore locates King in what he terms "the black revivalist tradition" in the South, a tradition that is "composed of eclectic, and not exclusively Christian, elements."[201] King combined this tradition's old-fashioned spirituality, its prophetic and protest dimensions, and its faith in the justice of the universe with his use of the

Enlightenment ideals of Tolerance, Reason, and Natural Law, thus affording a context for his deep appreciation of the Declaration of Independence and the Constitution. This blending of traditions in King's public faith could not have been more evident, especially given his deep roots in southern black Baptist Protestantism and his intense study of Jean Jacques Rousseau, Jeremy Bentham, Thomas Hobbes, John Locke, John Stuart Mill, and others.[202]

King was part of a black South that rejected much of the white South's blending of Christian principles and southern regional patriotism and chauvinism. As David Howard-Pitney has shown, African Americans, while sharing broad themes and symbols with whites (e.g., freedom, the Statue of Liberty, etc.), merged their own religious understandings of messianism, deliverance, and redemption with the nation's political ideals of democracy, freedom, and equality.[203] The black South also had its own unique set of sacred persons, events, beliefs, rituals, and symbols, all of which were rooted in a religion that stressed consistency between faith and praxis. Turned off by romanticized images of the Old South, and having virtually no interest in the Confederate tradition or the myth of the Lost Cause, King and other black southerners fashioned a public faith that largely rejected white southern notions of piety, honor, sacrifice, virtue, and morality, and which embodied the principles of creative nonviolence, redemptive love, altruism, respect for human differences, Christian optimism and hope, and participatory democracy.[204] Recognizing this significant difference between the public faiths of white and black southerners, the New South idealist James Dabbs commented:

> In brief, the old Southern community meant far less to the Negro than it did to the white, and when it fell apart he was but slightly tempted to worship the fragments, especially since he saw beyond the South the larger world of the nation looming on the horizon. Unlike the white southerner, he could accept this world wholeheartedly: he was no states'-righter who had to be brought back into the Union. . . . Never having been troubled seriously by the divisory Puritan conscience, never having had to hate the world because he publicly misused it in exploiting an entire race, the Negro possessed a freedom unknown to the white to absorb the more positive values of Southern life, to carry them with a re-

markable degree of perseverance through the collapse of the Southern order, and to hold them for the time when he should be able to speak with authority.[205]

King and the civil rights movement prepared the ground for what Charles Wilson calls "the transformation of the sacralized South from a whites-only vision of the Confederate Lost Cause into a post-1960s ideal of racial integration." Wilson also refers to this development as a shift from "the religion of the Lost Cause into a biracial southern civil religion."[206] Ralph McGill, Lillian Smith, James Dabbs, and other New South idealists also contributed in some ways to this shift. Although this transformation is not yet complete, it, even in its early stages, shows that King and others in the New South movement have had an enormous impact on how black and white southerners today view the relationship between religion, law, morality, politics, and social change.

Strangely enough, the power of this emerging "biracial southern civil religion" has been tested and challenged since King's death by a range of forces. First, there are white southerners who remain determined to sanitize and romanticize the Old South and the Confederate tradition. Segments of white southern society have continued to engage in reenactments of the Civil War and to celebrate Confederate heroes. Moreover, whites and blacks in Mississippi, South Carolina, Georgia, Alabama, and other areas of the South have consistently clashed over the singing of "Dixie" and the symbolic meaning and significance of the Confederate flag. During the presidential campaign of 2000, Republican candidates John McCain and George W. Bush contributed to the tensions by refusing to condemn the Confederate flag. The Bush campaign actually inspired those forces that celebrate the Confederate tradition and raise the banner of states' rights. This may well continue throughout the Bush presidency, thus undermining King's dream for a South that transcends all racial barriers in the interest of community.

A more extreme version of this southern attachment to the past is evident with the radical and violent racists in the South. These are Klanspersons, skinheads, neo-Nazis, and paramilitary groups that constitute a frightening but often ignored force. Such groups are openly committed to the preservation of white power and a white South, even to the point of preparing for a race war. Often they are perceived as a largely silent voice crying in the wilderness, but the continuing threats they pose to order and racial harmony in the South must not be over-looked. King was never oblivious to this reality.

A third force consists of white southern moderates and liberals who are increasingly subscribing to the notion that racism is a prob-lem of the past. Wedded to the politics of silence and even denial, they ignore the claims and complaints of African Americans and other minorities, and many vehemently oppose affirmative action and the call for reparations. They overlook the abundance of evidence that points to racial profiling, police brutality, hate crimes, and racism in the criminal justice system, while reminding African Americans that they should be pleased and grateful for the many strides they have made. For King, southerners of this variety were as much a bar-rier to racial progress as the hard-core racists.

Conservative politicians from the South make up yet another force that threatens the vitality of a truly biracial society and civil religion. They share the characteristics of southern moderates and liberals but differ in that they are able to use their political positions and power to reverse the civil rights gains made under the leadership of King and others. As stated earlier, they manipulate King's words to support their opposition to affirmative action, while uniting with black neo-conservatives to promote a conservative political, social, and economic agenda. Furthermore, these politicians, since the early 1970s when the Nixon administration made "law and order" a rallying cry, have used coded language about race (on topics of welfare, crime, illegitimacy, and so on) to heighten white fears, to stay in office, and to justify their failure to address issues such as affirmative action, reparations, racial profiling, and the disproportionate numbers of African Americans and other minorities in the prison system. Conservative Republicans, including President George W. Bush, are heavily represented within this group of southerners. Dan T. Carter is quite correct in viewing such politicians as part of the political legacy of George Wallace.[207]

Andrew M. Manis recently referred to an emerging "civil-religious conflict" or "culture war" in the South, rooted to a great extent in racial differences. This conflict, according to Manis, is evident in the battle between black and white southerners over the Confederate flag, in the different party affiliations of most black (Democratic) and white (Republican) southerners, and in the various perspectives that African

Americans and whites have on the long and complex history of the region.[208] These competing visions and allegiances often obscure the fact that the South can no longer live in isolation from the rest of the nation and the world. With immigration and the globalization of information technology and the economy, the South will increasingly become a microcosm of the world.

NOTES

1. James Baldwin, "The Dangerous Road Before Martin Luther King, Jr.," *Harper's Magazine*, vol. 222 (February 1961): p. 38.

2. This conclusion is supported by a reading of Lerone Bennett, Jr., "From Booker T. to Martin L.," *Ebony*, vol. 18 (November 1962): pp. 152–162; Peter C. Moore, "Journey Out of Egypt: The Development of Negro Leadership in Alabama," B.A. Thesis, Princeton University, Princeton, N.J. (1958), pp. 1–20; and Lewis V. Baldwin, *To Make the Wounded Whole: The Cultural Legacy of Martin Luther King, Jr.* (Minneapolis: Fortress Press, 1992), pp. 9–19.

3. My discussion of King's sense of regional identity and regional responsibility has been heavily influenced by Coleman B. Brown, "Grounds for American Loyalty in a Prophetic Christian Social Ethic—with Special Attention to Martin Luther King, Jr.," Ph.D. diss., Union Theological Seminary, New York (April 1979), pp. 48–62. Also see Lewis V. Baldwin, *There Is a Balm in Gilead: The Cultural Roots of Martin Luther King, Jr.* (Minneapolis: Fortress Press, 1991), pp. 15–90.

4. For excellent studies that treat the moral-religious dimensions of "the southern way of life," as defined by the white South, see Charles R. Wilson, *Baptized in Blood: The Religion of the Lost Cause, 1865–1920* (Athens: University of Georgia Press, 1980), pp. 12, 100, 119, 135, and 138–139; Charles R. Wilson, *Judgment and Grace in Dixie: Southern Faiths from Faulkner to Elvis* (Athens: University of Georgia Press, 1995), pp. 3–178; Gardiner H. Shattuck, Jr., *A Shield and Hiding Place: The Religious Life of the Civil War Armies* (Macon, Ga.: Mercer University Press, 1987), pp. 1–136; and Eugene D. Genovese, *A Consuming Fire: The Fall of the Confederacy in the Mind of the White Christian South* (Athens: University of Georgia Press, 1998), pp. 3–127.

5. Bennett, "From Booker T. to Martin L.," pp. 152–162; Philip S. Foner, ed., *The Voice of Black America: Major Speeches by Negroes in the United States, 1797–1973*, vol. 1 (New York: Capricorn Books, 1975),

pp. 608–612; Martin Luther King, Jr., "An Address at a Mass Meeting," Marks Mississippi (19 March 1968), Archives of the Martin Luther King, Jr. Center for Nonviolent Social Change, Atlanta, Georgia, pp. 5–6; and Baldwin, *There Is a Balm in Gilead,* pp. 80–90.

6. Gayraud S. Wilmore, *Black Religion and Black Radicalism: An Interpretation of the Religious History of Afro-American People* (Maryknoll, N.Y.: Orbis Books, 1983), pp. 136–137; and Martin Luther King, Jr., *Stride toward Freedom: The Montgomery Story* (New York: Harper & Row, 1958), pp. 32–34.

7. See Charles R. Wilson and William Ferris, eds., *Encyclopedia of Southern Culture* (Chapel Hill: University of North Carolina Press, 1989), pp. 146, 931–932, and 1113–1114; Samuel S. Hill, ed., *Encyclopedia of Religion in the South* (Macon, Ga.: Mercer University Press, 1984), p. 471; and Wilson, *Baptized in Blood,* pp. 84–85.

8. Wilson and Ferris, eds., *Encyclopedia of Southern Culture,* pp. 146, 247, 264–268, 931–932, and 1113–1114; Hill, ed., *Encyclopedia of Religion in the South,* p. 471; and Wilson, *Baptized in Blood,* pp. 84–85. Some studies show that Atticus G. Haygood first used the term "New South." Others note that the term was used as early as January 1874 by *Harper's New Monthly Magazine* and as early as March of that same year by Henry Grady in an editorial in the *Atlanta Daily Herald.* See Raymond B. Nixon, *Henry W. Grady: Spokesman of the New South* (New York: Alfred A. Knopf, 1943), p. 240 n6; and Nancy Keever Andersen, "Cooperation for Social Betterment: Missions and Progressives in the Methodist Episcopal Church, South, 1894–1921," Ph.D. diss., Vanderbilt University, Nashville, Tennessee (December 1999), p. 14.

9. King's New South ideal is discussed at some length in Baldwin, *There Is a Balm in Gilead,* pp. 63–90. King articulated his vision of the New South in a number of essays, sometimes using the term. See Martin Luther King, Jr., "Bold Design for a New South," *The Nation,* vol. 196 (30 March 1963): pp. 259–262; Martin Luther King, Jr., "Who Speaks for the South?" *Liberation,* vol. 2 (March 1958): pp. 13–14; and Martin Luther King, Jr., "The 'New Negro' of the South: Behind the Montgomery Story," *Socialist Call,* June 1956, pp. 16–19.

10. Judson C. Ward, ed., *The New South: Thanksgiving Sermon, 1880, by Atticus G. Haygood* (Atlanta: Library of Emory University, 1950), pp. v–xi; and Atticus G. Haygood, *The New South: Gratitude, Amendment, Hope: A Thanksgiving Sermon for November 25, 1880* (Oxford, Ga., 1880), pp. 3–12.

11. Virginius Dabney, *Liberalism in the South* (Chapel Hill: University of North Carolina Press, 1932), p. 160; Joel Chandler Harris, ed., *Life of Henry W. Grady, Including His Writings and Speeches: A Memorial Volume Compiled by Mr. Henry W. Grady's Co-Workers on "The Constitution"* (New York: Haskell House Publishers, 1972), pp. 83–93; Henry W. Grady, *The New*

South and Other Addresses: With Biography, Critical Opinions, and Explanatory Notes by Edna Henry Lee Turpin (New York: Haskell House Publishers, 1969), pp. 23–42; Edwin D. Shurter, ed., *The Complete Orations and Speeches of Henry W. Grady* (New York: Hinds, Noble & Eldredge, 1910), pp. 7–22; Harold E. Davis, *Henry Grady's New South: Atlanta, a Brave and Beautiful City* (Tuscaloosa: University of Alabama Press, 1990), pp. 133–166; Nixon, *Henry W. Grady*, pp. 237–260; James W. Lee, *Henry W. Grady: The Editor, the Orator, the Man* (Nashville: Publishing House of the M. E. Church, South, 1896), pp. 41–68 and 69–106; and Michael P. Darling, "Wither the New South?: The New South Dialectic of Henry W. Grady and Dr. Martin Luther King, Jr.," unpublished paper, Vanderbilt University, Nashville, Tenn. (28 April 1998), pp. 1–12.

12. Paul M. Gaston, *The New South Creed: A Study in Southern Mythmaking* (New York: Alfred A. Knopf, 1970), pp. 4–5, 7, and 11–13; D. Augustus Straker, *The New South Investigated* (New York: Arno Press, 1973), pp. iii–vi; C. Vann Woodward, *Origins of the New South, 1877–1913* (Baton Rouge, La.: Louisiana State University Press, 1951), pp. ix–x, 154–158, and 175; George B. Tindall, *The Persistent Tradition in New South Politics* (Baton Rouge, La.: Louisiana State University Press, 1975), pp. 3–72; James E. McCulloch, ed., *The Call of the New South: Addresses Delivered at the Southern Sociological Congress, Nashville, Tennessee* (7–10 May 1912), pp. 220–221; George B. Tindall, *The Emergence of the New South, 1913–1945* (Baton Rouge, La.: Louisiana State University Press, 1967), pp. 10–109; and Francis B. Simkins, *The South—Old and New: A History, 1820–1947* (New York: Alfred A. Knopf, 1947), pp. 3–527.

13. Gaston, *The New South Creed*, pp. 4–5.

14. Ibid., p. 5.

15. King, *Stride toward Freedom*, p. 22.

16. Haygood, *The New South*, pp. 8–10; Atticus G. Haygood, *Our Brother in Black: His Freedom and His Future* (New York: Phillips & Hunt, 1881), pp. 5–8, 17–23, 39–83, and 112–241; Atticus G. Haygood, *Pleas for Progress* (Nashville: Publishing House of the M. E. Church, South, 1889), pp. 5–24, 137–146, and 212–249; Shurter, ed., *The Complete Orations and Speeches*, pp. 7, 27, and 198; and Gaston, *The New South Creed*, pp. 137–141. Watterson, using stronger language than that of most New South advocates, called slavery "a curse," a description that sharply contrasts with Martin Luther King, Jr.'s image of that system as one resulting from a blatant misuse of human freedom and power. See Henry Watterson, *Compromises of Life and Other Lectures and Addresses: Including Some Observations on Certain Downward Tendencies of Modern Society* (New York: Fox, Duffield & Company, 1903), pp. 289 and 308; Henry Watterson, *"Marse*

Henry": An Autobiography, vol. I (New York: George H. Doran Company, 1919), pp. 49–51; Martin Luther King, Jr., "The Meaning of Hope," a sermon delivered at the Dexter Avenue Baptist Church, Montgomery, Alabama (10 December 1967), King Center Archives, pp. 1–2; and Baldwin, *There Is a Balm in Gilead*, pp. 46–47. But even as New South optimists rejoiced in the passing of the Old South, they were known to paint "idyllic pictures" of plantation life in those times. See Paul H. Buck, *The Road to Reunion, 1865–1900* (New York: Vintage Books, 1937), pp. 177–179.

17. Haygood, *Our Brother in Black*, pp. 112–127; Martin Luther King, Jr., "An Address at a Mass Meeting," Marks, Mississippi, pp. 5–6; and James M. Washington, ed., *A Testament of Hope: The Essential Writings and Speeches of Martin Luther King, Jr.* (San Francisco: HarperCollins, 1986), pp. 189–194, 315–316, 563–566, and 621–623.

18. Gaston, *The New South Creed*, pp. 137–141 and 224–225; Davis, *Henry Grady's New South*, pp. 132–166; Wilson and Ferris, eds., *Encyclopedia of Southern Culture*, pp. 931–932; and Arthur Krock, comp., *The Editorials of Henry Watterson* (New York: George H. Doran Company, 1923), pp. 313–315.

19. Gaston, *The New South Creed*, pp. 136–141; and Shurter, ed., *The Complete Orations and Speeches*, pp. 33–35.

20. Paul Gaston persuasively contends that "Following Haygood's admonition, the New South spokesmen pictured a harmonious biracial society in which white and black mingled and cooperated in mutual tasks but separated otherwise." See Gaston, *The New South Creed*, p. 139; Edward L. Wheeler, *Uplifting the Race: The Black Minister in the New South, 1865–1902* (Lanham, Md.: University Press of America, 1986), p. 58 n65; Haygood, *The New South*, pp. 8–10; Haygood, *Pleas for Progress*, pp. 10–14, 49–55, and 139–213; and Haygood, *Our Brother in Black*, pp. 115–157 and 182–252.

21. Buck, *The Road to Reunion*, pp. 304–305; and Gaston, *The New South Creed*, pp. 137–141.

22. Martin Luther King, Jr., *Why We Can't Wait* (New York: New American Library, 1964), p. 131.

23. Clayborne Carson, ed., *The Autobiography of Martin Luther King, Jr.* (New York: Warner Books, 1998), p. 90.

24. King adamantly rejected all segregationist and white supremacist arguments based on scripture, religious principles, philosophy, and genetics, a tendency that clearly separated him from Grady. See Gaston, *The New South Creed*, p. 137; From Martin Luther King, Jr. to Mr. William E. Newgent (20 October 1959), The Martin Luther King, Jr. Papers, Special Collections, Mugar Memorial Library, Boston University, Boston, Massachusetts, p. 1; and Baldwin, *There Is a Balm in Gilead*, pp. 51–52.

25. Gaston, *The New South Creed*, pp. 137–139. Clearly a white supremacist, Henry Grady felt that slavery "had provided a not-altogether-bad place for Negroes." With this in mind, one writer contrasts Grady's "conservatism" with the so-called "liberal thought" of Atticus Haygood, who, unlike Grady, felt that African Americans had great capacity for further development. Because major New South advocates, including Haygood, believed in white supremacy, the idea of a southern liberal tradition with roots in the late nineteenth century is not persuasive. See Davis, *Henry Grady's New South*, pp. 133–166; Dabney, *Liberalism in the South*, pp. 10–173; and Morton Sosna, *In Search of the Silent South: Southern Liberals and the Race Issue* (New York: Columbia University Press, 1977), pp. vii–xi.

26. Foner, ed., *The Voice of Black America*, vol. 1, p. 611; Gaston, *The New South Creed*, p. 139; Baldwin, *There Is a Balm in Gilead*, pp. 72–73; Martin Luther King, Jr., "To Chart Our Course for the Future," address delivered at SCLC retreat, Frogmore, South Carolina (29–31 May 1967), The King Center Archives, pp. 4–5; Baldwin, *To Make the Wounded Whole*, pp. 11–12; Martin Luther King, Jr., "Transforming the Neighborhood," unpublished sermon (10 August 1967), King Center Archives, pp. 5–6; and Dabney, *Liberalism in the South*, p. 173.

27. Haygood, *Our Brother in Black*, pp. 112–127; and Krock, comp., *The Editorials of Henry Watterson*, pp. 313–314.

28. Wilson and Ferris, eds., *Encyclopedia of Southern Culture*, p. 1114; James C. Cobb, *The Selling of the South: The Southern Crusade for Industrial Development, 1936–1990* (Urbana and Chicago: University of Illinois Press, 1993), p. 122; and Davis, *Henry Grady's New South*, p. 136. This tendency to resort to "the politics of denial and deceit"—to suggest that the South no longer had a serious race problem—should not be surprising, especially in view of the fact that even social gospelers like Josiah Strong and Walter Rauschenbusch either ignored or downplayed the significance of the problem.

29. Wilson and Ferris, eds., *Encyclopedia of Southern Culture*, pp. 1113–1114; and Cobb, *The Selling of the South*, p. 122.

30. Cobb, *The Selling of the South*, pp. 122–123, 138–141, and 148; Dabney, *Liberalism in the South*, p. 161; Gaston, *The New South Creed*, p. 7; Woodward, *Origins of the New South*, pp. 143–148, 168, and 174; and Henry Watterson, ed., *Oddities in Southern Life and Character* (Boston and New York: Houghton Mifflin Company, 1882), pp. 162–167.

31. Cobb, *The Selling of the South*, pp. 122–181.

32. Wilson and Ferris, eds., *Encylopedia of Southern Culture*, p. 1114.

33. Krock, comp., *The Editorials of Henry Watterson*, p. 313.

34. McCulloch, ed., *The Call of the New South*, pp. 222–225; Hill, ed., *Encyclopedia of Religion in the South*, pp. 820–821; John J. Ansbro, *Martin Luther King, Jr.: The Making of a Mind* (Maryknoll, N.Y.: Orbis Books, 1982), pp. 71–76; and Martin Luther King, Jr., "When a Negro Faces Southern Justice," *New York Amsterdam News*, 16 April 1966, p. 31.

35. Sosna, *In Search of the Silent South*, p. 197; Margaret R. Gladney, ed., *How Am I to Be Heard?: Letters of Lillian Smith—Gender & American Culture* (Chapel Hill: University of North Carolina Press, 1993), pp. xiii–xiv; Hill, ed., *Encyclopedia of Religion in the South*, p. 697; and Wilson and Ferris, eds., *Encyclopedia of Southern Culture*, pp. 929 and 1587–1588.

36. Wilson and Ferris, eds., *Encyclopedia of Southern Culture*, p. 220.

37. One must also remember that King's sense of the connection between the problems of race and economics in the southern context, one fully developed while he was still a teenager at Morehouse College, grew to some extent out of his knowledge that his paternal grandparents had been brutally exploited as sharecroppers in Georgia, and also out of his experiences with poor black playmates during the Great Depression. See King, *Stride toward Freedom*, p. 90; Clayborne Carson et al., eds., *The Papers of Martin Luther King, Jr.*, vol. 1: *Called to Serve, January 1929–June 1951* (Berkeley: University of California Press, 1992), pp. 359–360; and Baldwin, *There Is a Balm in Gilead*, pp. 19–20 and 96.

38. Martin Luther King, Jr., "A Speech at a Dinner Honoring Him as a Nobel Peace Prize Recipient," Dinkler Plaza Hotel, Atlanta, Georgia (27 January 1965), King Center Archives, pp. 6–7. Also see Gaston, *The New South Creed*, p. 1; Woodward, *Origins of the New South*, p. 166; Gladney, ed., *How Am I to Be Heard?*, pp. 195, 258, and 302; and Michelle Cliff, ed., *The Winner Names the Age: A Collection of Writings by Lillian Smith* (New York: W. W. Norton & Company, 1978), pp. 30–31 and 97–98.

39. Haygood, *The New South*, pp. 9–10; Haygood, *Pleas for Progress*, pp. 5–24, 98–117, and 157–190; Haygood, *Our Brother in Black*, pp. 144–157; Straker, *The New South Investigated*, p. 73; Dabney, *Liberalism in the South*, pp. 170–173; and Wilson and Ferris, eds., *Encyclopedia of Southern Culture*, pp. 931 and 1114.

40. Wilson and Ferris, eds., *Encyclopedia of Southern Culture*, p. 929.

41. Martin Luther King, Jr., "Address at a Mass Meeting," Clarksdale, Mississippi (19 March 1968), King Center Archives, p. 7; Baldwin, *To Make the Wounded Whole*, pp. 39–40; Martin Luther King, Jr., "Field of Education a Battleground," speech delivered before the United Federation of Teachers, New York, New York (15 July 1965), King Center Archives, pp. 1–2; Martin Luther King, Jr., "Revolution in the Classroom," address presented before the Georgia Teachers and Education Association, Atlanta, Georgia (31 April

1967), King Center Archives, pp. 2–8; and Martin Luther King, Jr., "An Address at Syracuse University," Syracuse, New York (15 July 1965), p. 1.

42. Harold E. Davis makes this claim with respect to Henry Grady, but it may well be made concerning Haygood, Dawson, Watterson, and other New South idealists. See Davis, *Henry Grady's New South*, p. 133.

43. See Haygood, *Our Brother in Black*, pp. 73–83 and 182–199; Shurter, ed., *The Complete Orations and Speeches*, p. 37; Krock, comp., *The Editorials of Henry Watterson*, pp. 312–313; Dabney, *Liberalism in the South*, p. 161; Haygood, *The New South*, p. 10; From Martin Luther King, Jr. to Harold Courlander (30 October 1961), King Papers, Boston University, p. 1; and From Harold Courlander to Martin Luther King, Jr. (30 August 1961), King Papers, Boston University, p. 1.

44. Baldwin, *There Is a Balm in Gilead*, pp. 63–90.

45. Quoted in Louis D. Rubin, Jr., et al., eds., *The History of Southern Literature* (Baton Rouge: Louisiana State University Press, 1985), p. 245.

46. For much of this idea, I am indebted to Gaston, *The New South Creed*, pp. 218–219.

47. From Martin Luther King, Jr. to Buford Boone (9 May 1957), King Papers, Boston University, p. 1; and Baldwin, *There Is a Balm in Gilead*, pp. 80–81.

48. King, *Why We Can't Wait*, p. 89. Interestingly enough, King read the works of these writers, sent them autographed copies of his own books, and also reviewed and endorsed their books. See From Martin Luther King, Jr. to Ralph McGill (6 May 1964), King Center Archives, p. 1; From Wyatt T. Walker to Ralph McGill (6 May 1964), King Center Archives, p. 1; From Ralph McGill to Dora McDonald (26 August 1963), King Center Archives, p. 1; From Anne Perkins to Martin Luther King, Jr. (26 February 1964), King Center Archives, p. 1; Martin Luther King, Jr., "Statement on Mrs. Sarah P. Boyle's *For Human Beings Only*, unpublished document (6 March 1964), King Center Archives, p. 1; From Sarah P. Boyle to Martin Luther King, Jr. (25 March 1964), King Center Archives, pp. 1–2; From Sarah P. Boyle to Martin Luther King, Jr. (22 June 1962), King Center Archives, p. 1; From Martin Luther King, Jr. to Mrs. Frances L. Phillips (3 July 1962), King Center Archives, p. 1; From Sarah P. Boyle to Martin Luther King, Jr. (16 July 1962), King Center Archives, p. 1; From Martin Luther King, Jr. to Harry Golden (30 April 1964), King Center Archives, p. 1; From Anne Braden to Martin Luther King, Jr. (25 January 1964), King Center Archives, pp. 1–3; From Anne Braden to Martin Luther King, Jr. (1 December 1962), King Center Archives, pp. 1–3; From Martin Luther King, Jr. to Anne Braden (6 April 1964), King Center Archives, p. 1; From Anne Braden to Martin Luther King, Jr. (21 March

1963), King Center Archives, pp. 1–4; From Anne Braden to Martin Luther King, Jr. (29 October 1963), King Center Archives, p. 1; From Anne Braden to Martin Luther King, Jr. (7 December 1961), King Center Archives, p. 1; From Lillian Smith to Martin Luther King, Jr. (7 July 1962), King Center Archives, p. 1; From Dora McDonald to Miss Lillian Smith (19 July 1962), King Center Archives, p. 1; and From Lillian Smith to Martin Luther King, Jr. (25 October 1964), King Center Archives, pp. 1–2. Strangely, King did not include Robert Penn Warren, the Pulitzer Prize–winning writer, among these New South prophets who were contributing to the civil rights crusade through their essays, books, poetry, plays, and short stories. Warren had said as early as 1956, during the early stages of the Montgomery bus boycott, that the South would one day be integrated, and he spent as much time interviewing King and following his activities as any other southern writer. See Robert P. Warren, *Segregation: The Inner Conflict in the South* (New York: Random House, 1956), pp. 3–66; and Robert P. Warren, *Who Speaks for the Negro?* (New York: Random House, 1965), pp. 203–222.

49. From King to McGill (6 May 1964), p. 1; and Harold H. Martin, *Ralph McGill, Reporter* (Boston: Little, Brown and Company, 1973), p. 80. King carried in his personal library issues of the journal *The New South* for the period July 1959 to December 1965.

50. Gladney, ed., *How Am I to Be Heard?*, pp. xiv, 14, and 347; Louise Blackwell and Frances Clay, *Lillian Smith* (New York: Twayne Publishers, 1971), pp. 91, 95, and 126; and Washington, ed., *A Testament of Hope*, pp. 91 and 93. One scholar claims that "by the 1930s, the term 'Southern liberal' came into its own," a development associated largely with Lillian Smith. See Sosna, *In Search of the Silent South*, pp. viii, xi, 196–197, and 208–209. One source claims that when Lillian Smith lectured for Dr. Benjamin E. Mays at Atlanta's Morehouse College in the 1940s, "criticizing laws separating the races," her "largely student audience included several future civil rights crusaders, among them Martin Luther 'Mike' King." See Wilson and Ferris, eds., *Encyclopedia of Southern Culture*, p. 220.

51. From King to Golden (30 April 1964), p. 1; Wilson and Ferris, eds., *Encyclopedia of Southern Culture*, p. 1316; From King to Braden (6 April 1964), p. 1; Anne Braden, *The Wall Between* (New York: Monthly Review Press, 1958), pp. 28, 30–31, 33, and 36; Anne Braden, *House on Un-American Activities Committee: Bulwark of Segregation* (Los Angeles: National Committee to Abolish the House on Un-American Activities Committee; reprinted with permission from "A Quarter-Century of Un-Americana," Marzani & Munsell, New York, 1963), pp. 5, 11, and 18; From Martin Luther King, Jr. to Sarah P. Boyle (6 April 1964), King Center Archives,

pp. 1–2; and From Martin Luther King, Jr. to Sarah P. Boyle (30 April 1964), King Center Archives, p. 1.

52. All of these southern white writers suffered abuse and rejection from large segments of the white South, but Smith and Braden suffered disproportionately, mainly because they were females. See Harry Golden, *Mr. Kennedy and the Negroes* (Cleveland and New York: The World Publishing Company, 1964), p. 20; Ralph McGill, *The South and the Southerner* (Boston: Little, Brown and Company, 1963), p. 275; Martin, *Ralph McGill, Reporter*, p. 238; Braden, *The Wall Between*, pp. 116–140; Cliff, ed., *The Winner Names the Age*, p. 218; and Anne C. Loveland, *Lillian Smith, A Southerner Confronting the South: A Biography* (Baton Rouge: Louisiana State University Press, 1986), p. 260.

53. Lillian Smith spoke for most New South idealists in the 1950s and 1960s when she attacked southern racists for "their servitude to the past." She "analyzed and condemned the southern tendency to mythologize the region's past." See Lillian Smith, "A Strange Kind of Love," *Saturday Review*, 20 October 1962, p. 18; and Wilson and Ferris, eds., *Encyclopedia of Southern Culture*, p. 1124.

54. Wilson and Ferris, eds., *Encyclopedia of Southern Culture*, pp. 1112, 1411–1412, 1529, and 1588; and Gladney, ed., *How Am I to Be Heard?*, pp. xv–xvii, 5, 9–10, 15, and 165.

55. Gladney, ed., *How Am I to Be Heard?*, pp. xiii–xvii, 5, 9–10, 15, and 165; and Blackwell and Clay, *Lillian Smith*, p. 94.

56. Wilson and Ferris, eds., *Encyclopedia of Southern Culture*, pp. 1411–1412; and Sarah P. Boyle, *The Desert Blooms: A Personal Adventure in Growing Old Creatively* (Nashville: Abingdon Press, 1983), pp. 76 and 78.

57. Martin Luther King, Jr., *The Trumpet of Conscience* (San Francisco: Harper & Row, 1989; originally published in 1968), pp. 69–70; King, "When a Negro Faces Southern Justice," p. 31; Washington, ed., *A Testament of Hope*, pp. 57, 520–521, 561, and 590; Martin Luther King, Jr., *Where Do We Go from Here: Chaos or Community?* (Boston: Beacon Press, 1968), pp. 13–17, 97–101, and 201–202. King described segregation as "little more than a new form of slavery covered up with certain niceties." See Martin Luther King, Jr., "Rally Speech," Gadsden, Alabama (21 June 1963), King Center Archives, p. 1.

58. McGill, *The South and the Southerner*, p. 270; Ralph E. McGill, "From a Tight Small Compartment," *Harvard Law School Bulletin*, vol. 12, no. 6 (June 1961): p. 6; Martin, *Ralph McGill*, p. 84; and Ralph McGill, *No Place to Hide: The South and Human Rights*, vol. 1 (Macon, Ga.: Mercer University Press, 1984), pp. 126–155. McGill's emerging perspective on segregation can also be detected from a reading of Barbara B. Clowse, *Ralph McGill: A*

Biography (Macon: Mercer University Press, 1998), pp. 180 and 187; Ralph McGill, *Southern Encounters: Southerners of Note in Ralph McGill's South*, ed. Calvin M. Logue (Macon, Ga.: Mercer University Press, 1983), pp. 91 and 284; Michael Strickland et al., *The Best of Ralph McGill: Selected Columns* (Atlanta: Cherokee, 1980), pp. 104, 107, 115, 121–123, 136–137, and 142; Ralph McGill, "Other Lessons Are Ahead of Us," unpublished manuscript (6 February 1961), pp. 1–2; and Ralph McGill, *A Church, A School* (New York and Nashville: Abingdon Press, 1959), p. 22.

59. Sosna, *In Search of the Silent South*, p. 197; and Golden, *Mr. Kennedy and the Negroes*, p. 20. Smith explored "the tragedy of segregation" in her book *Strange Fruit*, and the problem is addressed at some length in her other works. See Lillian Smith, *Strange Fruit: A Novel* (New York: Reynal & Hitchcock, 1944), pp. 1–371; Lillian Smith, *Killers of the Dream* (New York: Doubleday, 1963), pp. 1–227; Cliff, ed., *The Winner Names the Age*, pp. 30–31 and 94–98; Lillian Smith, *Now Is the Time* (New York: Viking, 1955), pp. 17, 20–23, 44, 100, 102–106, 108–118, and 120; Smith, "A Strange Kind of Love," pp. 18 and 20; Gladney, ed., *How Am I to Be Heard?*, pp. 146, 164–165, 195, 200–202, 256–302, 310, and 315; Blackwell and Clay, *Lillian Smith*, pp. 95 and 123; Loveland, *Lillian Smith*, pp. 154–155, 215–218, and 228; Lillian Smith, *The Journey* (Cleveland and New York: World, 1954), pp. 5–256; and Lillian Smith, *One Hour* (New York: Harcourt, Brace, 1959), pp. 1–440.

60. Washington, ed., *A Testament of Hope*, pp. 296–299.

61. Golden, *Mr. Kennedy and the Negroes*, p. 6; and Harry Golden, "The Future of the Civil Rights Movement: A Statement before the U.S. Senate on Urban Affairs" (27 June 1967), p. 2. Golden dedicated one of his books to Atlanta, Georgia, King's hometown, which, in his view, "led the South in the resolution of the desegregation crisis." See Harry Golden, *A Little Girl Is Dead* (Cleveland and New York: World, 1965), dedication page.

62. James M. Dabbs, *The Southern Heritage* (New York: Alfred A. Knopf, 1958), pp. 67–87. The problem of legalized segregation is also treated in James M. Dabbs, *Who Speaks for the South?* (New York: Funk & Wagnalls, 1964), pp. 272–273 and 379.

63. Braden, *The Wall Between*, p. 30.

64. Sarah P. Boyle, *The Desegregated Heart: A Virginian's Stand in Time of Transition* (New York: William Morrow, 1962), pp. xiii and 118.

65. Washington, ed., *A Testament of Hope*, pp. 342 and 546–548; King, *Where Do We Go from Here?*, pp. 55–56; Smith, *Now Is the Time*, pp. 111–113; and Cliff, ed., *The Winner Names the Age*, pp. 30–31.

66. King, "When a Negro Faces Southern Justice," p. 31.

67. Martin, *Ralph McGill*, pp. 85 and 150.

68. Gladney, ed., *How Am I to Be Heard?*, pp. xiv and 341.

69. King undoubtedly had such whites in mind when he spoke of "the terrible ambivalence in the soul of white America." Lillian Smith spoke of "the psychological ambiguities called 'the southern mind.'" See Martin Luther King, Jr., "Address to Mass Meeting at the Maggie Street Baptist Church," Montgomery, Alabama (16 February 1968), King Center Archives, p. 3; Blackwell and Clay, *Lillian Smith*, p. 95; and Cliff, ed., *The Winner Names the Age*, p. 216.

70. Martin Luther King, Jr., *Where Do We Go from Here?*, unpublished draft (1967), King Center Archives, pp. 9–10; and Baldwin, *There Is a Balm in Gilead*, p. 242.

71. McGill, who had been a part of the New South movement back in the World War II era, "was forced to reckon with an entirely new phase of the civil rights movement—direct action by Jim Crow's victims"—and he was at times very uncomfortable with it. He actually preferred to do by law and the courts what King and his followers were doing in the streets. See Martin, *Ralph McGill*, pp. 169 and 194; Clowse, *Ralph McGill*, p. 169; Strickland et al., *The Best of Ralph McGill*, pp. 121–123; and McGill, "From a Tight Small Compartment," p. 6.

72. Smith also spoke of the movement as one of "the good, creative forces in the South" that was challenging "people's apathy and complacency" and pricking "the consciences of people everywhere." See Loveland, *Lillian Smith*, pp. 139, 156, 222–223, and 229; Cliff, ed., *The Winner Names the Age*, p. 91; Smith, *Our Faces, Our Words*, pp. 17–99; and From Smith to King (25 October 1964), p. 1.

73. Harry Golden, *Our Southern Landsman* (New York: G. P. Putnam's Sons, 1974), p. 226.

74. Dabbs, *Who Speaks for the South?*, p. 312.

75. From Braden to King (1 December 1962), pp. 1–3; and From Braden to King (21 March 1963), pp. 2–3.

76. Boyle, *The Desegregated Heart*, pp. 93 and 118–119.

77. Martin, *McGill*, p. 274. McGill variously referred to King as "the spiritual leader" of student activists, as the one who "put the crusade in proper perspective," as a "manifestation of American promise," as "a phenomenon," as "the one prestigious voice that called for nonviolent action," as "the best-known leader of Negro opinion in the United States," and as "the nonviolent leader who could stir southerners to such paroxysms of rage that they committed violent acts." McGill also predicted that "the day will come when the South will appreciate what he has done." See McGill, *The South and the Southerner*, pp. 284–285; Strickland et al., *The Best of Ralph McGill*, pp. 120 and 140; McGill, *Southern Encounters*,

pp. 73–74; Martin, *Ralph McGill*, p. 169; and From Ralph McGill to Wyatt T. Walker (9 July 1964), King Center Archives, p. 1.

78. Smith referred to King in many of her writings as "a good friend," and on some occasions she used her influence in trying to secure his release from jail. See Gladney, ed., *How Am I to Be Heard?*, pp. 250, 252, 255, 257–258, 300, and 311–313; Loveland, *Lillian Smith*, p. 90; Blackwell and Clay, *Lillian Smith*, p. 125; and Baldwin, *There Is a Balm in Gilead*, pp. 81–82.

79. Smith reviewed King's first book, *Stride toward Freedom: The Montgomery Story* (1958), in *Saturday Review*, calling it "the most interesting book that has come out of the current racial situation." She clearly preferred King over militant writers like James Baldwin and militant activists such as Adam Clayton Powell, Jr., and the Black Muslims. She considered King and other nonviolent forces in the movement to be "our best defense against the Black Muslims who want black supremacy and will use violence when the time comes." Ralph McGill made a similar observation, insisting that "had a real hater—a Black Muslim—come along with Dr. King's power of speech and personality, the South long ago would have been bloodstained. The South is lucky to have Dr. King." See Loveland, *Lillian Smith*, pp. 223 and 238; Blackwell and Clay, *Lillian Smith*, p. 95; Gladney, ed., *How Am I to Be Heard?*, pp. xiv, 254, 301–303, and 347; and Martin, *Ralph McGill*, p. 195.

80. At other points, Golden referred to King as "the representative Negro leader" and "the preeminent leader of the cause of Southern Negroes." See Golden, *Mr. Kennedy and the Negroes*, pp. 30 and 119.

81. James M. Dabbs, "Quit You Like Men," address delivered at the fall session of the Southern Christian Leadership Conference (1 October 1959), King Center Archives, p. 3.

82. From Anne Braden to Martin Luther King, Jr. (19 February 1962), King Center Archives, p. 1.

83. From Sarah P. Boyle to Martin Luther King, Jr. (17 May 1964), King Center Archives, p. 1.

84. Martin Luther King, Jr., "Advice for Living," *Ebony*, vol. 13, no. 1 (November 1957): p. 106.

85. At one point in his writings, McGill declared that "nonviolence, like Christian soldiers in the old hymn, went on 'to victory and to victory,'" forcing many southern cities to alter their patterns of segregation. See Strickland et al., *The Best of Ralph McGill*, p. 140; McGill, *The South and the Southerner*, pp. 281 and 284–285; Martin, *Ralph McGill*, pp. 169, 175, 195, and 274; McGill, *Southern Encounters*, p. 74; Clowse, *Ralph McGill*, p. 182; and Loveland, *Lillian Smith*, p. 260.

86. Smith spent time in India, and she made numerous references to Gandhi in her writings. Sosna, *In Search of the Silent South*, pp. 196–197;

Loveland, *Lillian Smith*, pp. 155, 216, 223, and 237; Smith, *Our Faces, Our Words*, pp. 83–84 and 87; Blackwell and Clay, *Lillian Smith*, p. 90; and Smith, "A Strange Kind of Love," pp. 18–20.

87. Golden's remarks here are very similar to comments commonly made by McGill, who praised King for "preaching love instead of hate, passive resistance instead of fire and sword." McGill credited King with challenging white domination in the South "not with guns, not with dynamite, not with violence, but with prayer." Like Harry Golden and Lillian Smith, McGill spoke of King's methods in striking contrast to those of radicals like the Black Muslims. See Golden, *Mr. Kennedy and the Negroes*, pp. 25–26; and Martin, *Ralph McGill*, p. 195.

88. Wilson and Ferris, eds., *Encyclopedia of Southern Culture*, p. 1316; and Dabbs, "Quit You Like Men," pp. 3–11.

89. It seems that Braden was not as committed philosophically to King's nonviolent ethic as other New South advocates, a point perhaps open to debate. However, she "personally staked much of the emotional commitment of" her "own life on the belief" that King's SCLC, through its philosophy and methods, would ultimately transform the South. See Braden, *The Wall Between*, pp. 132–133, 291, and 294; and From Braden to King (1 December 1962), p. 1.

90. Boyle devoted a large section of her book *The Desegregated Heart* to a discussion of the Christian love ethic, and her treatment of the subject is quite consistent with King's. In a letter to King, She asserted that the book "is a really important step toward brotherhood and intergroup understanding in the South—the kind of approach which you strive so ably to induce." See Boyle, *The Desegregated Heart*, pp. 297–360; and From Boyle to King (22 June 1962), p. 1.

91. Quoted in Lerone Bennett, Jr., "Rev. Martin Luther King, Jr., Alabama Desegregationist, Challenges Talmadge," *Ebony*, vol. 12, no. 6 (April 1957): p. 79; Martin Luther King, Jr., "An Address to the National Press Club," Washington, D.C. (9 July 1962), King Papers, Boston University, p. 6; and Baldwin, *There Is a Balm in Gilead*, pp. 87–88. For other significant references by King to the New Negro, see Washington, ed., *A Testament of Hope*, pp. xv, 76–77, 101, 108, and 137; Martin Luther King, Jr., "The Burning Truth in the South," in *The Progressive*, Madison, Wisconsin (May 1960), pp. 8–10; Martin Luther King, Jr., "Statement on the Negroes' New Self-Respect," Montgomery, Alabama (27 April 1956), p. 1; and King, "The New Negro of the South," p. 17.

92. Foner, ed., *The Voice of Black America*, vol. 1, pp. 609–610; and Rayford W. Logan et al., eds., *The New Negro Thirty Years Afterward: Papers Contributed to the Sixteenth Annual Spring Conference of the Division of the Social Sciences* (Washington, D.C.: Howard University Press, 1955), p. 18.

93. Logan et al., eds., *The New Negro Thirty Years Afterward*, p. 18; and Washington, ed., *A Testament of Hope*, p. xv.

94. Tindall, *The Emergence of the New South*, p. 157.

95. For an example, King was quite mindful of the impact of black music, and indeed the African American freedom struggle, on the world. See Washington, ed., *A Testament of Hope*, pp. 24–25; Martin Luther King, Jr., "True Dignity," unpublished statement (n.d.), pp. 1–10; and Baldwin, *There Is a Balm in Gilead*, p. 57. Perhaps more than any other white New South idealist, James Dabbs shared with King a sense of the Negro's impact on the world through art. Dabbs referred to "Negro folklore and comedy, the spirituals and jazz," as "an American and an international language." See Dabbs, *The Southern Heritage*, p. 72.

96. Martin, *Ralph McGill*, p. 147; Clowse, *Ralph McGill*, p. 182; and McGill, *Southern Encounters*, pp. 69–74.

97. Loveland, *Lillian Smith*, pp. 222 and 229; Blackwell and Clay, *Lillian Smith*, p. 123; and Smith, "A Strange Kind of Love," p. 20.

98. White New South advocates generally agreed with King's contention that African Americans were, through their practical application of the ethics of love and nonviolence, injecting "a new spiritual dynamic" into Western civilization. See King, *Stride toward Freedom*, p. 224; and Golden, *Mr. Kennedy and the Negroes*, pp. 25, 119, and 257.

99. Dabbs, "Quit You Like Men," pp. 3–4, 8–9, and 11. Dabbs suggested that Negroes had "become better Christians than their teachers the whites." "It never occurred to" the white South, he added, "that God's grace might be so extravagant as this. The South, though religious, is still largely ignorant of the working of grace and judgment in society itself." Dabbs said at another point that "the enfranchised, the integrated Negro may bring to the white southerner a quality of balance, a wholeness the South has lacked in the past." See Dabbs, *Who Speaks for the South?*, p. 372; and Golden, *Mr. Kennedy and the Negroes*, p. 257.

100. Braden, *The Wall Between*, p. 291.

101. Boyle, *The Desegregated Heart*, pp. 83–84 and 118.

102. From Ralph McGill to Martin Luther King, Jr. (1 May 1967), King Center Archives, p. 1.

103. See Wilson and Ferris, eds., *Encyclopedia of Southern Culture*, pp. 957–958; and Rabbi Marc Schneier, *Shared Dreams: Martin Luther King, Jr. and the Jewish Community* (Woodstock, Vt.: Jewish Lights Publishing, 1999), pp. 23 and 57.

104. Wilson and Ferris, eds., *Encyclopedia of Southern Culture*, p. 1316; King, *Stride toward Freedom*, p. 32; and Golden, *Mr. Kennedy and the Negroes*, p. 257.

105. Interestingly enough, the African American students who staged a sit-in protest at a lunch counter in Greensboro, North Carolina, in February 1960, claimed Smith, Gunnar Myrdal, and Gandhi as major influences. Smith dedicated her book *Our Faces, Our Words* (1964) to "The Young in the Movement." See Sosna, *In Search of the Silent South*, p. 197; Gladney, ed., *How Am I to Be Heard?*, pp. xiv, 193–194, 202–203, 342–343; Loveland, *Lillian Smith*, pp. 156 and 222–223; and Blackwell and Clay, *Lillian Smith*, p. 126. In noting the inseparability of art and the struggle for freedom, Smith, called "a socially committed fiction writer," echoed the views of the great Paul Robeson. See Rubin et al., eds., *The History of Southern Literature*, p. 351; and Sterling Stuckey, *Slave Culture: Nationalist Theory and the Foundations of Black America* (New York: Oxford University Press, 1987), p. 318.

106. Washington, ed., *A Testament of Hope*, pp. 91–93.

107. Braden, *The Wall Between*, pp. 34 and 125; and From Braden to King (25 January 1964), p. 2.

108. From Boyle to King (25 March 1964), pp. 1–2; and From King to Boyle (6 April 1964), pp. 1–2.

109. Martin Luther King, Jr., "An Address at the First Annual Institute on Nonviolence and Social Change," Under the Auspices of the Montgomery Improvement Association, Holt Street Baptist Church, Montgomery, Alabama (3 December 1956), King Papers, Boston University, pp. 1–3; Martin Luther King, Jr., "A Statement to the South and Nation," issued by the Southern Leaders Conference on Transportation and Nonviolent Integration, Ebenezer Baptist Church, Atlanta, Georgia (10–11 January 1957), King Papers, Boston University, pp. 2–3; and Baldwin, *There Is a Balm in Gilead*, p. 67.

110. Martin Luther King, Jr., "Address at the Prayer Pilgrimage for Freedom," The Lincoln Memorial, Washington, D.C. (17 May 1957), King Papers, Boston University, p. 2.

111. See Sosna, *In Search of the Silent South*, pp. 208–209; and Baldwin, *There Is a Balm in Gilead*, pp. 78–80.

112. King, "Bold Design for a New South," pp. 260–261.

113. See McGill, *No Place to Hide*, pp. 126–133 and 196–210; and Strickland et al., *The Best of Ralph McGill*, p. 97.

114. Gladney, ed., *How Am I to Be Heard?*, pp. 193–194; Loveland, *Lillian Smith*, pp. 155–156; Smith, *Now Is the Time*, p. 113; and Baldwin, *There Is a Balm in Gilead*, p. 82.

115. See Dabbs, *The Southern Heritage*, pp. 32–35 and 66–87; and From Boyle to King (25 March 1964), pp. 1–2.

116. King, *Why We Can't Wait*, p. 89.

117. Carson, ed., *The Autobiography of Martin Luther King, Jr.*, pp. 172–173, 175–178, 180–181, and 210–212; King, *Why We Can't Wait*, pp. 101 and 104–105; and Washington, ed., *A Testament of Hope*, pp. 170, 281–282, and 526–534.

118. Washington, ed., *A Testament of Hope*, pp. 299, 310, 320, 373, and 608; and Carson, ed., *The Autobiography of Martin Luther King, Jr.*, pp. 200 and 254. King once noted that "such great philosophical thinkers as Aristotle, Hume, Kant, and Roscoe Pound have given us to know that this substantive justice is the ultimate standard of moral conduct and is consonant with the principle of giving every man his due." See King, "When a Negro Faces Southern Justice," p. 31; and King, "The Burning Truth in the South," p. 10.

119. McGill included southern politicians like Wallace and Maddox in what he called the "tradition of demagoguery." See Martin, *Ralph McGill*, pp. 195, 264, and 273; Clowse, *Ralph McGill*, p. 247; Strickland et al., *The Best of Ralph McGill*, p. 149; McGill, *Southern Encounters*, pp. 277–285 and 287–294; and McGill, "From a Tight Small Compartment," p. 7.

120. Smith, "A Strange Kind of Love," pp. 19–20; Cliff, ed., *The Winner Names the Age*, pp. 33, 90, and 97; Blackwell and Clay, *Lillian Smith*, p. 126; Smith, *Now Is the Time*, pp. 20, 99, 109, and 115; Loveland, *Lillian Smith*, pp. 226–227; and Smith, *Our Faces, Our Words*, p. 81. Lillian Smith actually got involved in the governor's campaign in Georgia in 1954, supporting Grace Wilkey Thomas, "the only gubernatorial candidate who stood for racial democracy," against the segregationist Samuel M. Griffin, who had the backing of former Governor Talmadge. The Democrat Griffin won the governorship. See Gladney, ed., *How Am I to Be Heard?*, p. 146.

121. Loveland, *Lillian Smith*, pp. 154–155; and Smith, *Now Is the Time*, p. 109.

122. Golden, *Mr. Kennedy and the Negroes*, pp. 23, 35, and 124.

123. Dabbs, "Quit You Like Men," pp. 7–8. Dabbs reduced the political system of segregation in the South to "a sort of Babylonian Captivity," a metaphor used over time by black religious leaders. See Dabbs, *Who Speaks for the South?*, p. 379.

124. From Braden to King (21 March 1963), p. 2.

125. From Boyle to King (25 March 1964), p. 1; and From Sarah P. Boyle to Martin Luther King, Jr. (6 August 1962), King Papers, Boston University, p. 1.

126. Washington, ed., *A Testament of Hope*, p. xvi; and Baldwin, *There Is a Balm in Gilead*, p. 76.

127. McGill's fleeting references to Paul Robeson and W. E. B. DuBois suggest that he was anticommunist, but he never used the communist label

in reference to King, even when he attacked the civil rights leader's position on Vietnam. See Strickland et al., *The Best of Ralph McGill,* p. 119; Martin, *Ralph McGill,* p. 178; McGill, *Southern Encounters,* pp. 87–94; Ralph McGill, "Says NAACP Follows Best Course in Rejecting Dr. King's Proposal," *Akron Beacon Journal,* 20 April 1967, p. A6; and From Ralph McGill to Martin Luther King, Jr. (1 May 1967), King Center Archives, p. 1.

128. The sources contend that from the 1930s and 1940s, Smith was deeply "distrustful of Communists and leftists." On one occasion, she scoffed at the idea of being labeled communist, noting that "they can't think I am communist for no one has fought communism more than I have." Smith also loathed what she called "red-baiting and McCarthyism," asserting that "I happened to be one of the first writers in this country to speak out against McCarthyism, long before it was 'the thing to do.'" In a statement that obviously supported King and others in the movement, Smith declared: "Long ago, Jesus Christ worked for peace. Does this make him, now, a Communist?" She felt that the Supreme Court decision in *Brown v. Board of Education* was "the most powerful political instrument against communism that the United States has. . . ." See Loveland, *Lillian Smith,* p. 157; Gladney, ed., *How Am I to Be Heard?,* pp. 146, 165, 254, and 260; Blackwell and Clay, *Lillian Smith,* p. 122; Smith, *Now Is the Time,* pp. 115–117; and Smith, "A Strange Kind of Love," p. 19.

129. From Harry Golden to Franklin D. Moran (27 April 1964), King Papers, Boston University, p. 1.

130. Braden, *House Un-American Activities Committee,* pp. 11 and 18.

131. Martin Luther King, Jr., "The South—a Hostile Nation," *New York Amsterdam News,* 11 May 1963, p. 19.

132. King, "An Address to the National Press Club," p. 3; Martin Luther King, Jr., "Address at March in Detroit," Cobo Hall, Detroit, Michigan (23 June 1963), King Center Archives, p. 4; and Martin Luther King, Jr., "Speech Made in Savannah," Savannah, Georgia (1 January 1961), King Center Archives, p. 8.

133. King, "Bold Design for a New South," pp. 259–260.

134. Braden, *The Wall Between,* pp. 294–295.

135. King, "Bold Design for a New South," p. 261; and Kenneth L. Smith and Ira G. Zepp, Jr., *Search for the Beloved Community: The Thinking of Martin Luther King, Jr.* (Valley Forge, Pa.: Judson Press, 1974), p. 121.

136. King, "An Address to the National Press Club," p. 4.

137. Coretta Scott King, *My Life with Martin Luther King, Jr.* (New York: Henry Holt, 1993), p. 239.

138. Dabbs, *Who Speaks for the South?,* p. 378; and Golden, "The Future of the Civil Rights Movement," p. 4.

139. The scholarship shows that both Braden and the later King leaned toward democratic socialism in advancing their visions of the ideal society. Here they disagreed with not only Booker T. Washington and other earlier advocates of a New South, who embraced the capitalistic ethic uncritically, but also with activists in the New South movement in their own time. See Wilson and Ferris, eds., *Encyclopedia of Southern Culture*, p. 1412; Braden, *The Wall Between*, p. 33; Kenneth L. Smith, "The Radicalization of Martin Luther King, Jr.: The Last Three Years," *Journal of Ecumenical Studies*, vol. 26, no. 2 (Spring 1989): pp. 270–288; Douglas Sturn, "Martin Luther King, Jr., as Democratic Socialist," *The Journal of Religious Ethics*, vol. 18, no. 2 (Fall 1990): pp. 79–105; and Michael Eric Dyson, *I May Not Get There with You: The True Martin Luther King, Jr.* (New York: Free Press, 2000), pp. 78–100. For an excellent essay which contrasts King's economic ethic with that of Booker T. Washington, his predecessor in the New South crusade, see Darryl M. Trimiew and Michael Greene, "How We Got Over: The Moral Teachings of the African-American Church on Business Ethics," *Business Ethics Quarterly*, vol. 7, no. 2 (1997): pp. 134–142.

140. King, "Bold Design for a New South," p. 261.

141. Washington, ed., *A Testament of Hope*, p. 93.

142. Clowse, *Ralph McGill*, p. 216; McGill, *No Place to Hide*, p. 134; and McGill, "Other Lessons Are Ahead of Us," p. 2.

143. Dabbs, "Quit You Like Men," p. 1.

144. David L. Chappell, *Inside Agitators: White Southerners and the Civil Rights Movement* (Baltimore: John Hopkins University Press, 1994), p. 257 n7.

145. King, "Field of Education a Battleground," pp. 1–2; King, "Revolution in the Classroom," pp. 2–8; McGill, "Other Lessons Are Ahead of Us," p. 1; Smith, *Now Is the Time*, pp. 104–106; Gladney, ed., *How Am I to Be Heard?*, p. 146; Cliff, ed., *The Winner Names the Age*, pp. 30–31; Golden, *Mr. Kennedy and the Negroes*, pp. 119–120; Dabbs, *The Southern Heritage*, pp. 77–78; Braden, *The Wall Between*, p. 35; and Boyle, *The Desegregated Heart*, pp. 189–196.

146. Baldwin, *There Is a Balm in Gilead*, p. 80; Michael K. Honey, *Southern Labor and Black Civil Rights: Organizing Memphis Workers* (Urbana and Chicago: University of Illinois Press, 1993), p. 118; and Chappell, *Inside Agitators*, p. 55.

147. King spoke at times of Horton's "creative endeavors," and he agreed to serve as a sponsor of the Highlander Folk School. Horton also thought highly of King, noting that "your moral support means a great deal to me personally." He once wrote King for "insights that would be helpful in shaping our Highlander Center Program." See Martin Luther

King, Jr., "A Look to the Future," unpublished speech (2 September 1957), King Papers, Boston University, p. 1; From Martin Luther King, Jr. to Myles Horton (23 August 1962), King Papers, Boston University, p. 1; From Myles Horton to Martin Luther King, Jr. (6 June 1962), King Papers, Boston University, p. 1; From Myles Horton to Martin Luther King, Jr. (24 August 1962), King Papers, Boston University, p. 1; and From Myles Horton to Martin Luther King, Jr. (6 February 1962), King Papers, Boston University, p. 1.

148. Jordan also held King in high regard, and the two men often exchanged letters. See From Martin Luther King, Jr. to Dr. Clarence L. Jordan (8 February 1957), King Papers, Boston University, p. 1; and From Clarence Jordan to the Friends of Koinonia Farm (April 1965), King Center Archives, p. 1. King is mentioned several times in Tracy E. K'Meyer, *Interracialism and Christian Community in the Postwar South: The Story of Koinonia Farm* (Charlottesville: University Press of Virginia, 1997), pp. 111, 136, 147, 150, 156, and 169.

149. K'Meyer, *Interracialism and Christian Community*, pp. 97 and 111.

150. Brown, "Grounds for American Loyalty," p. 54; and Baldwin, *There Is a Balm in Gilead*, pp. 70–72.

151. King actually said in 1966 that most white Americans "are unconscious racists." It is doubtful that any of the white writers in the New South movement would have agreed wholeheartedly with his perspective on white people at that particular point. See Dyson, *I May Not Get There with You*, pp. 30–31.

152. Loveland, *Lillian Smith*, pp. 236–238; and Gladney, ed., *How Am I to Be Heard?*, pp. 341 and 344.

153. Sosna, *In Search of the Silent South*, p. 197; Blackwell and Clay, *Lillian Smith*, p. 126; Loveland, *Lillian Smith*, pp. 223, 228, and 236–239; and Gladney, ed., *How Am I to Be Heard?*, pp. 341 and 344.

154. Sosna, *In Search of the Silent South*, p. 197; and Blackwell and Clay, *Lillian Smith*, p. 91. Smith viewed the black writer James Baldwin "as more dangerous than Malcolm X" because of the influence he seemed to exert on youngsters in the civil rights movement. But Smith never completely realized that many youngsters in SNCC and CORE, constantly brutalized by white bigots and left with little hope of radical, extensive change in the racial policies of government, "no longer viewed nonviolence as a philosophy based on 'a strange kind of love' that appealed to the conscience of white Americans and redeemed both activists and opponents." See Loveland, *Lillian Smith*, pp. 237 and 239.

155. See Gladney, ed., *How Am I to Be Heard?*, p. 341. For other remarks critical of King by Smith, see pp. 306–307 of the above source.

156. McGill, like Lillian Smith, actually expected too much of King and others in the movement, and the paternalism of these and other white writers clearly showed in their efforts to determine what African Americans were most suited to lead a movement to eliminate white racist structures. See Ralph McGill, "Charlatans: Black-White," *Atlanta Constitution*, 22 June 1967, p. 1; and Martin, *Ralph McGill*, p. 247.

157. McGill also attacked King for praising Muhammad Ali, a conscientious objector, whom the white writer said "is about as 'yellow' as they come." See From McGill to King (1 May 1967), p. 1; and McGill, "Says NAACP Follows Best Course in Rejecting Dr. King's Proposal," p. A6; and "Must End 'Tragic Adventure' in Vietnam, Dr. King Says," *Atlanta Constitution*, 1 May 1967, p. 15. Interestingly enough, King's anti-Vietnam position was in conflict with that of the massive Southern Baptist Convention. Studies toward the end of his life suggested that most Americans, including African Americans, disagreed with his views on Vietnam. See "Baptists Back War Till 'a Just Peace,'" *Atlanta Constitution*, 2 June 1967, p. 8; "Pulse of the Public: 'King Should Go to Vietnam,'"*Atlanta Constitution*, 4 May 1967, p. 4; and Lou Harris, "73 Pct. Oppose King's Stand on War; 60 Pct. Think It'll Hurt Rights Effort," *Atlanta Constitution*, 22 May 1967, pp. 1 and 13.

158. Interestingly enough, in a tribute to the late King, McGill, who died in 1969, contrasted the civil rights leader with "Negro militants" who opted for "apartheid in reverse." See McGill, *Southern Encounters*, pp. 69–74; and Martin, *Ralph McGill*, pp. 257–258.

159. Dabbs, *The Southern Heritage*, p. 33; and Dabbs, *Who Speaks for the South?*, p. 314. This "sense of place" is also discussed as a major theme in Baldwin, *There Is a Balm in Gilead*, pp. 30–44.

160. For King, white writers such as McGill, Smith, Golden, Dabbs, Braden, and Boyle had a much more positive and secure place in history than even William Faulkner, the Nobel Prize–winning author from Mississippi, who "encouraged Negroes to accept injustice, exploitation, and indignity for a while longer." Harry Golden called Faulkner "the best writer to come out of the South if not out of America," but Faulkner, he sadly acknowledged, was "trapped by the myth" which insists that "the Negro is happy." See Washington, ed., *A Testament of Hope*, p. 80; and Golden, *Mr. Kennedy and the Negroes*, p. 22.

161. I am indebted to Roger Hatch for much of this idea. From Roger D. Hatch to Lewis V. Baldwin (26 March 2000), p. 3; and Baldwin, *There Is a Balm in Gilead*, pp. 88–90.

162. Charles L. Sanders, "An Exclusive Interview: Has Gov. George Wallace Really Changed?," in *Ebony*, vol. 38, no. 11 (September 1983): pp. 44–46, 48, and 50.

163. By his own admission, Dees has received considerable support from black southerners in his quest to rid the South and the nation of the scourge of hate groups. See Bill Stanton, *Klanwatch: Bringing the Ku Klux Klan to Justice* (New York: Grove Weidenfeld, 1991), pp. 3–260; Morris Dees, *A Season for Justice: The Life and Times of Civil Rights Lawyer Morris Dees*, with the assistance of Steve Fiffer (New York: Charles Scribner's Sons, 1991), pp. 1–310; Morris Dees, *Gathering Storm: America's Militia Threat*, with the assistance of James Corcoran (New York: HarperCollins, 1996), pp. 1–235; and Marilyn Marshall, "Beulah Mae Donald: The Black Woman Who Beat the Ku Klux Klan," in *Ebony*, vol. 43, no. 5 (March 1988): pp. 148–149 and 152–153.

164. "Mobile Lawyer Fights Injustice with Center's Advice, Support," *SPLC Report*, vol. 30, no. 2 (June 2000): p. 4; "President Clinton, Former President Carter Tell: 'What Dr. Martin Luther King Means to Me,'" *Jet*, vol. 85, no. 11 (17 January 1994): pp. 4–6; "Clinton Speaks of King in Decrying Violence," *Jet*, vol. 85, no. 5 (29 November 1993): pp. 8–9; Mary F. Berry, "Pie in the Sky?: Clinton's Race Initiative Offers Promise and the Potential for Peril," *Emerge*, vol. 8, no. 10 (September 1997): pp. 68 and 70–71; "Keeps Promise to Name Most Diversified Cabinet Members in U.S. History," *Jet*, vol. 83, no. 12 (18 January 1993): pp. 6–7; and "Two Ex-Klansmen Charged with 1963 Church Bombing that Killed Four Girls," *Jet*, vol. 97, no. 26 (5 June 2000): pp. 22–24.

165. Donald E. Collins, *When the Church Bell Rang Racist: The Methodist Church and the Civil Rights Movement in Alabama* (Macon, Ga.: Mercer University Press, 1998), pp. 161–167. In a few instances, white United Methodists have confronted the racism issue in search of forgiveness, healing, and reconciliation, but they have not made significant steps beyond such gestures. See Paul McKay, "UMC Seeks Forgiveness for Racism," *The United Methodist Review: Tennessee Conference*, vol. 17, no. 11 (12 May 2000): pp. 3 and 6.

166. The Southern Baptists made such an apology in the form of its "Declaration of Repentance" in 1995, and the Tennessee Conference of the United Methodist Church in 1999. See Paul D. Escott et al., eds., *Major Problems in the History of the American South*, vol. 2: *The New South*, 2d ed. (Boston and New York: Houghton Mifflin, 1999), pp. 393–395.

167. Baldwin, *There Is a Balm in Gilead*, p. 334.

168. Efforts to distort King's dream since his death are discussed in Dyson, *I May Not Get There with You*, pp. 1–311; Luther D. Ivory, *Toward a Theology of Radical Involvement: The Theological Legacy of Martin Luther King, Jr.* (Nashville: Abingdon Press, 1997), p. 14; and Vincent Harding, *Martin Luther King, Jr.: The Inconvenient Hero* (Maryknoll, N.Y.: Orbis Books, 1996), pp. 1–141.

169. Baldwin, *There Is a Balm in Gilead*, p. 90; Cobb, *The Selling of the South*, pp. 254–281; Numan V. Bartley, *The New South, 1945–1980* (Baton Rouge: Louisiana State University Press, 1995), pp. 261–262; Lerone Bennett, Jr., "The Second Time Around: Will History Repeat Itself and Rob Blacks of the Gains of the 1960s?" *Ebony*, vol. 50, no. 11 (September 1995): pp. 86, 88, 90, and 144; and Douglas C. Lyons, "Selma: 25 Years Later—One Quarter of a Century After the March, Some Things Have Changed—and Some Haven't," *Ebony*, vol. 45, no. 5 (March 1990): pp. 110, 112, and 114.

170. Cobb, *The Selling of the South*, pp. 261–262. One recent source which is useful for critically analyzing King's position on the relationship between increased industrial-urban development and progress in race relations in the South is Timothy Minchin, *Hiring the Black Worker: The Racial Integration of the Southern Textile Industry, 1960–1980* (Chapel Hill: University of North Carolina Press, 1999), pp. 1–342.

171. Bartley, *The New South*, pp. 455–470; Cobb, *The Selling of the South*, pp. 254–281; King, "An Address to the National Press Club," p. 4; Bennett, "The Second Time Around," pp. 86, 88, 90, and 144; Walter Leavy, "What's Behind the Resurgence of Racism in America?," *Ebony*, vol. 42, no. 6 (April 1987): pp. 132–133, 136, and 138–139; and Charles Whitaker, "How to Survive the New Racism," *Ebony*, vol. 46, no. 12 (October 1991): pp. 106, 108, and 110.

172. "White Man, Black Wife Enjoy Life in New South," *Jet*, vol. 44, no. 6 (17 May 1973): p. 10.

173. Marshall, "Beulah Mae Donald," p. 148; and George E. Curry and Michelle McCalope, "Reduced to a Photo: A Family's Torment after the Tragic Dragging Death in Jasper, Texas," *Emerge*, vol. 10, no. 7 (May 1999): pp. 42–47.

174. There have been numerous battles between black and white southerners concerning the Confederate flag over the past two decades, extending through Alabama, Georgia, South Carolina, Kentucky, and other southern states. The use of the Confederate song "Dixie" has caused tensions between students at the University of Mississippi, and, in 1997, the Virginia legislature voted to retire the state song, "Carry Me Back to Old Virginny," which contains the lyrics "That is where this old darkey's heart am long'd to go/That's where I labored so hard for old Massa." See Leavy, "What's Behind the Resurgence of Racism in America," pp. 132–133.

175. Quoted in Baldwin, *There Is a Balm in Gilead*, p. 68.

176. This seems to be implied in John Egerton, *The Americanization of Dixie: The Southernization of America* (New York: Harper's Magazine Press, 1974), pp. 1–148.

177. Charles Whitaker, "The New Mississippi: Is It Really Better than 'Up North'?" *Ebony*, vol. 44, no. 10 (August 1989), p. 34.

178. Leavy, "What's Behind the Resurgence of Racism in America?" pp. 132–133, 136, and 138–139; Whitaker, "The New Mississippi," p. 30; Whitaker, "How to Survive the New Racism," pp. 106, 108, and 110; and Laura B. Randolph, "Black Students Battle Racism on College Campuses," *Ebony*, vol. 44, no. 2 (December 1988), pp. 126, 128, and 130. The statistics of the Southern Poverty Law Center documented more than four hundred hate groups in 1998, and by the beginning of the new millennium that number had exceeded five hundred. A striking number of these groups have emerged throughout the northern and western United States. See *Intelligence Report* (Montgomery, Ala.: The Intelligence Project of the Southern Poverty Law Center, Winter 1998), pp. 1–59.

179. King, "An Address to a Mass Meeting," Marks, Mississippi, pp. 5–6; and Baldwin, *There Is a Balm in Gilead*, pp. 79–80.

180. See King, "Field of Education a Battleground," pp. 1–2; and King, "Revolution in the Classroom," pp. 2–8.

181. Alex Poinsett, "The Drive for Economic Equality: The New Civil Rights Movement," *Ebony*, vol. 44, no. 10 (August 1989), pp. 74, 76, and 78.

182. Kenneth S. Tollett, "Southern Justice for Blacks: Legal System Is Dominated by Racist Police, Court Officials," *Ebony*, vol. 26, no. 12 (October 1971), pp. 58–60, 62, and 64.

183. Alex Poinsett, "Black Politics: An Unfulfilled Promise," *Ebony*, vol. 30, no. 10 (August 1975), pp. 96–98, 100, and 102; Alex Poinsett, "Why Blacks Don't Vote," *Ebony*, vol. 31, no. 5 (March 1976), p. 33; "Black Mayors: 136 Preside in Cities Ranging from Six to Nearly 3 Million," *Ebony*, vol. 31, no. 1 (November 1975), pp. 164–166, 168, 170, and 172–173; Carl T. Rowan, "Is There a Conspiracy against Black Leaders?," *Ebony*, vol. 31, no. 3 (January 1976), pp. 33–35, 37–40, and 42; "Black Mayors: A Growing Political Force," *Ebony*, vol. 37, no. 5 (March 1982), pp. 135–136 and 138; "The Big Ten of Black Vote Power: Southern States Lead the Way in the Number of Black Elected Officials," *Ebony*, vol. 39, no. 10 (August, 1984), pp. 128, 130, 132, 134, and 136; and Whitaker, "The New Mississippi," p. 33.

184. King, *Where Do We Go from Here?*, pp. 146–157.

185. See Daniel G. Reid et al., eds., *Dictionary of Christianity in America* (Downers Grove, Ill.: InterVarsity Press, 1990), pp. 281–283. For various definitions of civil religion—set forth by Robert N. Bellah, Sidney E. Mead, Will Herberg, and other scholars—see Russell E. Richey and

Donald G. Jones, eds., *American Civil Religion* (New York: Harper & Row, 1974), pp. 3–18; Robert N. Bellah and Phillip E. Hammond, *Varieties of Civil Religion* (San Francisco: Harper & Row, 1980), pp. 3–22; Gail Gehrig, *American Civil Religion: An Assessment*, Monograph Series Number 3 (Storrs, Conn.: Society for the Scientific Study of Religion, 1979), pp. 1–4; and Wilson, *Baptized in Blood*, pp. 12–13.

186. Bellah and Hammond, *Varieties of Civil Religion*, p. 194.

187. John D. Elder, "Martin Luther King and American Civil Religion," *Harvard Divinity Bulletin*, New Series, vol. 1, no. 3 (Spring 1968): pp. 17–18. A more fleeting but similar reference is made in Andrew Shanks, *Civil Society, Civil Religion* (Cambridge, Mass.: Blackwell Publishers, 1995), p. 6.

188. Elder, "Martin Luther King and American Civil Religion," p. 18.

189. Ibid; and Andrew M. Manis, *Southern Civil Religions in Con flict: Black and White Baptists and Civil Rights, 1947–1957* (Athens: University of Georgia Press, 1987), pp. 2–3 and 7. One scholar contends that King, like Frederick Douglass and other black leaders who preceded him, "employed a distinctly African American variation of a widespread American rhetoric of social prophecy and criticism known as the American jeremiad." See David Howard-Pitney, "'To Form a More Perfect Union': African Americans and American Civil Religion," unpublished paper, presented at the Public Influences of African American Churches' Project, Scholars Meeting 2000, held in connection with the Leadership Center of Morehouse College, Atlanta, Georgia (6 May 2000), pp. 1 and 34 n2; and David Howard-Pitney, *The Afro-American Jeremiad: Appeals for Justice in America* (Philadelphia: Temple University Press, 1990), pp. 1–100.

190. Wilson, *Baptized in Blood*, pp. 12–13.

191. Wilson, *Judgment and Grace in Dixie*, pp. 31–32.

192. This is why King referred to the civil rights crusade as "a spiritual movement," noting that "we feel that the universe is on the side of right." See Martin Luther King, Jr., "An Address at the 47th N.A.A.C.P. Annual Convention," San Francisco, California (27 June 1956), King Papers, Boston University, pp. 8–9.

193. Martin Luther King, Jr., "Address at the First Annual Institute on Nonviolence and Social Change," Holt Street Baptist Church, Montgomery, Alabama (3 December 1956), King Papers, Boston University, pp. 1–2; and Martin Luther King, Jr., "An Announcement of His Decision to Move from Montgomery to Atlanta," Dexter Avenue Baptist Church, Montgomery, Alabama (29 November 1959), King Papers, Boston University, p. 2.

194. Martin Luther King, Jr., "A Speech," delivered at the Dexter Avenue Baptist Church, Montgomery, Alabama (10 December 1967), King Center Archives, p. 2.

195. Dabbs, *Who Speaks for the South?*, pp. 371–372; Wilson, *Judgment & Grace in Dixie*, p. xv; and Baldwin, *There Is a Balm in Gilead*, pp. 64 and 68–69.

196. Dabbs, *Who Speaks for the South?*, p. 379.

197. See Lawrence W. Levine, *Black Culture and Black Consciousness: Afro-American Folk Thought from Slavery to Freedom* (New York: Oxford University Press, 1977), pp. 23, 37–38, 50–51, 57, 137, and 385; Martin Luther King, Jr., "The Church in the Frontier of Racial Tension," Southern Baptist Theological Seminary, Louisville, Kentucky (19 April 1961), p. 3; Baldwin, *There Is a Balm in Gilead*, p. 85; Washington, ed., *A Testament of Hope*, pp. 41–42; From Martin Luther King, Jr. to Major J. Jones (5 November 1960), King Papers, Boston University, p. 1; and "Sunday with Martin Luther King," transcribed interview, recorded on WAAF-AM Radio, Chicago, Illinois (10 April 1966), King Center Archives, p. 3.

198. Interestingly enough, the New South idealist Ralph McGill was among a minority of white southerners who launched a furious assault on the Confederate battle flag, the old war song "Dixie," and other symbols of the Confederate tradition. See Clowse, *Ralph McGill*, p. 246; and Martin, *Ralph McGill*, pp. 270–271.

199. King, *Where Do We Go from Here?*, p. 11; and Brown, "Grounds for American Loyalty," p. 288.

200. Manis, *Southern Civil Religions in Conflict*, p. 3; and Howard-Pitney, "'To Form a More Perfect Union,'" pp. 1–34.

201. Moore distinguishes between the white southern revivalist tradition of Billy Graham and the black southern revivalist tradition of King. See Edward Lee Moore, "Billy Graham and Martin Luther King, Jr.: An Inquiry into White and Black Revivalistic Triditions," Ph.D. diss., Vanderbilt University, Nashville, Tennessee (May 1979), 126–346.

202. Carson, ed., *The Autobiography of Martin Luther King, Jr.*, 17 and 24.

203. Howard-Pitney, "'To Form a More Perfect Union,'" pp. 1–33.

204. The "Lost Cause" refers to the white South's abandonment of its dream of a separate political nation (the Confederacy) after its defeat in the Civil War. See Wilson, *Baptized in Blood*, pp. 1–160.

205. Dabbs, *Who Speaks for the South?*, pp. 314–315 and 373.

206. Wilson, *Judgment & Grace in Dixie*, p. xx.

207. Special attention should be devoted to those parts of Carter's book that treat "the legacy of George Wallace" and President Richard Nixon, and "the Southernization of American Politics." See Dan T. Carter, *The Politics of Rage: George Wallace, the Origins of the New Conservatism, and the*

Transformation of American Politics (New York: Simon & Schuster, 1995), pp. 324–468.

208. Andrew M. Manis, "Culture Wars: The Southern Theater," an unpublished paper (2001), pp. 1–24. King had this and more in mind when he spoke of the need for "the darkness of the soul of the South" to be "fully dissipated." See Martin Luther King, Jr., "Introduction," in William B. Huie, *Three Lives for Mississippi* (New York: New American Library, 1968), pp. 7–8.

On the Relation of the Christian to the State

The Development of a Kingian Ethic

LEWIS V. BALDWIN

As Christians we must never surrender our supreme loyalty to any time-bound custom or earth-bound idea, for at the heart of our universe is a higher reality—God and his kingdom of love—to which we must be conformed.

—Martin Luther King, Jr.[1]

Questions concerning the proper relationship of the Christian to the state permeate the entire history of the church. Such questions have persisted in every age and in virtually every nation, beginning with the ancient Christians, who refused to render to the state a reverence due to God alone, and extending through the centuries-old struggle between the kings and popes of medieval Europe, the development of the Western conception of the separation of church and state, and contemporary debates about government-sponsored faith-based initiatives and the possible transgression of church-state boundaries by the political and Religious Right.[2] Martin Luther King, Jr., was keenly aware of how the issues of church-state relations had unfolded, in intellectual and practical terms, up to his time, and his knowledge of that history informed his sense of his own responsibility as a Christian in the American society.

Developing Attitude toward Law and Government:
Experiential and Intellectual Sources

Growing up in a society in which politics and government had long
tolerated and often sanctioned the oppression of African Americans,
King was mindful, even before he entered college, that the Christian
is often justified to resist the state in the interest of justice and the
common good. After all, the protest traditions of his own family and
church testified to this very principle. King's maternal grandfather,
A. D. Williams, and his father, Martin Luther King, Sr., both of whom
were Baptist preachers and pastors, courageously challenged state-
supported segregation laws in the South because those laws demanded submission that conflicted with the moral order and the
eternal will of God.[3] King was taught as a child never to be afraid to
answer a higher divine call, even when it contradicted the policies of
government and the laws of the land. Thus, his earliest understanding
of the responsibility of the Christian in a society occurred in the context of his family and church environments, and also in connection
with his people's struggle for basic constitutional rights.

Although born into a family heritage which affirmed the supremacy of the divine will and the sacred rights of the individual conscience over the policies of the state, King went through an intellectual
struggle with these principles long before he sought to translate them
into practical reality as a civil rights leader. That struggle began during
his student days at Morehouse College in Atlanta, Georgia, from 1944
to 1948. During this time frame, the young man read Henry David
Thoreau's celebrated essay "On the Duty of Civil Disobedience"
(1848) several times, and was "deeply moved" by Thoreau's concept of
noncooperation with a law or government judged to be evil and immoral.[4] Even more impressive for King was Thoreau's willingness to
accept imprisonment in 1846, rather than support a system that sanctioned slavery, the mistreatment of the Indians, and the war with
Mexico. King found such actions stimulating intellectually and spiritually, and Thoreau's challenge must have loomed large in his consciousness when he accepted the call to the ministry during his senior
year at Morehouse.[5] "Fascinated by the idea of refusing to cooperate
with an evil system," said King years later, "I became convinced that
noncooperation with evil is as much a moral obligation as is coopera-

tion with the good."[6] The impact of Thoreau's ideas and actions proved all the more important as young King reflected on how the Christian might meet the challenges of racial and economic injustice in America.[7]

When King entered Crozer Theological Seminary in Chester, Pennsylvania, in 1948, he began what he called "a serious intellectual quest for a method to eliminate social evil."[8] That intellectual quest extended beyond Crozer, from which he graduated in May 1951, through his doctoral studies at Boston University, from September 1951 to June 1955. During these years, King made important references to church-state relations in papers he wrote for courses in Bible, ethics, philosophy, theology, and church history, and his continuing interest in how Christians should relate to legal and political systems was quite evident.[9] In a paper he wrote at Crozer in the fall of 1948, entitled "The Significant Contributions of Jeremiah to Religious Thought," King addressed the relevance of the prophet's message for contemporary Christians, noting that "the worst disservice that we as individuals or churches can do is to become sponsors and supporters of the status quo."[10] In a paper on "Reinhold Niebuhr's Ethical Dualism," written for Professor L. Harold DeWolf's systematic theology class at Boston University in 1952, King affirmed the need for government but insisted that the Christian, "as a vicar of Christ," must always be mindful of the sharp boundaries that exist between loyalty to the orders of government and obedience to the commands of God. King declared:

> Niebuhr makes it quite clear that government, although holy as an instrument for restraining the sinful, must never be looked upon as divine. The individual's reverence for government extends only as far as the purpose for which that unit was created. When the government pretends to be divine, the Christian serves God rather than man. The Christian must constantly maintain a "dialectical" attitude toward government while the collective ego remains within its bounds, while being critical whenever these bounds are overpassed.[11]

It is clear that King, at least as far back as his graduate studies at Boston, found many of Niebuhr's ideas on government more acceptable than some of Thoreau's. King found it impossible to embrace the kind

of individualism and the notion of human perfectibility that led
Thoreau to conclude that government would ultimately have little significance in the daily activities of persons.[12] In the aforementioned
paper on Niebuhr, King elaborated the point:

> Actually, however, government is very necessary, for men in-
> evitably corrupt their potentialities of love through a lust for self-
> security which outruns natural needs. Men must be restrained by
> force, else they will swallow up their neighbors in a desperate
> effort to make themselves secure. In this sense government is ap-
> proved of God. "Government is divinely ordained and morally jus-
> tified because a sinful world would, without the restraints of the
> state, be reduced to anarchy by its evil lusts." The force of sinful-
> ness is so stubborn a characteristic of human nature that it can
> only be restrained when the social unit is armed with both moral
> and physical might.[13]

King generally accepted Niebuhr's view that democracy is the best
form of government, mainly because it embodies the right of the citizen to resist its unjust measures.[14] On the other hand, both of these
thinkers called totalitarianism the least desirable governmental form,
a view that accounted in part for King's rejection of communism
throughout his life. For King, the totalitarianism associated with communism not only undermined "the Christian doctrine of God, but also
the Christian doctrine of man." In more specific terms, he asserted:

> Communism attributes ultimate value to the state. Man is
> made for the state and not the state for man. One may object,
> saying that in Communist theory the state is an "interim reality,"
> which will "wither away" when the classless society emerges. True—
> in theory; but it is also true that, while it lasts, the state is the end.
> Man is a means to that end. Man has no inalienable rights. His
> only rights are derived from, and conferred by, the state. Under
> such a system, the fountain of freedom runs dry. Restricted are
> man's liberties of press and assembly, his freedom to vote, and his
> freedom to listen and to read. Art, religion, education, music, and
> science come under the gripping yoke of governmental control.
> Man must be a dutiful servant to the omnipotent state.[15]

But King's preference for democracy does not mean that he was oblivious to its limitations. Here again, Reinhold Niebuhr proved to be an immensely significant source for the young man. "Niebuhr makes it clear," wrote King at Boston, "that a perfect democracy is just as impossible to reach as either a perfect society or a perfect individual."[16] King shared Niebuhr's idea that democracy does not constitute the purely moral system because powerful political parties with special interests, not the people who vote, ultimately determine the issues of government. Thus, even the choices made under the most genuine democratic system are morally and ethically relative.[17] However, King, unlike Niebuhr, emphatically affirmed the power of the agape ethic to transform society, a position that, for King, had powerful implications for how the Christian should relate to politics and government.[18]

The analysis so far presented undermines the assumption that King did not seriously think of the responsibility of the Christian to the state until he emerged as a civil rights leader. This assumption can only be held by those who fail to properly connect King's studies in the academy with his activities in the sociopolitical arena. The academy provided the initial context for King to reflect seriously and critically on the prevailing values and practices of the state or the body politic, and on the implications of this for Christian social witness. The Montgomery bus boycott, occurring in 1955–1956, afforded the initial opportunity for him to translate into practical action what he had worked out in theoretical terms at Morehouse, Crozer, and Boston.

On the Christian and Civil Disobedience:
King's Conflicts with Fundamentalists and Evangelicals

The struggle between the African American community and the city fathers and bus officials in Montgomery compelled King to revisit with renewed interest Thoreau's piece on civil disobedience. While initially struggling with the possibility that the Montgomery protest "could be used to unethical and unchristian ends," such as forcing the bus company out of business, King ultimately concluded that the actions of the protesters were essentially moral and in the best tradition of Thoreau. He declared:

As I thought further, I came to see that what we were really doing was withdrawing our cooperation from an evil system, rather than merely withdrawing our support from the bus company. The bus company, being an external expression of the system, would naturally suffer, but the basic aim was to refuse to cooperate with evil. At this point I began to think about Thoreau's "Essay on Civil Disobedience." I became convinced that what we were preparing to do in Montgomery was related to what Thoreau had expressed. We were simply saying to the white community, "We can no longer lend our cooperation to an evil system." From this moment on I conceived of our movement as an act of massive noncooperation. From then on I rarely used the word "boycott."[19]

In terms that merit extended quotation, Alex Ayres describes one episode in Montgomery which clearly illustrated the influence of both Thoreau and Christian values on King's attitude toward law and government:

On September 3, 1958, King was arrested on the steps of the courthouse in Montgomery, Alabama, on a trumped-up charge of loitering. The arresting officers handled him roughly, in full view of many witnesses, and dragged him away. . . . Dr. King was found guilty of disturbing the peace. Standing before Judge Eugene Loe on September 5, in front of a crowded courtroom, King made this statement: "Your honor, you have found me guilty. My wife and I have talked and prayed over the course of action in the event this should happen. If I am fined, I must tell you that I cannot in good conscience pay a fine for an act I did not commit and for brutal treatment that I did not deserve. I am inwardly compelled to take this stand. We are commanded to resist evil by the God that created us all." The judge was visibly irritated, for he was not accustomed to being lectured to, especially not by a black man. "Although I cannot pay a fine, I will willingly accept the alternative which you provide, without malice," continued King. "I make this decision because of my deep concern for the injustices and indignities that my people continue to experience. I also make this decision because of my love for America and the sublime principles of liberty and equality upon which she is founded. I have come to see that America is in danger of losing her soul. Something must happen to awaken the dozing soul of America before it is too late." Judge Loe imposed a two-week jail sentence, but King was soon released when Police Commissioner Clyde Sellers, embarrassed by the entire episode, paid his fine. . . . This incident shows that King felt it was important to resist unjust laws, but that it was also important to accept the penalty for doing so. It was the acceptance of the penalty, he felt, that separated the activist who practices civil disobedience from the anarchist or the lawbreaker. The willingness to accept the penalty for breaking the unjust law is what makes civil disobedience a moral act and not merely an act of lawbreaking. "There comes a time when a moral man can't obey a law which his conscience tells him is unjust. And the important thing is that when he does that, he willingly accepts the penalty—because if he refuses to accept the penalty, then he becomes reckless, and he becomes an anarchist."[20]

Conservative Christians and other defenders of the status quo in Montgomery denounced the bus protest as un-Christian, and accused King of "bringing trouble where we've always had peace."[21] One source reports that white fundamentalist and evangelical clergy tried to browbeat King, Ralph Abernathy, and other black members of the Montgomery Improvement Association "with theological arguments in a futile attempt to get them to call off the boycott."[22] The Reverend E. Stanley Frazier, "one of the most outspoken segregationists in the Methodist Church," urged King and the other black preachers to "bring this boycott to a close and lead their people instead 'to a glorious experience of the Christian faith.'"[23] King even encountered conservative black preachers who insisted that religion and politics do not mix, and who felt that ministers and churches should focus on "the heavenly" instead of getting involved in "earthly, temporal matters."[24] It is important to add, though, that white fundamentalists and evangelicals were much stronger in their opposition to King than the black conservative Christians who rejected his wedding of biblical piety, theological liberalism, political advocacy, and social activism.

Throughout his thirteen-year career as a civil rights leader, King found himself in conflict with Christian conservatives, white and black, who did not share his understanding of the Bible and the faith, particularly around the question of the essential character of Christian witness. At the center of this conflict were questions of this nature: What is the proper role of a Christian in a society? Are ministers called and commissioned by God to be social and political activists, or to be merely soul winners? Doesn't Jesus' admonition—"render unto Caesar the things which are Caesar's and unto God the things which are God's"—suggest a clear line of demarcation between the civil and religious that every Christian should take seriously? How can one justify the African Americans' campaigns of active nonviolent resistance and civil disobedience in light of Paul's assertion that the civil magistrates are ordained of God and therefore must be obeyed? Doesn't the political witness of civil rights clergy, who seek the political implementation of their moral and religious visions, transgress the church-state boundary?[25]

King answered these questions directly and indirectly, not only in his books, essays, personal interviews, mass meeting speeches, sermons, and letters, but also by breaking laws and violating court injunctions which favored white supremacy and segregation. King held that the church and its leadership must always be in tension with the state, providing a prophetic critique of its values, institutions, and practices, especially in cases where injustice exists. This is what the civil rights leader had in mind when he referred to the church as "the conscience of the state."[26] "It has always been the responsibility of the church," he maintained, "to broaden horizons, challenge the status quo, and break the mores when necessary."[27] Church-based nonviolent direct action was King's way of fostering the kind of tension needed to force a stubborn and intransigent government to negotiate and to confront and eliminate an unjust situation:

> I must confess that I am not afraid of the word "tension." I have earnestly opposed violent tension, but there is a type of constructive, nonviolent tension which is necessary for growth. Just as Socrates felt that it was necessary to create a tension in the mind so that individuals could rise above the bondage of myths and half-truths to the unfettered realm of creative analysis and objective appraisal, so must we see the need for nonviolent gadflies to create the kind of tension in society that will help men rise from the dark depths of prejudice and racism to the majestic heights of understanding and brotherhood.[28]

The white fundamentalist and evangelical clergy who opposed King's view of the moral responsibility of the Christian in relation to the state fell into two categories as identified by Harvey Cox. The first were "the pietists, who believed that their duty was to proclaim the word of God and focus their congregation's attention on the afterlife and not involve themselves in protests they considered secular and political." Bob Jones, Jr., and Jerry Falwell, both clergy who represented old-line fundamentalism in the 1950s and 1960s, fitted well into this category. The second group consisted of "the theologically and politically conservative clergy," who felt that "religion, like politics, had a duty to uphold the status quo."[29] The popular televangelist Billy Graham, a spokesman for the evangelicals, epitomized this perspective. White clergy and laity in both categories were inclined to agree with Will Herberg's claim that King's ethic of civil disobedience "was not Christian at all but seriously deviant and heretical, since it did not have a foundation in the Christian tradition."[30] Perplexed and perhaps disturbed by King's challenge to the power structure in Montgomery, one white conservative of this persuasion, in a letter to King, asked: "How do you reconcile Paul's statements on obeying duly constituted authorities, Romans 13:1–7, with the Negro's campaign of passive resistance in the South?" King's response reflected, on the deepest level, his belief that the spirit of the times demanded a more critical and flexible attitude on the part of the Christian toward the state:

> Like many Biblical affirmations, the words of the Apostle Paul must be interpreted in terms of the historical setting and psychological mood of the age in which they were written. The Apostle Paul—along with all of the early Christians—believed that the world was coming to an end in a few days. Feeling that the time was not long, the Apostle Paul urged men to concentrate on preparing themselves for the new age rather than changing external conditions. It was this belief in the coming new age and the second coming of Christ which conditioned a great deal of Paul's thinking. Early Christianity was far from accepting the existing social order as satisfactory, but it was conscious of no mission to change it for the better. It taught its adherents neither to conform to the external framework of their time, nor to seek directly to alter it, but to live within it a life rooted in a totally different order. Today we live in a new age with a different theological emphasis;

consequently we have both a moral and religious justification for passively resisting evil conditions within the social order.[31]

King was determined to uphold the highest Christian standards in his political advocacy and in his challenge to unjust governmental authorities and policies. In contrast to his conservative critics in the white churches, he felt that his challenge to evil laws and to the immoral political structures of the state was grounded squarely in the Bible and the Jesus tradition. He saw himself walking in the path of Jesus, whom he called "the world's most dedicated nonconformist"—"one whose ethical nonconformity still challenges the conscience of mankind."[32]

For King, Jesus' commandment to render unto Caesar his due did not amount to an endorsement of the status quo as the highest order, especially since the man from Nazareth insisted during his Galilean ministry that the kingdom of God and its righteousness must be sought first. King accepted this view unequivocally, and made it one of the cornerstones of his resistance to the state. Like Jesus, his primary mission was to affirm and pursue the kingdom of God on earth, or what he termed "the beloved community," not to accept uncritically the power and jurisdiction of civil authorities. Thus, the southern religious historian Samuel S. Hill is correct in saying that King's Southern Christian Leadership Conference (SCLC), formed in 1957 to coordinate the activities of local protest organizations across the South, and "to give the total struggle a sense of Christian and disciplined direction," was actually an "intentional type of religious-political movement" which "sought the embodiment of the teachings of Jesus in the laws of American society."[33]

But it is equally true that King went through a stage when he was almost as reluctant as some of his white Christian critics to attack the federal government. Prior to his involvement in the Albany, Georgia, campaign in 1961–1962, the civil rights leader included the federal government and its enforcement agencies among the movement's "strongest and most supportive Allies."[34] After all, the Supreme Court had declared bus segregation in Montgomery unconstitutional, bringing to a successful climax the very first King-led civil rights campaign. This helps explain why King and his associates in the SCLC chose not to defy a federal injunction that called for the cessation of demonstrations in Albany for ten days.[35] But President John F. Kennedy's refusal to protect African Americans who were being brutalized in Albany caused King to view the government "more warily." After Albany, King became increasingly critical of the FBI, and the rift between him and the federal government gradually grew wider and eventually became irreparable.[36] Moreover, King's mounting criticism of, and conflict with, the state contributed to the growing rift between him and Christian conservatives.

King and his staff moved into Birmingham in 1963 with the determination to break even federal injunctions that contradicted their sense of Christian accountability. It was here that King's differences with white conservative clergy surfaced in very public ways. On April 12, 1963, King led a march in defiance of a state court order forbidding further demonstrations, a move that landed him in a Birmingham jail and exposed him to attack from both city officials and the religious establishment.[37] The act of civil disobedience immediately evoked a reaction from eight Alabama clergymen, who, in a statement printed in the local paper, called King "an outsider" and deemed his actions in Birmingham "unwise and untimely." They went on to express the conviction that "racial matters could properly be pursued in the courts, but urged that decisions of those courts should in the meantime be peacefully obeyed." "We appeal to both our white and Negro citizenry," the clergymen continued, "to observe the principles of law and order and common sense."[38] Their uneasiness with King's willingness to disobey court injunctions was shared by the television evangelist Billy Graham, who urged the civil rights leader to "put on the brakes a little bit."[39] But King was not persuaded by such appeals, especially since his faith in the American court system—in the independence of judges, the fairness of the jury system, the integrity of the oath, and the sanctity of the political process—had eroded significantly.[40]

King responded to the Alabama clerymen in his "Letter from the Birmingham City Jail," issued April 16, 1963. This much-acclaimed document is the best example of King's use of civil-religious rhetoric and symbols in an attempt to persuade white Christians that the faith demands noncooperation with unjust laws and political systems.[41] The sheer genius of King's letter rests in the fact that it drew on many of the very same sources that his critics cherished. King alluded to

Shadrach, Meshach, and Abednego, who refused "to obey the laws of Nebuchadnezzar because a higher moral law was involved." He referred to the Apostle Paul, who "carried the gospel of Jesus Christ to the far corners of the Greco-Roman world"; to Jesus, "who was an extremist for love"; and to the early Christians, "who were willing to face hungry lions and the excruciating pain of chopping blocks, before submitting to certain unjust laws of the Roman Empire." King also spoke of standing in the tradition of St. Augustine, who declared that "an unjust law is no law at all"; of Thomas Aquinas, who denied that the state has a moral right to pass legislation contrary to the *eternal law* and the *natural law;* of Martin Luther, who placed the word of God above the religious establishment and the German princes; of John Bunyan, who vowed to remain in jail for life before making a butchery of his conscience; and of Paul Tillich and Reinhold Niebuhr, whose writings provide moral and theological grounds for the Christian's challenge to evil persons and institutions.[42]

The emphasis on Judeo-Christian sources was brought together in King's letter with insights from Western philosophical streams and the traditions of American participatory democracy. This made his reflections on the moral responsibility of the Christian in an unjust state all the more convincing and provocative. King pointed to Socrates' willingness to die rather than surrender "his unswerving commitment to truth," and to the Declaration of Independence and the Constitution, which affirmed the citizen's "right to protest for right." "One day the South will know that when these disinherited children of God sat down at lunch counters," said King in the Birmingham letter, "they were in reality standing up for what is best in the American dream and for the most sacred values in our Judeo-Christian heritage."[43] Such reflections must have registered with great force on the minds of the Alabama clergymen, who would have acknowledged links between their religious faith and their patriotism. In any case, King's letter silenced his critics and challenged the white church with a more prophetic vision of ministry and mission.[44]

The content of King's "Letter from the Birmingham City Jail" was actually meant for all Christians who struggle with issues of church-state relations and with questions about their moral obligation toward society. King knew that the lack of social activism on the part of many churchpersons was rooted in their failure to understand that "each of us has certain basic rights that are neither derived from nor conferred by the state."[45] "In deep disappointment I have wept over the laxity of the church," he wrote. "Is organized religion too inextricably bound to the status quo to save our nation and the world?" he asked, to which the answer must be a resounding *yes*. With the failures of the Christian church etched deeply in his consciousness, King elaborated further:

> So often the contemporary church is a weak, ineffectual voice with an uncertain sound. So often it is an archdefender of the status quo. Far from being disturbed by the presence of the church, the power structure of the average community is consoled by the church's silent—and often even vocal—sanction of things as they are.[46]

The extent to which the state controlled and exploited elements of both the white and black churches for its own ends greatly disturbed King. It was clear to him that conservative black preachers like the National Baptist Convention leader Joseph H. Jackson, who denounced King-led civil rights campaigns for encouraging "lawlessness," were essentially no different from George M. Murray, Wallie A. Criswell, John R. Rice, Billy Graham, and other white fundamentalists and evangelicals who criticized his methods.[47] This explains why King was at times as critical of the black church as he was the white church.

But he clearly realized that there was a long tradition in the black church that encouraged resistance to unjust laws and governmental structures. In other words, he saw redeeming qualities in that institution that were not so evident in its white counterpart. This accounted for his refusal to completely lose faith in the power of the church as a vanguard in the struggle for much-needed social and political change. In his Birmingham letter, King expressed gratitude to God that "through the Negro church, the dimension of nonviolence entered our struggle."[48] The torture and destruction of numerous black churches in the South by white racists reinforced King's view of the power and potential of those institutions. The gracefulness of the black church in responding to such lawlessness and terror reminded King of the reactions of the early Christian martyrs to the persecutions and trials inflicted upon them by the imperial magistrates of the Roman state:

The role of the Negro church today, by and large, is a glorious example in the history of Christendom. For never in Christian history, within a Christian country, have Christian churches been on the receiving end of such naked brutality and violence as we are witnessing here in America today. Not since the days in the catacombs has God's house, as a symbol, weathered such attack as the Negro churches.[49]

King's civil disobedience in Birmingham was not completely devoid of moral dilemmas. Many Christian conservatives wondered how he could urge white southerners to obey the laws of the land and the orders of the courts while he chose, at the same time, to engage in civil disobedience in the name of God and righteousness. But King denied that he and his followers were "anarchists advocating lawlessness," for it was obvious to them "that the courts of Alabama had misused the judicial process in order to perpetuate injustice and segregation." "Consequently, we could not, in good faith, obey their findings," King maintained.[50] Referring to himself and fellow activists in Birmingham as "political prisoners" whose First Amendment right to protest had been disregarded, King argued that "going to jail for disobeying an unjust law was the highest form of fidelity to the Constitution."[51] As he saw it, this is what distinguished the advocates of civil disobedience "from the racists who practiced uncivil disobedience," and a person who "breaks, circumvents, flouts, and evades the law but is unwilling to pay the penalty."[52] Thus, King called upon persons of all religious faiths to resist both segregation laws and the courts' "maliciously effective, pseudo-legal way of breaking the back of legitimate moral protest."[53]

Questions about the moral legitimacy of King's civil disobedience were raised continuously by Christian conservatives throughout the nation. This was particularly true of the South, where most of the King-led civil rights campaigns occurred, and where many white Christians viewed segregation as a godly ordained social order. When King went to St. Augustine, Florida, in 1964 to lead the last major crusade "against segregation in public accommodations facilities," he and his followers were met with white mob violence of unspeakable proportions, and with a city mayor and biblical fundamentalist who tolerated such lawlessness while insisting that "God segregated the races when he made the skins a different color."[54] King always found it difficult to understand how white Christians could cloak themselves in such a false view of God and of biblical revelation.

When King and his Southern Christian Leadership Conference set up operations in Selma, Alabama, in 1965, to struggle for the right to vote, conservative voices in the white church emerged again in ways that recalled Birmingham. White clergymen such as Bob Jones, Jr., Jerry Falwell, and Billy Graham found it virtually impossible to reject the claim, made earlier by Senator Jesse Helms of North Carolina, that "King's outfit is heavily laden at the top with leaders of proven records of communism" and "socialism."[55] Jones, the Alabama-born fundamentalist militant and separatist, and president of the university in Greenville, South Carolina, which bears his name, openly rejected King's interpretation of scripture and the faith. Convinced that the mission of the Christian did not involve challenging government and transforming the laws and moral codes of the society, Jones dismissed the social gospel preached by King and others as "pure socialism."

> *There is no such thing as a social Gospel.* That's a joke! There is only the Gospel of the Grace of God, and it's an individual Gospel. Whosoever comes, whosoever believes. The Lord's message is always a message to the individual.[56]

Jones's idea that one can change society by merely converting individuals clashed with King's notion that the Christian must take the lead in transforming both persons and institutions. Jerry Falwell espoused Jones's view during the Selma campaign, and both men felt that King was one of the greatest threats to biblical Christianity in the United States. In a sermon called "Ministers and Marches," delivered from his Lynchburg, Virginia, pulpit one Sunday night in 1965, Falwell, the southern Baptist preacher, attacked King and other activist preachers for getting tangled up in transitory social and political problems:

> As far as the relationship of the church to the world, it can be expressed as simply as the three words which Paul gave to Timothy— "Preach the Word." Nowhere are we commissioned to reform the externals. We are not told to wage wars against bootleggers, liquor

stores, gamblers, murderers, prostitutes, racketeers, prejudiced persons and institutions, or any other existing evil as such. . . . Our only purpose on this earth is to know Christ and to make Him known. Believing the Bible as I do, I would find it impossible to stop preaching the pure, saving gospel of Jesus Christ, and begin doing anything else—including fighting communism, or participating in civil rights reforms. . . . Preachers are not called to be politicians but soul-winners.[57]

While more receptive to King's idea of social gospel than Bob Jones, Jr., and Jerry Falwell, Billy Graham was very uncomfortable with the civil rights leader's statements about the possible need for massive acts of civil disobedience in Selma. Without mentioning King specifically, Graham asserted in Montgomery in June 1965, three months after the Selma campaign, "that racial harmony could be achieved" if "the extremists in the civil rights organizations would give Alabama time to digest the new civil rights laws."[58] The tone of Graham's remarks was quite insensitive, especially since King had "walked a careful line" on state laws and the injunction issue. In March 1965, King had refused to lead the Selma to Montgomery march until the event received federal court approval.[59] The more than two hundred Catholic, Protestant, and Jewish leaders involved in that march presented a healthy challenge to status quo preachers like Graham. But instead of viewing the ecumenical character of the Selma to Montgomery march as a model of Christian activism, Graham expressed fear that "evil forces" were exploiting "the race problem" to "overthrow the American government," a statement that supported King's view that large segments of white society were more concerned about the status quo, about law and order, than about justice and humanity.[60] King's concerns were well-founded in that Graham absolutely refused to strongly condemn Alabama's segregation laws and the violence used against nonviolent demonstrators by the Ku Klux Klan and other racist elements in Selma.[61]

The fact that young black evangelicals were beginning to publicly express their support for King and the movement made leaders like Graham all the more uneasy. This shift toward a social gospel resulted in a spiritual and intellectual struggle for John Perkins, whose "Christian experience" had "led him to focus on the necessity of personal salvation" and other faith issues that "gave him kinship with white evangelicals."[62] But Perkins turned to civil rights activism in the 1960s, embracing aspects of King's nonviolent ethic and crusading for racial reconciliation as the central message of the gospel.[63] Tom Skinner, the Harlem gangster who became a militant black evangelical, heavily criticized "the hypocrisy of middle-class white America and the complacency of Evangelical churches," accusing them of contributing "to institutionalized racism and poverty."[64] Other young black evangelicals also stated their case for a more prophetic understanding of the faith. Columbus Salley launched a blistering assault on "evangelical racism, based on biblical principles, historical evidence, contemporary social realities, and the positive elements of Black Power." William Pannell, who later served with Skinner as a trustee at Fuller Theological Seminary, "demanded that evangelicals repudiate the traditional Christ of white, suburban America and its civil religion in favor of the universal, risen Lord Jesus Christ who liberates and reconciles an oppressed humanity."[65] Echoes of King's own challenge to the religious, social, and political establishments could be heard in the voices of all of these proponents of an evangelical theology of social change.

The young black evangelicals developed a radical activist interpretation of the gospel that made it much easier for them to relate to King and the movement than to the predominantly white National Association of Evangelicals (NAE). In 1963, two years before proclaiming their support for King's efforts in Selma, Skinner, Salley, and Pannell joined William H. Bentley, another African American evangelical, in forming what became the National Black Evangelical Association (NBEA). This group espoused a theology that was quite conservative on some levels, and it embraced political perspectives that ranged from the apolitical to King's political liberalism to the nationalistic.[66] Its leaders stood as living proof that evangelicals in America were not monolithic in terms of their perspectives on the relationship of the Christian to the state. Indeed, the ideas of the most militant and prophetic members of the NBEA provided a much-needed critique of Billy Graham, Joseph H. Jackson, and other evangelical Christians who capitulated to power structures and bowed to the established norms and customs of the society.

King's involvement in the Chicago Freedom Movement in 1966–1967 brought other challenges from Christian leaders who rejected his politics of confrontation. Determined to eliminate slum conditions and to strike down segregated housing policies in Chicago, King encountered hostile white and black ministers who were either intimidated by, or controlled by, the powerful political machine of Mayor Richard J. Daley. Archbishop James P. Cody, the Catholic prelate of Chicago, was one of the very few white ministers to voice support for the movement, but doubts about his sincerity surfaced when he refused to appear at King's Soldier Field rally, and actually urged activists to call off their march into segregated neighborhoods like Cicero.[67] The Reverend James Bevel, one of King's staff members, publicly denounced Cody for abandoning the cause, noting that "When there's trouble, Daley sticks up his liberal bishop to say, 'You've gone far enough.'" "But we've got news for the man," Bevel continued. "If the bishop doesn't have the courage to speak up for Christ, let him join the devil."[68]

King's "consistent adversary" and greatest nemesis among the clergy in Chicago was Joseph Jackson, who maintained that the proper role of the church and its leaders involves spreading God's word to the flock, saving souls for Jesus, and effecting change through exemplary conduct.[69] Still resentful of King's influence on the hundreds of progressive black preachers who severed ties with the National Baptist Convention back in 1961, Jackson joined Mayor Daley in labeling King "an outsider" and "a troublemaker." Moreover, the National Baptist president dismissed King's nonviolent direct action campaigns as premeditated actions designed to cause "civil disruption," and charged that King's challenge to local laws and court authority "was not far removed from open crime."[70] In Jackson's estimation, "Chicago needed no help from King" as long as it had "such true-hearted friends of black people as Richard J. Daley." King casually scoffed at such sentiments, asserting that "I don't think Dr. Jackson speaks for one percent of the Negroes in this country."[71] Be that as it may, Jackson's influence accounted largely for the refusal of many churches and preachers to support King's efforts in Chicago, a problem that contributed to the movement's failure.[72] However, King's lack of success also stemmed from his inability to "understand big city power politics, and so he was hopelessly outmaneuvered by Mayor Daley."[73]

Grinding poverty and the growing cycle of urban riots led King to more radical solutions that virtually assured his continuing conflicts with both the federal government and the most conservative wings of the religious establishment. As King and his staff planned for the proposed Poor People's Campaign in late 1967, there was talk of the need for "prolonged and massive civil disobedience" in Washington, D.C. King even raised the possibility of disrupting "the functioning of the city" if the government failed to act promptly and constructively.[74] This type of nonviolent sabotage "was to include transportation tie-ups, school boycotts, and appearances at major government buildings," actions that King deemed "risky" but morally responsible and necessary to dramatize the conditions of the poor.[75] The federal government and enforcement agencies like the FBI, which had long had King and his associates under surveillance, would not have tolerated such actions. Furthermore, King's efforts to broaden the boundaries of civil disoobedience clashed with the pronouncements of conservative clergy about the "dangers of encouraging" disregard for "established laws."[76]

This conflict continued as King equated the goals of the Poor People's Campaign with the concerns of the hundreds of black men involved in the Memphis Sanitation Strike. King joined the garbage workers in Memphis, Tennessee, in March 1968, insisting that the struggle there signaled "the beginning of the Poor People's Campaign."[77] Although black ministers and laypersons in the Community on the Move for Equality, an organization formed "to coordinate support for the strike," embraced King's call for massive civil disobedience as an option, many fundamentalists and evangelicals nationwide found such tactics intolerable and even frightening. Joseph H. Jackson, Jerry Falwell, and Billy Graham were among those who continued to criticize King and his followers for encouraging unwarranted civil disobedience in the name of Christian social reform. Graham spoke in dramatic terms about "false prophets in the church," and essentially denied that there is something inherently *moral* or *Christian* about resisting the laws of the state.[78] "We should realize that though the law must guarantee human rights and restrain those who violate those rights," Graham explained, "whenever men lack sympathy for the law they will not long respect it, even if they cannot repeal it." It is clear that Graham was censuring even those "who chose to violate existing laws for what they thought to be higher standards."[79] His position was essentially no different from that of Noel Smith, the Southern Baptist leader and longtime editor of *The Baptist Bible Tribune*, who insisted that King was "guilty of a palpable falsehood" when he suggested "that the New Testament and the practices of the early Christians" authenticated "his objectives and methods."[80]

King's Poor People's Campaign and mounting opposition to U.S. involvement in Vietnam afforded ammunition for white Christian conservatives who had long sought to attach the communist label to him. In a period when McCarthyite hysteria was still quite pervasive in the United States, King's statements about the evils of capitalism and the killing of "little brown children in Vietnam" were destined to be misunderstood and falsely labeled.[81] His concern for the uplift of the poor led him to advocate basic structural changes in the capitalistic system, a position equated in the minds of fundamentalist and evangelical clergy with the whole train of Marxist-Leninist-Stalinist thought. King's interest in international peace drove him to call for negotiations with the Vietcong, a position most conservative Christians associated with communist sympathizers.[82] White fundamentalists and evangelicals nationwide were inclined to accept Billy Graham's claim that "communism is inspired, directed, and motivated by the Devil himself," a view that made them all the more prone to denounce King as a traitor who needed to be silenced.[83]

Although faced with growing opposition from white Christians during the last three years of his life, King never ceased to address publicly the weaknesses of capitalism and the shame of his government's role in Vietnam. For him, the issues were inseparable. In response to Christian conservatives who identified the capitalistic ethic with Christian values, King defined capitalism as largely unethical and un-Christian because it encourages unscrupulous competition, selfish ambition, and an excessive profit motive.[84] As Billy Graham and other televangelists praised U.S. involvement in Vietnam as a fight against communism, King denounced the whole adventure as further proof that his government "was the greatest purveyor of violence in the world today."[85] While many white clergymen labeled communism the tool of Satan, King saw in that system's concern for the underprivileged an indictment against and challenge to the Christian church.[86] The civil rights leader adamantly rejected the claim that his positions on such issues constituted acts of treason, insisting instead that they were expressions of Christian duty.

But King was equally emphatic in refuting the charge that the civil rights movement was communist infiltrated, supported, and controlled. He repeatedly noted that communism is evil to the extent that it upholds atheism, ethical relativism, totalitarianism, and a materialistic and humanistic view of life and history, ideas carefully outlined in his sermon "How Should a Christian View Communism."[87] "Communism and Christianity are fundamentally incompatible," King wrote. "A true Christian cannot be a true Communist, for the two philosophies are antithetical and all the dialectics of the logicians cannot reconcile them."[88] In other writings, he dismissed communism as inconsistent with the religious heritage, the patriotic spirit, and the political aspirations of African Americans. "You must realize that a very great part of Negro life is church-centered," King explained, "and thusly, his native religious appetite would not be prone to a godless system such as communism."[89] For King, this was the most important reason for the failure of communism among African Americans. Interestingly enough, he also attributed the lack of success of the communist movement among his people to "the whole grain of" their "natural patriotism," and "to the fact that the vast majority of Negroes have found a ray of hope in the framework of American democracy."[90]

But King always had problems with the blind patriotism of the fundamentalists and evangelicals who consistently attacked his views on the responsibility of the Christian toward the state. He felt that Noel Smith, Billy Graham, Joseph H. Jackson, and other Christian conservatives stood as living symbols of how the state often exploits the power of the church for its own ends. King reminded these supporters of the status quo that "there comes a time when one must take a position that is neither safe nor politic nor popular, but he must do it because Conscience tells him it is right":

> Let us not forget, in the memories of the six million who died, that everything Adolph Hitler did in Germany was "legal," and that everything the Freedom Fighters in Hungary did was "illegal." In spite of that, I am sure that I would have aided and comforted my Jewish brothers if I had lived in Germany during Hitler's reign, as some Christian priests and ministers did do, often at the cost of their lives. And if I lived now in a Communist country where principles dear to the Christian's faith are

suppressed, I know that I would openly advocate defiance of that country's anti-religious laws—again, just as some Christian priests and ministers are doing today behind the iron curtain. Right here in America today there are white ministers, priests and rabbis who have shed blood in the support of our struggle against a web of human injustice, much of which is supported by immoral man-made laws.[91]

In a similar statement, issued in January 1968, three months prior to his death, King applauded black South Africans for refusing to bow to state control. He referred specifically to Albert J. Luthuli, a committed Christian and the nonviolent leader of the African National Congress, who suffered daily because of his resistance to the apartheid system and the repressive measures of the South African government. "I'm convinced that if I had lived in South Africa I would have joined Chief Luthuli, the late Chief Luthuli," King commented, "as he had his campaigns, openly to disobey those laws, and to refuse to comply with the pass system, where people had to have passes and all that stuff to walk the streets."[92]

Some of the "critics of King's civil disobedience" accused him of not relying sufficiently "on litigation and petitions to achieve his goals."[93] This accusation was made repeatedly by Billy Graham and, to a lesser degree, Joseph H. Jackson. In brilliant and provocative terms, John J. Ansbro has answered such critics:

They have ignored the fact that, in his attempts to transform the political and economic structures, he did make appeals to the courts. These critics have also disregarded his many petitions to Federal, state, and municipal authorities. Petitions were developed for all of his crusades. At times he tried to dramatize the significance of these petitions. In the Selma Movement he arranged for a delegation to attempt to present a petition to Governor George Wallace. In the Chicago Movement, in a manner reminiscent of Martin Luther, he posted on a church door his demands upon the city officials. Apart from his crusades and his books, he presented petitions through a variety of channels, including the Prayer Pilgrimages to Washington, D.C.; the March on Washington; speeches at universities, conventions, and press clubs and before the Platform and Resolutions Committees of the Democratic and Republican National Conventions; sermons; interviews; numerous articles in journals, magazines, and newspapers, especially articles in *The Nation;* a detailed petition to President Kennedy, and discussions with him and with Presidents Eisenhower and Johnson. However, he soon became painfully aware that only when he reinforced the petitions with nonviolent direct actions could he secure some of the necessary legislation, and even its partial implementation.[94]

King believed deeply in "strong and aggressive leadership from the federal government," but he insisted also that "our government must depend more on its moral power than on its military power." He also asserted that "government action" around the issues of racial and economic injustice constituted only "an important partial answer." King further remarked: "Negroes must therefore not only formulate a program; they must fashion new tactics which do not count on government goodwill but serve, instead, to compel unwilling authorities to yield to the mandates of justice."[95]

The importance of the law in transforming life and culture for the better never escaped King, even as he defended the right of the Christian to engage in acts of civil disobedience under certain conditions. Although opposed in many instances to coercive political power to influence morality, he agreed nevertheless with the many Western philosophers, political theorists, and religious thinkers who, from ancient times, had argued that government has a responsibility to help control antisocial and immoral behavior through the processes of law. King wrote:

> It is true that laws cannot change internal prejudiced attitudes, but they can control the external effects of bad attitudes. While a law cannot make an employer have compassion for an employee, it can keep him from refusing to hire individuals because of the color of their skin. Laws do not change attitudes, but at least they control behavior. We need laws to change the habits of men while we wait on religion and education to change their hearts.[96]

King frequently said that Christians who always felt compelled to sanction the status quo needed to reconsider their views on the proper roles of law and government in a society. He also reasoned that they needed to develop a more prophetic sense of the responsibility of the Christian toward the state. He put this challenge before the Southern Baptist Convention, one of America's largest white evangelical groups, with piercing clarity, noting that its constituents had become far too comfortable with southern conservative politics, including the segregation of the races.[97] For King, the reactions of the early Christian martyrs to imperial oppression and persecution provided the ideal model for how Christians today might relate to the state:

> There was a time when the church was very powerful. It was during that period when the early Christians rejoiced when they were deemed worthy to suffer for what they believed. In those days the church was not merely a thermometer that recorded the ideas and principles of popular opinion; it was a thermostat that transformed the mores of society. Wherever the early Christians entered a town the power structure got disturbed and immediately sought to convict them for being "disturbers of the peace" and "outside agitators." But they went on with the conviction that they were "a colony of heaven," and had to obey God rather than man. They were small in number but big in commitment. They were too God-intoxicated to be "astronomically intimidated."[98]

The powerful challenge of this early Christian minority to the Roman state loomed large in King's consciousness as he considered the role that African Americans were playing as a creative minority in the United States. Through their willingness to suffer nonviolently for the common good, King thought, African Americans were improving the nation while projecting upon it a new image of the church and a fresh awareness of the possibilities inherent in the Christian faith.[99] King recognized in the church-centered civil rights campaigns of the 1950s and 1960s not only the fulfillment of a divine plan, but also the realization of Henry David Thoreau's idea regarding "the effectiveness of a creative minority who serve the state by resisting it with the intention of improving it."[100] In these respects, King thought, the black church recalled the church of the apostles.

Much of the power of King's legacy rests in the fact that he successfully challenged a conservative religious establishment that had long failed to properly distinguish between obedience to God and loyalty to the state. Indeed, King challenged all Christians with a fresh vision of what it means to follow Christ in the contemporary world. C. Eric Lincoln has put it best:

> The late Dr. Martin Luther King, Jr. did more than anyone in modern times to exemplify the spirit of Christianity and this tremendous benefit was to all of Christendom, not just the black church. Christianity itself was against the wall and King's moral leadership and eventual martyrdom did more to re-establish credibility and interest in the faith than all of the councils and pronouncements of the last hundred years. The late Dr. King demonstrated that being is more substantial than words, and doing is more convincing than good intention.[101]

False Images of the King Legacy:
The Confusion of the Religious and Political Right

The assassination of Martin Luther King, Jr., on April 4, 1968, evoked a range of responses from conservative, Bible-believing Christians across the United States. Christian conservatives in the African American community responded with alarm and disbelief, and even those who had strongly opposed King's philosophy and methods offered prayers and sincere expressions of sympathy and sorrow. Among white Christian conservatives, reactions to the tragedy were not as monolithic in tone and spirit. Billy Graham is said to have grieved for King and his family, while praying "for a person whose philosophy and strategy he had ceased to understand, much less condone."[102] Brady Whitehead's study shows that in the immediate aftermath of King's death, many conservative white clergy either chose not to mention him in their sermons, or spoke unfavorably of him.[103] Bob Jones, Jr., referred to King as "an apostate," and refused to lower his university's flag to half-mast in memory of the civil rights leader.[104] A white independent Baptist clergyman from Alabama, echoing the thoughts of political conservatives like Jesse Helms and Strom Thurmond, maintained that King "loaded the gun of his own destruction by making himself the symbol of resistance to law and order." Referring to King's crusade as "anti-Christian," the segregationist pastor questioned those who would make a martyr of one "who rejected the cardinal tenets of biblical Christianity for the heathen philosophy of Mahatma Gandhi."[105]

Some of the reactions of white evangelicals to King's murder defied logic and even the most elementary standards of decency. A group of young white evangelicals at Los Angeles Baptist College cheered loudly when informed of the assassination.[106] "God answered my prayers when Communist Rev. Martin Luther King (nigger) was shot," said one Bible-believer in a letter to James Earl Ray, the accused assassin. Hundreds of others congratulated Ray in letters and telegrams, and packages containing Bibles and religious pamphlets were sent to him.[107] Such extreme reactions reflect what Stephen Berk describes as the "animosity" that existed "between the evangelical churches and the civil rights movement."[108]

But King had had a noticeable effect on even those white fundamentalists and evangelicals who found satisfaction in his death. Indeed, he had forced them to confront their own moral and spiritual impotence, despite their failure to properly come to terms with it. He taught them the absurdity of separating religion from politics, and of divorcing the mission of the church from the affairs of the state. Moreover, King reminded Christian conservatives that obedience to God must always take precedence over even the most heartfelt loyalty to humanly contrived legal and political structures.[109]

The impact of King on the emerging social and political consciousness of white evangelical and fundamentalist clergy in the 1970s and 1980s has not been adequately recognized. King's challenge accounted largely for Billy Graham's public statements against racism in the 1970s.[110] Jerry Falwell's shift toward a more *politicized* interpretation of Christian responsibility, which found institutionalized expression in the Moral Majority, Inc. in 1979, also owed much to the influence of King and the civil rights crusade.[111] Having "learned a lesson in strategy from Martin Luther King, Jr., and other black ministers," Falwell asserted in the late 1970s that "Our Founding Fathers separated church and state in function, but never intended to establish a government void of God."[112] This outlook was embraced by many other white and black religious leaders who experienced an acknowledged about-face on the validity of Christian participation in civic affairs. This politicization of fundamentalist and evangelical Christians crystallized in the 1980s as Falwell, Pat Robertson, and others in the so-called Religious Right united with Ronald Reagan, Strom Thurmond, Jesse Helms, and others in the political right to restore what they perceived to be the biblical and moral foundations of American life and culture.

In 1980, Falwell dismissed "Ministers and Marches," a sermon preached against King and other activist preachers fifteen years earlier, as "false prophecy." He went on to proclaim that "in recent months, God has been calling me to do more than just preach—He has called me to take action. I have a divine mandate to go right into the halls of Congress and fight for laws that will save America."[113] Falwell acted on this claim in the 1980s by joining millions of other religious and political conservatives in calling for government action to outlaw abortion, to discourage homosexuality and pornography, to encourage prayer and the teaching of creationism in schools, to oppose feminism and the Equal Rights Amendment, and to ensure a strong military and pro-Israeli policies. Falwell actually applauded Christian antiabortionists and antigay activists who took their fight to the streets. Although the controversial televangelist stated in 1981 that "I feel that what King was doing is exactly what we are doing," it is highly unlikely that he and the civil rights leader would have seen eye-to-eye on most of these concerns.[114]

Some sources raved in the 1980s about the growing "measure of admiration" that Falwell and other white religious conservatives felt toward King. One account reasoned that because of the change in Falwell's "views toward Martin Luther King's methods, it is possible that acts of nonviolence and civil disobedience will be entertained by the Religious Right, a violation of civil law under the claims of a higher moral law."[115] This is precisely what occurred in some instances with Randall Terry and other politicized fundamentalists in the pro-life movement, who insisted that "their protests follow in the tradition of Martin Luther King, Jr.'s civil rights movement."[116] Assessing the logic of such a comparison, Daniel C. Maguire has remarked:

> One of the principal complaints of the New Rightists is that they are being criticized for doing what "liberal" religionists have always done—mixing religion and politics. They cite the work of

Martin Luther King, Jr. Clearly he did not preach a privatized religion. He went from pulpit to polling booth. He took the ideals that were bred in evangelical piety and made them the basis of a movement that eventually yielded civil rights legislation and affirmative action executive orders. How dare we now complain, after cheering Martin Luther King, Jr., when another stripe of evangelicals make their own attempt to influence politics.[117]

Religious and political conservatives in the 1980s sought to politically implement moral visions that conflicted with King's beloved community ideal—with his dream of a totally integrated society based on love, mutual acceptance, true intergroup and interpersonal living, and shared power.[118] Many in the Christian and political right used some of King's most famous words in their arguments against government aid for the poor and oppressed, noting, for example, that his call for a nation in which persons are judged by character rather than skin color suggests opposition to affirmative action.[119] Well into the 1990s, rabid anti-affirmative action advocates like Newt Gingrich, Dick Armey, and Clint Bolick actually invoked "King's struggle in support of *their* specious arguments."[120] This misrepresentation of King's words is difficult to understand, especially since he consistently called for "special" and "compensatory measures" or "concessions" for "the deprived" and "disadvantaged" in the American society.[121] Jerry Falwell, Pat Robertson, and others in the political and Religious Right totally ignored the long history of racial and economic injustice and its continuing impact on poverty among African Americans and other racial-ethnic groups in this country. This is why they supported government cutbacks in aid for the poor and the oppressed while, at the same time, agreeing with the massive military budgets of the Reagan-Bush years. Nothing could contrast more with King's vision:

> Here again is the difference between a religiously motivated Martin Luther King, Jr., and the New Right. The Hebrew and Christian scriptures from which King drank are obsessed with the needs of the poor and the powerless in society. How the New Right can read those scriptures and support elitist monopolies, weaken civil rights enforcement, and cut back on aid to poor children is an epic of hypocrisy that must be called by its name.[122]

The contradictions became all the more glaring because many Christian conservatives who claimed to be pro-life, who took bold and uncompromising stands against abortion, also favored the death penalty. This tragic ambivalence did not exist in King's spirit. Moreover, King made significant strides toward transforming society and culture without resorting to the kind of force and intimidation occasionally used by antiabortionists. As Bea Blair once put it: "Martin Luther King and his followers never screamed and yelled at people. They were sitting, they were quiet, and they never interfered with other people's rights."[123]

Religious and political conservatives have been determined since the 1980s to strengthen and reinforce the structures of white male supremacy in the United States. This not only explains their refusal to seriously engage the problem of racism, but also their fierce opposition to feminism and government action to enhance the quality of life for women. Daniel Maguire speaks graphically to the issue:

> The ferocious resistance of the New Right to such matters as the Equal Rights Amendment has been telling. They claim credit for defeating it in many states, and in this case their claims may indeed be largely true. Since they defend patriarchal rights for men, equal rights for women are subversive in their worldview. If the New Right has its way, the white male monopoly that from the founding of this country has demanded and gotten a 90 to 100 percent monopoly on positions of power and prestige in church, state, business, the professions, and the academic world will continue. Affirmative action, a modest effort to ease that historic monopoly, is targeted against by the New Right. Success for them here means the further *disabling* and *disempowering* of women. To compare that achievement to that of Martin Luther King, Jr., is an obscenity.[124]

The central questions in distinguishing King from the political and Religious Right of contemporary America are: *What is the relationship between religion and politics in a diverse and multicultural society? Should they be utilized to "disempower and disable or to empower and enable?"* The charge that Christian conservatives are using religion in "antipolitical and subversive" ways to hurt people who are not *white, male,* and *masculine* is difficult to refute. In suggesting a deeper contrast between King and the Christian Right around this concern, Daniel Maguire writes:

> There is all the difference imaginable between what Martin Luther King, Jr., brought to the political order and what the Falwells bring. When King left his pulpit and ceased his political activism, many who had lacked rights before had come to possess those rights. People were voting who could not vote before, were getting hired and educated who would have known only rejection, and were finding decent housing who could not before. In short, King's interventions in politics were *enabling* and *empowering*. . . . However, when the Falwells of the New Right leave their pulpits and end their political activism, inasmuch as they are successful, people who had rights will have lost them. Their interventions are *disabling* and *disempowering*.[125]

One scholar has made significant references to the "multiple and competing images of King" which continue to generate "mass public confusion," and another has poignantly described "the profound sense of national amnesia that has distorted so much of America's approach to" the civil rights leader.[126] Both concerns are relevant to any discussion of King's meaning for the political and Religious Right. It should be noted that while a few of these conservatives refer to King in defending the moral legitimacy of their cause, most have consistently sought to diminish his significance as a national hero. This became most evident in the 1980s when Jesse Helms, the dean of conservative Republicanism, staged a virtual one-man, protracted tirade in an unsuccessful attempt to prevent Senate approval of the King Holiday Bill. Helms, with the silent approval of many Christian Rightists, raved about "King's communist associates," and labeled him an advocate of subversive means rather than a symbol of Americanism.[127] This portrayal of King as one who was fundamentally *un-American*, in both his outlook and actions, represented one extreme over against the tendency of some to cast him in the image of the gentle, harmless preacher who embraced uncritically the American dream.[128]

Despite the powerful outbursts of anti-King propaganda, the U.S. Senate voted overwhelmingly, on October 19, 1983, to designate the third Monday in January, beginning in 1986, as a federal holiday in memory of King.[129] But this did not end the drive in conservative political and religious circles to destroy King's image. Throughout much of the eighties, leaders such as Governor Evan Mecham of Arizona resisted "the rising tide of public support" for a King holiday in states that still rejected the idea. Although President Ronald Reagan signed the holiday bill in November 1983, he never wholly disassociated himself from Mecham, Jesse Helms, and other King detractors in white churches and in government.[130] In 1988, the Reverend Curtis W. Caine of Jackson, Mississippi, an "extreme fundamentalist" in the Southern Baptist Convention, condemned King as "a fraud." Such a characterization of King, though repudiated by a few in the convention, was widely accepted by most Southern Baptists, thus calling into question the sincerity of the public apologies they made to blacks for racism.[131] In 1989, Patrick Buchanan, the conservative Republican, went a step further than Caine, denouncing King as a womanizer and declaring that he, despite his achievements, "was not remotely so great a man or historic figure as George Washington, who led the army of independence, presided at our constitutional convention, and became our first president."[132] Apparently, Buchanan failed to see that King freed Americans in ways that Washington never imagined.

Organized efforts to counter such images of King have not been very strong up to this point. In 1997, Martin Luther King III founded Americans United for Affirmative Action to dispel the notion, propagated by white and black conservatives, that his father's "dream would not have countenanced racial preferences."[133] George E. Curry, the editor in chief of *Emerge*, an African American news magazine, has also contributed to this effort, refuting the claims of former California Republican Governor Pete Wilson, and of black political conservatives like Clarence Thomas and Ward Connerly, who persist in twisting King's words to legitimize their opposition to affirmative action.[134] But most black and white politicians and churchpersons, who emphasize the need to preserve King's legacy, have done surprisingly little to discourage those in the political and Religious Right from molding King to fit their own special interests and agenda.

Black fundamentalists and evangelicals have done even less to keep their counterparts from sanitizing, and in some cases demonizing, the image of King. John Perkins and William Pannell, who still identify with the traditions of evangelical Christianity, constitute important exceptions. In the spirit of King, they are challenging white Christian conservatives, through their writings and speeches, to recognize and help solve the lingering problems of institutional racism. Perkins, the founder of Mendenhall Ministries in Mississippi, and of the California-based Harambee Christian Family Center and the John M. Perkins Foundation for Reconciliation and Development, is still struggling to reconcile black Christians with traditionally conservative, white evangelicals. He is also encouraging white evangelical Christians to translate biblical principles into social reform ministries that seriously address the problems of racism and poverty.[135] Pannell warns of "the coming race wars" that could haunt the nation in the future if white evangelicals continue to ignore King's legacy and its implications for addressing an urban crisis that involves unresolved racial and economic issues.[136]

King's dream and legacy are not compatible with the current strategies put forth by the political and Religious Right for the redemption and transformation of American life and culture. King ultimately had in mind the creation of a democratic socialist society, the political and economic equivalent of the ethical ideal of the beloved community and the theological ideal of the kingdom of God on earth.[137] As Kenneth L. Smith has indicated, King's dream

> moved beyond civil rights for blacks to the need for basic structural changes within the capitalistic system: the nationalization of basic industries, massive federal expenditures to revive center cities and to provide jobs for ghetto residents, and a guaranteed annual income for every adult citizen of the U.S.[138]

This sense of a more just and inclusive society still stands as a challenge to religious and political conservatives who feel that their greatest battle is against secular humanism and theological liberalism, not poverty and injustice, and who exclude the disadvantaged, abused, and marginalized from their vision of *the truly moral and virtue-based society*. During the 1980s and 1990s, a few white evangelical voices emerged to counter the so-called Christian Right, among them Ronald J. Sider, the founder of Evangelicals for Social Action, and Tony Campolo, a counselor to President Bill Clinton. Sider and Campolo have expressed a devotion to the principles of the beloved community as articulated by King, but the power of their visions is still undermined by their failure to engage in the kind of militant, aggressive action for which King became so widely known.[139] King's life and work should be a reminder that no true follower of Christ can compromise, follow the path of passive acquiescence, or join in a conspiracy of silence when a nation affirms and uplifts some of its citizens while leaving others defeated, destitute, and defenseless.

NOTES

1. Martin Luther King, Jr., *Strength to Love* (Philadelphia: Fortress Press, 1981), p. 18.

2. Numerous scholarly works have been produced on church-state relations and on the role of the Christian in an unjust society, but very little has been written on how King approached this issue. See Agnes Cunningham, ed., *The Early Church and the State* (Philadelphia: Fortress Press, 1982), pp. 1–114; Roland H. Bainton, *Christian Attitudes toward War and Peace: A Historical Survey and Critical Reevaluation* (Nashville: Abingdon Press, 1985), pp. 13–268; Robert G. Clouse, ed., *War: Four Christian Views* (Downers Grove, Ill.: InterVarsity Press, 1981), pp. 10–196; Ernst Helmreich, ed., *Church and State in Europe, 1864–1914* (St. Louis, Mo.: Forum Press, 1979), pp. 1–111; Robert L. Cord, *Separation of Church and State: Historical Fact and Current Fiction* (Grand Rapids, Mich.: Baker Book House, 1988), pp. 3–303; Thomas J. Curry, *The First Freedoms: Church and State in America to the Passage of the First Amendment* (New York: Oxford University Press, 1986), pp. 1–222; M. Stanton Evans, *The Theme Is Freedom: Religion, Politics, and the American Tradition* (Washington, D.C.: Regnery Publishing, 1994), pp. 3–323; Robert M. Grant, *Early Christianity and Society: Seven Studies* (New York: Harper & Row, 1977), pp. 1–163; Brian Tierney, *The Crisis of Church and State, 1050–1300* (Englewood Cliffs, N.J.: Prentice-Hall, 1964), pp. 1–210; and Gabriel Fackre, *The Religious Right and Christian Faith* (Grand Rapids, Mich.: William B. Eerdmans, 1982), p. xi.

3. "Face to Face: John Freeman of BBC Interviews Martin Luther King, Jr.," U.K., London (transcribed from a TV telediphone recording (29 October 1961), The Archives of the Martin Luther King, Jr. Center for Nonviolent Social Change, Atlanta, Georgia, p. 1; Martin Luther King, Sr., *Daddy King: An Autobiography*, with Clayton Riley (New York: William

Morrow and Company, 1980), pp. 23–136; Martin Luther King, Jr., *Stride toward Freedom: The Montgomery Story* (New York: Harper & Row, 1958), pp. 19–20; and Lewis V. Baldwin, *There Is a Balm in Gilead: The Cultural Roots of Martin Luther King, Jr.* (Minneapolis: Fortress Press, 1991), pp. 94–95 and 120–122.

4. King, *Stride toward Freedom*, p. 91.

5. This conclusion is not difficult to sustain since young King, in his own words, felt "a desire to serve God and humanity" through "the ministry." The very idea of service to God and humanity is consistent with Thoreau's concept of the responsibility of the truly "moral" person in a society. See Hugo A. Bedau, ed., *Civil Disobedience: Theory and Practice* (New York: Pegasus, 1970), pp. 15–48; Clayborne Carson et al., eds., *The Papers of Martin Luther King, Jr., volume 1: Called to Serve, January 1929–June 1951* (Berkeley: University of California Press, 1992), p. 39; Clayborne Carson, ed., *The Autobiography of Martin Luther King, Jr.* (New York: Warner Books, 1998), pp. 13–16; and Baldwin, *There Is a Balm in Gilead*, pp. 279–280.

6. Carson, ed., *The Autobiography of Martin Luther King, Jr.*, p. 14.

7. King, *Stride toward Freedom*, p. 91; and Carson, ed., *The Autobiography of Martin Luther King, Jr.*, pp. 13–16.

8. King, *Stride toward Freedom*, p. 91.

9. See Carson et al., eds., *The Papers of Martin Luther King, Jr.*, volume 1, pp. 181–195, 245–251, 272–273, 281–289, and 438–439; and Clayborne Carson et al., eds., *The Papers of Martin Luther King, Jr.*, volume 2: *Rediscovering Precious Values, July 1951–November 1955* (Berkeley: University of California Press, 1994), pp. 144–151, 167–170, and 214.

10. Quoted in Carson et al., eds., *The Papers of Martin Luther King, Jr.*, volume 1, pp. 181 and 194.

11. Carson et al., eds., *The Papers of Martin Luther King, Jr.*, volume 2, pp. 144 and 147.

12. John J. Ansbro contrasts King with Thoreau on this point, but Ansbro's claim that Thoreau "at times revealed himself to be a political anarchist" is rejected by some scholars. Hugh A. Bedau argues that "Thoreau is not so much an anarchist or revolutionary as he is a utopian. His vision is not of men ruled by no law at all, or only by a law of each man's own devising, but of a life in which the claims of government have little significance in the day-to-day activities of the individual." Bedau goes on to contend that "Thoreau is not so much opposed to government as he is unimpressed by and uninterested in it." See John J. Ansbro, *Martin Luther King, Jr.: The Making of a Mind* (Maryknoll, N.Y.: Orbis Books, 1982), p. 113; and Bedau, ed., *Civil Disobedience*, p. 21.

13. Carson et al., eds., *The Papers of Martin Luther King, Jr.*, vol. 2, p. 147.

14. Ansbro, *Martin Luther King, Jr.*, p. 156.

15. Carson et al., eds., *The Papers of Martin Luther King, Jr.*, vol. 2, p. 147; and King, *Strength to Love*, pp. 98–99.

16. Carson et al., eds., *The Papers of Martin Luther King, Jr.*, vol. 2, p. 148.

17. Ansbro, *Martin Luther King, Jr.*, pp. 156–157; and Carson et al., eds., *The Papers of Martin Luther King, Jr.*, vol. 2, p. 148.

18. Ansbro, *Martin Luther King, Jr.*, p. 157–158; King, *Stride toward Freedom*, pp. 97–100; and Carson et al., eds., *The Papers of Martin Luther King, Jr.*, vol. 2, pp. 150–151.

19. Carson, ed., *The Autobiography of Martin Luther King, Jr.*, pp. 53–54.

20. Quoted in Alex Ayres, ed., *The Wisdom of Martin Luther King, Jr.* (New York: Penguin Books USA, 1993), pp. 133–135.

21. Franklin H. Littell, *From State Church to Pluralism: A Protestant Interpretation of Religion in American History* (New York: MacMillan Company, 1971), pp. 161–162; and Mark B. Friedland, *Lift Up Your Voice like a Trumpet: White Clergy and the Civil Rights and Antiwar Movements, 1954–1973* (Chapel Hill: University of North Carolina Press, 1998), p. 28.

22. Friedland, *Lift Up Your Voice like a Trumpet*, p. 28. Scholars today tend to distinguish between fundamentalism and evangelicalism while pointing to their similarities. While both fundamentalists and evangelicals are conservative Christians who subscribe to the basics of the Christian faith, the former tends to be less ecumenical-minded and more militant in their assault on liberal theology and cultural modernity than the latter. For important reflections on the terms "fundamentalism" and "evangelicalism," see George M. Marsden, *Understanding Fundamentalism and Evangelicalism* (Grand Rapids, Mich.: William B. Eerdmans, 1991), pp. 1–6.

23. King, *Stride toward Freedom*, pp. 116–117.

24. Ibid., pp. 35–36.

25. Martin Luther King, Jr., "Advice for Living," *Ebony*, vol. 12, no. 12 (October 1957): p. 53; and Martin Luther King, Jr., *Why We Can't Wait* (New York: New American Library, 1964), pp. 76–95.

26. "Hugh Downs's Interview with Martin Luther King, Jr.," NBC "Today" Show (18 April 1966), King Center Archives, p. 2. Michael Dyson is right in saying that "thanks to his religious beliefs, King refused to idolize the state." See Michael E. Dyson, *I May Not Get There with You: The True Martin Luther King, Jr.* (New York: Free Press, 2000), p. 4.

27. Martin Luther King, Jr., "Beyond Discovery, Love," an address delivered at the International Convention of Christian Churches (Disciples of Christ), Dallas, Texas (25 September 1966), King Center Archives, p. 1.

28. King, *Why We Can't Wait*, pp. 79–80. Here the influence of the ancient Greek philosopher Heraclitus and the German philosopher Georg Hegel on King is quite evident. Heraclitus held that "justice emerges from the strife of opposites," and Hegel that growth comes through the kind of struggle that involves pain. See James M. Washington, ed., *A Testament of Hope: The Essential Writings and Speeches of Martin Luther King, Jr.* (San Francisco: HarperCollins, 1986), p. 135; and Ansbro, *Martin Luther King, Jr.*, pp. 50–51 and 119–120.

29. Cox also lists "the new breed" of liberal white clergy whose views on the responsibility of the Christian toward the state closely approximated King's. See Harvey Cox, "The 'New Breed' in American Churches: Sources of Social Activism in American Religion," *Daedalus*, no. 96 (Winter 1967): p. 137; and Friedland, *Lift Up Your Voice like a Trumpet*, p. 6.

30. See Will Herberg, "A Religious Right to Violate the Law," *National Review*, vol. 16, no. 28 (14 July 1964): p. 579; and Ansbro, *Martin Luther King, Jr.*, p. 297 n42.

31. King, "Advice for Living," p. 53.

32. King, *Strength to Love*, p. 18.

33. See Samuel S. Hill, "Religion and Politics in the South," in Charles R. Wilson, ed., *Religion in the South* (Jackson, Miss.: University Press of Mississippi, 1985), p. 144.

34. William D. Watley, *Roots of Resistance: The Nonviolent Ethic of Martin Luther King, Jr.* (Valley Forge, Pa.: Judson Press, 1985), p. 70.

35. Alan F. Westin and Barry Mahoney, *The Trial of Martin Luther King: The Landmark Birmingham Case and Its Meaning for Today* (New York: Thomas Y. Crowell Company, 1974), pp. 45–46; King, *Why We Can't Wait*, pp. 70–71; and Watley, *Roots of Resistance*, p. 72.

36. Watley, *Roots of Resistance*, p. 70.

37. Westin and Mahoney, *The Trial of Martin Luther King*, pp. 73–86; and "Letter from a Birmingham Jail," *Christian Century*, vol. 80 (12 June 1963): pp. 767–773; and "Letter from a Birmingham City Jail: Wait Almost Always Means Never," *New Leader*, vol. 46 (24 June 1963): pp. 3–11.

38. "Letter from a Birmingham Jail," pp. 767–773; "Letter from a Birmingham City Jail: Wait Always Means Never," pp. 3–11; and King, *Why We Can't Wait*, pp. 76–95.

39. See "Billy Graham Urges Restraint in Sit-ins," *New York Times*, 18 April 1963, p. 21; and Edward L. Moore, "Billy Graham and Martin Luther King, Jr.: An Inquiry into White and Black Revivalistic Traditions," Ph.D. diss., Vanderbilt University, Nashville, Tennessee (May 1979), p. 458.

40. For some of King's most important statements on the limitations of legislation and the judicial process in addressing racial issues,

see King, "Beyond Discovery, Love," pp. 6–7; Martin Luther King, Jr., "Statement Concerning the Court System in Alabama" (3 December 1965), King Center Archives, pp. 1–2; Martin Luther King, Jr., "People in Action" (3 February 1962), King Center Archives, p. 1; and Martin Luther King, Jr., An Address at the Nashville Consultation," Nashville, Tennessee (27 December 1962), King Center Archives, pp. 14–15.

41. Support for this view is afforded in Malinda Snow, "Martin Luther King's 'Letter from Birmingham Jail' as Pauline Epistle," *Quarterly Journal of Speech*, vol. 71, no. 3 (1985): pp. 318–334; and Douglas Surm, "Crisis in the American Republic: The Legal and Political Significance of Martin Luther King's *Letter from a Birmingham Jail*," *Journal of Law and Religion*, vol. 2 (1984): pp. 309–324.

42. King had a high regard for the normative authority of the ancient church, and his sense of the strict discipline and devotion of the early Christians was one of the prime motivations for his acts of civil disobedience. He held that civil disobedience was "practiced superbly by the early Christians." However, the extent to which Christian thinkers like Paul, Augustine, Aquinas, Luther, and Bunyan would have supported King's civil disobedience is clearly open to debate. See King, *Why We Can't Wait*, pp. 77, 80, 82–84, 88–89, and 91–94; Washington, ed., *A Testament of Hope*, pp. 290, 293–294, 297–298, 300, and 302; Ansbro, *Martin Luther King, Jr.*, pp. 115–119; and King, *Strength to Love*, p. 18.

43. King, *Why We Can't Wait*, pp. 79–80, 85, and 93–94.

44. In his "Letter from a Baltimore Jail," written while he was serving a term for destroying draft files in the late 1960s, Father Philip Berrigan noted that "Dr. King's letter silenced his critics, most of whom were Christians and some of whom were Catholics." It is also important to recognize that King was not excessively and unsympathetically critical of the eight Alabama clergymen and white Christians in general, for he commended the Reverend Earl Stallings for welcoming blacks to his "worship service on a non-segregated basis," and Catholic leaders of Alabama "for integrating Spring Hill College several years ago." See Philip Berrigan, *Prison Journals of a Priest Revolutionary* (New York: Ballantine Books, 1971), p. 15; and King, *Why We Can't Wait*, p. 89.

45. Martin Luther King, Jr., "Segregation Is Not Just a Southern Problem," interview in Chicago, Illinois (28 July 1965), King Center Archives, p. 2; and Martin Luther King, Jr., "Speech Made in Savannah," Savannah, Georgia (1 January 1961), King Center Archives, p. 5.

46. King, *Why We Can't Wait*, pp. 92–93. King wrote extensively about the white church and its spiritual emptiness and moral failings, and he consistently challenged white Christians to engage in a more radical

interpretation of the faith and of the Judeo-Christian heritage. Thinking that perhaps white religious institutions were too tied to the status quo to be a force for positive change, King concluded that "maybe I must turn my faith to the inner spiritual church, the church within the church, as the true *ecclesia* and the hope of the world." See Martin Luther King, Jr., "Love, Law, and Civil Disobedience," in Washington, ed., *A Testament of Hope*, pp. 43–53 and 300; Martin Luther King, Jr., "Who Is Their God?," *Nation*, vol. 195 (13 October 1962): pp. 209–210; and Martin Luther King, Jr., "The Church and the Race Crisis," *Christian Century*, vol. 65 (8 October 1958): pp. 1140–1141. King actually felt that the church should be in a position to achieve what "the force of law" could not promote. While he recognized the importance of "legislation and judicial decrees" in striking down barriers between people, he held that "the churches" should "lead men along the path of true integration, something the law cannot do." See King, "Beyond Discovery, Love," pp. 6–7.

47. J. H. Jackson, *A Story of Christian Activism: The History of the National Baptist Convention, U.S.A., Inc.* (Nashville: Townsend Press, 1980), p. 486; David L. Lewis, *King: A Critical Autobiography* (New York: Praeger Publishers, 1970), p. 336; and Baldwin, *There Is a Balm in Gilead*, pp. 214 and 222–223. For interesting treatments of the reactions of white fundamentalists and evangelicals to King and the civil rights movement, see Andrew M. Manis, " 'Dying from the Neck Up': Southern Baptist Resistance to the Civil Rights Movement," *Baptist History and Heritage*, vol. 34, no. 1 (Winter 1999): pp. 33–48; and Bill J. Leonard, "A Theology for Racism: Southern Fundamentalists and the Civil Rights Movement," in ibid., pp. 49–68.

48. King, *Why We Can't Wait*, p. 87; and Washington, ed., *A Testament of Hope*, p. 297. A similar statement by King can be found in Mathew Ahmann, ed., *Race: A Challenge to Religion* (Chicago: Henry Regnery, 1963), pp. 164–165.

49. Quoted in Washington, ed., *A Testament of Hope*, pp. 346–347.

50. King, *Why We Can't Wait*, p. 71.

51. Westin and Mahoney, *The Trial of Martin Luther King*, pp. 79 and 152; and Watley, *Roots of Resistance*, pp. 72–73; and Martin Luther King, Jr., "Crisis and Political Rally in Alabama," reprint of speech delivered at the Sixteenth Street Baptist Church, Birmingham, Alabama (3 May 1963), in Charles V. Hamilton, *The Black Experience in American Politics* (New York: G. P. Putnam & Sons, 1973), pp. 162–163.

52. Martin Luther King, Jr., "A Message from Jail" (14 July 1962), King Center Archives, pp. 3–4.

53. King, *Why We Can't Wait*, p. 70.

54. King called St. Augustine "the most lawless" city that he and the SCLC had ever seen in the course of their activities. See Westin and Ma-

3; and Adam Fairclough,
ian Leadership Conference
of Georgia Press, 1987),
onding to the claim, set
d segregation, a position
ches in relation to slavery
vhite southerners' use of
other biblical passages in
ntation of what the scrip-
for Living," *Ebony*, vol. 13,
Jr., "Rev. Martin Luther
Talmadge," *Ebony*, vol. 12,
alm in Gilead, pp. 51–52;
E. Newgent (20 October
ecial Collections, Mugar
assachusetts, p. 1. On one
a man can be a Christian
men, created alike in the
This is at the very heart of
g, Jr., "Advice for Living,"

Terror: The Fundamentalist
nd Our Private Lives (New

nderstanding of the Bible
f Bob Jones University. See
y and the Power: The Funda-
on: Beacon Press, 1992),
the Power," a series of film
PR (June 1992). The view
not a Christian, was widely
icals. See Manis, "'Dying
, "A Theology for Racism,"

p. 85–86; Fackre, *The Reli-*
Neuhaus and Michael Cro-
Fundamentalists Confront the
olicy Center, 1987), pp. 12,
s Right: Piety, Patriotism, and
Press, 1994), p. 202; Lewis V.
n *Luther King, Jr., and South*
2; and Lewis V. Baldwin, *To*

Make the Wounded Whole: The Cultural Legacy of Martin Luther King, Jr. (Minneapolis: Fortress Press, 1992), pp. 237–238. Even Clarence Jordan, the rather liberal white southern leader who founded the interracial community called Koinonia Farm in Americus, Georgia, in 1942, criticized King, "calling him a political rather than a spiritual leader." See Tracy E. K'Meyer, *Interracialism and Christian Community in the Postwar South: The Story of Koinonia Farm* (Charlottesville: University Press of Virginia, 1997), p. 156.

58. See Stanley Mooneyham, "Graham Crusade Draws 100,000 in Montgomery," *Crusade Information Service News* (23 June 1965), p. 1; and Moore, "Billy Graham and Martin Luther King, Jr.," pp. 461–462.

59. Watley, *Roots of Resistance*, pp. 84–85; and Westin and Mahoney, *The Trial of Martin Luther King, Jr.*, pp. 152–153 and 165.

60. Mooney, "Graham Crusade Draws 100,000," p. 1; Moore, "Billy Graham and Martin Luther King, Jr.," pp. 462–463; and *Dr. Martin Luther King, Jr.: An Amazing Grace*, sixty-two-minute film produced by WABC-TV (Del Mar, Caif.: McGraw Hill Films, 1978).

61. Graham merely suggested that the Klan should "quiet down," advice that meant essentially nothing since Jimmie Lee Jackson, the Reverend James Reeb, and Viola Liuzzo had already been murdered earlier in the Selma campaign. Graham's tendency to speak in terms of what one source calls "fervent generalities" proves that he was not willing to take the kind of prophetic stand that would have undoubtedly destroyed his credibility among whites nationwide. See Mooneyham, "Graham Crusade Draws 100,000," p. 1; "Be Specific, Mr. Graham," *Christian Century*, vol. 82, no. 35 (1 September 1965): p. 1035; and Moore, "Billy Graham and Martin Luther King, Jr.," pp. 461–463.

62. Stephen E. Berk, *A Time to Heal: John Perkins, Community Development, and Racial Reconciliation* (Grand Rapids, Mich.: Baker Books, 1997), p. 73.

63. See David Hazard, "John Perkins Speaks Out on Racial Reconciliation, Leadership Development, and the Welfare State," *Kingdom Lifeline: The Christian Magazine Committed to Racial Reconciliation* (September–October 1986): pp. 8–13; and John Perkins, *Let Justice Roll Down* (Glendale, Calif.: Regal Books, 1978), pp. 65–223.

64. Richard Quebedeaux, *The Young Evangelicals: The Story of the Emergence of a New Generation of Evangelicals* (New York: Harper & Row, 1974), pp. 92–93 and 115–118. Skinner's publications clearly reflected his agreement with many of the ideas and protest methods employed by King and the black power advocates, positions that set him very much at odds with his fellow white evangelicals, who "either ignored or out-and-out rejected King, his Southern Christian Leadership Conference, and the black

church-based civil rights movement because of the liberal influences on them." See Tom Skinner, *Black and Free* (Grand Rapids, Mich.: Zondervan Publishing House, 1968), pp. 87–158; Tom Skinner, *How Black Is the Gospel?* (Philadelphia and New York: A. J. Holman Company, 1970), pp. 7–123; and Berk, *A Time to Heal*, pp. 73 and 150.

65. Quebedeaux, *The Young Evangelicals*, p. 116. Also see Columbus Salley and Ronald Behm, *Your God Is Too White* (Downers Grove, Ill.: Inter-Varsity Press, 1970).

66. William H. Bentley, *National Black Evangelical Association: Evolution of a Concept of Ministry*, rev. ed. (Chicago: William H. Bentley, 1979), pp. 1–15; Mary R. Sawyer, *Black Ecumenism: Implementing the Demands of Justice* (Valley Forge, Pa.: Trinity Press International, 1994), pp. 113–133; and Daniel G. Reid et al., eds., *Dictionary of Christianity in America* (Downers Grove, Ill.: InterVarsity Press, 1990), p. 795.

67. Fairclough, *To Redeem the Soul of America*, pp. 294, 298–299, and 306; and David J. Garrow, *Bearing the Cross: The Southern Christian Leadership Conference and Martin Luther King, Jr.* (New York: William Morrow and Company, 1986), pp. 460–461, 495, and 508.

68. Quoted in Fairclough, *To Redeem the Soul of America*, p. 299.

69. Lewis, *King: A Critical Biography*, p. 333; Garrow, *Bearing the Cross*, p. 491; Baldwin, *There Is a Balm in Gilead*, p. 214; Charles H. King, "Quest and Conflict: The Untold Story of the Power Struggle between King and Jackson," *Negro Digest* (May 1967): pp. 71–79; and J. H. Jackson, *A Story of Christian Activism: The History of the National Baptist Convention* (Nashville: Townsend Press, 1980), pp. 424–425 and 485–486.

70. Lewis, *King: A Critical Biography*, p. 336; Baldwin, *There Is a Balm in Gilead*, p. 214; and Garrow, *Bearing the Cross*, p. 491. Jackson's attack was largely aimed at a very controversial decision King made in the course of the Chicago Freedom Movement in February 1966. The civil rights leader "assumed trusteeship of a slum tenement," a building owned by an elderly white man, insisting that he would collect rents and "use the money to clean and renovate" it. King called these actions "supralegal," meaning that moral considerations figured more prominently than legal ones. Jackson detected in King's actions an arrogance which suggested that he was "above the law." With this in mind, Jackson asked: "How could one appeal to a sense of right when there was no commitment to the right?" See Jackson, *A Story of Christian Activism*, p. 424. The city court ultimately barred King from the building and made him account for all money collected. See Watley, *Roots of Resistance*, pp. 94–95.

71. Quoted in Garrow, *Bearing the Cross*, p. 491.

72. Baldwin, *There Is a Balm in Gilead*, p. 223.

73. James W. McClendon, *Biography as Theology: How Life Stories Can Remake Today's Theology* (Nashville and New York: Abingdon Press, 1974), p. 70; and Watley, *Roots of Resistance*, pp. 95–98.

74. Fairclough, *To Redeem the Soul of America*, pp. 357–358; and Martin Luther King, Jr., "Why We Must Go to Washington," unpublished manuscript (15 January 1968), King Center Archives, pp. 13–15.

75. Walter Rugaber, "Dr. King Plans to Disrupt Capital in Drive for Jobs," *New York Times*, 5 December 1967, pp. 1 and 32; and Moore, "Billy Graham and Martin Luther King, Jr.," pp. 464–465.

76. Edward Lee Moore says this in highlighting King's differences with Billy Graham, but the point can easily be made concerning King's conflicts with other conservative white and black ministers. See Moore, "Billy Graham and Martin Luther King, Jr.," p. 464.

77. Fairclough, *To Redeem the Soul of America*, p. 371.

78. Moore, "Billy Graham and Martin Luther King, Jr.," p. 465.

79. Ibid.

80. Leonard, "A Theology for Racism," pp. 51 and 61.

81. James H. Cone, *Martin and Malcolm and America: A Dream or a Nightmare* (Maryknoll, N.Y.: Orbis Books, 1991), p. 239.

82. King, *Strength to Love*, pp. 102–103; Washington, ed., *A Testament of Hope*, pp. 250 and 629–630; David Halberstam, "When 'Civil Rights' and 'Peace' Join Forces," in C. Eric Lincoln, ed., *Martin Luther King, Jr.: A Profile* (New York: Hill and Wang, 1986), p. 207; Kenneth L. Smith, "Equality and Justice: A Dream or Vision of Reality," in *Report from the Capital*, vol. 39, no. 1 (January 1984): p. 5; Kenneth L. Smith, "The Radicalization of Martin Luther King, Jr.," *Journal of Ecumenical Studies*, vol. 26, no. 2 (Spring 1989): pp. 270–278; and Kenneth O'Reilly, *"Racial Matters": The FBI's Secret File on Black America, 1960–1972* (New York: Free Press, 1989), p. 243.

83. Neuhaus and Cromartie, eds., *Piety and Politics*, p. 73.

84. King, *Strength to Love*, pp. 102–103; Washington, ed., *A Testament of Hope*, pp. 250 and 629–630; and Martin Luther King, Jr., *Where Do We Go from Here: Chaos or Community?* (Boston: Beacon Press, 1968), pp. 186–188.

85. Quoted in Washington, ed., *A Testament of Hope*, p. 233.

86. King, *Strength to Love*, pp. 99–105.

87. Ibid., pp. 96–99.

88. Ibid., pp. 96–97.

89. From Martin Luther King, Jr. to Mr. David C. Dautzer (9 May 1961), King Papers, Boston University, p. 1. It is also important to note that King defined the civil rights movement as "a spiritual movement,"

thus setting it apart from communist theory. See Martin Luther King, Jr., "An Address at the 47th NAACP Annual Convention," San Francisco, California (27 June 1956), King Papers, Boston University, pp. 8–9; and Baldwin, *There Is a Balm in Gilead*, p. 77.

90. King to Dautzer, p. 1. King declared that "I can see no greater tragedy befalling the Negro than a turn to either Communism or Black Nationalism as a way out of the present dilemma." See From Martin Luther King, Jr. to Mr. Edward D. Ball (14 December 1961), King Papers, Boston University, pp. 1–2; From Martin Luther King, Jr. to Mr. Joseph B. Cumming, Jr. (22 December 1961), King Center Archives, pp. 1–2; "Complete Text of Dr. Martin Luther King, Jr.'s Statement on Governor Ross Barnett's Claims against the Civil Rights Movement," released to the *Atlanta Journal and Constitution* (13 July 1963), King Center Archives, p. 1; and "King Answers Southern Editor's Blast," press release from the Southern Christian Leadership Conference, Atlanta, Georgia (14 December 1961), King Center Archives, pp. 1–2.

91. Martin Luther King, Jr., "An Address to the Ministers' Leadership Training Program," Miami, Florida (19–23 February 1968), King Center Archives, pp. 2–3; and Washington, ed., *A Testament of Hope*, pp. 50, 294–295, and 356–357.

92. King, "Why We Must Go to Washington," pp. 14–15; Washington, ed., *A Testament of Hope*, p. 50; and Baldwin, *Toward the Beloved Community*, pp. 55 and 213 n.117. The five typical answers that H. Richard Niebuhr provides to the Christian's struggle to set the relation between the Christ he represents and the culture which nurtures him are applicable to King. See H. Richard Niebuhr, *Christ and Culture* (New York: Harper & Row, 1975), pp. 45–229. Interestingly enough, King argued that nonviolent civil disobedience employed by an "international coalition of socially aware forces, operating outside governmental frameworks," remained the best approach to South Africa's "entrenched problems." See Martin Luther King, Jr., *The Trumpet of Conscience* (San Francisco: Harper & Row, 1968), p. 63.

93. Ansbro, *Martin Luther King, Jr.*, p. 134.

94. Ibid., pp. 134–135.

95. Ayres, ed., *The Wisdom of Martin Luther King, Jr.*, p. 99; King, *Stride toward Freedom*, p. 198; King, *The Trumpet of Conscience*, p. 14; and King, *Where Do We Go from Here?*, p. 133.

96. Martin Luther King, Jr., "Advice for Living," *Ebony*, vol. 14, no. 2 (December 1958): p. 154.

97. Martin Luther King, Jr., "A Knock at Midnight," sermon delivered at the All-Saints Community Church, Los Angeles, California (25 June

1967), King Center Archives, p. 1; and Baldwin, *Toward the Beloved Community*, p. 28.

98. King, *Why We Can't Wait*, p. 91; and Washington, ed., *A Testament of Hope*, p. 300.

99. Gayraud Wilmore makes this claim regarding King, but it should be made with respect to the larger African American community. See Gayraud S. Wilmore, *Black Religion and Black Radicalism: An Interpretation of the Religious History of African Americans* (Maryknoll, N.Y.: Orbis Books, 1998), p. 204.

100. See Ansbro, *Martin Luther King, Jr.*, p. 111. King also saw in the movements of his people for change clear proof of the validity of what W. E. B. DuBois, Arnold J. Toynbee, Mohandas K. Gandhi, and Reinhold Niebuhr had said about the potential of African Americans as a humanizing force. By acknowledging a messianic role for his people, King was standing in what Cornel West calls "the Exceptionalist Tradition." See Baldwin, *There Is a Balm in Gilead*, pp. 231–233; and Cornel West, *Prophesy Deliverance!: An Afro-American Revolutionary Christianity* (Philadelphia: Westminster Press, 1982), pp. 70 and 72–78.

101. C. Eric Lincoln, "The Black Church and a Decade of Change," part II, *Tuesday at Home* (March 1976), p. 7; and Baldwin, *There Is a Balm in Gilead*, pp. 227–228.

102. Moore, "Billy Graham and Martin Luther King, Jr.," pp. 465–466.

103. See Brady B. Whitehead, Jr., "Preaching Response to the Death of Martin Luther King, Jr.," Ph.D. diss., Boston University School of Theology, Boston, Massachusetts (1972), pp. 120–239.

104. "The Glory and the Power," series of film and radio documentaries; and Leonard, "A Theology for Racism," p. 63.

105. Leonard, "A Theology for Racism," p. 63.

106. Berk, *A Time to Heal*, pp. 150 and 195.

107. William B. Huie, *He Slew the Dreamer: My Search, with James Earl Ray, for the Truth about the Murder of Martin Luther King* (New York: Delacorte Press, 1970), pp. 207–212.

108. Berk, *A Time to Heal*, p. 73.

109. One scholar rightly observes that "the nation's most profound confrontation with Christian public testimony in the twentieth century was precipitated by the sermons/speeches of Martin Luther King, Jr., and his colleagues, in which evangelical themes were prominent." This, too, must be considered in any discussion of King's meaning and significance for conservative Christians in America. Mark A. Noll, *The Scandal of the Evangelical Mind* (Grand Rapids, Mich.: William B. Eerdmans, 1994), p. 156.

1 1 0. " 'We All Need a New Heart': Rev. Graham to S. Africa," *Jet*, vol. 44, no. 2 (5 April 1973): p. 13; and Baldwin, *Toward the Beloved Community*, pp. 83–84. One scholar makes the unpersuasive claim that during the 1960s, Graham embraced a "prophetic social position" on "racial justice and love" that put him "far ahead of his Evangelical constituency." The evidence shows that Graham was always a very reluctant critic when it came to racism and the unjust laws and governmental practices of the state. See Quebedeaux, *The Young Evangelicals*, p. 86.

1 1 1. Falwell himself has not sufficiently acknowledged his indebtedness to King. This failure speaks to the continuing impact of racism in America. See Jerry Falwell, *Listen, America!* (New York: Doubleday, 1980), pp. 3–266; and Baldwin, *There Is a Balm in Gilead*, p. 334.

1 1 2. Quoted in Carol Flake, *Redemptorama: Culture, Politics, and the New Evangelicalism* (New York: Penguin Books, 1984), p.226.

1 1 3. Conway and Siegelman, *Holy Terror*, p. 86; Neuhaus and Cromartie, eds., *Piety and Politics*, p. 310; Fackre, *The Religious Right and Christian Faith*, p. 14; George Marsden, ed., *Evangelicalism and Modern America* (Grand Rapids, Mich.: William B. Eerdmans, 1984), p. 60; and Leo P. Ribuffo, *The Old Christian Right: The Protestant Far Right from the Great Depression to the Cold War* (Philadelphia: Temple University Press, 1983), p. 264.

1 1 4. Falwell, *Listen America!*, pp. 69–266; Richard N. Ostling et al., "Jerry Falwell's Crusade: Fundamentalist Legions Seek to Remake Church and Society," *Time*, vol. 126, no. 9 (2 September 1985): pp. 48–52, 55, and 57; and Ansbro, *Martin Luther King, Jr.*, p. 315 n.115.

1 1 5. Marsden, ed., *Evangelicalism and Modern America*, p. 60; Neuhaus and Cromartie, eds., *Politics and Piety*, p. 310; and Fackre, *The Religious Right and Christian Faith*, p. 28.

1 1 6. James D. Hunter, *Culture Wars: The Struggle to Define America* (New York: Basic Books, 1991), p. 17.

1 1 7. Daniel C. Maguire, *The New Subversives: Anti-Americanism of the Religious Right* (New York: Continuum Publishing Company, 1982), pp. 38–39. For an interesting treatment of King and Pat Robertson and their "use of religious beliefs in the political realm," see David J. Marley, "Martin Luther King, Jr., Pat Robertson, and the Duality of Modern Christian Politics," *Fides et Historia*, vol. 32, no. 2 (Summer/Fall 2000): 67–81.

1 1 8. Martin Luther King, Jr., "To Chart Our Course for the Future," address delivered at SCLC retreat, Frogmore, South Carolina (29–31 May 1967), pp. 4–5; and Baldwin, *There Is a Balm in Gilead*, pp. 72–73.

1 1 9. See "Group Criticize Civil Rights Appointee," *Tennessean*, 28 June 1997, p. 11A; George E. Curry, ed., *The Affirmative Action Debate* (Reading, Mass.: Addison-Wesley Publishing Company, 1996), pp. 60, 63, 133, and

212; and George E. Curry, "Preserving Dr. King's Legacy: Editor's Note," *Emerge*, vol. 8, no. 9 (July/August, 1997): p. 8.

120. Obey M. Hendricks, Jr., "The Domestication of Martin Luther King, Jr.," *The A.M.E. Church Review* (April–June 1998): pp. 53–54. This disturbing tendency on the part of "right-wing conservatives" to "quote King's speeches" in opposition to affirmative action is strongly condemned in Michael E. Dyson, *I May Not Get There with You: The True Martin Luther King, Jr.* (New York: Free Press, 2000), pp. ix.

121. King, *Why We Can't Wait*, pp. 136–141; King, *Where Do We Go from Here?*, pp. 196–199; and Curry, "Preserving Dr. King's Legacy," p. 8. Cornel West has rightly observed that the "hard-line conservatives" who oppose affirmative action are "the same ones who opposed" King and the civil rights movement. Victoria Valle has said that those conservatives who read selectively from King's "I Have a Dream" speech (1963) to make their case against affirmative action should note also those parts that outline reasons why such a program is needed in the first place. Quoted in Curry, ed., *The Affirmative Action Debate*, pp. 32 and 212.

122. Maguire, *The New Subversives*, p. 42.

123. Quoted in Hunter, *Culture Wars*, p. 17.

124. Maguire, *The New Subversives*, pp. 40–41.

125. Ibid., p. 40. One important source for assessing how African Americans, in the post-King era, view Jerry Falwell's Moral Majority and its stand on issues of race, class, and economic injustice is William Willoughby, *Does America Need the Moral Majority?* (Plainfield, N.J.: Haven Books, 1981), pp. 127–142.

126. Luther D. Ivory, *Toward a Theology of Radical Involvement: The Theological Legacy of Martin Luther King, Jr.* (Nashville: Abingdon Press, 1997), pp. 14–15; and Vincent Harding, *Martin Luther King: The Inconvenient Hero* (Maryknoll, N.Y.: Orbis Books, 1996), p. vii.

127. Eric Breindel, "King's Communist Associates," *New Republic*, vol. 190, no. 4, issue 3 (30 January 1984): p. 14; and David J. Garrow, "The Helms Attack on King," *Southern Exposure*, vol. 12, no. 2 (March/April 1984): pp. 12–15.

128. One scholar rightly notes that the image of King "as a gentle minister" enables our "nation to create a comforting icon out of the career of a political iconoclast." See Robert Weisbrot, "Celebrating Dr. King's Birthday: A Legacy of Confrontation and Conciliation," *New Republic*, vol. 190, no. 4, issue 3 (30 January 1984): p. 10.

129. "Katie Hall Leaves House but Claims Victory in King Bill and Vows to Return," *Jet*, vol. 67, no. 13 (3 December 1984): pp. 38–40; and "The Continuing Struggle for a National King Holiday," *Ebony*, vol. 43, no. 3 (January 1988): pp. 27–28, 30, and 32.

130. "The Continuing Struggle for a King Holiday," p. 27; "Arizona Governor's Stance on King Holiday May Cost State $18 Million Loss," *Jet*, vol. 72, no. 13 (22 June 1987): p. 36; "Arizona Finally Gets a M.L. King State Holiday," *Jet*, vol. 77, no.1 (9 October 1989): p. 18; and "President Reagan Declares Martin Luther King, Jr. Day," *Jet*, vol. 75, no. 16 (23 January 1989): p. 6.

131. Ray Waddle, "Critic of King Should Resign, Baptists Urge," *Tennessean*, 18 January 1989, pp. 1B and 3B; David T. Morgan, *The New Crusades, the New Holy Land: Conflict in the Southern Baptist Convention, 1969–1991* (Tuscaloosa: University of Alabama Press, 1996), p. 116; Oran P. Smith, *The Rise of Baptist Republicanism* (New York: New York University Press, 1997), p. 222; and "Southern Baptists Apologize to Blacks for Racism," *Jet*, vol. 88, no. 9 (10 July 1995): pp. 26–27.

132. Patrick Buchanan, "A Rascal's Bedroom Escapades Diminish His Status as a Saint," *Tennessean*, 22 October 1989, p. 5G; and Baldwin, *To Make the Wounded Whole*, p. 297.

133. Kevin Sack, "Sheen of the King Legacy Dims on New, More Profitable Path," *New York Times*, 19 August 1997, p. A16; and Cokie and Steven V. Roberts, "Martin Luther King, III: Can He Step Forward?" *Tennessean: USA Weekend*, 16–18 January 1998, pp. 4–5.

134. Curry, "Preserving Dr. King's Legacy," p. 8; and Curry, ed., *The Affirmative Action Debate*, pp. 29, 86, 112, 155–156, 161, 191, 280, 290, 293–294, 296, 300, 305, 317, 323, and 326.

135. Berk, *A Time to Heal*, pp. 291–408.

136. William Pannell, *The Coming Race Wars?: A Cry for Reconciliation* (Grand Rapids, Mich.: Zondervan Publishing House, 1993), pp. 23–143.

137. Smith, "The Radicalization of Martin Luther King, Jr.," pp. 270–288.

138. Smith, "Equality and Justice," p. 5.

139. Sider, the editor of *Prism Magazine*, challenged white evangelicals in the 1980s to come up with a theology of liberation and social change, but his voice remains unheard. He persists in seeing himself as "America's alternative Evangelical voice," but his failure to embrace militant action for social change shows that he is not essentially different from other white evangelicals and fundamentalists. See Ronald J. Sider, ed., *Evangelicals and Development: Toward a Theology of Social Change* (Philadelphia: Westminster Press, 1981), pp. 15–101; and From Josh Perry to Lewis V. Baldwin (13 January 1999).

American Political Traditions and the Christian Faith

King's Thought and Praxis

LEWIS V. BALDWIN

I can say without the slightest hesitation, and yet in all humility, that those who say that religion has nothing to do with politics do not know what religion means.

—Mohandas K. Gandhi[1]

Martin Luther King, Jr.'s interest in politics developed and found expression long before he became a civil rights leader. His early feelings of curiosity about the political traditions of the United States surfaced naturally, for he was born and raised in a society that extolled the virtues of democratic politics while denying African Americans the fundamental right to vote and hold public office. The black experience provided much of the inspiration and the context not only for King's lifelong interest in American political life, but also for his efforts in combining politics and religion for the creation of a more peaceful, just, and inclusive society.

For a More Perfect Union:
On the Sacred Documents in American Political Life

The Declaration of Independence, the Constitution, and the Emancipation Proclamation figured prominently in King's understanding and articulation of what he called "the American Dream." These documents embodied the principles and values of the natural rights tradition to which he appealed in his struggle against racial injustice. Having studied the social contract theories of Thomas Hobbes and John Locke, King found in the Enlightenment ideals of Tolerance, Reason, and Natural Law much of the context for his appreciation of the Declaration of Independence and the Constitution.[2] Moreover, King discovered in these founding documents, and in the Emancipation Proclamation, the same basic values and norms that permeated African American religion, literature, and art.[3] In his appeal to these sources, he was following a time-honored tradition that stretched back to Frederick Douglass and other African American leaders. But most problematic was King's seemingly uncritical appeal to the Declaration of Independence and the Constitution, especially since the "all men are created equal" and the "inalienable rights" language of these documents did not include black people. King acknowledged this much and more toward the end of his life, when he, having become more radical, noted that the Declaration of Independence "has never had any real meaning in terms of implementation in our lives."[4]

King had a very nuanced understanding of the complexities of American history and of her documents of freedom. He knew that the Declaration of Independence, the Constitution, and the Emancipation Proclamation are fraught with contradictions, but he valued the noble ideals they embodied, and they were among the sources he used to validate a movement for freedom. When it came to the Declaration of Independence and the Constitution, what mattered to King most was not the original intent of the founding fathers, but, rather, the ways in which the principles embodied in those documents could best be universalized in the present and future. In repeatedly saying that "the goal of America is freedom," King was evoking a particular myth that found expression in the Declaration of Independence, the Constitution, and the Emancipation Proclamation. Indeed, "freedom," for him, became America's mythic meaning and ideal.

While King's appeals to the Declaration of Independence, the Constitution, and the Emancipation Proclamation were always informed by his religious faith, he was never completely comfortable with the idea of using religion as a basis for political decision making. For King, the problems with such a strategy had become all too real in the case of white Christian conservatives who grounded their politics in a particular understanding of scripture and the faith. But even "liberal" and so-called "progressive-minded" Christians did this as well, and so did King. King simply had a different understanding of scripture and the faith—one which was more appropriate to the traditions of early Hebrew prophecy, the gospel, and the heritage of the black church, and one that was also morally and ethically credible in light of the best of Christian principles.[5]

In April 1944, in his junior year at Atlanta's Booker T. Washington High School, the fifteen-year-old King won an oratorical contest with a speech on "The Negro and the Constitution." In this speech, which "reflected King's early political views," the young man spoke of the affinity between America's constitutional principles and her biblical faith. He quoted the Declaration of Independence, as he did repeatedly in later years: "We hold these truths to be self-evident, that all men are created equal, that they are endowed by their Creator with certain unalienable Rights, that among these are Life, Liberty and the pursuit of Happiness."[6] When Thomas Jefferson wrote these words, King often said as a civil rights leader, "the first government of the world to be based on" the "theory of natural rights," the "justification of revolution," and the "ideal of a society governed by the people" was "established on American soil."[7]

For King, the words of the Declaration of Independence were consistent with what he termed "the sublime principles of our Judeo-Christian tradition."[8] More specifically, that document affirmed values that King inherited from both the black church tradition and the personal idealism of Edgar S. Brightman and L. Harold DeWolf. "It is a profound, eloquent and unequivocal expression of the dignity and worth of all human personality," King often declared.[9] But he was more a sentimentalist than a hardheaded realist on this point, because this concept of humanity, as articulated by Jefferson and other pioneers, included only white people. In any case, King believed that the "amazing universalism" and the "inviolable character of personal rights" expressed in the Declaration of Independence provided intellectual support for his practical quest for the beloved community, a position clearly vulnerable to criticism.[10]

What disturbed King most was white America's failure to embody the true meaning of the Declaration of Independence in its relationships with persons of color. In "The Negro and the Constitution," and in his writings and speeches throughout the 1950s and 1960s, King pointed to what he called "this terrible ambivalence in the soul of white America":

> Ever since the signing of the Declaration of Independence, America has manifested a schizophrenic personality on the question of race. She has been torn between selves—a self in which she has proudly professed democracy and a self in which she has sadly practiced the antithesis of democracy. The reality of segregation, like slavery, has always had to confront the ideals of democracy and Christianity. Indeed, segregation and discrimination are strange paradoxes in a nation founded on the principle that all men are created equal.[11]

King traced this "moral dilemma" back to the founders of the nation, whose politics accounted in part for "the state we are in now."

> Virtually all of the Founding Fathers of our nation, even those who rose to the heights of the Presidency, those whom we cherish as our authentic heroes, were so enmeshed in the ethos of slavery and white supremacy that not one ever emerged with a clear, unambiguous stand on Negro rights. . . . George Washington, Thomas Jefferson, Patrick Henry, John Quincy Adams and Abraham Lincoln were great men, but—that "but" underscores the fact that not one of these men had a strong unequivocal belief in the equality of the black man.[12]

Some of the words of the Constitution revealed this dilemma in the most disturbing fashion, for they called into question the very humanity of African Americans. "When the Constitution was written," King wrote, "a strange formula to determine taxes and representation declared that the Negro was 60 percent of a person."[13] But for much of his public career, King refused to stress the view, put forth by Malcolm X and the nationalist wing of the movement, that the framers of the Constitution never meant to include black people—that the document was written by white people for white people. In his "I Have a Dream" speech, delivered in Washington, D.C., in August 1963, King declared:

When the architects of our republic wrote the magnificent words of the Constitution and the Declaration of Independence, they were signing a promissory note to which every American was to fall heir. This note was a promise that all men, *yes*, black men as well as white men, would be guaranteed the unalienable rights of "Life, Liberty and the pursuit of Happiness."[14]

King held that by protesting in the streets "and there giving practical lessons of democracy's defaults and shortcomings," he and other activists were "bringing our nation back to those great wells of democracy which were dug deep by the founding fathers in their formulation of the Constitution and the Declaration of Independence."[15] It was his hope that all freedom-loving Americans would join him in continuing "that noble journey toward the goals reflected in the Preamble to the Constitution, the Constitution itself, the Bill of Rights, and the Thirteenth, Fourteenth, and Fifteenth Amendments."[16] King's belief in the spirit and power of the Constitution and other sacred documents in American political history made it all the more difficult for him to understand how white lawmakers and the court system could interfere with the First Amendment rights of peaceful protesters, as was the case in Montgomery, Albany, and numerous other southern cities.[17] Even so, the civil rights leader maintained that "we will win our freedom because the sacred heritage of our nation and the eternal will of God are embodied in our echoing demands."[18]

This faith in the ultimate flowering of true democracy in America was rooted primarily in a Christian theology of hope, but it was also inspired as much by the spirit of the Emancipation Proclamation as by the traditions of the Constitution and the Declaration of Independence. Drawing on Frederick Douglass's insights on "the world significance of the Emancipation Proclamation," King called that document "the offspring of the Declaration of Independence," and noted that "it used the force of law to uproot a social order which sought to separate liberty from a segment of humanity."[19] King also included the Emancipation Proclamation, signed by President Abraham Lincoln in 1863, in the "great tradition of executive actions," to be equated in significance with Franklin D. Roosevelt's war decree prohibiting employment discrimination (1941), Harry S. Truman's order ending segregated armed forces units (1948), John F. Kennedy's mandate banning discrimination in federally aided housing (1962), and Lyndon B. Johnson's signing of the Civil Rights Act (1964) and the Voting Rights Act (1965).[20] More specifically, the Emancipation Proclamation was for King America's third major document of freedom, a document designed to extend the notion of *rights* affirmed earlier in the Declaration of Independence and the Constitution.[21] "This momemtous decree," King declared, "came as a great beacon light of hope to millions of Negro slaves, who had been seared in the flames of withering injustice. It came as a joyous daybreak to end the long night of their captivity."[22]

King insisted that the centennial celebration of the Emancipation Proclamation afforded the nation an excellent opportunity to rededicate herself to the principles of human freedom. Recalling the Emancipation Proclamation in numerous speeches from 1961 to 1963, he approached President John Kennedy concerning "the need for a sort of second Emancipation Proclamation declaring all segregated facilities unconstitutional and illegal on the basis of the Fourteenth Amendment of the Constitution." "Just as the first Emancipation Proclamation was an executive order," King reasoned, "I don't think it is too much to ask for a second Emancipation Proclamation bringing an end to segregation almost 100 years after the first Emancipation Proclamation was issued." Kennedy agreed to carefully consider the proposal, but he was assassinated before he could completely follow through on his promises.[23]

While providing a model for more contemporary documents of freedom, the 1863 Emancipation Proclamation also proved to be yet another reflection of what King often termed "America's chief moral dilemma."[24] President Lincoln revealed this dilemma in ways that recalled the founding fathers of the nation. "Morally, Lincoln was for black emancipation," King maintained, "but emotionally, like most of his white contemporaries, he was for a long time unable to act in accordance with his conscience." King elaborated further:

> A civil war raged within Lincoln's own soul, a tension between the Dr. Jekyll of freedom and the Mr. Hyde of slavery, a struggle like that of Plato's charioteer with two headstrong horses each pulling in different directions. . . . But Lincoln was basically honest and willing to admit his confusions. He saw that the nation could not survive half slave and half free; and he said, "If we could

first know where we are and whither we are tending, we could better judge what to do and how to do it." Fortunately for the nation, he finally came to see "whither we were tending." On January 1, 1863, he issued the Emancipation Proclamation, freeing the Negro from the bondage of chattel slavery. By this concrete act of courage his reservations of the past were overshadowed. The conclusion of his search is embodied in these words: "In giving freedom to the slave, we assure freedom to the free,— honourable alike is what we give and what we preserve."[25]

Clearly, one notices some inconsistencies in King's reflections on the actions of Lincoln. On the one hand, he spoke of "the spirit of Lincoln"—"that spirit born of the teachings of the Nazarene, who promised mercy to the merciful, who lifted the lowly, strengthened the weak, ate with publicans, and made the captives free."[26] On the other, the civil rights leader referred to Lincoln as "a vacillating president" who was compelled by political ambition and expediency to sign the Emancipation Proclamation.[27]

In any case, the document became as much an act of disappointment as it was a symbol of hope, for it accepted African Americans as a legal fact while failing to accept them as human beings with the same rights as white Americans.[28] Moreover, said King, "what the Emancipation Proclamation proscribed in a legal and formal sense has never been eliminated in human terms."[29] Thus, while agreeing that the one-hundredth birthday of the document should be celebrated, King, quoting Lyndon B. Johnson, reminded the nation in 1963 that "Emancipation was a Proclamation but not a fact":

> But one hundred years later, the Negro still is not free. One hundred years later, the life of the Negro is still sadly crippled by the manacles of segregation and the chains of discrimination. One hundred years later, the Negro lives on a lonely island of poverty in the midst of a vast ocean of material prosperity. One hundred years later, the Negro is still languished in the corners of American society and finds himself in exile in his own land.[30]

Using biblical imagery, King held that "the Emancipation Proclamation brought" his people "nearer to the Red Sea, but it did not guarantee" their "passage through parted waters."[31] In his estimation, the power of that document of freedom was undermined by the Supreme Court's "separate but equal" doctrine in *Plessy v. Ferguson* in 1896.[32] Moreover, its essential meaning and significance had been continuously ignored since that time by American political leaders— by "the Pharoahs," who "have employed legal manoeuvres, economic reprisals, and even physical violence to hold the Negro in the Egypt of segregation."[33] With this in mind, King could speak of "the Negro revolution" as a sustained or protracted effort to actualize the promises made in America's great political documents. It is "an epic," King said of the freedom movement, and it fits squarely "in the American tradition, a much delayed salute to the Bill of Rights, the Declaration of Independence, the Constitution, and the Emancipation Proclamation."[34]

Equally important for King were the ways in which the values coursing through these documents also find expression in America's great tradition of songs. Indeed, he discovered in "The Battle Hymn of the Republic," "The Star Spangled Banner," and "The Negro National Anthem" the values of freedom, resistance, and self-determination— core values that stood at the very heart of the movement.[35] The fact that King constantly appealed to these sources, in inspiring Americans to greater heights in the quest for freedom, is but another indication of how fundamentally *American* he was in his outlook and aspirations, despite his basic quarrel with the American society.

King held that the sacred documents of America's political heritage had much to teach other nations in their struggles to establish freedom and independence. He highlighted the fact that the Vietnamese people, after proclaiming their independence under Ho Chi Minh in 1945, "quoted the American Declaration of Independence in their own document of freedom." President Truman's decision not to recognize them, King thought, was but another example of America's failure to bridge the chasms between creed and deed, a problem all the more evident since "the Constitution and the Declaration of Independence" are today "America's greatest claim to moral and political stature in the world."[36] When King spoke of the *will* of the American people, he had in mind a nation that lives its creed out of moral convictions, and not simply on the basis of what is politically feasible and acceptable.

King and the Powers That Be: Presidential Politics,
Political Parties, and the Civil Rights Cause

Martin Luther King, Jr., met, talked, and tried to work with Presidents Dwight D. Eisenhower, John F. Kennedy, and Lyndon B. Johnson. In dealing with these men, he was neither *status quo* nor *radical* in most respects, but a *moderate* who did not want to set himself and his agenda against them and theirs. Concerning his relationship with these chief executives, King reported that he became "increasingly aware of the play of their temperaments on their approach to civil rights, a cause that all three have espoused in principle."[37] King's dealings with Eisenhower, Kennedy, and Johnson, and with the political parties they represented, are a vital part of the story of American politics in the 1950s and 1960s. On a few occasions, King appeared before the Platform, the Credentials, and the Resolutions committees of the Democratic and Republican Parties, and he made numerous appeals to U.S. presidents.[38]

King always felt that moral leadership and support from the highest levels of the federal government were needed to ensure the success of the struggle for equal rights and social justice in the United States. But from the time of the Montgomery bus protest in the mid-1950s, he doubted the willingness of America's major political parties to serve as a vital force in resolving her racial dilemma. Knowing that political machines typically function as if power, love, and justice are polar opposites, and as if morality is irrelevant in political affairs, King never allowed himself to become too closely aligned with the leadership and the partisan politics of either the Democratic or the Republican party.[39] In October 1956, in response to a letter from Earl Kennedy, chairman of the First Congressional District of the Michigan Citizens for Eisenhower, King explained why he was "not taking any public position in this" presidential election:

> In private opinion I find something to be desired from both parties. The Negro has been betrayed by both the Democratic and the Republican Party. The Democrats have betrayed us by capitulating to the whims and caprices of the southern dixiecrats. The Republicans have betrayed us by capitulating to the blatant hypocrisy of conservative right wing northerners. This coalition of

southern dixiecrats and right wing northern Republicans defeats every move toward liberal legislation in Congress. So we confront the problem of choosing the lesser of two evils. At this point I might say, however, that I feel that the Negro must remain an independent voter, not becoming unduly tied to either party. He should seek to vote for the party which is more concerned with the welfare of all the people.[40]

King strongly believed that all of the major branches of government—the executive, congressional, and judicial wings—had a moral duty to take the lead in establishing true interracial democracy on a solid foundation. As early as January 1957, soon after the reelection of Eisenhower, King and the other founders of the Southern Christian Leadership Conference (SCLC) moved to secure presidential leadership in the struggle for civil rights in the South:

> We wired President Dwight D. Eisenhower, asking him to come south immediately, to make a major speech in a major Southern city urging all Southerners to accept and to abide by the Supreme Court's decisions as the law of the land. We further urged him to use the weight of his great office to point out to the South the moral nature of the problems posed at home and abroad by the unsolved civil rights issue.[41]

In his first national speech, given at the Prayer Pilgrimage in the nation's capitol on May 17, 1957, King challenged the Eisenhower administration on another level. "Give us the ballot," he cried, and "we will fill our legislative halls with men of goodwill." "Give us the ballot and we will place judges on the benches of the South who will 'do justly and love mercy,' and we will place at the head of the southern states governors who have felt not only the tang of the human but the glow of the divine."[42]

President Eisenhower never really met these challenges, though he did take steps which suggested that he was willing to address the civil rights issue on some levels. His decision to use force to integrate Little Rock's Central High School, in September 1957, proved wise and necessary, and was applauded by King. Of the decision, King wrote:

I thought it was quite regrettable and unfortunate that young high school students in Little Rock, Arkansas, had to go to school under the protection of federal troops. But I thought it was even more unfortunate that Arkansas Governor Orval Faubus, through irresponsible actions, left the President of the United States with no other alternative. I believe firmly in nonviolence, but, at the same time, I am not an anarchist. I believe in the intelligent use of police force. And I think that was all we had in Little Rock. It wasn't an army fighting against a nation or a race of people. It was just police force, seeking to enforce the law of the land. It was high time that a man as popular in the world as Eisenhower—a man with his moral influence—speak out and take a stand against what was happening all over the South. So I backed the President, and I sent him a telegram commending him for the positive and forthright stand that he took in the Little Rock school situation. He showed the nation and the world that the United States was a nation dedicated to law and order rather than mob rule.[43]

Eisenhower made several other moves which appeared pro–civil rights at first glance. Also in September 1957, he signed a Civil Rights Act into law, giving "the Attorney General considerable authority in local cases," with "some provisions on voting rights."[44] King endorsed the measure, but felt that it afforded further proof that African Americans could not rely solely on the institutions of government for freedom.[45] On June 23, 1958, in response to calls for "an immediate conference" with African American leaders, Eisenhower met with King, Roy Wilkins of the NAACP, the labor leader A. Philip Randolph, and Lester B. Granger of the National Urban League. The "symbolism of the high level meeting was impressive," despite the president's mild reaction to proposals for more federal action in support of civil rights initiatives.[46] In May 1960, Eisenhower signed a new Civil Rights Act, which he hailed as "an historic step forward in the field of civil rights." This piece of legislation strengthened "the authority of the FBI in investigating violence and provided for federal voting referees and mandatory retention of voting records for five years," but it did not honor the black leaders' request for federal action against white mob violence in the South, for protection of voting rights, and for federal disapproval of the use of government funds to support agencies and businesses that practiced discrimination.[47] King left "the meeting un-ruffled," but now convinced that Eisenhower was too conservative po-litically to assume moral leadership in the civil rights cause.[48]

King ultimately questioned the Republican leader's commitment to the creation of a genuinely democratic and racially inclusive so-ciety. With some disappointment, King stated:

> I thought Eisenhower believed that integration would be a fine thing. But I thought he felt that the more you push it, the more tension it would create, so, just wait a few more years and it will work itself out. I didn't think that Eisenhower felt like being a cru-sader for integration. President Eisenhower was a man of integrity and goodwill, but I am afraid that on the question of integration he didn't understand the dimensions of social change involved nor how the problem was to be worked out.[49]

Moreover, King came to see that Eisenhower would not be moved to act by moral convictions nor by the ever-changing political exigen-cies and considerations. In short, Eisenhower was a reluctant chief ex-ecutive who spoke eloquently about equal rights under the law, while doing little or nothing to transform words into concrete action:

> No one could discuss racial justice with President Eisenhower without coming away with mixed emotions. His personal sincerity on the issue was pronounced, and he had a magnificent capacity to communicate it to individuals. However, he had no ability to translate it to the public, or to define the problem as a supreme domestic issue. I have always felt that he failed because he knew that his colleagues and advisors did not share his views, and that he had no disposition to fight even for cherished beliefs. More-over, President Eisenhower could not be committed to anything which involved a structural change in the architecture of Ameri-can society. His conservatism was fixed and rigid, and any evil de-facing the nation had to be extracted bit by bit with a tweezer because the surgeon's knife was an instrument too radical to touch this best of all possible societies.[50]

As Eisenhower's second term drew to a close in 1960, King ex-pressed the hope that his successor would take a stronger civil rights stand. The race was between Republican candidate Richard M. Nixon, who had served as Eisenhower's vice president, and Democratic nominee John F. Kennedy, a senator from Massachusetts, both of whom had weak records on civil rights. Although King had known Nixon longer, he felt that the vice president "was an opportunist at many times who had no real grounding in basic convictions." "Very frankly," King remarked, "I did not feel at that time that there was much difference between Kennedy and Nixon."[51] Nixon had voted consistently "with the right wing of the Republican Party," and Kennedy, King felt, seemed willing to "compromise basic principles to become president." King's decision regarding the presidential race came in May 1960, after he was sentenced to "six months of hard labor" at Georgia's Reidsville Prison for driving without a state license.[52] While Nixon acted like he "had never known" King during that time, Senator John Kennedy became "a great force" in making the civil rights activist's release from Reidsville possible after only a few days of incarceration. That action figured prominently in King's decision to vote for Kennedy.[53]

King's support for Kennedy was solidified when the two met in New York in June 1960. While he never publicly endorsed Kennedy, King admitted that "I was very impressed by the forthright manner in which he discussed the civil rights question." Interestingly enough, Kennedy won the presidency in November 1960 with a substantial majority of the black vote, but did not respond immediately with a strong civil rights program. "In 1961 the Kennedy administration waged an essentially cautious and defensive struggle for civil rights against an unyielding adversary," King noted. "As the year unfolded, executive initiative became increasingly feeble," King added, "and the chilling prospect emerged of a general administration retreat."[54] This pattern extended through much of 1962, as Kennedy refused to intervene on behalf of King and others in their mass movement against segregation in Albany, Georgia.[55]

King viewed Kennedy's actions as symptomatic of a larger problem which extended to the other branches of government as well. In other words, the Washington establishment refused to respond morally and ethically to the civil rights challenge. King noted, for example, how the Supreme Court had not only failed to honor its 1954 decree to end school segregation "with all deliberate speed," but was actually retreating from its own antisegregation stance. At the end of

1962, eight years after *Brown v. Board of Education,* "approximately 9 percent of southern Negro students were attending integrated schools," King lamented. At this pace, he argued, "it would be the year 2054 before integration in southern schools would be a reality."[56]

Equally problematic was the fact that the Democratic and Republican Parties had "been generous" in their "convention vows on civil rights" in 1960, only to mark "time in the cause of justice" after the election. King pointed to the problem in America's major political parties in some detail, giving weight to his claim that African Americans were still being used as pawns in a political game between northern and southern congressmen:

> In the Congress, reactionary Republicans were still doing business with the Dixiecrats. And the feeling was growing among Negroes that the administration had oversimplified and underestimated the civil-rights issue. President Kennedy, if not backing down, had backed away from a key pledge of his campaign—to wipe out housing discrimination "with the stroke of a pen."[57]

A shift in administration policy began to take shape in November 1962, when Kennedy issued an executive order barring religious and racial discrimination in federally funded housing. Although King detected "a serious weakness" in the failure of the order "to attack the key problem of discrimination in financing by banks and other institutions," he promptly deemed its terms "praiseworthy."[58] In December 1962, Kennedy met with King, James Farmer, Roy Wilkins, and other civil rights leaders to discuss civil rights and the possibility of government sanctions against the apartheid regime in South Africa.[59] The experience was such that King began to detect a change in Kennedy's attitude toward the race problem. By the beginning of 1963, the civil rights leader was speaking of the rise of a different president, a claim that was more prudent and political than substantive:

> President Kennedy was a strongly contrasted personality. There were, in fact, two John Kennedys. One presided in the first two years under pressure of the uncertainty caused by his razor-thin margin of victory. He vacillated, trying to sense the direction his leadership could travel while retaining and building support

for his administration. However, in 1963, a new Kennedy had emerged. He had found that public opinion was not in a rigid mold. American political thought was not committed to conservatism, nor radicalism, nor moderation. It was above all fluid. As such it contained trends rather than hard lines, and affirmative leadership could guide it into constructive channels.[60]

Sensing what appeared to be a changing mood in the White House, King felt that the time had come to apply more pressure around civil rights initiatives. In a statement released on March 24, 1963, King challenged the Kennedy administration "to replace its timorous programs with new patterns of bold design" since a large part of the South was "ready for extensive change." While recognizing that "the government has been unable to make the Constitution functional for human rights in many parts of the South," King held that the administration "should place its weight behind the *dynamic* South, encouraging and facilitating its progressive development":

> The Administration is at an historic crossroad. It has at stake its moral commitment, and with it its political fortunes. It will not weaken its international posture, but strengthen it, if it takes the road to democratization of the South in active unity with the enlightened South—white and Negro.[61]

King's challenge did not go unheard. On June 11, 1963, after violence had broken out between blacks and whites in Birmingham, Kennedy made a national television appearance during which he called civil rights "a moral issue," one "as old as the Scriptures and as clear as the American Constitution." The central issue, Kennedy asserted, "is whether all Americans are to be afforded equal rights and equal opportunities." The president then announced his plan to challenge Congress "to make a commitment it has not fully made in this country to the proposition that race has no place in American life or law."[62] King reacted to Kennedy's speech with joy and excitement, calling it "the most earnest, human and profound appeal for understanding and justice that any President has uttered since the first days of the Republic."[63] King was further encouraged when Kennedy sent his Civil Rights Bill to Congress on June 19, eight days after the speech. Three days later, Kennedy met with King and other civil rights activists to discuss this piece of legislation and the upcoming March on Washington.[64] Kennedy's shifting attitude toward civil rights helps explain why King, Bayard Rustin, A. Philip Randolph, and other moderate civil rights leaders chose not to attack the administration publicly at the March on Washington on August 28, 1963.

The administration's new approach to civil rights probably owed more to pressure from various emerging elements in the movement than to any moral considerations.[65] In private, King is said to have admitted this much and more. He and Kennedy shared a concern regarding the rise of militant groups such as the Black Muslims, who preached racial separatism and retaliatory violence, and who seemed determined at times to turn the nonviolent crusade into one based on a preference for counterviolence or self-defense tactics. In May 1963, Kennedy had warned the "people of Birmingham, and of the South . . . that if they do not accept Dr. King's way they will get the Muslims' way," a view echoed by King in his speeches and writings.[66] King responded to Kennedy's "concern about Negro extremism" a month later, highlighting the potential for Negro retaliation against white mob violence, and reminding the president that government action on the civil rights front was the best answer to the problem:

> I have learned from authentic sources that Negroes are arming themselves in many quarters where this reign of terror is alive. I will continue to urge my people to be nonviolent in the face of the bitterest opposition, but I fear that my counsel will fall on deaf ears if the Federal Government does not take decisive action. If Negroes are tempted to turn to retaliatory violence, we shall see a dark night of rioting all over the South.[67]

The assassination of Kennedy in November 1963 shook King, coming as it did at a time when the administration was pushing what would have become the strongest civil rights legislation in the nation's history. While King always had questions about the nature and extent of Kennedy's commitment to black people, he eulogized the chief executive in the most sympathetic and generous terms:

> President Kennedy was not given to sentimental expressions of feeling. He had, however, a deep grasp of the dynamics of and

the necessity for social change. His work for international amity was a bold effort on a world scale. . . . Uniting his flair for leadership with a program of social progress, he was at his death undergoing a transformation from a hesitant leader with unsure goals to a strong figure with deeply appealing objectives.[68]

King initially had serious doubts about Lyndon B. Johnson's ability to pursue the course started by Kennedy. The civil rights leader had met Johnson when the Texas native was serving as vice president under Kennedy. Almost from the beginning, King viewed Johnson, Kennedy's successor, as part of what he called "the *dynamic* South," meaning those white southerners who were ready for positive and concrete changes in race relations. Concerning Johnson, King wrote:

> His approach to the problem of civil rights was not identical with mine—nor had I expected it to be. Yet his careful practicality was nonetheless clearly no mask to conceal indifference. His emotional and intellectual involvement were genuine and devoid of adornment. It was conspicuous that he was searching for a solution to a problem he knew to be a major shortcoming in American life. I came away strengthened in my conviction that an undifferentiated approach to white southerners could be a grave error, all too easy for Negro leaders in the heat of bitterness. Later, it was Vice-President Johnson I had in mind when I wrote in *The Nation* that the white South was splitting, and that progress could be furthered by driving a wedge between the rigid segregationists and the new white elements whose love of their land was stronger than the grip of old habits and customs.[69]

Having become the nation's president on the day of the Kennedy assassination, Johnson set out to build on the civil rights legacy of his predecessor. In his first speech as president, delivered on November 27, 1963, five days after the assassination, Johnson declared that "no memorial oration or eulogy could more eloquently honor President Kennedy's memory than the earliest possible passage of the civil rights bill for which he fought so long."[70] King found much hope in Johnson's speech. Less than a month later, a meeting between the two men further eased some of the civil rights leader's misgivings about the extent of Johnson's commitment to the elimination of discrimination and poverty.[71] This accounted primarily for King's early assessment of the Johnson presidency:

> The dimensions of Johnson's leadership have spread from a region to a nation. His recent expressions, public and private, indicate that he has a comprehensive grasp of contemporary problems. He has seen that poverty and unemployment are grave and growing catastrophes, and he is aware that those caught most fiercely in the grip of this economic holocaust are Negroes. Therefore, he has set the twin goal of a battle against discrimination within the war against poverty. . . . I have no doubt that we may continue to differ concerning the tempo and the tactical design required to combat the impending crisis. But I do not doubt that the President is approaching the solution with sincerity, with realism and, thus far, with wisdom. I hope his course will be straight and true. I will do everything in my power to make it so by outspoken agreement whenever proper, and determined opposition whenever necessary.[72]

It soon became clear to King that Johnson was not as committed to civil rights as he originally implied. When King wired the president in June 1964, requesting federal marshals to protect himself and other black activists from white mob violence in St. Augustine, Florida, Johnson refused to act responsibly.[73] Although Johnson signed the Civil Rights Bill passed by Congress a month later, with its fair employment and public accommodation sections, King felt that this achievement was far less important to the movement than Freedom Summer (1964), the "massive voter registration and political education campaign" led by black and white students in Mississippi.[74] Even so, King, who was invited to the signing, expressed the hope that the bill would end unfair employment practices and discrimination in public accommodations, a hope dashed later by Congress's failure "to enforce it in all its dimensions."[75]

Although generally unhappy with Johnson's civil rights record, King supported his campaign for the White House in 1964. Clearly, the preference for Johnson over the Republican candidate Barry Goldwater, whom King associated with racists, was rooted in politics rather than in any personal commitment to Johnson.[76] In the course of the campaign, in the summer of 1964, King met with the Platform Committees of the Democratic and Republican Parties, arguing for a stronger civil rights agenda. His efforts to seat delegates from the mostly black Mississippi Freedom Democratic Party (MFDP) at the Democratic National Convention in Atlantic City failed, mainly because of the opposition of Johnson, Vice President Hubert H. Humphrey, and United Auto Workers' president Walter Reuther, who threatened to cease financial support for the SCLC.[77] In any case, Johnson was elected in a landslide in November 1964, with heavy support from African Americans. Equally important for King was the fact that "the elections of 1964 broke the decades-old Congressional alliance of Dixiecrats and Northern conservatives, and sent to the Congress some fifty new Representatives who were receptive to fresh thinking."[78]

But new faces in Washington did not immediately translate into a change in the federal government's direction on civil rights. King continued to press for stronger presidential leadership and more legislation, with a particular focus on the political enfranchisement of blacks in the South. Awarded the Nobel Peace Prize in December 1964, which brought worldwide recognition of the nonviolent movement he led, King then had an even stronger base from which to challenge the government around both domestic and foreign policy concerns. Soon after receiving the award, the civil rights leader met with President Johnson and raised the issue of voting rights, only to be told that a voting rights bill could not make it "through this session of Congress"— that "it's just not wise or the politically expedient thing to do."[79] King was reminded once again that the president would not act without pressure from the movement.

King insisted that the Voting Rights Act passed by Congress in 1965 "was born in violence in Selma, Alabama," not on "the polished mahogany desk" of the president.[80] Hundreds of blacks and whites were brutalized during the struggle for the ballot in Selma, which lasted from January to March 1965, and Jimmie Lee Jackson, James Reeb, and Viola Liuzzo were killed by racists. "Our nation has declared war against totalitarianism around the world," King commented in a statement to the press, "and we call upon President Johnson, Governor Wallace, the Supreme Court, and the Congress of this great nation to declare war against oppression and totalitarianism within the shores of our country."[81] On March 5, 1965, King met with Johnson again, urging him "to expedite the new Voting Rights Bill and" to "make sure that it provided for *federal* registrars of voting applicants."[82] But Johnson acted only after the violence erupted in Selma. Less than two weeks after the audience with King, the president addressed the Congress, noting that the time had come for all Americans to have access to the ballot and other fundamental rights. Though still cautiously optimistic, King praised the speech in the most glowing terms:

> In his address to the joint session of Congress, President Johnson made one of the most eloquent, unequivocal, and passionate pleas for human rights ever made by a President of the United States. He revealed a great understanding of the depth and dimension of the problem of racial justice. His tone and his delivery were disarmingly sincere. His power of persuasion has been nowhere more forcefully seen. We are happy to know that our struggle in Selma has gone far beyond the issue of the right to vote and has focused the attention of the nation on the vital issue of equality in human rights.[83]

King wept softly as he listened to Johnson, who ended his speech with the pledge, "We shall overcome," words that affirmed the movement.[84] On August 6, 1965, Johnson signed into law the Voting Rights Act, guaranteeing the right to vote with special provisions for the protection of black voters from physical attack and discriminatory examinations.[85] Although elated with this significant legislative achievement, King would later express disappointment that the measure was "permitted to languish with only fractional and halfhearted implementation."[86]

The violence that exploded in the Watts section of Los Angeles, five days after the signing of the Voting Rights Bill, signaled the beginning of problems that would later result in an irreparable breach between Johnson and King. The Watts riot left thirty-four people dead, thousands arrested, and whole blocks of buildings destroyed, and it touched off a spirit of rebellion that triggered riots in black ghettoes throughout the urban North. Johnson reduced the riots to essentially irrational acts of violence and hooliganism, and his lan-

guage often contained veiled threats of retaliation against those involved. King saw the riots as the cries of the unheard, and he reminded the president that strong measures to eliminate poverty in the
urban North and the rural South, not police action against rioters,
constituted the most moral and practical response to the problem.[87]
"We don't need President Johnson" to remind us that "Negro rioters"
are "outnumbered ten to one," King observed.[88] King wondered why
the president seemed more concerned about black rioters than about
"the white backlash," which involved "the surfacing of old prejudices,
hostilities and ambivalences that have always been there."[89]

King believed that the riots testified to the essential failure of Johnson's Great Society reforms to address the economic roots of racism.
The president's plan for "rebuilding entire slum neighborhoods"—for
turning decaying cities into "the masterpieces of our civilization"—was
presented to the Congress in 1965, but was passed in a watered-down
form a year later.[90] Johnson's so-called war on poverty was designed to
promote open housing, the enhancement of ghetto areas, job training, and the recruitment, hiring, and promotion of more minorities by
federal contractors, but the problem for King was the lack of the enforcement of these affirmative action measures.[91] The civil rights
leader also criticized Johnson's expressed hope that his policies would
"become the realities of the twenty-first" century, noting that "on this
timetable many Negroes not yet born and virtually all now alive will not
experience equality."[92] Convinced that "we are grappling with basic
class issues between the privileged and the underprivileged," King
called for an "Economic Bill of Rights for the Disadvantaged" in 1966.
His contention was that the provisions of such a bill should be need-
based, extending compensatory treatment to blacks and whites alike,
and not race-based.[93] Thus, he anticipated debates concerning affirmative action that would occur in political circles, the academy, and in
the public square for the next three decades and beyond.

King held that much of the resources needed to ensure the success of Johnson's Great Society reforms were being consumed by the
war in Vietnam. He pointed to the fact that the administration's war
budget "amounts to $10 billion for a single year," "more than five
times the amount committed to antipoverty programs." "The bombs
in Vietnam explode at home," King lamented, "they destroy the hopes
and possibilities for a decent America."[94] In his controversial address,

"A Time to Break Silence," delivered at New York City's Riverside Church in April 1967, King linked the war to the civil rights movement and publicly denounced Johnson's war policy.[95] Moreover, King called upon the administration to stop the bombing in Vietnam, to declare a unilateral cease-fire, to prevent other battlegrounds in Southeast Asia, to allow the Vietnamese self-determination, and to withdraw all American troops from Vietnam in compliance with the 1954 Geneva agreement.[96]

The need for more prophets to rise up in opposition to Johnson's Vietnam strategy could not have been more pressing for King. "I think our policy is absolutely wrong, from a moral point of view, from a political point of view, and from a practical point of view," he observed. He chided those religious leaders who eagerly attacked him while supporting American aggression in Southeast Asia. "There have been too many instances where individual clergymen and the church in general gave a kind of moral sanction to war as if it was a holy venture," King complained. At the same time, he praised the National Council of Churches, Pope Paul, and the many Jewish rabbis who were "very vocal and forthright" in "calling for a negotiated settlement" in the Vietnam conflict.[97]

The decision to break with Johnson on Vietnam did not come easy for King. He thought long and hard before delivering "A Time to Break Silence," and his hesitation was rooted in his knowledge of the power embodied in the U.S. presidency. He had no personal commitment to Johnson, and he knew that he would risk losing the support the federal government had previously given him, a development that occurred as predicted.[98] King's antiwar statements, participation in the peace movement, and attempts at peacemaking disappointed and infuriated Johnson. Moreover, many in the administration felt that by advising young men to file as conscientious objectors, to avoid service in Vietnam, King was crossing the line that divided loyal, patriotic dissent from the advocacy of treasonable action. On one occasion, Johnson lashed out at the civil rights leader: "What is that preacher doing to me? We gave him the Civil Rights Act of 1964, we gave him the Voting Rights Act of 1965, we gave him the War on Poverty. What more does he want?"[99] In time, King became "*a persona non grata* to President Johnson" and lost much of his influence with white and black supporters in Congress. He was never again invited to the White

House, and his appeals to Johnson to protect marchers in the South went unheard, as had been the case earlier in cities like St. Augustine and Selma.[100]

King saw Vietnam as reflective of the weaknesses inherent in the Johnson administration's foreign policy. Equally disturbing to him was the administration's failure to impose strong sanctions against apartheid South Africa, to push for the seating of Red China in the United Nations, and to develop a Marshall Plan for the economic uplift of Africa, Latin America, and other parts of the so-called Third World. What King had in mind was a foreign policy not based on political expediency and an arrogant show of military might, but one grounded in the biblical principle of the sacredness of all human personality and the interrelatedness of all life.[101] His sense of what should be the true character of political ethics and government morality made conflict between him and the Washington establishment inevitable— more especially because those who ruled America came to see that he was willing to risk all for a complete restructuring of the capitalistic society.

King's plans regarding the Poor People's Campaign in 1967–1968 further alienated him from the political establishment. With coalition politics in mind, the civil rights leader and the SCLC staff set out to unite poor whites, African Americans, Hispanic Americans, and other so-called minorities into a nonviolent army, with the purpose of converging on the nation's capitol to dramatize the problem of poverty. President Johnson hated the idea, and encouraged a number of prominent blacks and whites to denounce King's views on both this campaign and the Vietnam War. Of particular concern to the administration was King's call for massive civil disobedience and nonviolent sabotage. Powerful figures in the Congress, the FBI, and other areas of government viewed King's activities with anger and alarm, and the charge that the civil rights leader was influenced by communists grew louder and more widespread.[102] By early 1968, various power elites had emerged to discredit and ultimately silence him.

But King reached the point where he was not willing to sacrifice principle and conscience merely to maintain the halfhearted support of the federal government. In "A Testament of Hope," an essay published posthumously, he was no longer careful and prudent in his criticisms of the Washington establishment:

The past record of the federal government, however, has not been encouraging. No president has really done very much for the American Negro, though the past two presidents have received much undeserved credit for helping us. This credit has accrued to Lyndon Johnson and John Kennedy only because it was during their administrations that Negroes began doing more for themselves. Kennedy didn't voluntarily submit a civil rights bill, nor did Lyndon Johnson. In fact, both told us at one time that such legislation was impossible. President Johnson did respond realistically to the signs of the times and used his skills as a legislator to get bills through Congress that other men might not have gotten through. I must point out, in all honesty, however, that President Johnson has not been nearly so diligent in *implementing* the bills he has helped shepherd through Congress.[103]

The lines of communication between the federal government and the civil rights movement had been all but severed when King succumbed to an assassin's bullet in April 1968. A few in the various branches of government were undoubtedly touched deeply by the tragedy, and offered genuine expressions of sorrow and regret. Many others reacted with appalling silence, and breathed a deep sigh of relief. This is always the case when great disturbers of the political order pass from the scene. President Johnson eulogized King with the words of a shrewd politician and the graceful manner of an aged priest, giving no indication of the storm that had at times raged between them:

> The dream of Dr. Martin Luther King, Jr. has not died with him. Men who are white, men who are black, must and will now join together as never in the past to let the forces of divisiveness know that America shall not be ruled by the bullet but only by the ballot of free and of just men.[104]

The Power to Achieve Purpose:
King's Political Proposals and Recommendations

Gayraud S. Wilmore's characterization of King as "the high priest of the civil rights movement" is widely accepted and virtually impossible to refute by most standards.[105] What is often ignored is that King was also what Coleman B. Brown calls "a consummate politician." Brown says of King:

> He offended moralists of various types by his openness to compromise. He seems to have understood compromise, not primarily as a sign of moral or political weakness, but, first as a means of retaining or increasing power necessary for the accomplishment of justified basic objectives; and, second, as a means for keeping doors open to opponents.[106]

King is said to have "expressed his political beliefs far more frankly and explicitly in private than he did in public."[107] This helps explain the many different opinions among scholars and activists regarding his roles and significance as a political thinker and leader. Some are apt to view King as a political conservative who operated within the system while decrying revolution. Others see him as a political liberal who fought for social change without wandering too far from the political mainstream. Still others associate King with a political radicalism that undermined American values and threatened her institutions.[108]

King's political convictions and actions developed and matured over time as he confronted white America's personal and institutional racism at various levels. "Neither by experience nor reading is King a political radical," declared one of his biographers in 1959. This image contrasts sharply with Adam Fairclough's claim, set forth thirty years later, that King embraced a "deep political radicalism" that was often concealed by his "placid exterior, his orotund manner, and his sober clerical mien."[109] The powerlessness of African Americans in a complex and hypocritical land—in a nation claiming to be the citadel of freedom while denying civil rights to its citizens of color—led King to combine what might be termed *conservative, liberal,* and *radical* elements in his politics. The situation he addressed proved in many respects so ambiguous, even anomalous, that he, given his high intellect and integrity, had to be politically flexible, adjusting his thinking and activities toward the changing realities on the racial scene.

"The logic of growth" for King necessarily involved African Americans moving from protest in the nation's streets to "equal participation in the political process."[110] Only in this manner could they significantly influence national policy, a concern King raised most often with respect to southern blacks. "Few people in America realize the seriousness of the burden imposed upon our democracy by the disfranchisement of Negroes in the deep South," he explained. Black political power and representation were essential to his conception of freedom, and those who sacrificed life and limb to that end were, as he put it, among "the real saviors of democracy."[111]

King equated political power at its best with the right to vote and hold public office. While understanding that voting always has an indirect influence upon social policy, he felt nonetheless that his people had to exercise that right as both a civic responsibility and a sign of their new and emerging sense of personal dignity.[112] For the Negro, he held, voting is not only "a badge of full citizenship" and "a source of power," but also "the foundation stone of political action":

> With it the Negro can eventually vote out of office public officials who bar the doorway to decent housing, public safety, jobs and decent integrated education. It is now obvious that the basic elements so vital to Negro advancement can only be achieved by seeking redress from government at local, state and Federal levels. To do this the vote is essential.[113]

Noting that "one of the most significant steps that the Negro can take at this hour is that short walk to the voting booth," King agonized over the fact that his people had "not scratched the surface . . . in this all-important area." In 1967, he wrote:

> The Negro vote presently is only a partially realized strength. It can still be doubled in the South. In the North, even where Negroes are registered in equal proportion to whites, they do not vote in the same proportions. Assailed by a sense of futility, Negroes resist participating in empty ritual. However, when the Negro citizen learns that united and organized pressure can achieve measurable results, he will make his influence felt. Out of this consciousness the political power of the aroused minority will be enhanced and consolidated. . . . Up to now that power has been inconsequential because, paradoxically, although Negroes vote with great discernment and traditionally as a bloc, essentially

we are unorganized, disunited and subordinated in the decision-making process. There is no correlation between the numerical importance of the urban Negro vote to the party it supports and the influence we wield in determining the party's program and policies, or its implementation of existing legislation.[114]

King suggested a number of steps as an avenue to the full realization of black political power. One involved increasing the black registration and vote, most especially in the border and deep southern states.[115] Another had to do with African Americans becoming more politically sophisticated and responsible. King recommended setting up voting clinics throughout the community to assist persons with registration and voting procedures, a cause to which churches could contribute financially and morally.[116] He also urged each church to establish "a social and political action committee" to keep people politically aware and active.[117] Beyond that, according to King, African Americans could realize their "true power potential" by combining educational competence and social involvement with political action, a tradition more than adequately established by Jewish Americans.[118]

Yet another step involved the creation of leaders who embody virtues that the masses can respect—"who have moral and ethical principles we can applaud with an enthusiasm that enables us to rally support for them based on confidence and trust." King further elaborated the point:

> We will have to demand high standards and give consistent, loyal support to those who merit it. We will have to be a reliable constituency for those who prove themselves to be committed political warriors in our behalf. When our movement has partisan political personalities whose unity with their people is unshakable and whose independence is genuine, they will be treated in white political councils with the respect those who embody such power deserve.[119]

This need to develop "genuinely independent and representative political leaders" could not have been more pressing for King, especially since most black politicians tended to collaborate with their white counterparts in preserving the racist system. As King put it,

The majority of Negro political leaders do not ascend to prominence on the shoulders of mass support. Although genuinely popular leaders are now emerging, most are selected by white leadership, elevated to position, supplied with resources and inevitably subjected to white control. The mass of Negroes nurtures a healthy suspicion toward these manufactured leaders.[120]

King himself often brushed aside suggestions that he should officially get involved in electoral politics. The civil rights leader was approached by persons who felt that he should become a candidate for the office of president of the United States, but he had no ambition along these lines. Moreover, he knew that it was virtually impossible for one to remain prophetic when one becomes intimately involved with the system. King included himself among those hybrids in the black community "who lead civil rights groups, churches, unions and other social organizations," and who "bargain for political programs" while generally operating "outside of partisan politics." As he put it: "In Negro life there is a unique and unnatural dichotomy between community leaders who have the respect of the masses and professional political leaders who are held in polite disdain."[121]

Despite all his talk about the need for independent and responsible black politicians to serve the African American community, King was opposed to the idea of voting for and supporting candidates for office solely on the basis of race. He also rejected the thought of an all-black political party as an end in itself, on both moral and practical grounds. This was essentially King's problem with many black power advocates, who, in his estimation, advocated the illegitimate use of power based on racial separatism.[122] As he stated in an interview with Rabbi Abraham Heschel in March 1968:

> Whether we like it or not and whether the racist understands it or not, our music, our cultural patterns, our poets, our material prosperity and even our food, are an amalgam of black and white, and there can be no separate black path to power and fulfillment that does not ultimately intersect white routes. There can be no separate white path to power and fulfillment, short of social disaster, that does not recognize the necessity of sharing that power with black aspirations for freedom and justice.[123]

King insisted that the primary black political goal was to eliminate "racism as an electoral issue." In other words, the goal was to contribute to a more progressive democracy by promoting the cause of all Americans.[124] The radicalization of King's vision and methods in the period from 1965 to 1968 did not lead to a change in his perspective on this matter.[125]

Convinced that "integration in political terms" is "shared power," King urged his people "to master the art of political alliances."[126] More specifically, he encouraged African Americans to become the "natural allies" of reform and independent political organizations comprised of other races and ethnic groups, for "they are the keys to political progress." For King, the Poor People's Campaign (1967–1968), designed to bring together blacks, Appalachian whites, Mexican Americans, Puerto Ricans, and other groups to fight for economic justice, afforded the best model for what might happen in political circles. He believed that such alliances or coalitions of conscience would allow for considerably more "political freedom" than the "old-line machine politicians," who typically used African Americans as pawns. Moreover, alliances of this nature, "based upon some self-interest of each component group and a common interest into which they merge," would displace bigoted politicians "and with them racism as a political issue."[127]

Also included among King's political recommendations was "an expanding advocate role for the federal government" and the federal courts "in the struggle for human rights."[128] In this sense, King was what Obey M. Hendricks, Jr., calls *a political liberal*.[129] However, his focus on the need for an alliance "with the federal government" shifted during the last three years of his life, as he became increasingly alienated from the centers of power, and he spoke more about "an expanded emphasis upon self help development."[130] King had come to realize that his people could not always depend on the federal government to defend, protect, and promote their political and citizenship rights.

It is difficult to avoid the conclusion that King had become something other than a friend to the American political establishment. After all, he had moved from the "idea of reforming the existing institutions" to the belief that "a reconstruction of the entire society" was essential. He concluded that it was unwise to integrate his people into the existing capitalistic structure. While he did not publicly advocate socialism, he did speak of the need for a "synthesis" of the best elements of capitalism and communism, "a socially conscious democracy which reconciles the truths of individualism and collectivism."[131] Even so, he stopped short of advocating political anarchy, despite claims to the contrary. He simply felt that the democratic socialist model was more consistent with his idea of a political order based on high moral and ethical standards. Moreover, he never abandoned the view that the norms of Christian morality had to be related to some degree to politics, government, and to social policy and programs. It was in this sense that King became what Andrew Young calls "a political theologian."[132]

To Serve the Present Age:
Reflections on King's Political Legacy

Martin Luther King, Jr.'s political impact on American life and culture was phenomenal. Emerging in a time of restless political ferment and change, he was a political philosopher who articulated and pursued an alternative model of society. The movement he led not only helped hasten the decline and virtual demise of all-white political primaries in the South, but also contributed to the erosion of much of the racism from electoral politics. Although African Americans were still encountering difficulties in registering, voting, and holding public office at the time of King's death, the barriers to such rights had been legally struck down, and Americans had become a democratically stronger people.[133]

King's political legacy can be evaluated on several levels. First, it rests on the conviction that *political rights should be extended to all qualified Americans, irrespective of race, class, gender, or national origin.* For King, all artificial human barriers to political access and participation had to be eliminated. This invariably meant that African Americans should have the privilege of holding political office at all levels, including the cabinet level in the federal government.[134] This is how he understood participatory democracy at its best. Significantly, this part of his legacy has found fulfillment in the sense that every American who wishes to be involved in the political process can exercise that right without being arrested, castigated, physically attacked, maimed, or killed. Thus, Charles V. Hamilton is right in saying that "the focus today is not so much on the *right* of black Americans to participate, but rather on the search for *reasons* to participate and on the *means* of that participation."[135]

But despite the trends toward a more participatory democracy in recent decades, *race* is still a powerful force in politics and in the electoral process. To be sure, it is often a factor in determining how African Americans, whites, and other racial and ethnic groups vote on the local, state, and national levels. It also figures prominently into the kinds of issues and concerns that different groups find politically significant. Furthermore, the problem of race also surfaces in cases where redistricting or gerrymandering occurs, a process that tends to hurt blacks more than whites.[136] King's call for the elimination of racism as a political and electoral issue may never be achieved, but it remains a challenge in any society where different peoples fail to understand the ways in which their political destinies are interconnected.

Second, King's legacy challenges us concerning *the need to learn and implement the techniques and art of coalition politics.* Since his death, African Americans have not been very successful in achieving what he termed "partners in power" with liberal whites and with other minorities.[137] This is not surprising in view of the racism that still permeates the body politic. Once the 1965 Voting Rights Act passed, the issues turned in a more economic direction, and most white liberals, who trembled at the idea of sharing material resources and economic power with blacks, abandoned the civil rights cause. The coalition of conscience King tried to develop in the 1960s—consisting of African Americans, liberal whites, representatives of organized labor, Protestants, Catholics, Jews, and members of other minority groups—had faded by the time of his death. Even the alliance that developed between blacks and Jews, symbolized most profoundly in the friendship between King and Rabbi Abraham J. Heschel, steadily declined and degenerated into outright conflict in some quarters in the 1970s, 1980s, and 1990s, mainly because of growing nationalistic sentiments in both groups, disputes concerning quotas and affirmative action, disagreements over the Palestinian question, tensions over South African–Israeli relations, differences over big-city election campaigns, and the bigoted statements of leaders on both sides.[138] Although Jesse Jackson succeeded in reviving this coalition of conscience to some degree during his presidential campaigns in 1984 and 1988, the effort ultimately failed as Jackson lost favor with many in the Jewish community.

Because African Americans remain a minority in a predominantly white racist society, King's idea of coalition politics is still perennially relevant to their quest for both political and economic empowerment.[139] The SCLC, the National Association for the Advancement of Colored People (NAACP), the Urban League, and other civil rights organizations that lay claim to King's legacy should do more to translate this idea into practical reality and action. Even the Congressional Black Caucus (CBC), formally organized as a voice of advocacy for African American concerns in 1971, has failed at critical points to promote King's concept of alliance politics on practical levels, a reality difficult to face since some black congresspersons marched and worked with the civil rights leader. The same can be said of related groups of black elected officials, such as the Joint Center for Political and Economic Studies, which, like the CBC, "emerged in the late 1960s out of a perceived need to develop new organizational forms to deal with post-civil rights era problems."[140] Powerful political coalitions between blacks and other groups are not likely to be established in the near future, especially given the disturbing trends in the polarization and tensions that exist between the growing ethnic populations in the central cities of America's metropolitan areas, but the idea should survive as a possible avenue to change in the twenty-first century.

A third dimension of King's legacy involves *the need to combine mass social protest with electoral politics.* During the more than three decades after King's death, black participation in American politics and the electoral process has been emphasized to the neglect of organized social protest.[141] King knew that much-needed and lasting change could not occur without a proper emphasis on both. He was as concerned about those African Americans who retreated into an apolitical posture as he was about those who shunned social activism. Of the former, he commented:

> They tend to hold themselves aloof from politics as a serious concern. They sense that they are manipulated, and their defense

rest. To safeguard themselves on this front from
hat torments them in so many areas, they shut
cal activity and retreat into the dark shadows of
nse of futility is deep, and in terms of their bitter
astified. They cannot perceive political action as
It will take patient and persistent effort to eradi-
ut the new consciousness of strength developed
rring agitation can be utilized to channel con-
tivity into political life and eliminate the stagna-
an outdated and defensive paralysis. . . . In the
ecome intensive political activists. We must be
ection because we need political strength more
any other group in American society. Most of us
ave adequate economic power, and many of us
the culture to be part of any tradition of power.
us toward the power inherent in the creative

of new black voters began to elect politicians of
ast three decades of the twentieth century, parti-
o many African Americans remained apathetic
e African Americans who still refuse to take ad-
von political privileges would do well to remem-
d statement that freedom entails responsibility.
he said on one occasion, and on another he as-
must be the primary force in determining his
lso challenged those who believed that prayer
fficient substitute for sociopolitical activism, in-
st always be combined with hard work, intelli-
ction. To those who would casually and carelessly
nal political privileges at the expense of the
still quite applicable. Said he: "There must be a
aure in the Negro community that scorns the
k up his citizenship rights and add his strength
luntarily to the accumulation of power for him-

eating political leaders of character who are devoted
et another aspect of King's legacy. The civil

rights leader had little patience with politicians who exploited the power of the black vote only to ignore the needs of the community, and he was especially critical of black political leaders who were more concerned about personal gain than about the empowerment and liberation of their people. King also knew that the mere election of African Americans to political office would not radically change the black condition, a point more than sufficiently demonstrated in the case of big-city black mayors over the past four decades. He pressed the thought further: "A black face that is mute in party councils is not political representation; the ability to be independent, assertive and respected when the final decisions are made is indispensable for an authentic expression of power."[145] These thoughts are particularly relevant for our times, all the more because black and white neoconservatives in politics are employing rhetoric that obscures continuing racial inequity while threatening the future progress of African Americans.

Finally, King's legacy embraces *the need to apply high moral and ethical standards to politics and government.* In the current political context, one still informed by scandals at the highest levels of our nation's life, "high moral and ethical standards" usually refer to "personal morality," not so much social and political ethics. But King had both in mind. Opposed to a Machiavellian approach to political power, King called upon politicians and governments to use power "humanely and morally for improving the lot of those who have few, if any, other resources."[146] Moreover, King believed that the Christian ethic should have some role in democratic politics, lawmaking, and government-based social policy, a position that flowed naturally out of his conviction that power, love, and justice, in their most authentic expression, are inextricably linked. Here he owed much to his cultural experience and to Reinhold Niebuhr's examination of the interface between the Christian faith and American political life. While King stopped short of calling for a theocracy or a holy commonwealth, the separation of politics from religion remained as foreign to him as the isolation of art from the human struggle. For King, the very survival of the nation ultimately hinged on the capacity of government and religion to work together for the common good.

NOTES

1. Mohandas K. Gandhi, *Autobiography: The Story of My Experiments with Truth*, trans. Mahadev Desai (New York: Dover Publications, 1983), p. 454.

2. Clayborne Carson, ed., *The Autobiography of Martin Luther King, Jr.* (New York: Warner Books, 1998), pp. 17 and 24.

3. Lewis V. Baldwin, *There Is a Balm in Gilead: The Cultural Roots of Martin Luther King, Jr.* (Minneapolis: Fortress Press, 1991), p. 87.

4. Quoted in Michael E. Dyson, *I May Not Get There with You: The True Martin Luther King, Jr.* (New York: The Free Press, 2000), pp. 38–39.

5. For this idea, I am indebted to Rufus Burrow, an ethicist who explored aspects of the moral and political dimensions of King's thought in this volume. From Rufus Burrow, Jr. to Lewis V. Baldwin (17 August 1999), p. 1.

6. Clayborne Carson et al., eds., *The Papers of Martin Luther King, Jr.*, vol. 1: *Called to Serve, January 1929–June 1951* (Berkeley: University of California Press, 1992), pp. 36 and 108–111; "Contest Winner, M. L. King, Jr.," *Atlanta Daily World,* 16 April 1944, p. 2; Martin Luther King, Jr., "Segregation Is Not Just a Southern Problem," an interview in Chicago, Illinois (28 July 1965), Archives of the Martin Luther King, Jr. Center for Nonviolent Social Change, Atlanta, Georgia, p. 2; and Coleman B. Brown, "Grounds for American Loyalty in a Prophetic Christian Social Ethic— with Special Attention to Martin Luther King, Jr.," Ph.D. diss., Union Theological Seminary, New York, New York (April 1979), pp. 188, 248, and 253–254.

7. Martin Luther King, Jr., *Where Do We Go from Here: Chaos or Community?* (Boston: Beacon Press, 1968), p. 70.

8. Martin Luther King, Jr., "The Negro and the American Dream," speech at a public meeting of the Charlotte branch of the NAACP, Charlotte, North Carolina (25 September 1960), Martin Luther King, Jr. Papers, Special Collections, Mugar Memorial Library, Boston University, Boston, Massachusetts, p. 2.

9. Ibid., p. 1; Martin Luther King, Jr., "Draft of an Address to be Delivered at the March on Washington for Jobs and Freedom" (28 August 1963), King Center Archives, pp. 1–2; and Martin Luther King, Jr., "Moral and Religious Imperatives for Brotherhood," excerpts from an address delivered at the Congregation B'nai Jeshurun, New York, New York (9 September 1963), King Center Archives, pp. 1–3.

10. Brown, "Grounds for American Loyalty," p. 248; and King, "Segregation Is Not Just a Southern Problem," p. 2. I am highly indebted to Dr. Rufus Burrow, Jr., for much of this idea.

11. Martin Luther King, Jr., *Stride toward Freedom: The Montgomery Story* (New York: Harper & Row, 1958), pp. 190–191; King, "Segregation Is Not Just a Southern Problem," pp. 2–3; Martin Luther King, Jr., *The Trumpet of Conscience* (San Francisco: Harper & Row, 1989), p. 26; King, *Where Do We Go from Here?*, pp. 70–71; Martin Luther King, Jr., *Strength to Love* (Philadelphia: Fortress Press, 1981), pp. 20–21, 28, and 80; Martin Luther King, Jr., *The Measure of a Man* (Philadelphia: Fortress Press, 1988), pp. 29–30; Martin Luther King, Jr., *Why We Can't Wait* (New York: New American Library, 1964), pp. 93–94, 128, and 131; Martin Luther King, Jr., "Address at a Mass Meeting," Maggie Street Baptist Church, Montgomery, Alabama (16 February 1968), King Center Archives, p. 4; and Baldwin, *There Is a Balm in Gilead*, p. 50.

12. King, *Where Do We Go from Here?*, pp. 75–76; Martin Luther King, Jr., "America's Chief Moral Dilemma," address at the United Church of Christ—General Synod, Palmer House, Chicago, Illinois (6 July 1965), pp. 1–20; Brown, "Grounds for American Loyalty," p. 107; and Baldwin, *There Is a Balm in Gilead*, p. 50.

13. King, *Where Do We Go from Here?*, p. 6.

14. Carson, ed., *The Autobiography of Martin Luther King, Jr.*, p. 224; and James M. Washington, ed., *A Testament of Hope: The Essential Writings and Speeches of Martin Luther King, Jr.* (San Francisco: Harper Collins, 1986), p. 217.

15. Martin Luther King, Jr., *Where Do We Go from Here: Chaos or Community?*, unpublished draft (1967), pp. 9–10; King, *Why We Can't Wait*, p. 94; and Baldwin, *There Is a Balm in Gilead*, p. 242.

16. King, *Why We Can't Wait*, p. 25.

17. Carson, ed., *The Autobiography of Martin Luther King, Jr.*, pp. 60, 167, and 272; Alan F. Westin and Barry Mahoney, *The Trial of Martin Luther King* (New York: Thomas Y. Crowell Company, 1974), pp. 45–46, 59–60, 151–153, 158–159, 187–188, and 193–194; and King, *Why We Can't Wait*, pp. 70–71.

18. King, *Why We Can't Wait*, p. 93; Carson, ed., *The Autobiography of Martin Luther King, Jr.*, p. 202; Martin Luther King, Jr., "Negro Gains in Rights—1965," speech at the Atlanta Press Club, Atlanta, Georgia (10 November 1965), King Center Archives, p. 19; and Martin Luther King, Jr., "An Address," delivered to a joint convention of the two houses of the General Court of Massachusetts (22 April 1965), King Center Archives, p. 13.

19. Martin Luther King, Jr., "Statement on the Declaration of Independence, the Constitution, and the Emancipation" (December 1962), King Center Archives, pp. 1–3; Martin Luther King, Jr., "An Address," delivered before the New York Civil War Centennial Commission, the Park

Sheraton Hotel, New York, New York (12 September 1962), King Center Archives, pp. 1, 3, 5–10, and 12; Martin Luther King, Jr., "Emancipation Proclamation," article prepared for the *New York Amsterdam News,* 10 September 1962, King Center Archives, pp. 1–3; and Martin Luther King, Jr., "The Luminous Promise," unpublished essay (December 1962), King Center Archives, pp. 1–3.

20. Carson, ed., *The Autobiography of Martin Luther King, Jr.,* pp. 243–244; and King, *Where Do We Go from Here?,* pp. 1–3, 34, 58, 81, and 119.

21. Coleman Brown rightly argues that "for King, Lincoln's Emancipation Proclamation—confirmed and extended by the 13th, 14th, and 15th Amendments—was both integral and essential to the 'sacred' American 'obligation' entered upon in the Declaration of Independence and the Constitution." See Brown, "Grounds for American Loyalty," p. 289.

22. Washington, ed., *A Testament of Hope,* p. 217; and Carson, ed., *The Autobiography of Martin Luther King, Jr.,* p. 223.

23. Martin Luther King, Jr., "A Second Emancipation Proclamation," a brief statement given in San Francisco, California (16 October 1961), King Center Archives, p. 1; Martin Luther King, Jr., "A Statement on the Second Emancipation Proclamation," prepared for the *Afro-American* (24 March 1962), King Center Archives, p. 1; and "MLK/JFK on Abolition of Segregation," Washington, D.C. (16 October 1961), King Center Archives, p. 1.

24. King, "America's Chief Moral Dilemma," pp. 1–20.

25. King, *Where Do We Go from Here?,* pp. 77–78; and Brown, "Grounds for American Loyalty," pp. 109–110.

26. Carson et al., eds., *The Papers of Martin Luther King, Jr.,* vol. 1, p. 111. King spoke of Lincoln as one who followed a "divine example," as one who manifested a dangerous altruism when he signed the Emancipation Proclamation. Here his view of Lincoln is essentially the same as that revealed in the narratives and tales of many ex-slaves. See Eugene D. Genovese, *Roll, Jordan, Roll: The World the Slaves Made* (New York: Pantheon Books, 1974), pp. 118–119; and John J. Ansbro, *Martin Luther King, Jr.: The Making of a Mind* (Maryknoll, N.Y.: Orbis Books, 1982), p. 31.

27. Carson, ed., *The Autobiography of Martin Luther King, Jr.,* p. 359; Washington, ed., *A Testament of Hope,* pp. 279–280; and King, *Strength to Love,* pp. 80–81. This view of Lincoln is supported by recent scholarship on slavery. See Robert W. Johannsen, *Lincoln, the South, and Slavery: The Political Dimension* (Baton Rouge: Louisiana State University Press, 1991), pp. 13–124.

28. Ansbro, *Martin Luther King, Jr.,* pp. 161–162; Brown, "Grounds for American Loyalty," pp. 112 and 289; King, *Where Do We Go from Here?,*

pp. 78–79; King, *Strength to Love,* p. 81; and Washington, ed., *A Testament of Hope,* p. 271.

29. Martin Luther King, Jr., "The South—A Hostile Nation," *New York Amsterdam News,* 11 May 1963, p. 12.

30. King, *Why We Can't Wait,* pp. 22–23; From Martin Luther King, Jr. to Mrs. Anne Braden (2 October 1962), King Papers, Boston University, p. 1; Carson, ed., *The Autobiography of Martin Luther King, Jr.,* pp. 223–224; and Washington, ed., *A Testament of Hope,* pp. 217 and 271.

31. King, *Strength to Love,* p. 81.

32. Ibid.

33. Ibid.

34. Carson, ed., *The Autobiography of Martin Luther King, Jr.,* p. 219.

35. Washington, ed., *A Testament of Hope,* p. 230; and Baldwin, *There Is a Balm in Gilead,* p. 87.

36. King, *The Trumpet of Conscience,* p. 26; and Martin Luther King, Jr., "True Dignity," unpublished paper (n.d.), King Center Archives, p. 8.

37. King, *Why We Can't Wait,* p. 143.

38. See Martin Luther King, Jr., "Statement before the Credentials Committee of the Democratic National Committee" (22 August 1964), King Center Archives, pp. 1–4; Martin Luther King, Jr., "Statement before the Platform Committee of the Democratic National Convention," Atlantic City, New Jersey (August 1964), King Center Archives, pp. 1–14; Martin Luther King, Jr., "Statement before the National Democratic Platform and Resolutions Committee" (11 August 1956), King Center Archives, pp. 1–2; and Martin Luther King, Jr., "Statement concerning an Appeal to Vice President Richard M. Nixon" (13 June 1957), King Center Archives, pp. 1–2.

39. King felt that political parties in the United States tended to be to some degree Nietzschean and Machiavellian when in power, especially when confronted with the issue of racial justice. That is to say that they not only tended to exercise power not rooted in love and a commitment to justice, but also typically maintained power by acting on the basis of political expediency instead of moral considerations. A careful reading of King makes this conclusion virtually inescapable. See Ansbro, *Martin Luther King, Jr.,* pp. 1–2.

40. From Martin Luther King, Jr. to Mr. Earl Kennedy (30 October 1956), King Papers, Boston University, p. 1. One scholar rightly claims that King was always "skeptical of both major American political parties." See Brown, "Grounds for American Loyalty," p. 123.

41. Carson, ed., *The Autobiography of Martin Luther King, Jr.,* pp. 100–101.

42. Washington, ed., *A Testament of Hope,* pp. 197–198; and Martin Luther King, Jr., "Prayer Pilgrimage for Freedom," *Congressional Record,* 103 (28 May 1957): pp. 7822–7824.

43. Carson, ed., *The Autobiography of Martin Luther King, Jr.*, pp. 100 and 109–110. Interestingly enough, King, with some exaggeration, compared Eisenhower's actions in Little Rock to those of Mohandas K. Gandhi, who "not only spoke against the caste system," but "took 'untouchables' by the hand and led them into the temples from which they had been excluded." Said King: "To equal that, President Eisenhower would take a Negro child by the hand and lead her into Central High School in Little Rock." See Washington, ed., *A Testament of Hope*, p. 28.

44. Thomas R. Peake, *Keeping the Dream Alive: A History of the Southern Christian Leadership Conference from King to the Nineteen-Eighties* (New York: Peter Lang Publishing, 1987), pp. 51–52.

45. Taylor Branch, *Parting the Waters: America in the King Years, 1954–63* (New York: Simon and Schuster, 1988), pp. 221–222.

46. Peake, *Keeping the Dream Alive*, p. 60; and Carson, ed., *The Autobiography of Martin Luther King, Jr.*, p. 100. For some sense of the content of the proposal presented to Eisenhower, see Roy Wilkins, Martin Luther King, Jr., and A. Philip Randolph, "Statement regarding Little Rock, Arkansas Decision and Other Matters" (23 June 1958), King Center Archives, pp. 1–4.

47. Peake, *Keeping the Dream Alive*, pp. 60 and 76–77.

48. Ibid., pp. 60–61; and Coretta Scott King, *My Life with Martin Luther King, Jr.*, rev. ed. (New York: Henry Holt and Company, 1993), pp. 147 and 149. One scholar rightly contends that Eisenhower's "private sympathies" rested with white southerners when it came to many of the issues raised by blacks. See Branch, *Parting the Waters*, p. 221.

49. Carson, ed., *The Autobiography of Martin Luther King, Jr.*, p. 110.

50. King, *Why We Can't Wait*, p. 143.

51. Carson, ed., *The Autobiography of Martin Luther King, Jr.*, pp. 148–150.

52. King had only recently moved from Montgomery, Alabama, and had not obtained a Georgia license. King reported that the lawyers and the judge "later admitted in court that they had never fined or arrested anybody on a charge like that, and they really had nothing on the statute to reveal how long you had to be in Atlanta before changing your license." So King concluded that "it was obviously a case of persecution." See ibid., pp. 147–150.

53. Ibid., pp. 145–150; and Martin Luther King, Jr., "Statement on SCLC Policy regarding the Endorsement of Presidential Candidates" (1 November 1960), King Center Archives, p. 1.

54. Carson, ed., *The Autobiography of Martin Luther King, Jr.*, pp. 143 and 152; King, *Why We Can't Wait*, pp. 143–144; Martin Luther King, Jr., "Statement concerning the President and the Secretary of Defense,"

released to Carl Fleming, *Newsweek*, and to Prindle, *Inquirer* (9 November 1961), King Center Archives, p. 1; and Martin Luther King, Jr., "Fumbling on the New Frontier: Report on Civil Rights," reprinted from *The Nation* (3 March 1962), King Center Archives, pp. 1–4.

55. William D. Watley, *Roots of Resistance: The Nonviolent Ethic of Martin Luther King, Jr.* (Valley Forge, Pa.: Judson Press, 1985), p. 70; and "Dr. King on President Kennedy's Stand on Negotiations in Albany," press release from the city jail, Albany, Georgia (1 August 1962), King Center Archives, p. 1.

56. King, *Why We Can't Wait*, pp. 18–19.

57. Ibid., pp. 19–20.

58. Ibid. For other important sources, see Martin Luther King, Jr., "President Kennedy's Record," unpublished document (17 February 1962), King Center Archives, pp. 1–3; Martin Luther King, Jr., "The President on Civil Rights," a statement given in Washington, D.C. (19 July 1962), King Center Archives, p. 1; From Martin Luther King, Jr. to President John F. Kennedy (December 1962), King Center Archives, p. 1; and Martin Luther King, Jr., "JFK's Executive Order on Housing," unpublished document (13 December 1962), King Center Archives, pp. 1–4.

59. From the American Negro Leadership Conference on Africa to John F. Kennedy (17 December 1962), King Papers, Boston University, pp. 1–2; and Lewis V. Baldwin, *Toward the Beloved Community: Martin Luther King, Jr. and South Africa* (Cleveland: Pilgrim Press, 1995), pp. 40–41 and 207 n64.

60. King, *Why We Can't Wait*, pp. 143–144; Carson, ed., *The Autobiography of Martin Luther King, Jr.*, p. 150; and Martin Luther King, Jr., "Statement concerning President Kennedy," released to *Time* (12 January 1962), King Center Archives, p. 1.

61. "King Urges JFK to Support Dynamic South in Civil Rights," news release from the Southern Christian Leadership Conference (24 March 1963), King Center Archives, pp. 1–2.

62. *New York Times*, 12 June 1963, p. 20; and James H. Cone, *Martin and Malcolm and America: A Dream or a Nightmare* (Maryknoll, N.Y.: Orbis Books, 1991), p. 82.

63. Cone, *Martin and Malcolm and America*, p. 82; and King, *Why We Can't Wait*, p. 144.

64. Cone, *Martin and Malcolm and America*, p. 82.

65. Recent research on the Kennedy administration makes it virtually impossible to avoid such a conclusion, especially since King became the target of FBI surveillance and a counterintelligence agenda during the Kennedy years. See Kenneth O'Reilly, *"Racial Matters": The FBI's Secret File*

on Black America, 1960–1972 (New York: Free Press, 1989), pp. 101–104 and 122.

66. *New York Times,* 19 May 1963, p. 10E; *New York Times,* 15 May 1963, p. 26; and Cone, *Martin and Malcolm and America,* pp. 264–265.

67. Cone, *Martin and Malcolm and America,* p. 264; and Carson, ed., *The Autobiography of Martin Luther King, Jr.,* p. 166.

68. King, *Why We Can't Wait,* p. 144. Also see Martin Luther King, Jr., "Comments on John F. Kennedy," the Berlin Festival, Berlin, Germany (13 September 1964), King Center Archives, pp. 1–6.

69. "King Urges JFK to Support Dynamic South," pp. 1–2; and King, *Why We Can't Wait,* pp. 145–146.

70. Westin and Mahoney, *The Trial of Martin Luther King,* p. 155.

71. Peake, *Keeping the Dream Alive,* p. 145.

72. King, *Why We Can't Wait,* p. 146.

73. Adam Fairclough, *To Redeem the Soul of America: The Southern Christian Leadership Conference and Martin Luther King, Jr.* (Athens: University of Georgia Press, 1987), p. 185; and From Martin Luther King, Jr. to President Lyndon B. Johnson (29 May 1964), King Center Archives, pp. 1–2.

74. Westin and Mahoney, *The Trial of Martin Luther King,* p. 156; King, *My Life with Martin Luther King, Jr.,* p. 229; Fairclough, *To Redeem the Soul of America,* p. 194; and King, *Where Do We Go from Here?,* p. 81.

75. King, *Where Do We Go from Here?,* pp. 81 and 119; and Westin and Mahoney, *The Trial of Martin Luther King,* p. 156.

76. Carson, ed., *The Autobiography of Martin Luther King, Jr.,* pp. 246–248; and Martin Luther King, Jr., "Civil Right No. 1—The Right to Vote," *New York Times Magazine,* section 6, part 1 (14 March 1965): pp. 25–27. During the presidential campaign in 1964, King actually suggested that New York Republican Governor Nelson Rockefeller, due to his "humanitarian history," would make a good president. King was disturbed by Senator Barry Goldwater's "right wing conservatism." When Goldwater was nominated by the Republican Party, King felt that he and his people had no choice but to support the ticket of President Johnson. See Martin Luther King, Jr., "The Republican Presidential Nomination," unpublished statement (1 April 1964), King Center Archives, pp. 1–4.

77. King, *My Life with Martin Luther King, Jr.,* pp. 128 and 230; Fairclough, *To Redeem the Soul of America,* pp. 200–204; Baldwin, *Toward the Beloved Community,* pp. 43–44; From D. McDonald to Mr. George Houser (1 July 1964), King Papers, Boston University, p. 1; King, "Statement before the Platform Committee of the Democratic National Convention," pp. 1–14; King, "Statement before the Credentials Committee of the Democratic National Committee," pp. 1–4; and Martin Luther King, Jr.,

"Statement before the Platform Committee of the Republican National Convention," San Francisco, California (7 July 1964), King Center Archives, pp. 1–2.

78. Martin Luther King, Jr., "Freedom's Crisis: The Last Steep Ascent," *Nation* (14 March 1966): p. 289. King noted that the results of the election preserved his "faith in this great nation of ours." See Martin Luther King, Jr., "Statement on the Election of Lyndon B. Johnson," unpublished document (4 November 1964), King Center Archives, pp. 1–2. Also, King insisted at that point that "President Johnson has the opportunity to complete the job which was started by Roosevelt and interrupted by the war." See Martin Luther King, Jr., "Address to the Southern Association of Political Scientists" (13 November 1964), King Center Archives, p. 3.

79. Cone, *Martin and Malcolm and America*, pp. 87 and 215–216.

80. King, *Where Do We Go from Here?*, pp. 1 and 34.

81. Carson, ed., *The Autobiography of Martin Luther King, Jr.*, p. 275.

82. King, *My Life with Martin Luther King, Jr.*, p. 241. Just prior to the March 5 meeting, King declared that "I would certainly say that the President is committed on civil rights. I have no doubt about that." During the meeting, King and Johnson discussed the need for federal registrars as part of the Voting Rights Bill, for it was his conviction that blacks in many counties in the black-belt South would not be registered "unless you have federal registrars." Martin Luther King, Jr., "Comments at a Press Conference," held at the International Airport, Crown Room of Satellite No. 6, Delta Airlines (24 February 1965), King Center Archives, p. 7; and Martin Luther King, Jr., "On White House Conference," Washington, D.C. (6 March 1965), King Center Archives, p. 1.

83. Washington, ed., *A Testament of Hope*, p. 127.

84. King, *Where Do We Go from Here?*, pp. 1–2; and King, *My Life with Martin Luther King, Jr.*, pp. 245–246.

85. Carson, ed., *The Autobiography of Martin Luther King, Jr.*, pp. 288–289; King, *My Life with Martin Luther King, Jr.*, pp. 252–253; and Watley, *Roots of Resistance*, p. 87.

86. King, *Where Do We Go from Here?*, p. 81; Hugh D. Graham, *The Civil Rights Era: Origins and Development of National Policy* (New York: Oxford University Press, 1990), p. 4; and Ansbro, *Martin Luther King, Jr.*, p. 213.

87. King, *Where Do We Go from Here?*, pp. 2–3 and 32–39; Washington, ed., *A Testament of Hope*, pp. 396–397 and 322–323; and Martin Luther King, Jr., "Showdown for Nonviolence," *Look*, vol. 32, no. 8 (16 April 1966): pp. 23–25.

88. King, *Where Do We Go from Here?*, p. 56; and Carson, ed., *The Autobiography of Martin Luther King, Jr.*, p. 329.

89. King, *Where Do We Go from Here?*, pp. 68–101.

90. Ibid., p. 82.

91. Graham, *The Civil Rights Era*, pp. 4 and 258; Melvin I. Urofsky, *A Conflict of Rights: The Supreme Court and Affirmative Action* (New York: Charles Scribner's Sons, 1991), pp. 17–18; Cone, *Martin and Malcolm and America*, p. 286; and King, *Where Do We Go from Here?*, pp. 87–88.

92. King, *Where Do We Go from Here?*, p. 88.

93. Cone, *Martin and Malcolm and America*, p. 286; Washington, ed., *A Testament of Hope*, pp. 64–72; and King, *Why We Can't Wait*, pp. 136–140.

94. King, *Where Do We Go from Here?*, p. 86.

95. Washington, ed., *A Testament of Hope*, pp. 231–243; and King, *Where Do We Go from Here?*, p. 86.

96. Washington ed., *A Testament of Hope*, p. 239.

97. Martin Luther King, Jr., "Doubts and Certainties Link: An Interview," London, England, aired 4 April 1968, King Center Archives, p. 8; "Hugh Downs's Interview with Martin Luther King, Jr.," NBC "Today" Show (18 April 1966), p. 3; and Washington, ed., *A Testament of Hope*, pp. 239–240. Clearly, King had become very critical of the Johnson administration by 1967. See "Transcript of an Interview with Martin Luther King, Jr.," on "Face the Nation," with news correspondents Martin Agronsky of CBS News, Ted Poston of the *New York Post*, and Robert Schakne of CBS News (16 April 1967), King Center Archives, p. 10; and Martin Luther King, Jr., "Sleeping through a Revolution," delivered at the Sheraton Hotel, Chicago, Illinois (10 December 1967), King Center Archives, p. 3.

98. Watley, *Roots of Resistance*, pp. 102–103.

99. Ansbro, *Martin Luther King, Jr.*, p. 252; Fairclough, *To Redeem the Soul of America*, pp. 272 and 340–341; and Watley, *Roots of Resistance*, pp. 100 and 102–103.

100. Ansbro, *Martin Luther King, Jr.*, p. 256; David J. Garrow, *Bearing the Cross: Martin Luther King, Jr., and the Southern Christian Leadership Conference* (New York: William Morrow and Company, 1986), p. 445; and Fairclough, *To Redeem the Soul of America*, pp. 273 and 340–341.

101. Baldwin, *Toward the Beloved Community*, pp. 44 and 47; King, *Where Do We Go from Here?*, pp. 173–191; and King, *The Trumpet of Conscience*, pp. 69–70.

102. Cone, *Martin and Malcolm and America*, p. 233; and Fairclough, *To Redeem the Soul of America*, pp. 367–369.

103. Washington, ed., *A Testament of Hope*, p. 320.

104. Quoted in Lerone Bennett, Jr., *What Manner of Man: A Biography of Martin Luther King, Jr.* (New York: Pocket Books, 1968), p. 145.

105. Lewis V. Baldwin, *To Make the Wounded Whole: The Cultural Legacy of Martin Luther King, Jr.* (Minneapolis: Fortress Press, 1992), p. 84. Also see the outstanding chapter "Martin Luther King, Jr.—20th

Century Prophet," in Choan-Seng Song and Gayraud Wilmore, *Asians and Blacks*, Joseph Cook Memorial Lectures, Sixth Series (Spring 1972), pp. 65–81.

106. Brown, "Grounds for American Loyalty," p. 194. When asked on one occasion if he was "a Negro political leader," King refused to answer in the negative, but noted that "my first and . . . deepest commitment" is "to my calling as a Christian minister." See King, "Doubts and Certainties Link," p. 3. For significant references to King's own reasons for not running for U.S. president or any other political office, see Martin Luther King, Jr., "Statement on the 1968 Elections," Atlanta, Georgia (25 April 1967), King Center Archives, pp. 1–2; and Martin Luther King, Jr., "Statement on the New Left and Presidential Campaign," unpublished document (10 July 1967), King Center Archives, pp. 1–2.

107. Adam Fairclough, "Was Martin Luther King a Marxist?" in David J. Garrow, ed., *Martin Luther King, Jr.: Civil Rights Leader, Theologian, Orator*, vol. 2 (Brooklyn: Carlson Publishing, 1989), p. 302.

108. Ibid., pp. 301–302.

109. Lawrence D. Reddick, *Crusader without Violence: A Biography of Martin Luther King, Jr.* (New York: Harper & Brothers, 1959), p. 233; and Fairclough, "Was Martin Luther King a Marxist?," pp. 301–302. According to Andrew Young, King represented "a socio-politico-religion which in a real sense is a fulfillment promised in the dreams of our ancestors." From Andrew J. Young to Harry Belafonte (28 February 1966), King Center Archives, p. 1.

110. King, "Freedom's Crisis: The Last Steep Ascent," p. 288.

111. King, "Civil Right No. 1," p. 25; and King, "The Negro and the American Dream," p. 2.

112. King, "Civil Right No. 1," p. 25.

113. King, *Where Do We Go from Here?*, p. 147; and King, "Civil Right No. 1," p. 25.

114. King, "The Negro and the American Dream," p. 3; From Martin Luther King, Jr. to Mr. Simeon Booker (20 October 1959), African American Collection, Amistad Research Center, Tulane University, New Orleans, Louisiana, pp. 1–2; and King, *Where Do We Go from Here?*, p. 147.

115. King wrote and spoke often about the importance of the ballot for his people. See "King Says Mississippi Can Elect Five Negro Congressmen," news release from the Southern Christian Leadership Conference, Atlanta, Georgia (8 February 1962), King Center Archives, p. 1; Martin Luther King, Jr., "Statement to the Press" (5 April 1962), King Center Archives, p. 1; Martin Luther King, Jr., "The Ballot" (17 July 1962), King Center Archives, pp. 1–3; Martin Luther King, Jr., "A Statement on

Voting," for radio station WLIB, New York City, via station WAOK, Atlanta, Georgia (6 September 1962), King Center Archives, p. 1; Martin Luther King, Jr., "The Terrible Cost of the Ballot," *Newsletter of the Southern Christian Leadership Conference*, vol. 1, no. 7 (September 1962): pp. 1–3; Martin Luther King, Jr., "More Negroes in Jail than on Voting Rolls," *New York Amsterdam News*, 27 February 1965, p. 8; and Martin Luther King, Jr., "Whose Right to Vote—Selma: The Shame and the Promise" (March 1965), King Center Archives, pp. 1–17. For King's thoughts on the various methods used to keep blacks from voting, see Martin Luther King, Jr., "New Harassment: The Lunacy Test," unpublished paper (23 June 1962), King Center Archives, pp. 1–2.

116. Martin Luther King, Jr., and Ralph D. Abernathy to the Friends of the Montgomery Improvement Association (27 November 1956), King Papers, Boston University, p. 1; Martin Luther King, Jr., "Civil Rights at the Crossroads," address to the Shop Stewards of Local 815, Teamsters and Allied Trades Council, New York, New York (2 May 1967), King Center Archives, p. 4; and King, *Where Do We Go from Here?*, pp. 148–149.

117. King had set up such a committee during his early days at Dexter Avenue Baptist Church in Montgomery (1954–1959). See Zelia S. Evans and J. T. Alexander, eds., *The Dexter Avenue Baptist Church, 1877–1977* (Montgomery, Ala.: The Dexter Avenue Baptist Church, 1978), p. 75; and Martin Luther King, Jr., "Speech Made in Savannah," Savannah, Georgia (1 January 1961), King Center Archives, p. 13.

118. King, *Where Do We Go from Here?*, pp. 154–156; and Martin Luther King, Jr., "Revolution in the Classroom," speech to the Georgia Teachers and Education Association, Atlanta, Georgia (31 May 1967), King Center Archives, pp. 1–8.

119. King, *Where Do We Go from Here?*, pp. 149–150.

120. Ibid., pp. 148–150. King appeared at times to view Congressman Adam Clayton Powell, Jr., of Harlem as an exception, though he did not express this view as adamantly and consistently as the black nationalist Malcolm X. See Washington, ed., *A Testament of Hope*, pp. 309 and 606; George Breitman, ed., *By Any Means Necessary: Speeches, Interviews and a Letter by Malcolm X* (New York: Pathfinder Press, 1970), pp. 72–73; and Steve Clark, ed., *February 1965: The Final Speeches—Malcolm X* (New York: Pathfinder Press, 1992), pp. 130–131.

121. King, *Where Do We Go from Here?*, p. 149.

122. "Black Power for Whom?," *Christian Century*, vol. 83, no. 29 (20 July 1966): pp. 903–904; and King, *Where Do We Go from Here?*, pp. 23–66. King's opposition to certain black power advocates does not mean that he opposed the concept of black power. He saw black power as "pooling

black political resources in order to achieve our legitimate goals." Clearly, he saw black power in terms of the mobilization of political and economic resources. See Washington, ed., *A Testament of Hope*, pp. 664–665; and Martin Luther King, Jr., "Speech at Operation Breadbasket Meeting," Chicago Theological Seminary, Chicago, Illinois (25 March 1967), King Center Archives, p. 4. On one occasion, King actually chided the Freedom Now Party for using his "photograph to forward its aims," noting that "I have never advocated the formation of an all Negro political party." See Martin Luther King, Jr., "A Statement of a Position on the Freedom Now Party" (30 October 1964), King Center Archives, p. 1.

123. Washington, ed., *A Testament of Hope*, pp. 665–666. One scholar perceptively contends that "the idea of a mutually dependent, even symbiotic, liberation for oppressed and oppressor is an important and unique component of King's thought and praxis." See Leila A. Meier, "The Symbiotic Relationship of Oppressed and Oppressor in the Thought of Martin Luther King, Jr.," unpublished paper, Vanderbilt University, Nashville, Tennessee (30 April 1992), pp. 1–12.

124. King, "Civil Right No. 1," p. 25.

125. See Kenneth L. Smith, "The Radicalization of Martin Luther King, Jr.: The Last Three Years," *Journal of Ecumenical Studies*, vol. 26, no. 2 (Spring 1989): pp. 270–288.

126. Washington, ed., *A Testament of Hope*, p. 666; Martin Luther King, Jr., "To Chart Our Course for the Future," address at SCLC retreat, Frogmore, South Carolina (29–31 May 1967), King Center Archives, pp. 1–2; Frank L. Morris, "A Dream Unfulfilled: The Economic and Political Policies of Martin Luther King, Jr.," in Garrow, ed., *Martin Luther King, Jr.: Civil Rights Leader, Theologian, Orator*, vol. 3, pp. 662 and 664–665; King, *Where Do We Go from Here?*, p. 150; and King, "Doubts and Certainties Link," pp. 7–8.

127. King, *Where Do We Go from Here?*, pp. 150–157; Washington, ed., *A Testament of Hope*, pp. 664–666; "Miscellaneous Interviews with Martin Luther King, Jr. Regarding *Why We Can't Wait*, Violence in Mississippi, and U.S. Elections," London, England (21 September 1964), King Center Archives, p. 2; *I Am a Man: Photographs of the 1968 Memphis Sanitation Strike and Dr. Martin Luther King, Jr.* (Memphis, Tenn.: Memphis Publishing Company, 1993), pp. 64 and 66; Martin Luther King, Jr., "The Need to Go to Washington," press conference at Ebenezer Baptist Church, Atlanta, Georgia (16 January 1968), King Center Archives, p. 6; King, "America's Chief Moral Dilemma," p. 19; King, "An Address," p. 13; and "Hugh Downs's Interview with Martin Luther King, Jr.," p. 2.

128. Morris, "A Dream Unfulfilled," pp. 665–667.

129. Hendricks, "The Domestication of Martin Luther King, Jr.," pp. 54–55. King obviously believed that political liberalism in the United States was more consistent with democratic values and the Christian ethic.

130. Morris, "A Dream Unfulfilled," pp. 665–666; King, *Why We Can't Wait*, pp. 147–151; and King, "Speech at an Operation Breadbasket Meeting," pp. 5–6.

131. Smith, "The Radicalization of Martin Luther King, Jr.," pp. 270–288; Fairclough, "Was Martin Luther King a Marxist?," pp. 301–307; and Douglas Sturm, "Martin Luther King, Jr., as Democratic Socialist," *Journal of Religious Ethics*, vol. 18, no. 2 (Fall 1990): pp. 79–103.

132. See Andrew Young, "Martin Luther King as Political Theologian," in Theodore Runyon, ed., *Theology, Politics, and Peace* (Maryknoll, N.Y.: Orbis Books, 1989), pp. 79–85.

133. Baldwin, *To Make the Wounded Whole*, p. 300.

134. King actually suggested that "Negroes may use their political power at the polls" to "defeat Congressmen who allowed the race question to sabotage one of the most cherished dreams of the Negro community— a Negro in the Federal Government at the cabinet level." See Martin Luther King, Jr., "A Statement on the Negro and the Federal Government," released to *Newsweek* (26 February 1962), King Center Archives, p. 1.

135. Quoted in Michael B. Preston et al., eds., *The New Black Politics: The Search for Political Power* (New York: Longman, 1982), p. xvii. King's friendship with Heschel is discussed in Abraham J. Heschel, *Moral Grandeur and Spiritual Audacity*, ed. Susannah Heschel (New York: Farrar Straus Giroux, 1996), pp. xxiii–xxiv.

136. See John O'Loughlin, "Racial Gerrymandering: Its Potential Impact on Black Politics in the 1980s," in Preston et al., eds., *The New Black Politics*, pp. 241–262.

137. King, *Where Do We Go from Here?*, p. 54; and Morris, "A Dream Unfulfilled," pp. 662–665.

138. See Joseph R. Washington, Jr., *Jews in Black Perspectives: A Dialogue* (Cranbury, N.J.: Associated University Presses, 1984), pp. 19–208; Jonathan Kaufman, *Broken Alliance: The Turbulent Times between Blacks and Jews in America* (New York: Simon & Schuster, 1995), pp. 1–299; Michael Lerner and Cornel West, *Jews and Blacks: Let the Healing Begin* (New York: G. P. Putnam's Sons, 1995), pp. 1–276; Jack Newfield, "Blacks and Jews: The Tragedy of Jackson, the Logic of Coalition," *Voice*, vol. 29, no. 12 (20 March 1984): pp. 1 and 13–16; Playthell Benjamin, "African Americans and Jews: A Tattered Alliance," *Emerge*, vol. 2, no. 1 (October 1990): pp. 73–78; and Cornel West, "Blacks vs. Jews: The Traps of Tribalism," *Emerge*, vol. 4, no. 5 (March 1993): pp. 42–44.

139. King spoke of politics as "the key that opens the door to economic opportunity." See Martin Luther King, Jr., "Negro Americans and Political Maturity," unpublished statement (13 February 1963), King Center Archives, pp. 1–2.

140. See Marguerite R. Barnett, "The Congressional Black Caucus: Illusions and Realities of Power," in ibid., pp. 28–53; and Robert C. Smith, *We Have No Leaders: African Americans in the Post-Civil Rights Era* (Albany: State University of New York Press, 1996), pp. 105–122.

141. This trend actually began in the 1970s, as indicated in William E. Nelson, Jr., "Cleveland: The Rise and Fall of the New Black Politics," in Preston et al., eds., *The New Black Politics*, pp. 187–205.

142. King, *Where Do We Go from Here?*, p. 154.

143. King, "The Negro and the American Dream," p. 4; and Martin Luther King, Jr., "Suggested Preamble for the Southern Christian Leadership Conference," unpublished document (n.d.), King Center Archives, pp. 1–2.

144. King, *Strength to Love*, pp. 131–132; and King, *Where Do We Go from Here?*, p. 156.

145. King, *Where Do We Go from Here?*, pp. 148–150; Alvin J. Schexnider, "Political Mobilization in the South: The Election of a Black Mayor in New Orleans," in Preston et al., eds., *The New Black Politics*, pp. 221–236; and Manning Marable, *Black American Politics from the Washington Marches to Jesse Jackson* (London: Verso, 1985), pp. 125–190.

146. Morris, "A Dream Unfulfilled," p. 662.

King, the Constitution, and the Courts

Remaining Awake through a Great Revolution

BARBARA A. HOLMES

AND SUSAN HOLMES WINFIELD

When Rip Van Winkle went up into the mountain the sign had a picture of King George III of England. When he came down twenty years later, the sign had a picture of George Washington, the first president of the United States. When Rip Van Winkle looked up at the picture of George Washington . . . he was amazed—he was completely lost—he knew not who he was. And this reveals to us that the most striking thing about the story of Rip Van Winkle is not merely that Rip slept twenty years, but that he slept through a revolution.

—Martin Luther King, Jr. [1]

This chapter focuses on the role of Martin Luther King, Jr., in reshaping American society and its jurisprudence. At a critical stage in history, King's approach to social change made abstract legal pronouncements and mystical religious principles tangible and relevant to a nation accustomed to shadowboxing with the truth. A revolution had begun. Standing at the crossroads of law, religion, and morality, King stirred the intractable bastions of racism in a manner that precipitated a shift in the national consciousness. Although he was not the first to envision an egalitarian society and the full citizenship of African Americans, King was uniquely situated to dramatize the anomalies of law, the potentialities of religion, and the shape of public morality.

King's relationship to the law and the judiciary has not received the same attention as his theology. The reasons are apparent to historians and the witnesses who remain. Mythmakers and media hagiographers who distort reality until fallen leaders are one-dimensional enough to fit on a postage stamp have convinced us that it would be sacrilege to connect King to anything other than ethereal "dream" language. Nothing could be further from the truth. To the contrary, if King's theories are to remain relevant to future generations, his political strategies and legal perspectives must also be considered in conjunction with his theological and moral precepts.

In this article, three areas of focus emerge: (1) a historical view of the American Constitution, its limitations, and King's legal perspectives on both; (2) King's higher-law values as a catalyst for legal and moral transformation; and (3) King's performative civil disobedience and the Supreme Court's response. King's utilization of dramatic street actions achieved a singular effectiveness in the historical quest for civil rights by presenting to the nation and the courts an undeniable and dignified plea for equality. The whole world was watching as demonstrators were confronted by the hideousness of hatred in its most illogical and virulent forms. When nonviolence was met by violence, observers from all camps, including legal theorists, mainline Christians, and detached jurists, were forced to reconsider the contours of justice in every realm.

This chapter analyzes the historical and legal underpinnings of twentieth-century injustice, as inherited by King. This analysis unveils a perpetual vacillation by the courts between protector and instrumentality of oppression during the periodic assaults on African American civil liberties. King was largely realistic about the courts' limitations, yet publicly and steadfastly faithful to the premises upon which the justice system stands.

The strength of King's belief in the law, his abiding faith in love as praxis, and the force of his performative acts forged crosscultural alliances and inspired even the courts to interpret the law in a manner that for a time changed the face of the nation. Ultimately, however, the untimely death of Dr. King left African Americans first shocked and then complacent. Many expected continued successes in the courts, even though those successes had come primarily in response to King's leadership and nationwide acts of civil disobedience. As the most visible signs of public segregation began to crumble, the black community began to rely, to its detriment, on the perpetual benevolence of the federal judiciary. As a consequence, it failed to develop new strategies of engagement to combat the Supreme Court's conservative pendulum shift and the culture's affirmative action backlash. After King's death, demonstrations faltered and the courts retreated.

However, King's civic vision, despite its subsequent containment, remains equally potent today. His belief in the salvific effects of love and the inherent morality of humankind offers the same quiescent ability to change hearts and minds. A fresh look at King's full spectrum of initiatives—legal, theological, and moral—may provide insights into strategies that will again advance the civil rights movement toward justice in the new millennium.

Another Great Awakening

King's "I Have a Dream Speech"[2] was a powerful and prophetic exposition of his civic vision of a flourishing and integrated future for the nation.[3] However, King's "dream" speech was not the quintessential summary of his lifework. Although he reported his rhetorical vision using dream language, he never intended these references to become the primary metaphor for his challenge to the courts and the churches. More likely than not, he would be shocked to know that at the turn of the century, we are still teaching our children that he was a "dreamer." His own words refute that characterization. In fact, the title of his last Sunday-morning sermon, just prior to the assassination, was "Remaining Awake through a Great Revolution." King knew that if the founding documents of the nation were to have any meaning, and if America was to survive its pluralism, the courts, the churches, and the moral priorities of the nation would have to undergo cataclysmic changes.

In this last sermon, King used the story of Rip Van Winkle to make the coming paradigm shift more accessible. He said of Rip's long sleep,

> While he was peacefully snoring up in the mountain a revolution was taking place that at points would change the course of history. . . . And one of the great liabilities of life is that all too many people find

themselves living amid a great period of social change and yet they fail to develop the new attitudes, the new mental responses—that the new situation demands. They end up sleeping through a revolution.[4]

King was a visionary whose activism brought the entire nation into a full awareness of its potential future. Even nonviolent revolutions require a wide-awake methodology to wrest freedom from oppression's grasp.

To fully comprehend the magnitude of the changes brought about by King's nonviolent movement, one must have an understanding of the stormy off-and-on relationship between this nation and its "darkest" citizens. We use the term "darkest" not in the descriptive sense, but to evoke racism's social and cultural obliteration of the human particularities of the African American community. In the pre-King years, even well-meaning whites had difficulty grasping the contours of black personhood. Inevitably, this murkiness was reflected in local and federal legislative and judicial proceedings. Although African Americans had access to the courts, available remedies and judicial opinions often reflected prevailing racial and cultural biases.

It took the dramatism of the civil rights movement and King's performative leadership to confront the glaring disparities that existed between America's narrative of equality, law, and justice and the stark reality of oppression. "Dramatism" should not be confused with theatricality or playacting. Kenneth Burke, an eclectic cultural analyst, inscribed the term on the culture in the 1960s. Rather, dramatism describes life as an interactive event and space where people perform assigned roles and construct a social reality.

King's activism initiated a stunning political drama. One commentator describes it as "the confrontation of a 'powerless, moral, courageous people . . . by a larger, more powerful, decadent society.'"[5] When activists took to the streets, the political, social, and identity crises that had been imposed on the black community since slavery were no longer invisible to the majority culture. In a series of peaceful confrontations, King "helped to create a national perception of a 'moral crisis' that resulted in some of the most far-reaching civil rights legislation since the Civil War."[6] The crisis had been ongoing since slavery. However, until the nation saw a reflection of its own image amid snarling dogs and water hoses, it was "peacefully snoring" on the eve of a revolution. Like an early morning wake-up call, King sounded the alarm. The nonviolent revolt had begun and it would be televised.

The first acts of resistance seemed innocuous. Ordinary black folks asked for a desk in a properly equipped classroom, a seat at a public lunch counter, a view from the front of the bus. In simple but dignified demonstrations of their exclusion, protesters presented a panoramic tableau of suffering and love-in-action. These simple, repeated public acts of nonviolence unleashed tidal waves of venom and violence. Under King's leadership, activists exposed the human tragedy endemic to segregation.

In response to this activism, courts used the rhetoric of fairness, but consistently refused to declare that black people had the fundamental right to participate fully in the American society. The failure of the courts to dismantle American apartheid left King few choices. He challenged the nation in the court of pubic opinion, and shifted jurisprudential reasoning almost one hundred eighty degrees. Ultimately, the demonstrations held a mirror to the obscenity of racism in the culture as well as in the courts. The image was more than most could bear. It was certainly more than the courts could allow. King's performative leadership broke open the wound of racism and exposed the festering historical disparities that had been encoded into the founding documents of the nation.

The Constitution: Slain in the House of Its Friends?

Frederick Douglass's words resound throughout the centuries as an indictment of the Constitution:

> I now undertake to say that neither the original Constitution nor the Constitution as amended since the War is the law of the land. That Constitution has been slain in the house of its friends. So far as the colored people of the country are concerned, the Constitution is but a stupendous sham. . . . Keeping the promise to the eye and breaking it to the heart . . . , they have promised us law and abandoned us to anarchy.[7]

In this excerpt, Douglass infers that there are aspects of the Constitution that exceed its written constraints. That which can be slain must surely still be alive: "In a word, the [C]onstitution is a plan for a way of life, and this entails an enunciation of those values that would support a certain conception of the good life, and also a certain conception of justice."[8] For King, the Constitution was alive with the intent of its founders and with the inherent potential to inspire the interpretive vitality of generations to come. Yet, "before the historic *Brown* decision, the Constitution was a document that frequently legitimated and sanctioned the second-class citizenship of African Americans."[9] As Douglass so poignantly concludes, the chasm between lofty words and ineffectual promises became a wound that would not heal.

Other founding documents suffered from a similar malady. Most people are familiar with the language of the Declaration of Independence: "We hold these truths to be self-evident, that all men are created equal. They are endowed by their Creator with certain inalienable rights and that among these are life, liberty and the pursuit of happiness."[10] At face value, these words declare that not only is the equality of men a truth, but one that is self-evidently so. Similar sentiments were written into the preamble to the Constitution, which reads in pertinent part:

> We the people, of the United States, in order to form a more perfect union, establish justice, ensure domestic tranquillity, provide for the common defense, promote the general welfare, and secure blessings of liberty to ourselves and our posterity, do ordain and establish this Constitution of the United States of America.[11]

Just who are "the people"?[12] What could be more self-evident than that "people" includes men and women, free persons and slaves, natives and immigrants? The political reality, however, was that neither Native Americans nor women were allowed to participate in the affairs of the Union. Slaves were compromised to count as only fractions of human beings with no rights at all.[13] What of free black men? Most of us assume that the framers of the Constitution made their intentions shamefully clear, intending to include all persons of color in the fractional calculation. Unfortunately, many African Americans were and are too offended by the express language of the Constitution to explore the unspoken intentions of the drafters concerning the rights of free black persons.

Justice Benjamin R. Curtis of the Supreme Court, however, brilliantly argued what we ignore. In a seldom-quoted dissenting opinion in the infamous *Dred Scott v. Sandford* decision (1857), his logic is compelling.[14] According to Curtis, the new federal government was the anticipated product of a confederation of states whose intention was to consolidate their territories for protection against an outside oppressor while maintaining maximum autonomy within their borders. These states had already made independent determinations as to who were their voting citizens entitled to the privileges and immunities of the state governments. Among these were five states—New Hampshire, Massachusetts, New York, New Jersey, and North Carolina—which had already granted the right to vote in state government affairs to all free males, including free Negroes.

It is undisputed that the original states did not intend to relinquish any states' rights of their citizens to the federal government,[15] and it is equally clear that the citizens of the states intended that the acquisition of federal citizenship would be self-actualized upon the adoption and ratification of the Constitution. This is the irony. As white male drafters of the Constitution were busily compromising and redacting the rights of slaves, Native Americans, and women from federal citizenship, the voting citizens of the original states, including free black men, were automatically acquiring those same benefits. Moreover, they were voting to ratify the Constitution and establish the union.[16] By its silence, the Constitution bestowed upon all free voters, black and white, equal rights of federal citizenship.

Few would disagree that the quest for justice was derailed when the founders ignored the presence of free black citizens and attempted to protect the institution of slavery. Yet, the express language of the founding documents held promise for potentially transformative interpretations. King recognized this potential and was willing to hold America to those promises. In a salient statement about the Declaration of Independence, he described civil rights protesters not only as heirs, but also as the symbolic progeny of the nation's founders, living out their best hopes of freedom. In this regard he said,

> One hundred eighty-four years ago a bold group of men signed the Declaration of Independence. If their struggle had been lost they had signed their own death warrant. Nevertheless, though explicitly regretting that King George had forced them to this extreme by a long "train of abuses," they resolutely acted and a great new society was born. The Negro students, their parents, and their allies are acting today in that imperishable tradition.[17]

King's critics point to statements of this type as examples of his inability to perceive the inherent malevolence of the system. They argue that even before the ink had dried on any of the originating documents, the framers knew that the "truths" were neither self-evident nor true. At a later date, King readily admitted that racism and colonialism were not the missteps of a just and righteous nation; rather, they were examples of evil systems operating exactly as they were intended to operate.[18] However, he refused to abandon a basic belief in the God-given affinity of humans, one for another, or in the redemptive potential of people, nations, and even founding documents. This incurable faith and hope owed much to his cultural roots, especially the black church.

In recent years, the retreat of the Supreme Court on issues of race and the reentrenchment of violent forces in the culture (church burnings are just one example) have brought King's moral assumptions and practices into question. It seems almost naive in retrospect to hear his attestations of reliance on the founding documents of the nation. Yet it was this reliance that obliterated decades of degradation. King accomplished this Herculean task by anchoring his civil rights activism to the entitlements of the Constitution and the Declaration of Independence. Such rhetorical boldness announced that neither local traditions nor ad hoc legal interpretations would define the African American community. Instead, the creedal language of the founding documents would suffice to define us all.

King's strategies were drawn from many resources. Among other influences, Swedish economist Gunnar Myrdal's two-volume treatise on race helped to shape King's thinking. King agreed with Myrdal that "the moral distance between creed (all men are created equal) and deed (segregation) created a dissonance, or what King called 'tension,' that could be resolved only by progressively moving toward an extension of human rights."[19] Nonviolence was a tactic that accomplished this end and ensured that the moral advantage would remain with the besieged community. Nonviolence also put segregationists on the defensive, both morally and intellectually. "Thus paralyzed, the white man's laws could be changed, and once changed, the heart would follow. It was a formula that offered hope and encouraged suffering and ultimately the love of one's enemy."[20] Ultimately, such strategies would shatter the cocoon of denial that many Americans used to justify the status quo. Segregation had done its job. It shielded the nation from the horror of its abuse of African Americans. Now, King's prayerful drama would unveil the night riders, challenge the laws, and press the courts and legislatures into action.

Derailing the Train of Abuses: King and the Law

When lofty language in founding documents fails, societies rely on systems of laws that obligate, proscribe, and protect. In the United States, a country of competing interests and conflicting rights, the courts emerged early on as the centrifugal force around which the remaining two branches of government and the citizenry would revolve.[21] The courts, particularly the Supreme Court, arrogated to themselves the role of arbiter of the authority of federal, state, and local governments. Over time, the Supreme Court became the bastion of original intent, declaring who really was created equal and who was entitled to enjoy freedom and the privileges of citizenship. Because of the immutable hierarchy of the judicial and legal construct, lower-court judges and the entire bar of lawyers nationwide were constrained to embrace the law as ordained by nine white male justices without regard to their often transparent race, class, and gender biases. When King arrived on the political scene, the growing gap between high-court rhetoric and local civic realities had reached a critical point.

Notwithstanding the routine and pernicious deprivations of civil liberties and inconsistent applications of the law, African Americans never abandoned the option of judicial intervention to redress their grievances. The courts were by definition available to hear the claims of the individual, including the black claimant. By default, the courts became the primary venue of formal protest for black Americans. Unlike the other branches of government, the courts could not easily deprive black people of their rights without having to make some effort to explain the reasoning of their decisions and the consistency of that reasoning with controlling precedents. The legal principle of *stare decisis*,[22] the Holy Grail of legal analysis and reasoning, requires courts to act consistent with, and in conformity to, decisions made in earlier cases. As a result, Supreme Court justices must take care that a decision involving the rights of a black person not be made with such indifference as to negatively impact the future claims of a white person. Despite its power, the majority culture could ill afford a racially "appropriate" but universally damaging precedent. The Court is compelled to consider the many, while deciding the issues of the few. In theory, then, the rule of *stare decisis* became an important ally in each civil rights case.

Unfortunately, some of the cases brought by African Americans were unique to their social status and experiences as functional non-citizens. These cases presented clearer opportunities for the courts to make decisions that could be restricted to black people with little or no impact on white Americans. In many such instances, the Supreme Court has reacted by shaming itself and besmirching the legal history of this country. Under the guise of applying only the framers' intent, the Supreme Court issued several pronouncements that continue to shock and embarrass entering classes of first-year law students.

In one of the more notorious of these cases, Dred Scott, a slave, sued to be declared a free man after he lived for two years (with his slave master) on a federal army base that had barred slavery.[23] The Supreme Court, through Chief Justice Roger B. Taney, held that all Negroes (including free, voting black persons)[24] "were so far inferior, that they had no rights which the white man was bound to respect."[25] In so concluding, Taney, with a stroke of his pen, obliterated the rights of black persons to U.S. citizenship, relegated them to "less than human" status, and ensconced himself in historical ignominy.[26] His justification was that the Court was constrained by the constitutional interpretive process. Taney declared:

> It is not the province of the court to decide upon the justice or injustice, the policy or impolicy, of these laws. The decision of that question belonged to the political or law-making power; to those who formed the sovereignty and framed the Constitution. The duty of the court is to interpret the instrument they have framed, with the best lights we can obtain on the subject, and to administer it as we find it, according to its true intent and meaning when it was adopted.[27]

Of *Dred Scott,* King remarked,

> The famous *Dred Scott* decision of 1857 well illustrates the status of the Negro during slavery. In this decision the Supreme Court of

the United States said in substance that the Negro is not a citizen of the United States, he is merely property subject to the dictates of his owner.[28]

Defenders of the Supreme Court did not agree with King's assessment. They argued that in matters of constitutional interpretation, the Court is not free to declare its own view of how a case should be decided. This would inevitably lead to unacceptable inconsistencies as the persons appointed to the Court change over the years. Instead, the Court is faced with competing concepts of constitutional analysis: whether to glean and remain faithful to the intentions of the original authors or to evaluate the document, not as a statement of intentions, but as a broad statement of purpose and goals. The former approach requires one to study the persons who were individually responsible for the words and phrases and to do no more than those persons appear to have envisioned originally. The other requires the current Court to study the Constitution as a document in the context of its history and current events and discern from those contributing factors what the words and phrases seem to permit.[29] Justices still struggle with these interpretive approaches.[30]

Black litigants confronted the vagaries of the law often with the assistance of black lawyers. Trained in historically black and often segregated law schools, minority attorneys frequently dedicated their careers to the cause of equal rights and justice.[31] In fact, all of the cases heard by the Supreme Court between 1923 and 1940 that involved civil rights issues included at least one black lawyer on the team.[32] At the turn of the twentieth century, the National Association for the Advancement of Colored People (NAACP) provided a supportive environment for lawyers to pool their talents and resources in the quest for justice.

In some instances, minority lawyers were joined by white lawyers who, like abolitionists and social protesters before them, could not or would not ignore the chasm over which self-evident truth had been suspended. These specially skilled lawyers were available to assist victims of discrimination and to effectively navigate the maze of legal obstacles. Although King recognized and appreciated the talents of lawyers who supported minority causes, he opined that they were merely tapping into a deep wellspring of justice, righteousness, and morality that permeates the very fabric of the universe.

King's engagement with the courts was set against the historical backdrop of constitutional amendments and the case law that construes their meaning. A brief review of the Supreme Court opinions from *Dred Scott* to *Brown v. Board of Education* (1954) reveals the high court's alternating cycles of myopia and insightfulness when confronted with liberation cases and controversies. Given this pattern, it should have been apparent that the judiciary could not provide a permanent respite from racism.

After the Civil War, the Thirteenth, Fourteenth,[33] and Fifteenth Amendments essentially overruled Taney's decision in *Dred Scott*. Nonetheless, the Supreme Court initially found reasons to limit the effect of these protections. In two well-known cases, the Court severely restricted the effect of the entire Thirteenth Amendment (banning slavery) as well as the privileges and immunities clause and the equal protection clause of the Fourteenth Amendment.[34] The Court held that the Thirteenth and Fourteenth Amendments proscribed only acts of discrimination that were either "badge[s] of slavery" or actions taken "under color of state law." Private acts were neither. Thus, the Supreme Court held that Congress could not constitutionally interdict the acts of private persons. Private violence and segregation were thereby immunized from Court sanctions and moved beyond the ongoing constitutional discourse.

In a similar stance, the Court decided a case that devastated the movement toward equality and freedom for persons of color in this country. In *Plessy v. Ferguson* (1896),[35] the Court proclaimed the "separate but equal doctrine." In so doing, the Supreme Court gave its imprimatur to Jim Crow[36] laws and put shared public accommodations beyond the enjoyment of black Americans for decades. Speaking for the Court and ignoring the patent inequality of segregated facilities, Justice Henry B. Brown wrote:

> Legislation is powerless to eradicate racial instincts or to abolish distinctions based upon physical differences, and the attempt to do so can only result in accentuating the difficulties of the present situation. If the civil and political rights of both races be equal, one cannot be inferior to the other civilly or politically. If one race be inferior to the other socially, the Constitution of the United States cannot put them upon the same plane (Id. 163 U.S. at 551).

By contrast, King stated this of *Plessy:*

> The enforcement of this *Plessy* doctrine ended up making for tragic inequality and ungodly exploitation. There was a strict enforcement of the "separate" with not the slightest intention to abide by the "equal." So the old *Plessy* doctrine ended up plunging the Negro across the abyss of exploitation where he experienced the bleakness of nagging justice.[37]

King argued further that even if external equalities were afforded, this would not suffice so long as hearts and minds remained unchanged. Under the separate but equal doctrine, the Supreme Court protected racially segregated schools, restaurants, street- and railcars, hotels, elevators, sport facilities, public parks, and even some fishing holes. Either the justices failed to inform themselves of how unequal the separate facilities were or they intentionally exalted rhetoric over reality. Either way, the Court was guilty of perpetrating a premeditated fiction upon the people who persisted in their belief in the supremacy of the law over social evil.

The separate but equal doctrine was reaffirmed in a number of cases over the next fifty years, notwithstanding its patent flaws.[38] In some of the cases, the doctrine was maintained even in the face of nonexistent facilities for blacks.[39] In *Cumming v. Richmond Co. Board of Education* (1899), the Court concluded that the separation of facilities at the outset was proper and that the financial "need" to close a "colored" facility, but not a white one, was a rational exercise of civic governance. The Court further held that there was no recognizable right of the beneficiaries of the closed facility to enjoy the only open one(s), even though the facility in question was a local high school.

Although the courts continued to be available to minorities, they were consistently unavailing. Each of the Supreme Court decisions that perpetuated segregation and discrimination thickened the fog, obscuring the truth—that there remained a treacherous breach between the words on the constitutional page and the acts of its interpreters. During these bleak years of Supreme Court decision making, the black bar struggled to regain lost ground, while the majority of the legal community conceptually endorsed the opinions and tried to justify and apply the Court's reasoning.

In retrospect, the only reasonable response to unjust laws is resistance. Yet, taken in context, King deemed civil rights issues to be issues of the heart and spirit. Judges and lawyers were accustomed to intellectual and legalistic issues bandied about in sterile courtrooms. Few white lawyers and judges witnessed crying black women removing their "forbidden fruit" from the lynching trees. Few experienced first-hand the pangs of hunger, thirst, and fatigue that had to be accommodated long enough to find available public facilities. Few had to struggle to educate their children in schools with little or no funding. As such, the plight of black people remained safely abstract to most lawyers and judges, who remained unaccountable for their lack of compassion.[40]

After the turn of the century, the political and social landscape began to change for African Americans.[41] African Americans participated in two world wars and afterwards found increased opportunities and jobs in the North. The demand for more freedom and respect could not be ignored. With these demands came more responsiveness on the part of the Supreme Court. As the Court lumbered toward fairness, few foresaw the dangers that lay ahead for the country as a whole. For the time being, there was much to celebrate. The Supreme Court invalidated "grandfather" clauses,[42] desegregated voting primaries,[43] and began to forecast the coming *Brown v. Board of Education* decision[44] by determining that separate education was more and more patently unequal.[45]

Finally, in 1954, the doctrine of "separate but equal" came crumbling down in the *Brown* case. Reminiscent of the words of Frederick Douglass, the Court declared that segregation of black children on the basis of race "may affect their hearts and minds in a way unlikely ever to be undone." The Court concluded that the "separate but equal" doctrine was no longer defensible because when viewed in the context of race relations, separate accommodations are inherently unequal.

What could go wrong on this journey toward justice? The highest court in the land declares over and again that segregation is a dead letter in the South and throughout the country. Blacks achieve one court victory after another and are finally recognized as equal members of the wider community. But something did go very wrong. There was a cataclysmic white backlash and a powerful conservative paranoia that gripped the country both in the North and the South.[46] Boldly and fervently, the South made a last-gasp attempt to save its "heritage" against the encroachment of equal rights and integration.

The *Brown* decision presaged a tidal wave of violence. The Ku Klux Klan began riding more frequently at night. Black homes and churches were bombed.[47] Eugene "Bull" Connor led a particularly violent and repressive response to civil rights demands. In Mississippi, Governor Ross Barnett defied an injunction ordering him to permit James Meredith to enroll at the University of Mississippi, and racists murdered and mutilated fourteen-year-old Emmett Till.

Victory became the catalyst for violence and African Americans turned in mass to their churches for solace. Since slavery, the black church had been the microcosmic black "government" in which "citizen" church members could hold office, wield power, redress social grievances, and receive protection and guidance. The church gave hope and comfort, and validated the worth of its members. Within its safety, congregations were being prepared for freedom through the biblical narratives of deliverance.

At this moment in history, Martin Luther King, Jr., arrived. He was a man of the church and therefore understood the place to which his people had withdrawn. He also had a deep appreciation for the role of the courts in securing basic civil liberties. Poised at the intersection of religion, morality, and the law, King ignited combustible but seemingly unrelated events and players. Professors Ronald Collins and David Skover describe King's emergence in the public sphere as "an emerg[ing] human voice, the proper name, the local drama."[48] Speaking about King, the playwright James Baldwin observed:

> [King] has succeeded in a way no Negro before him has managed to do, to carry the battle into the individual heart and make its resolution the province of the individual will. He has made it a matter, on both sides of the racial fence of self-examination. [49]

Clearly, Baldwin agreed with Douglass that although the rhetoric is law and order, the real issue is the struggle for the hearts and minds of both the powerful and the powerless. King sought a closer alignment of the spirit and a rhetoric of liberation. Accordingly, he extended his activism from the streets to the courts, to legislative and executive

branches of government, where he found unexpected allies. Yet he reserved his deep regard, trust, and praise for the federal courts:

> So far only the judicial branch of the government has evinced this
> quality of leadership. If the executive and legislative branches of
> the government were as concerned about the protection of our
> citizenship rights as the federal courts have been, then the transi-
> tion from a segregated to an integrated society would be infinitely
> smoother.[50]

King viewed the federal courts as champions of the rights of the
individual and credited the courts and judges with good intentions. In
glowing terms, he spoke of how "the majesty of federal law must assert
its supremacy over the reign of evil and illegality dominating defiant
southern communities."[51] A realist, nonetheless, King understood that
the court had a very limited ability to maintain social change once
opinions were pronounced:

> Legislation and court orders tend only to declare rights; they can
> never thoroughly deliver them. . . . A catalyst is needed to breathe
> life experience into a judicial decision by the persistent exercise
> of the rights until they become usual and ordinary in human con-
> tact.[52]

Through his public demonstrations, King became the catalyst that infused new life into judicial edicts. Because the civil rights move ment
drew resources from religion and law, King presented stunning
new options that allowed justices to begin to write a different story, to
tell truer truths. These truths would challenge comfortable assumptions about both law and religion. While the law preferred to remain
dispassionate and intellectual, and religion preferred to remain spiritual and emotional, King acknowledged that law and religion have
always been historically intertwined and interdependent. He declared
that they are not divergent realms; rather, they are coterminus parts of
a moral order and a fulfillment of the original premises of the Constitution.

As history recounts, King declared the efficacy of love gleaned
from Christian principles, manifested in law, and made practical

through morality. In so doing, he crystallized the issues that had plagued the nation for decades. King knew that freedom could not be fully implemented by the courts. Freedom will have meaning when unconditional love, demonstrated under the most harrowing of circumstances, has its way with us.

"What's Love Got to Do with It?": King's Higher Law

Martin Luther King, Jr., asserted that "man-made laws assure justice, but a higher law produces love."[53] Here King was clearly distiguishing between the legal structures that humans create and often sustain and the moral laws of God. This distinction proved enormously important to him as he developed a beloved community ideal that embraced people across the boundaries of race, class, and nationality.

One might ask, as songstress Tina Turner did, "What's Love Got to Do with It?" What has love to do with slavery, Jim Crow, apartheid, or ethnic cleansing? Love preaches well and in some economies, love even sells well. But can one rely upon it during extreme historical circumstances? When we are confronted by the infrastructures of malignant social systems, love seems frail at best and irrelevant at worst. Yet, the lessons of history teach just the opposite. In defiance of our logic, love has sustained whole communities. With nothing more than love, besieged people confront radical evil, endure losses, bury their dead, and console each other during and after the devastation.

Are we talking about the same phenomenon? Tina called it a "secondhand emotion." We combat the impulse to agree with her by explaining agape in a New Testament context. King went further and asserted that agape love is a foundational principle for social change.[54] When King emerged on the public scene, his theory of love tackled a virulent opponent. A nation that incorporated God into its founding documents, its money, and its pledge of allegiance ignored the commandments of that same God with regard to the treatment of fellow human beings. Moreover, America inculcated into its civic myths and personal narratives a mantra of liberty and justice that refused to recognize the gaps between rhetoric and performance.

King was boxed in. Had he approached the problem of denial of rights on an intellectual or legal basis, the response would have been

intellectual and legal resistance. Had he approached the problem theologically, he would have been snared by the national paranoia over
the separation of church and state. King chose the option of perform-
ing higher-law principles in the public sphere:

> I have also decided to stick to love. . . . I'm not talking about emo-
> tional bosh. I'm talking about a strong demanding love. And I
> have seen too much hate. . . . I know that it does something to
> [segregationists'] faces and their personalities. And I say to myself
> that hate is too great a burden to bear. I have decided to love.[55]

He explained his use of the word "love" as an agape action based
more on faith and will than on emotion or sentiment. In King's words,
it is "not even an affection sort of thing."[56] For King, love is synonymous with ethics. It is a moral principle that provides context, norms,
rules of engagement, and a vision of moral flourishing.[57] The love that
King offered as a tool to pry open the doors of opportunity is sensitive
and selfless.

King's concept of love as method and as integrating civic force
can be attributed in large part to his experiences in the black church.
In the common vernacular, love is often deemed to be an uncritical
and emotional human marker. King held no such opinion. Early on,
he viewed emotionalism and scriptural literalism with a critical eye.[58]
However, this thoughtful critique of his own tradition did not erode
King's love for the black church or his family's Baptist legacy. Historian Paul Johnson credits King's Baptist upbringing with the "pioneering exponents of a distinctively African-American version of
social gospel Christianity."[59]

An African American version of the social gospel must account for
communal crisis and survivalism. Its historical responses to an often
chaotic social milieu are rooted in a prophetic pragmatism and agape
love. Survival requires synthesis. One could never hold to radically resolute positions in a society that wields power in erratic and unpre-
dictable ways. Under those circumstances, malleable perspectives and
flexible psyches are the mark of health. In the tradition of the Hebrew
Bible, besieged communities looked "to the hills from whence came
their help," and then responded to unexpected situations with prayer
and resolute action.

King's higher-law values were steeped in the ethos of the black community. Most of the ethics that guided his theological formation are evinced from practical experience and local traditions. He expressed this mix of advanced theological training and "mother wit" in the traditional black homiletical style that renders Christian texts accessible to every member of the congregation regardless of their education.

King's values deemed service to God and one another worthier than economic wealth or personal gain. The recent consumer lust that has ravaged the black community stands in direct opposition to his prescient warning: "If we are to go forward, if we are to make this a better world in which to live, we've got to go back. We've got to rediscover these precious values that we've left behind."[60] King was urging a theological and narrative recovery of the historical memory of a resilient people. Recovery always dares the myth of liberal progression to pause for a moment of reflexivity—that is to say, a moment to dialogue with and incorporate the past into the nuances of the future. King believed that the future is love.

To speak of higher-law values in terms of love sometimes reduces the concept to the constraints of the human imagination, or worse. Those who now argue that King's love methodology was an accommodationist capitulation to renegade social forces miss the point. Higher values cannot be reduced to a self-righteous subtext for individual earthly pursuits or desires. Rather, higher-law values, as King envisioned them, propose the practical implementation of ideal moral attributes that are efficacious for the entire community.[61] These values also act as uncomfortable restraints on human egotism and pride. One cannot claim to be operating with higher-law values unless a constant self-critique is part of the process. Can we actually love our neighbors as ourselves? If we ever achieve full justice in American society, can we be just to others? The questions overwhelm us.

And yet, one need not wrestle with the demons of injustice when love can contend for itself. King knew that love is never captive to human shortcomings, but instead prevails in unlikely ways under unexpected circumstances. King opined that love had a voice that had to be heard and witnessed in public. He also believed that peaceful demonstrations were, in fact, love speaking to the nation. The opportunity for the nation to answer in kind was always available. However,

King did not defer his acts of conscience out of fear that they might evoke an evil response. Instead, he urged the nation to look and listen at the embodiment of love and commitment. He said, "Justice is what love sounds like when it speaks in public. Civic piety is love's public language, equality its tone of voice, and freedom its constant pitch."[62]

Within the context of the civil rights movement, love's reach far exceeded the maudlin self-conscious altruism of which King is sometimes accused. To the contrary, he was aware that love as a tool of liberation and reconciliation will induce a cultural crisis. Of love as methodology, King observed, "The purpose of our direct-action program is to create a situation so crisis-packed that it will inevitably open the door to negotiation."[63]

A nonviolence that inevitably elicited violence did not "sit well" with some members of the judiciary. They did not agree with King's street action protests, and argued that only the law provides society with a sturdy shelter against the storms of the self-righteous.[64] One judge from the Criminal Court of New York City predicted that "[l]aw-breaking in civil rights demonstrations will result in anarchy."[65] King responded to all detractors with the famous statement that "an unjust law is no law at all."[66]

A number of classical philosophical and theological threads were also interwoven into King's methodology. Notwithstanding these well-tested referents, the choice of higher-law principles as the core of civil disobedience is surprising given the historical circumstances. A culture that elevates violence to a fine art is not usually the best medium within which to test the Christian principles of agape love. No one can imagine that Jews in concentration camps or slaves on whipping posts could have, by their love of the oppressor, changed their immediate situations significantly. Even the most dedicated advocates of nonviolence must admit that, in some situations, radical evil eludes all avenues other than divine intervention. However, King's ideology presents the daunting prospect of loving an enemy toward fairness and reconciliation as the only option.

In one line of the song that frames this discussion, Tina Turner asks, "Who needs a heart when a heart can be broken?" King knew that love crucified, but not broken, was the only model that could redeem the dignity of those who sought freedom and those who conspired to deny it. King was grieved by this reality, but could not let the probability of his own death or the deaths of others forestall change. He confronted a violent culture with prophetic words, concerted action, and optimism. Moreover, he insisted that the rhetoric of Christianity embedded in constitutional language was indicative of an internalized national conscience that was still inclined toward God and was therefore redeemable.

King's higher-law values succeeded on several levels. He required that African Americans translate the human dignity that had been affirmed in their churches into a secular context:

> The Negro must boldly throw off the manacles of self-abnegation and say to himself in the world, "I am somebody. I am a person. I am a man [woman] with dignity and honor. I have a rich and noble history, however painful and exploited that history has been."[67]

Although false humility dictates otherwise, the first act of love is toward self. This is an uncomfortable private proposition and an even more problematic public strategy. Those emerging from "invisibility" weren't quite sure about self-love. What would it look like? How would it sound? King proposed that Christians embrace the unlovable self and the unlovable neighbor. Such acts in their simplicity and boldness forecast the advent of a new civic order.

Notwithstanding its occasional losses, this love that King relied on is not a pushover. It is not narcissism writ large, but an embrace of God's embodied image reflected in the mirror. Love insists on dignity, but is willing to absorb rather than inflict abuse. In the African American preaching tradition, the prayer that precedes a sermon often ends with a phrase that expresses the earnest desire, "We would see Jesus." Higher-law values would urge the listeners to turn to the left and right and catch a glimpse of divinity in the eyes of the other. Such practices make retaliation and retribution impossible.

To language analysts, every "discourse bears within itself the anonymous and repressed actuality of highly particular arrangements of power and knowledge."[68] The discourse of love is not different. However, it confounds the deconstructionists and "power" police because its power is gleaned from the inverted principles of bottom-up liberation Christology. "Like a telescope, language allows us to peer out into the universe of the divine, but we can see only as much as our telescope can contain."[69] King challenged the nation to try mutual love as a pragmatic and expansive solution to the issue of race relations.

King's higher-law values also challenged the theory articulated by W. E. B. DuBois that double consciousness separated the public and private lives of black people.[70] DuBois referred to a survival technique that required blacks to present varied facades in public life so as not to exacerbate the fears or potential violence of the white majority. Such survival techniques kept black personhood out of public view. King offered to present, in a public way, the dignity that black folks already held privately in their close communities and sacred rituals. Without presenting theological treatises or legal arguments against unjust legislation, King engaged the willingness of the black community to absorb palpable abuse as an act of radical love and obedience to the higher laws of God's order. Inevitably, these acts would impact upon secular laws.

King's call to love was not synonymous with a call to arms. For the call to love is a reflective activity in its first stage. Those who responded, regardless of race, had to reconsider personal moral perspectives and the theological precepts that informed their lives. Although it is not immediately apparent, there is a connection between self-reflection and changed laws. Laws reflect the delegated authority and transcribed preferences of the governed. Moreover, laws constitute a microcosm of the social order and a repository of past wisdom gleaned from solved problems. A crisis in the social order is precipitated when the values of the people are no longer reflected in the laws that govern them. King's call to love challenged the laws that supported the antithesis of love. Once the challenge was issued, and the national process of self-reflection began, the shift toward justice was inevitable.

Legal scholar David Luban suggests that "the real theology required by King is not a biblical or even Socratic doctrine of conscience, but rather an understanding of the essentially redemptive character of political action itself."[71] Luban is correct to the extent that this political action has a guiding ethics. King's guiding ethics, his religious, moral, and legal inclinations, were subsumed in the mandate to love. For him, love expressed in civil disobedience was more than a "secondhand emotion," it constituted an objective moral standard.[72] As scholar Anthony Cook writes:

> What then are the guiding principles of love for those living in community? The answer requires an understanding of the overlapping duties to God, to oneself and to others in the community.[73]

King saw what the nation and the courts could not. The condition that defines human existence is influenced by, but not limited to, categories of race, sex, class, and gender. Rather, we are overlapping people in an overlapping universe of multiple realities, constrained to see the bigger picture through a limited lens. What's love got to do with it? If King had been asked, he might have answered, "Everything!"

"Who Can Say What Discord Lies Ahead?"

Martin Luther King, Jr., once wrote: "Nonviolent direct action seeks to create such a crisis and establish such creative tension that a community that has constantly refused to negotiate is forced to confront the issue. It seeks so to dramatize the issue that it can no longer be ignored."[74] This assertion, influenced heavily by Socrates, Heraclitus, and Hegel, reflected King's deeper conviction that change ultimately results from a continuous conflict between the forces of progression and the forces of retrogression.

King's civil disobedience initiatives confronted a nation that had not discerned "the signs of the times." Though the resolve of activists was clear, legal and political structures recoiled at the moral insurgency and at the threat to the authority of the majority. The threats were intensified by the symbolic power of the marches and civil disobedience initiatives.

The courts took particular exception to civil rights demonstrations. Perhaps this resistance was rooted in their implicit understanding that law often functions to protect the interests of the ruling class and to curtail social behavior that threatens the status quo.[75] Our national love affair with egalitarian principles makes us recoil from such assertions, yet they are proven in history. This is the language of the court:

> Is there any wonder . . . that there have been riots and expanding
> lawlessness? And who can say what discord lies ahead? . . . Can we
> reasonably expect throngs in the street to understand and observe
> subtle differences between peace protest, disorderly conduct, and
> mob violence?[76]

Here, Lewis Powell, soon to be appointed to the Supreme Court,
expressed its skepticism about the ability of street activists to distinguish peaceful resistance from mob action, when in fact, distinctions
were being made on a daily basis under crisis conditions. The entire
civil rights movement was undergirded by the willingness of participants to adhere to the tenets of nonviolence. Distinctions were also
being made by the entire nation. They could see for themselves the
disparities between the discourse of freedom and the debasement of
subjugated lives.

King knew that the power of dramatic enactments would affect
the culture on several levels—it would reveal injustice and point to
the transcendent possibilities of mutuality and common goals. Demonstrations at lunch counters and bus boycotts were always more than
the piecemeal effort to be accepted by the majority culture. Rather,
the stirrings of this movement brought constitutional and sacred precepts to life. This was rhetorical performance at its best. As Mark De-
Forrest observes:

> Civil disobedience has certain utilitarian benefits in society. It
> serves to reinforce the dignity of the human person by pointing to
> the inviolability of the individual conscience. . . . [It] also serves to
> reinforce a limited view of governmental power by pointing to a
> standard above the positive law by which the acts of government
> can be judged.[77]

King studied philosophers, theologians, and historians, and understood, as did Erasmus, that human life is "a continuous performance
in which all go about wearing different masks in which everyone acts a
part assigned to him [her] until the stage director removes him [her]
from the boards."[78] King credited Thoreau's essay on civil disobedience as the motivator of his performative acts and the inspiration for
a "legacy of creative protest." He commented:

During my early college days I read Thoreau's essay on civil dis-obedience for the first time. Fascinated by the idea of refusing to cooperate with an evil system, I was so deeply moved that I re-read the work several times. [79]

King added: "Whether expressed in a sit-in at lunch counters, a freedom ride into Mississippi, a peaceful protest in Albany, Georgia, a bus boycott in Montgomery, Alabama, it is an outgrowth of Thoreau's insistence that evil must be resisted."[80] What better means of resist-ance than the dramatic rituals, songs, and music of the black church? King led black church folk who were ready to translate their rituals and music into the reality and praxis of freedom. Their message was clear. The incongruity of their lives would no longer be tolerated.

The discourse of rhetorical performance is one with which both law and religion are familiar, for as Harold Berman said, "We must see our highest expectations enacted before our eyes in order for us to incorporate it into our belief systems."[81] Litigation is acted out in courtrooms. We accept the outcome of institutional decision making because we have seen the claims of power displayed. Once depicted, these events become an integral part of our existence.[82] Likewise, in any church or religious gathering, the rituals and liturgy offer the ad-herents of faith a tangible grasp of the Christian narrative so as to contextualize the mystical tenets of the faith. Civil disobedience was the quintessential dramatization of the potential of the Constitution, the failures of the civil order, and the fulfillment of public morality. For King,

> the non-violent strategy has been to dramatize the evils of our so-ciety in such a way that pressure is brought to bear against those evils by the forces of good will in the community and change is produced. The student sit-ins of 1960 are a classic illustration of this method.[83]

Yet, King also expressed reservations that wholesale reliance on the courts might breed passivity. He noted:

> When legal contests were the sole form of activity the ordinary Negro was involved as a passive spectator. His interests were stirred, but his energies were unemployed.[84]

Civil disobedience actions fully stirred the passions of the world and the energies of the African American community by starkly contrasting innocence with brutality, peaceful protest with lawlessness, and obscenity with morality. No one could turn away from the television screens or the photographs in the newspapers. Yet no one could bear to watch. King brought thousands of adults at first, and later children, to be arrested for singing freedom songs and praying while walking peacefully. The response of the political powers was to use water cannons and police dogs to attack protesters. As President Kennedy remarked, "it was sickening."[85]

Despite the riveting events occurring on the streets of the South, the Supreme Court clung to its view of the primacy of the law over the moral appeal of the petitioners. In a pivotal moment of the civil rights movement, Martin Luther King planned a large demonstration in Birmingham during the Lent/Easter season in 1963. He had been repeatedly denied a permit to march, which was a requirement of a local ordinance. Nonetheless, he and the demonstrators marched and were arrested for violating the local law. After King's release, another march was planned. Days before, however, local authorities sought and obtained a federal court injunction ordering King to refrain from marching.

King was faced with a profound dilemma: to obey the federal courts that he deeply respected and risk losing momentum in the movement, or disobey the law and seemingly lose the high moral ground. After studiously assessing his options and his beliefs, King decided to march anyway, submit himself to the arrest that would surely follow, and accept whatever punishment was meted out. King's decision to disobey unjust laws was made out of a deep respect for the legal system:

> In no sense do I advocate evading or defying the law, as would the rabid segregationist. That would lead to anarchy. One who breaks an unjust law must do so openly, lovingly, and with a willingness to accept the penalty. I submit that an individual who breaks a law that conscience tells him is unjust, and who willingly accepts the penalty of imprisonment in order to arouse the conscience of the community over its injustice, is in reality expressing the highest respect for the law.[86]

While King was grappling with the balance of law and faith, the Supreme Court was cleaving to a principle of law that guaranteed his conviction and sentence.[87] The "collateral bar" rule provides that a facially valid ordinance may not be challenged in court after an injunction requiring obedience of the ordinance has been violated. Before a challenge may be made to a law that is the subject of an injunction, the injunction must first be obeyed. The only challenge that may properly be lodged against a disobeyed injunction is to the jurisdiction of the issuing court.[88] The theory is that one who disobeys the injunction, even if it validates a patently unjust law, is in contempt of court and may therefore not be heard to challenge the validity of the underlying ordinance.

Thus, King had the option of either obeying the injunction and retaining the right to file a legal challenge to the ordinance or disobeying the injunction and foregoing any legal challenge after his arrest. As it happened, King's time spent in jail provided him with the opportunity to ponder his internal conflict between respect for the law and a determination to be equal under it.[89]

As King accepted an arrest and jail term in Birmingham, thousands of child demonstrators participated in the demonstrations on the "front lines" for the first time. When Bull Connor attacked the children with the same arsenal with which he had assailed the adults, King's supporters and the Supreme Court recoiled in fear, doubting the wisdom of the sacrifice. In particular, the Court expressed its concern about the ability of the movement to repeatedly meet mounting violence with nonviolence. In *Cox v. Louisiana, supra* (1965), Justices Arthur J. Goldberg, Tom C. Clark, and Hugo Black expressed concerns about where the demonstrations might lead. Even Black, a champion of the rights of the disenfranchised, dissented with these words:

> Experience demonstrates that it is not a far step from what to many seems the earnest, honest, patriotic, kind-spirited multitude of today, to the fanatical, threatening, lawless mob of tomorrow. And the crowds that press in the streets for noble goals today can be supplanted tomorrow by street mobs pressuring the courts for precisely opposite ends. [90]

As the demonstrators acted, the Supreme Court and federal appellate courts responded despite their fears that the nonviolent movement would unravel. The pathos of the demonstrations spoke with more eloquence than the rhetoric of all the ministers and lawyers that had come before. Compelled by the demonstrations to address obvious inequities, the Supreme Court held that state enforcement of restrictive covenants (excluding black persons from purchasing certain property) constituted state action subject to constitutional oversight.[91] In another case, segregation of public buses was held unconstitutional.[92] Train stations likewise could no longer constitutionally remain separate and unequal.[93] Public recreational facilities were ordered desegregated.[94] The poll tax was ruled unconstitutional.[95] Convictions for criminal trespass, and aiding, abetting, and disturbing the peace were invalidated because they were based upon unconstitutional local segregation laws.[96] In the areas of voting, employment, and housing, the Court upheld the right of black people to equal participation in their political and social communities.[97]

Then, the Supreme Court announced a new weapon in the arsenal of antidiscrimination justifications—the commerce clause. In *Heart of Atlanta Motel, Inc. v. United States* (1964),[98] the Court held that Congress could regulate even private conduct that had a significant impact on interstate commerce.[99] Using the commerce clause, the Court had a basis to reach private action in many public accommodations cases. As the violent confrontations between children and water cannons continued, the Supreme Court spoke clearly and often, holding that the Constitution unequivocally endowed the demonstrators with rights and protections which could not be abridged.

Clearly, the courts were backing King, until he began moving toward a more radical view of human rights and economics. As King began to focus in this direction, he also lost centrist, white Protestant ministers, young black power advocates, and upwardly mobile black and white communities who were unwilling to put their buckets down with the poor. Soon, both blacks and whites became uncomfortable with the street actions. They declared that progress meant moving away from demonstrations. By 1970, two years after King's assassination, the Supreme Court began a slow but clear retrenchment from its civil rights opinions. It soon became clear that there was a direct relationship between the jurisprudential movement toward fairness and the demonstrations that crystallized the effects of injustice. For when African Americans stopped demonstrating the gritty unpleasantness of racism, the Court went back to abstraction and theory.

It is chic these days to recite all of the reasons that integration was a poor choice for degraded people. Suggestions for alternatives range from a movement West, to repatriation and nationhood within the nation, similar to the status of Native Americans. Critics are responding to the failure to implement the spirit and the letter of civil rights legislation. However, the reason for this retreat from King's civic vision is that King did not live long enough to lead performative acts that would have seared the contours, expectations, and moral parameters of integration into the national consciousness. He set up the initial paradigm and was assassinated soon thereafter. Integration thus became an abstraction relegated to educational initiatives, legal gains, and employment opportunities. If King had lived, he might have cautioned against this nuts-and-bolts approach to integration.

At the turn of this century, the tools of liberation are close at hand. They are theological, legal, and moral. To appropriate and utilize these resources is to take seriously King's reminder to develop new attitudes and new mental responses for the new situations that we will face. Newness in this context does not assume unfamiliarity. Rather, the black community's renewal may lie in the reclamation of the moral strengths that King revealed to the world.

Had King arrived on the public scene in this country even twenty years earlier, he would have confronted a world that was not quite ready for his methodology of performative acts. Although the nation was being nudged by savvy servicemen and urbanized black populations toward a more level playing field, the timing was not right. Had King arrived twenty years later, Camelot would have already eroded, and Vietnam would have stolen center stage. Who would have appreciated the force of water canons against the backdrop of napalm?

Instead, King emerged in his beloved South just as the murmur for equality was increasing and the oppression was extreme. The social revolution that he led shook the courts and revitalized the meaning of the Constitution. Yet, the lessons of history are clear: the courts will not save, the politicians and preachers will disappoint, but agape love seldom fails. Using love's untapped potential, King awakened a nation to its shortcomings and African Americans to the fullness of their humanity. But more important, he refused to let us "peacefully snore" through a great revolution.

NOTES

1. Excerpt from Martin Luther King, Jr.'s Passion Sunday speech given on 31 March 1968 at the National Cathedral (Episcopal) in Washington, D.C., reprinted in *A Testament of Hope: The Essential Writings and Speeches of Martin Luther King Jr.*, ed. James M. Washington (San Francisco: HarperCollins, 1986), 268–278.

2. Speech given before the Lincoln Memorial on 28 August 1963 during the keynote address of the March on Washington, D.C., for civil rights, also reprinted in Washington, *A Testament of Hope*, 217–220.

3. Compare Barbara Jordan's concept of a national community in Barbara Holmes, *A Private Woman in Public Spaces: Barbara Jordan's Speeches on Ethics, Public Religion and Law* (Harrisburg, Pa: Trinity Press International, 2000).

4. Washington, ed., *A Testament of Hope*, 268, 269.

5. John F. Cragan, "Rhetorical Strategy: A Dramatistic Interpretation and Application," *Central States Speech Journal*, vol. 26 (Spring 1975): 9.

6. Carolyn Calloway-Thomas and John Louis Lucaites, *Martin Luther King Jr., and the Sermonic Power of Public Discourse* (Tuscaloosa, Ala. and London: University of Alabama Press, 1993), 21.

7. Frederick Douglass, "Speech on the Occasion of the 24th Anniversary of Emancipation in the District of Columbia, Washington, D.C., 1886," in *The Life and Writings of Frederick Douglass*, ed. Philip S. Foner, 4 vols. (New York: International Publishers, 1950), vol. 4, *Reconstruction and After* (1955), 431.

8. Simeon C. R. McIntosh, "Reading *Dred Scott, Plessy* and *Brown*: Toward a Constitutional Hermeneutics," 38 *Howard L. J.* 53 (1994).

9. Michael W. Combs, "The Supreme Court, African Americans and Public Policy Changes and Transformations," in *Blacks and the American Political System*, ed. Huey L. Perry and Wayne Parent (Gainesville: University of Florida Press, 1995).

10. Thomas Jefferson, "In Congress, July 4, 1776. The unanimous Declaration of the Thirteen United States of America." Drafted between June 11 and June 28, 1776.

11. U.S. Constitution, preamble, 1787.

12. In the infamous *Dred Scott v. Sandford* decision, 60 U.S. (19 How.) 393, p. 404 (1856), chief Justice Taney opined:

The words "people of the United States" and "citizens" are synonymous terms, and mean the same thing. They both describe the political body who, according to our republican institutions, form the sovereignty, and who hold the power and conduct the Government through their representatives. They are what we familiarly call the "sovereign people," and every citizen is one of this people, and a constituent member of this sovereignty.

13. See U.S. Constitution, Article I, section 2, which provides: "Representatives and direct taxes shall be apportioned among the several states . . . according to their respective numbers, which shall be determined by adding the whole number of free persons . . . and excluding Indians not taxed, three-fifths of all other persons." When this language was written, there were several thousand free black people living in both the North and the South of the country. See Don E. Fehrenbacher, *The Dred Scott Case: Its Significance in American Law and Politics* (New York: Oxford University Press, 1978), 61.

14. See n12, above.

15. U.S. Constitution, Amendment X: "The powers not delegated to the United States by the Constitution, nor prohibited by it to the States, are reserved to the States respectively, or to the people."

16. See n12, above, 60 U.S. (19 How.) at 572–4 (Curtis, J., dissenting opinion). In this powerful dissent, Justice Curtis reasoned:

By the Articles of Confederation, a Government was organized, the style whereof was "The United States of America." This Government was in existence when the Constitution was framed and proposed for adoption, and was to be superseded by the new Government of the United States of America, organized under the Constitution. When, therefore, the Constitution speaks of citizenship of the United States, existing at the time of the adoption of the Constitution, it must necessarily refer to citizenship under the Government which existed prior to and at the time of such adoption. . . . [I]t may safely be said that the citizens of the several States were citizens of the United States under the Confederation. . . . There were free persons, descended from Africans held in slavery, who were citizens of the states of New Hampshire, Massachusetts, New York, New Jersey and North Carolina. They "were not only citizens of those States, but such of them as had the other necessary qualifications possessed the franchise of electors, on equal terms with other citizens."

Curtis went on to cite the fourth article of the Articles of Confederation, which provided: "The free inhabitants of each of these States, paupers, vagabonds, and fugitives from justice, excepted, shall be entitled to

all the privileges and immunities of free citizens in the several States."
Curtis recounted that an attempt had been made to add the word "white"
in the description of "free inhabitants" in this article, but the proposed
amendment was voted down by a majority of the states. Thus, Curtis concluded that

> [the] Constitution was ordained and established by the people of
> the United States, through the action, in each State, of those per-
> sons who were qualified by its laws to act thereon, in behalf of
> themselves and all other citizens of that State. . . . In at least five of
> the States [colored persons] had the power to act, and doubtless
> did act, by their suffrages, upon the question of [the Constitu-
> tion's] adoption. It would be strange, if we were to find in that in-
> strument anything which deprived of their citizenship any part of
> the people of the United States who were among those by whom
> it was established.

See also James Miller, *Democracy Is in the Streets* (New York: Simon and
Schuster, 1987), 101. For a comprehensive analysis of these issues of citizenship for free black men, see the following symposium article by Donald G. Neiman, "Bondage, Freedom and the Constitution: The New Slavery
Scholarship and Its Impact on Law and Legal Historiography: Emancipation and the New Conception of Freedom: From Slaves to Citizens:
African-Americans, Rights, Consciousness, and Reconstruction," 17 *Car-
dozo Law R.* 2115 (1996).

17. King, "Who Speaks for the South," printed in the *Progressive*,
24 May 1960, reprinted in Washington, *A Testament of Hope*, 98.

18. King, "A Time to Break Silence," speech given at Riverside
Church, New York City, 4 April 1967. See also D. Halberstam, "The Second
Coming of Martin Luther King Jr.," *Harper's Magazine*, 19 August 1997.

19. Calloway-Thomas and Lucaites, "Public Discourse," 20.

20. Ibid.

21. See, *Marbury v. Madison*, 5 U.S. 137, 178 (1 Cranch 137) (1803),
in which the Supreme Court declared: "It is emphatically the province
and duty of the judicial department to say what the law is. Those who
apply the rule to particular cases, must of necessity expound and interpret
that rule. If two laws conflict with each other, the courts must decide on
the operation of each. . . . The judicial power of the United States is extended to all cases arising under the Constitution."

22. *Stare decisis* is a Latin phrase that means "to abide by, or adhere to,
decided cases," according to *Black's Law Dictionary*, 5th ed. (St. Paul, Minn:
West Publishing Company, 1979). It stands for the proposition that courts
should avoid disturbing previously resolved legal principles.

Stare decisis is a "doctrine that, when [a] court has once laid down a principle of law as applicable to a certain state of facts, it will adhere to that principle, and apply it to all future cases, where [the] facts are substantially the same; regardless of whether the parties and property are the same." *Id.*; *Horne v. Moody*, 146 S.W.2d 505, 509–10 (Tex. App. 1940). "When a point of law has been settled by decision, it forms precedent which is not afterwards to be departed from, and while it should ordinarily be strictly adhered to, there are occasions when departure is rendered necessary to vindicate plain, obvious principles of law and remedy continued injustice." *Colonial Trust Co. v. Flanagan*, 25 A.2d 728, 729 (Pa. 1942).

23. Dred Scott sought a court order declaring that he had acquired his freedom during a two-year period when he lived with his master, Dr. Emerson, on a federal army base at Ft. Snelling, Louisiana. Although he subsequently moved back to a slave state (Missouri), Scott argued that once he had acquired his freedom, it could not be relinquished by a move to a slave state. Amazingly, Scott won his case in state court before a jury of all white men. The state appealed, however, and won a reversal in the Missouri Supreme Court. Scott then took his case to federal court, where he lost at all levels. See n12 above.

24. Taney said, "The court must be understood as speaking in this opinion of . . . those persons who are the descendants of Africans who were imported into this country, and sold as slaves." See n12 above, 403.

25. See n12 above, 407.

26. Thomas Ross, *The Rhetorical Tapestry of Race ("Rhetorical Tapestry")*, 32 *William and Mary Law Review* 1, 9–12, 1990. Notably, all nine justices for the first time in history wrote individual opinions. The dissenters included Justice Curtis of Massachusetts, who reminded Chief Justice Taney that blacks had participated in the vote for the establishment of the federal government and had thereby acquired United States citizenship, which could not be so easily written off. The status of African Americans was nonetheless rewritten by the words of one judge.

27. Id., 404–405.

28. King, "Facing the Challenge of a New Age," address before the First Annual Institute on Nonviolence and Social Change, December 1956, Montgomery, Alabama, reprinted in Washington, *A Testament of Hope*, 136.

29. In the end, though, under either approach to constitutional analysis, the rights of an entire group of people can be suppressed or exalted if the motivation is there and the opinion is written persuasively. The author's own view of the outcome of the case informs the approach he takes. If, for example, Chief Justice Taney had believed in a different outcome for Dred Scott, he may well have recited the history of free black

men in this country from their early arrival to the present time. He might then have written convincingly that the black man played such an integral part in the establishment and protection of our federal government that it must have been intended by the original authors of the Constitution that at least those free black men who already enjoyed citizenship rights in their respective states were to be included among those entitled to United States citizenship. Taney might further have declared that it was always the intention of the framers to bestow citizenship upon anyone born in the United States, thereby including the children of slaves as potential citizens. Depending on his inclination, Taney could have concluded that Dred Scott's former owner intended to grant freedom to his slaves by moving with them to a territory that outlawed slavery. Thus, it may have been decided that Scott's freedom, once acquired, could not be and was not abrogated merely by his return to a slaveholding state. The point is, whatever the analytic approach, the truth lies in the pen of the author.

30. Simeon C. R. McIntosh, "Constitutional Founding," see n4 above, quoting Justice Holmes in *Missouri v. Holland,* 252 U.S. 416 (1920).

Professor McIntosh crystallizes the duality of constitutional adjudications as follows:

> [T]he Constitution is a special type of intentional object, it is the founding document of our constitutional democratic order; our charter for collective life. Thus, although the interpretation of the Constitution consistent with the intentions of the Founding Fathers might lend assurance that constitutional interpretation is not an arbitrary exercise of the Judge's personal will, it bears emphasis that, given the Constitution's evident purpose as our founding document, the problem of intention could not plausibly be conceived solely in biographical terms. . . . Thus, the questions remains: what interpretive approach would best account for the Constitution as an intentional object, and yet remain sensitive to its evident nature and purpose and its principal commitments, as the central text of an enduring republic? (53)

31. Howard University opened its integrated law school in 1897.

32. All were members of the National Bar Association, a professional organization of black lawyers. Between 1910 and 1920, the number of black lawyers increased from approximately 800 to 950. By 1940, there were 1,350 black lawyers serving 13 million black Americans. By 1950, the total number of black lawyers had increased to 1,450 and by 1960 there were 2,000 black lawyers. Darlene Clark Hines, "Black Lawyers and the

Twentieth-Century Struggle for Constitutional Change," *African Americans and the Living Constitution,* ed. John Hope Franklin and Genna Rae McNeil, (Washington and London: Smithsonian Institution Press, 1995).

33. The Fourteenth Amendment provides:

> All persons born or naturalized in the United States, and subject to the jurisdiction, are citizens of the United States and of the state wherein they reside. No state shall make or enforce any law which shall abridge the privileges and immunities of citizens of the United States; nor shall any state deprive any person of life, liberty or property, without due process of law; nor deny to any person within its jurisdiction the equal protection of the laws.

34. *Slaughter-House Cases,* 83 U.S. (16 Wall.) 36 (1872); *Civil Rights Cases of 1883,* 109 U.S. 3 (1883).

35. 163 U.S. 532 (1896).

36. Jim Crow was reportedly a minstrel character in road shows in the early 1800s.

37. Martin Luther King, Jr., " The Role of the Church in Facing the Nation's Chief Moral Dilemma," speech 25 April 1957, Nashville, Tennessee.

38. *McCabe v. Atchison, Topeka & Santa Fe Railway Co.,* 235 U.S. 151 (1914) (Oklahoma separate coach law upheld).

39. The Supreme Court permitted a county to close one black high school for reasons of lack of funding while denying access to those dispossessed black students to the white high school that remained fully funded. *Cumming v. Richmond Co. Bd. of Ed.,* 175 U.S. 528 (1899). The Court also upheld separate school accommodations in *Berea v. Kentucky,* 211 U.S. 45 (1908).

40. Thomas Ross discusses the theory of white innocence and black abstraction in "Rhetorical Tapestry." See n26 above.

41. The National Association for the Advancement of Colored People (NAACP) was founded along with CORE (the Congress of Racial Equality) and the National Urban League. The National Bar Association, an organization of minority attorneys, expanded its ranks considerably. World War I brought blacks into the armed forces and, through migration, to the urban north. The NAACP improved its ability to identify and argue test cases, which began to pay off in victories in housing and voting laws. Thurgood Marshall and Charles Hamilton Houston became rising stars in the NAACP constellation of exquisitely trained attorneys. The Great Depression equalized some of the poverty issues facing blacks and whites all over the country. President Franklin Roosevelt made new

appointments to the Supreme Court, including Hugo Black, which had an impact on the decisions made by the Court. World War II brought even larger numbers of blacks into the military, including some who were trained for highly skilled positions, like the Tuskegee Airmen. When these men returned from fighting in such close proximity to their white counterparts, the fire for equality was inevitable.

42. *Guinn v. United States*, 238 U.S. 268 (1939); *Lone v. Wilson*, 307 U.S. 268 (1939).

43. *United States v. Classic*, 313 U.S. 299 (1941) and *Smith v. Allwright*, 321 U.S. 649 (1944).

44. 163 U.S. 53 (1954).

45. *Missouri ex rel. Gaines v. Canada*, 305 U.S. 337 (1938); *Sipuel v. Board of Education Regents of the University of Oklahoma*, 332 U.S. 631 (1948); *Sweatt v. Painter*, 339 U.S. 629 (1950).

46. Note that during this time, in the 1950s, Senator Joseph McCarthy began his infamous campaign to identify and root out communism wherever it was suspected. This exposed all races and classes of people to the terror of irrational victimization. In a perverse but real way, this reign of character assassination had a unifying effect on the nation as more and more individuals were swept up in the net that spread across all races, genders, political parties, and economic strata.

47. On September 15, 1963, four black girls were murdered when a bomb exploded at the Sixteenth Street Baptist Church as they attended Sunday school. Charles Morgan, Jr., *A Time to Speak* (New York: Holt, Rinehart and Winston, 1964), 890–891.

48. Ronald K. L. Collins and David M. Skover, *Paratexts*, 44 Stan. L.R. 509, 510, 1992.

49. Washington, ed., *A Testament of Hope*, p. xvi, quoting from James Baldwin, "The Highroad to Destiny," C. Eric Lincoln, ed., *Martin Luther King, Jr.: A Profile* (New York: Hill and Wang, 1970), 111.

50. King, " Give Us the Ballot—We Will Transform the South," keynote address in front of the Lincoln Memorial during the Prayer Pilgrimage for Freedom on 17 May 1957, in Washington, ed., *A Testament of Hope*, 198.

51. Id., 104.

52. King, "An Address before the National Press Club," Washington, D.C., 19 July 1962, reprinted in Washington, *A Testament of Hope*, 103.

53. Martin Luther King, Jr., "The Ethical Demands for Integration," speech delivered before a church conference in Nashville, Tennessee, on 27 December 1962.

54. King offers an expansive definition of agape love, which includes "understanding, creative, redemptive good will for all men," in "The

Power of Nonviolence" a speech given at the University of California at Berkeley, 4 June 1957, Berkeley, Californian, reprinted in Washington, ed., *A Testament of Hope*, 12–15.

55. In Washington, ed., *A Testament of Hope*, 250.

56. King, "The Power of Nonviolence," 13.

57. When love rules, social-action initiatives must sometimes wait. On one occasion, when Harry Belafonte and Miriam Makeba were refused service in Atlanta at the King's Inn Restaurant, King delayed social protests to share in the communal grief at the loss of many members of the Atlanta art community in an air crash. King, "Statement regarding the refusal of restaurant to serve Harry Belafonte," June 1961, Atlanta, Georgia.

58. Paul E. Johnson, *African-American Christianity: Essays in History* (Berkeley: University of California Press, 1994),160.

59. Ibid., 161.

60. King, "Rediscovering Precious Values" 28 February 1954, included in *Papers of Martin Luther King, Jr.,* vol. 2, ed. Clayborne Carson et al. (Berkeley: University of California Press, 1992), also quoted in Johnson's *African-American Christianity* (Berkeley: University of California Press, 1994), 171.

61. See discussion of the effects of love on community formation and conflict in an essay by Barbara A. Holmes and Susan Holmes Winfield entitled "II Corinthians 1–11: Considering the Paradox of Conflict and Consolation in Faith Communities," in *Conflict and Community in the Corinthian Church* (New York: Women's Division of the General Board of Global Ministries, United Methodist Church, 2000).

62. Michael Dyson, *Reflecting Black: African-American Cultural Criticism* (Minneapolis: University of Minnesota Press, 1993), 365.

63. King, "Is It All Right to Break the Law?" *U.S. News and World Report,* August 12, 1963.

64. Matthew Lippman, "Liberating the Law: The Jurisprudence of Civil Disobedience and Resistance," 2 *San Diego Justice Journal,* 299–393, at 303 (1994).

65. Ibid.

66. King, "Letter from a Birmingham City Jail," April 16, 1963, reprinted in Washington, ed., *A Testament of Hope*, 289–302.

67. Alex Ayres, ed., *The Wisdom of Martin Luther King, Jr.* (New York: Meridian Press, 1993), 11.

68. David Tracy, *Plurality and Ambiguity: Hermeneutics, Religion, Hope* (New York: Harper & Row, 1987), 79.

69. Paul F. Knitter, "Toward a Liberative Interreligious Dialogue," *Cross Currents* (Winter 1995): 454.

70. W. E. B DuBois, *The Souls of Black Folk: Essays and Sketches* (Nashville, Tenn.: Fisk University Press, 1979).

71. David Luban, "Difference Made Legal: The Court and Dr. King," 87 *Michigan L. Rev.* 2152–2224, (1987).

72. Mark Edward DeForrest, "Civil Disobedience: Its Nature and Role in the American Legal Landscape," 33 *Gonzaga L. Rev.* 653, 668 (1997/98).

73. Anthony E. Cook, " The Death of God in American Pragmatism and Realism: Resurrecting the Value of Love in Contemporary Jurisprudence," 82 *The Georgetown L. J.* 1431, 1492 (1994).

74. "Letter from a Birmingham City Jail," reprinted in Washington, *A Testament of Hope,* 289–302.

75. James F. Klumpp and Thomas A. Hollihan, " Rhetorical Criticism As Moral Action," *Quarterly Journal of Speech* 75 (1989): 86.

76. Lewis F. Powell, Jr., "A Lawyer Looks at Civil Disobedience," 23 *Wash. and Lee L. Rev.* 205, 225–226 (1966).

77. DeForrest, "Civil Disobedience," 668.

78. See Nicholas Evreinoff's discussion, containing the quotation from Erasmus, in "The Never Ending Show," in *The Theatre in Life,* ed. and trans. Alexander I. Nazaroff (New York: Brentanos, 1927), 46–55.

79. King, "Stride toward Freedom," reprinted in Washington, ed., *A Testament of Hope,* 429.

80. King, " A Legacy of Creative Protest," 7 September 1962, reprinted in *The Massachusetts Review* (Autumn 1962). At first blush, Thoreau seems to be an odd choice for King. He might well have gleaned resources for resistance from those who fought slavery at the cost of their lives. The names Denmark Vesey, Gullah Jack, Sojourner Truth, Harriet Tubman, and others come to mind. King was not unaware of these resources within the black community, but attributed his theories to philosophers integral to his training. He also used philosophical references as yet another tool to wake the masses. Blacks and whites took notice as King appropriated philosophical resources on behalf of an "outcast" community.

81. Harold Berman, *Faith and Order: The Reconciliation of Law and Religion* (Atlanta: Scholars Press, 1993).

82. Whatever one's impression of the outcome of many celebrated trials, including the criminal case against O. J. Simpson, observers were able to inculcate the reality of the experience because they witnessed the drama unfold.

83. King, *Where Do We Go from Here: Chaos or Community?* (New York: Harper & Row, 1976).

84. Ibid., 566.

85. David J. Garrow, *Bearing the Cross* (New York: W. Morrow, 1986), 250. See also David B. Oppenheimer, 26 *U.C. Davis L. Rev.* 790 (Summer 1993).

86. "Letter from a Birmingham Jail," reprinted in Washington, ed., *A Testament of Hope*, 289–302.

87. *Walker v. City of Birmingham*, 388 U.S. 307 (1967). The Court upheld Dr. King's conviction for contempt on the grounds that he had disobeyed a facially valid injunction issued by a court of competent jurisdiction. Ultimately, the Supreme Court ruled that segregation ordinances such as the one involved here were unconstitutional. See cases cited in n98, below.

88. *In re Debs*, 158 U.S. 564 (1895).

89. This was the occasion on which Dr. King wrote the "Letter from a Birmingham City Jail."

90. *Cox v. Louisiana*, n78 above, 379 U.S. at 584 (dissenting opinion).

91. *Hurd v. Hodge*, 334 U.S. 24 (1948); *Shelley v. Kraemer*, 334 U.S. 1 (1948).

92. *Browders v. Gayle*, 352 U.S. 903 (1956).

93. *Baldwin v. Morgan*, 251 F.2d 780 (5th Cir. 1958).

94. *Muir v. Louisville Park Theatrical Assn.*, 347 U.S. 971 (1955).

95. *Harper et al. v. Virginia Board of Elections et al.*, 383 U.S. 663 (1966).

96. *Bell v. Maryland, 378 U.S. 226 (1964); Gober v. City of Birmingham*, 373 U.S. 374 (1963); *Shuttlesworth v. City of Birmingham*, 373 U.S. 262 (1963); *Lombard et al. v. Louisiana*, 373 U.S. 267 (1963); *Peterson v. City of Greenville*, 373 U.S. 244 (1963).

97. See *Brown v. Louisiana*, 368 U.S. 157 (1961); *Garner v. Louisiana*, 368 U.S. 157 (1961). (The Court struck down criminal convictions of defendants who had violated local ordinances and statutes that empowered the police to order protesters to leave an area.); *Taylor v. Louisiana*, 370 U.S. 154 (1962); *Hamm v. Rock Hill*, 379 U.S. 306 (1964). (The Civil Rights Act of 1964 prohibited discrimination in public accommodations. The efforts to use these accommodations could therefore not be prosecuted as criminal trespass.); *Cox v. Louisiana*, n78, above. (The Court reversed a conviction of one who had protested "near" a local courthouse in violation of a city ordinance.); *Shuttlesworth v. City of Birmingham*, 394 U.S. 147 (1969). (The Court struck down a city ordinance that vested an unconstitutional amount of discretion in local politicians to deny parade permits to civil rights activists.) See also, Matthew Lippman, *Civil Disobedience and Resistance*, 2 *San Diego Justice Journal* 299, 328–341.

98. 379 U.S. 241 (1064).

99. See *Katzenbach v. McClung*, 379 U.S. 294 (1964), in which the Court upheld the right of Congress to eliminate a voter-literacy qualification on the grounds of the impact of the ordinance on interstate commerce.

F I V E

Personalism, the Objective Moral Order, and Moral Law in the Work of Martin Luther King, Jr.

RUFUS BURROW, JR.

[God] has placed within the very structure of this universe certain absolute moral laws. We can neither defy nor break them. If we disobey them, they will break us. The forces of evil may temporarily conquer truth, but truth will ultimately conquer its conqueror.

—Martin Luther King, Jr. [1]

Martin Luther King, Jr., frequently talked about just and unjust laws in the United States and other parts of the world. A theologian by training and a committed minister of the Christian faith, he judged civil law and political policies and practices by the more fundamental objective moral law. Any civil law that was contrary to moral law was deemed by King to be unjust. King was not a classroom theologian. Therefore, he was vigilant in his efforts to create a society and world that more nearly approximates the requirements of moral law. His belief in the existence of moral laws was grounded in the further conviction that there is an objective moral order that is caused and sustained by God. This conviction is important because the taproot of King's theological social ethic, namely, the Beloved Community, is grounded in the principle that reality hinges on moral foundations. This means that although persons are created in freedom, and therefore may choose to do good or evil, they have essentially been created for good and to do good.

This chapter discusses the significance of King's conviction that there exists an objective moral order and objective moral laws in the universe. It will first be necessary to address the impact of the philosophy

213

of personalism,[2] for these were basic personalistic ideas that were consistent with what he learned while growing up in the black church. Because some King scholars, for example, David Garrow, downplay the importance of personalism on his formal theological development,[3] it is important to remember that King affirmed that it was his fundamental philosophical point of departure:

> This personal idealism remains today my basic philosophical position. Personalism's insistence that only personality—finite and infinite—is ultimately real strengthened me in two convictions: it gave me metaphysical and philosophical grounding for the idea of a personal God, and it gave me a metaphysical basis for the dignity and worth of all human personality.[4]

Notice that King did not say that he first came to believe in a personal God and the dignity of persons through the formal study of personalism. These were beliefs that were instilled in him through his family upbringing and teachings at the Ebenezer Baptist Church in Atlanta, Georgia, pastored by his father, Martin Luther King, Sr. Therefore, King brought these beliefs to the study of personalism, which in turn provided the metaphysical foundation he sought. Susan Harlow makes the point in a paper she wrote recently on King.

> The church of his parents and grandparents had imparted an understanding of God and of the purposes of Christian ministry that could not be displaced by theological sophistication. *His study of personalism reinforced his beliefs rather than supplanted them.* It gave him a metaphysical basis for the dignity and worth of all persons.[5] (Emphasis added)

I am not only interested in showing the significance of personalism and its chief progenitors for King. It is also important to note how *he* impacted and enriched that school of thought.

King contributed significantly to personalism. He also put flesh on the doctrine that the universe is friendly to value, or as he liked to say: The universe hinges on moral foundations. This means that one has to focus on the objectivity of moral value and moral law, and that there is something in the very nature of things that sides with the good, love, justice, beauty, and truth. King grounded a number of his strongly held views on this, for example, his conviction that some things are right and some things are wrong, whether one is seen doing them or not, and his view that the nature of reality is such that justice must be done for everybody, or for nobody. Indeed, even his oft-stated view that persons possess inherent and inviolable dignity is to a large extent grounded in the conviction that the universe is solidly grounded on a moral foundation, that is, is charged with value, and that the God of the eighth-century prophets and of Jesus Christ is the source.

This is also the case of the indisputable keystone of King's theological ethics, the *Beloved Community* ideal. The philosophical roots of this term are traceable to the absolutistic personalist Josiah Royce (1855–1916).[6] Its biblical foundation can be traced to the Kingdom of God ideal in the New Testament, and its theological roots to the social gospel espoused by the likes of Walter Rauschenbusch and Reverdy C. Ransom.[7] The term may also be traced to Howard Thurman's ideal of community.[8] African Americans have been searching for the Beloved Community ever since they were forced to come to this country as slaves.[9] Because King believed that reality hinges on moral foundations, he clearly saw the reasonableness of seeking the actualization of the Beloved Community, the basis of which is his conviction that the universe is friendly to value.

I begin with a brief discussion of the meaning and development of personalism, followed by consideration of several of its chief tenets and how King interpreted them. I also briefly discuss what I call King's "homespun personalism" as the basis for his formal study of personalism and how he transcended his teachers. This is followed by consideration of the significance of King's belief in the existence of an objective moral order and the moral law system. These and related ideas contributed to King's faith in the possibility of the achievement of the Beloved Community, and his insistence on nonviolence as a way of life. The chapter ends with a consideration of socioethical implications of King's doctrine of the objective moral order and moral laws. The particular focus will be on the meaning of these for African Americans.

The Meaning and Development of Personalism

Fundamentally a metaphysics, personalism is the view that reality is personal and persons are the highest—not the only—intrinsic values. It is a type of idealism which maintains that *person* is the supreme philosophical principle—that principle without which no other principle can be made intelligible. The type of personalism which prompted King to claim it as his fundamental philosophical standpoint maintains that the universe is a society of interacting and intercommunicating selves and persons with God at the center. Personalism provided for King a philosophical framework to support his long-held beliefs in a personal God, the idea of the absolute dignity of persons, and the belief in the existence of an objective moral order and moral laws.

The term "personalism" was first introduced by the German theologian Friedrich Schleiermacher in 1799, although he did not develop it philosophically. Both English and American scholars[10] used the term in their writings in the mid-nineteenth century. However, like Schleiermacher, they did not develop its philosophical meaning.

Personalism was made a going concern in the United States by Borden Parker Bowne (1847–1910), "the father of American personalism." Called to Boston University in 1876, Bowne reacted vigorously against impersonalistic and naturalistic philosophies like that of Herbert Spencer.[11] Using Spencer's work as a kind of philosophical cadaver in his courses, Bowne argued persuasively and emphatically that the personal (or mind) can never be derived from an impersonal "Unknown," and that only mind or intelligence can produce intelligence. Indeed, for Bowne the most acute argument for theism is the argument from intelligibility.[12] Much influenced by the idealism of René Descartes, Bishop George Berkeley, and Immanuel Kant, Bowne gave primacy to self-certainty, the immaterialism of all phenomenal objects (which led to the view that all objects in nature are the manifestation of God's will and thought), the practical reason, a dualistic and activistic epistemology, the primacy of the good will, and the intrinsic dignity of the person.

Bowne's systematic development of personalism as a worldview and as a way of living in the world led to the characterization of his philosophy as "systematic methodological personalism."[13] This meant that Bowne, more than any of his contemporaries, with the possible exception of George Holmes Howison,[14] pushed the personalistic argument to its logical conclusions in metaphysics, epistemology, philosophy of religion, and ethics. As a result of Bowne's leadership,

Boston University was known as the great bastion of personalistic studies until roughly the end of the 1960s. I date the decline of personalism from the year of King's assassination in 1968. I do so because King was the chief social personalist in this country who both explicitly identified himself as a personalist and was devoted to making personalism a reality in human relations.

Homespun Personalism

To the extent that it is possible to say it of one whose life *was* the civil and human rights struggle, Martin Luther King, Jr., was a thoroughgoing personalist. In this sense he was able to reason personalism out to its logical conclusions in metaphysics, epistemology, the philosophy of religion, and ethics. Long before he was introduced to the term "personalism" or to the work of any of its chief representatives, he was exposed to some of its basic tenets by his parents and grandparents.

As a boy, King learned from his mother that he was as good as anybody, regardless of race; indeed, that he was *somebody*. This was so because he was a child of God and a being of infinite worth to God. This was reinforced by his father, who modeled for him what it meant to be in touch with one's own sense of dignity. Daddy King refused to allow white racists to insult his personhood with impunity, and he always stood up for himself and his people—at times in the presence of his young son.[15]

King also learned from his parents a corollary of this principle, namely, that persons should love and respect each other as children of God. In addition, King learned from the example of his father and maternal grandfather the need for his people to work together cooperatively and with God in order to assert their humanity and dignity and to *demand* that they be treated accordingly. He was taught by them the necessity of struggle if one desired to gain one's rights as a human being and citizen of the United States. It was his father and grandfather who introduced him to the basic Hegelian principle that progress and growth come through struggle.[16] Years later King would critically examine this principle as a graduate student at Boston University, and would ultimately recite it in numerous speeches, sermons, and writings. He also developed from his upbringing a strong belief in a personal and loving God, who cares about the well-being of persons in the world and who is always working on their behalf.

As important as Boston University was for King's theological development, it did not make him a personalist. By definition he was a personalist long before he began seminary and graduate theological studies. That is, his personalism was initially spun in his parents' home, in Sunday school classes and worship services at Ebenezer Baptist Church, in courses under the instruction of Benjamin E. Mays and George Kelsey at Morehouse College, through the witness and example of his father and maternal grandfather, and in other areas of the black community. King's home- and church-grown personalism was thoroughly mixed with strong family and community values. However, what Boston University did was crucial for his subsequent work in the civil and human rights movement. King's study with prominent personalists such as Edgar S. Brightman and L. Harold DeWolf provided a sound philosophical basis for his homespun personalistic convictions.

Before proceeding to the discussion on King's conviction that the universe is grounded on a moral foundation and that its source is cosmic, it will be helpful to clarify the formal influence of personalism on his thought, inasmuch as a number of King scholars have sought to discount its significance.

King and the Formal Influence of Personalism

At Boston University, King was a student under Brightman for a brief period. He wrote of the latter's strong influence on his character development.[17] Since King also studied under DeWolf, who became his major adviser when Brightman died suddenly in 1953, there is no question that he was familiar with all of the basic concepts of personalism. What Brightman and DeWolf gave King was a name and a philosophical grounding for ideas that were conveyed to him by his parents, grandparents, and college professors. Since King acknowledged personalism or personal idealism as his fundamental philosophical point of departure, it is reasonable to say that he was, in the academically formal sense, a personalist.

While in graduate school, King wrote papers on the Bowne-Brightman type of personalism, comparing and contrasting it with other types, for example, the atheistic personalism of John M. E. Mc-Taggart.[18] He also compared Brightman's personalism to the philosophies of other thinkers, such as William Ernest Hocking.[19] King wrote a number of papers like this, a practice which culminated in his dissertation: "A Comparison of the Conceptions of God in the Thinking of Paul Tillich and Henry Nelson Wieman" in 1955. He chose to write on the doctrine of God because of the central place it occupies in religion and because it is one of the perennial issues begging for further clarification.[20] He selected Tillich and Wieman primarily because they represented vastly different philosophical standpoints, which was conducive to his desire to compare and contrast at least two theological systems. Although King learned much from his study, Tillich and Wieman were essentially foils for highlighting the significance of a personalistic conception of God. Indeed, Bowne's was for him the more reasonable doctrine of God. Arguing that God is both omnipotent and omnibenevolent, Bowne's view was closest to that of the vast majority of African American religionists, including King's.[21]

King was influenced by personalism's doctrine of the personal God of love and reason[22] as well as its emphasis on the objective moral order, moral laws, and the inherent sense of the dignity of persons as such. In light of this, it is baffling that King scholars such as David Garrow[23] and Keith D. Miller[24] try to undermine the importance of personalism as a major influence on him. Peter J. Paris errs in this regard as well in his otherwise fine chapter on King.[25] These scholars imply that personalism played but a minor role in King's theological development.

Garrow[26] and Taylor Branch[27] have pointed out that a number of King's speeches and essays were ghostwritten. For Garrow this means, in part, that we should not give much weight to references in many of King's speeches and writings to the key role of personalism in his theological development. In addition, Garrow argues that a limitation of much early scholarship on King was the failure to give serious—indeed any!—attention to the more formative and preacademic influences, such as the importance of being brought up in an African American family under a father who was an outstanding pastor of one of the largest churches in Atlanta. So rather than begin, as most early studies on King did, with the written and formal academic influences on him, Garrow argues for the need to begin much earlier.[28]

No reasonable person can doubt the importance of this aspect of Garrow's concern. But what I take issue with is the implication that because a number of King's speeches and writings were ghostwritten, we should be apprehensive about accepting as truth his published claims about the importance of personalism for his theological and philosophical development. The problem with this part of Garrow's criticism is that long before King became so popular and busy that he needed others to write speeches, articles, and chapters in his books, he had already spoken and written of the fundamental role of personalism in his intellectual development.

Garrow is quite right to criticize early King scholars for their failure to stress the black church and familial influences on King's development, for these laid the foundation for what was to come during his formal seminary and graduate school training. But Garrow—as well as Miller and Paris—could have made his criticism without also downplaying the importance of personalistic idealism as King's basic philosophical framework.

In addition, there is no evidence that King ever denied the importance of personalism for his way of thinking about and doing theology and social ethics. King was a very good and incisive thinker. It is therefore preposterous to think that he would not have challenged the published accounts of ghostwriters regarding his basic philosophical standpoint, if they in fact misrepresented him. Were he in basic disagreement with ghostwritten statements in this regard, he would very likely have taken issue with them verbally and/or through his own writings. There is no evidence that he disagreed with written statements about the influence of personalism on his thought. Not only did King acknowledge personalism as his fundamental philosophical starting point, but his wife wrote that he was "wholeheartedly committed"[29] to it.

Furthermore, one gets a sense of the significance of personalism for King from papers he wrote as a seminary and graduate student. After all, had he not gone to Boston University precisely for the purpose of studying personalism under Brightman?[30] King agreed with chief proponents of personalism that there are one of two ways to characterize God: as *impersonal* or *personal.* In addition, King insisted, against Wieman and Tillich, that the term "personality" as applied to God is theomorphic, not anthropomorphic. It is in God, not in human beings, that we get our best idea of the essence of *person.* The human person gives us our best clues to the meaning of *person,* to be sure. But the true essence of *person* is to be found only in God or the Absolute.[31] Following Bowne, King maintained that essential *person* is not commensurate with corporeality. Rather, *person* essentially "means simply self-consciousness and self-direction."[32] In God, these reach a perfection that far surpasses that of human persons, who are but faint images of essential personhood.

God, then, is the chief exemplification of what it means to be *person*. In addition, and also in his dissertation, King quoted approvingly from Albert C. Knudson a statement that Thomas Aquinas made about God and essential *person:* "As Thomas Aquinas says: 'The name *person* is fittingly applied to God; not, however, as it is applied to creatures, but in a more excellent way (*via eminentiae*).'"[33]

Through the formal personalistic framework provided by the instruction of Brightman and DeWolf and his reading of Bowne, King was able to critically reflect on the meaning and value of his homespun personalism. In addition, he was able to draw out the deeper implications of the meaning of human dignity, the need for self-love and respect for others, belief in the existence of an objective moral order and moral laws, the necessity of cooperative endeavor between persons and God while working to achieve the Beloved Community, and his long-held conviction that God is personal. Therefore, what the formal study of personalism contributed to King's theological and philosophical development was large indeed.

In any event, there is no question that *King was both a metaphysical and an ethical personalist.* That is, he believed in a personal God who is the ground of all things, and he was a staunch believer in the sacredness of all persons: "Every man is somebody because he is a child of God. . . . Man is a child of God, made in His image, and therefore must be respected as such."[34] Despite the tendency of some King scholars to downplay the significance of personalism in his intellectual development, an examination of his writings confirms its importance for him. And yet there was a particular type of personalism to which King adhered.

The Personalism That Appealed to King

There is not one, but nearly a dozen types of personalism.[35] Yet even within the most systematically developed type, "theistic personalism," which King studied, there are divergent viewpoints. For example, not all adherents to this type of personalism accept the idea of an omnipotent-omnibenevolent God. Nor do all adhere to the idea of the temporality of God (i.e., that God is in, and thus affected by, time). But differences notwithstanding, there are a number of distinguishing features shared by all schools of personalism.

First, personalism maintains that *person* is prominent both metaphysically and ethically. This means that the Supreme Reality (God) is both personal and the cause and sustainer of human and nonhuman life-forms. This doctrine has important implications for how persons should be treated in the world, for it implies that because the Supreme Person *chooses* or wills to create persons they are of infinite value to the Creator, and thus should be respected and treated like beings who possess infinite worth. King maintained that persons should be loved and respected precisely because God loves them. "The worth of an individual," he said, "does not lie in the measure of his intellect, his racial origin, or his social position. Human worth lies in relatedness to God. An individual has value because he has value to God."[36] For King, the biblical tradition of the Jewish-Christian faith points to the quality of innate dignity in persons, an idea he believed to be implicit in the concept of the image of God. This led him to conclude that

> This innate worth referred to in the phrase the image of God is universally shared in equal portions by all men. There is no graded scale of essential worth; there is no divine right of one race which differs from the divine right of another. Every human being has etched in his personality the indelible stamp of the Creator.[37]

Every person is of inestimable value to God. This necessarily implied for King the obligation of persons to treat self and others with respect. The idea of an inborn ideal of worth is prominent in the ethical system of Bowne,[38] the black church, and the Jewish-Christian traditions, each of which influenced King.

Second, the type of personalism that appealed to King is *theistic*. Personalists believe in a personal God who is the creator and sustainer of the created order. In theistic personalism, we find metaphysical grounding for the biblical claim that in God we live and move and have our being. This personal God is perceived as infinitely loving, caring, responsive, active, righteous, and just. We get a sense of the thoroughgoing nature of theistic personalism in Bowne's contention that God is the only foundation of truth, knowledge, and morals.[39] Although he argued that it is impossible to demonstrate the existence of God, Bowne was eager to show that the problems of the world and life cannot be solved without God as the fundamental assumption.[40]

King believed the universe to be under the guidance of a personal and loving Creator God. Nowhere did he express this more clearly than in his reflections on some of the hardships and threats made against him and his family during the civil rights movement.[41] King believed God to be "a Personal Being of matchless power and infinite love," and that "creative force" in the universe who "works to bring the disconnected aspects of reality into a harmonious whole."[42]

Third, in addition to holding that reality is personal, personalism is *freedomistic*. In fact, its two organizing principles are *person* and *freedom*. Accordingly, all being is both personal and free. To be is to be free and to act or have the potential to do so (although it is more than this!). At bottom, to be free is what it means to be a person; to be a person is to be free, or an agent capable of acting, whether for good or evil. This sense of self-determination is what the Creator intends, a view which has important implications for the ethical and political freedom of persons in the world and what they ought to be willing to do to assert, protect, and defend their essential freedom.

Persons are not first created and then *given* freedom. Rather, the nature of person is freedom. That is, it is the intention of the Creator that persons come into existence as free beings and with the capacity to be self-determined moral agents. That some persons lack moral agency because they are retarded or imbecilic raises the theodicy question. That the extent of the existence of moral agency in some persons is questionable because of the denial of basic life chances also raises fundamental problems that have both moral and sociopolitical implications. For example, to what extent can we say that young African American males who engage in intracommunity violence and murder are *morally* responsible for their behavior? There is no question that the one who pulls the trigger in a drive-by shooting, for example, is legally responsible. But morally? At any rate, it is because of essential freedom that *all* persons who are moral agents[43] are morally obligated to resist fiercely anybody and anything that undermines or seeks to crush their freedom.

King said three things about this fundamental freedom. First, freedom is the capacity to be self-determined and self-directed. It is "the capacity to deliberate or weigh alternatives." Secondly, freedom "expresses itself in decision." Once one chooses a particular alternative one necessarily cuts off other choices. And thirdly, freedom implies responsibility. Once a person makes a choice, she is responsible both for it and its most foreseeable consequences.[44] It may also be reasoned that any practice that threatens one's freedom is a threat to one's personhood and impinges on one's ability to weigh alternatives, to make decisions, and to be responsible for choices.

So important was freedom for King that he concluded with Brightman that without it there can be no persons. Freedom is a capstone of personalism. Following Brightman and Bowne, King emphasized both the ethical and the speculative significance of freedom. Without freedom neither morality nor knowledge is possible, since each depends on the capacity to deliberate and choose. In graduate school, King wrote an essay on the personalism of the British philosopher John M. E. McTaggart (1866–1925). He argued against McTaggart's rejection of freedom. "In rejecting freedom," he said, "McTaggart was rejecting the most important characteristic of personality."[45] For King, freedom is an abiding expression of the higher spiritual nature of persons. "Man is man," he said, "because he is free to operate within the framework of his destiny. . . . He is distinguished from animals by his freedom to do evil or to do good and to walk the high road of beauty or tread the low road of ugly degeneracy."[46]

Finally, personalism conceives of *reality as through and through social, relational, or communal.* Accordingly, it views the universe as a society of selves and persons who interact and are united by the will and love of God. The individual never experiences self in total isolation. Instead, the self always experiences something which it did not invent or create, but finds or receives from her "interaction and communication with other persons."[47] Here we see the dual emphasis on the autonomous individual *and* the community, a stance that is both personalistic and African. Kwame Gyekye, a Ghanaian philosopher, argues against the earlier tendency of African scholars, political leaders, and literary artists to stress the significance of the community at the expense of the individual. He argues instead for a soft or restricted communitarianism where the value and claims of both the individual and the community are acknowledged and respected.[48] This is also how we must understand the relationship between the individual and the group in King's Beloved Community ethic.

In any event, the emphasis on the communal nature of reality has been present in personalism since the time of Bowne. The focus on the personal was never intended to point to individuals in a vacuum. Instead, in the type of personalism that appealed to King the reference has always been to "persons set in relations to one another, which relations are as much a fact as is the separate existence of the individuals."[49] Walter Muelder expressed this idea in his term "persons-in-community." He writes that "man is a socius with a private center. . . ."[50] This description effectively holds in tension the primacy of both the *person* and the *community*, neither of which can be adequately understood apart from the other.

King's belief in the communal nature of reality and persons, and his Beloved Community ideal, was grounded in his doctrine of God and his conviction that reality is value-fused. Although he followed more closely Bowne's concept of God than Brightman's, he had deep affinity with the latter's view that while God does not need humans for God's existence as we need God for ours, God is love, and love is a social category. Persons cannot love to the fullest in isolation. Rather, they are created to live together and can be fully human and achieve the highest good only cooperatively and in community. Brightman seemed to have this in mind when he said, "The maxim, 'Think for yourself,' is basic; but the further maxim, 'Think socially,' must be added if philosophy is to do its whole duty."[51] This implies that the nature of persons is such that we need relationship with like beings and thus possess a natural urge toward community.

King maintained that this is what is required of Christians. "The real Christian world," wrote Albert C. Knudson, "is a world of mutually dependent beings. It is a social world, a world of interacting moral beings; and in such a world love is necessarily the basic moral law."[52] For King love is the essence of the Christian faith. "I think I have discovered the highest good," he said. "It is love. This principle stands at the center of the cosmos. As John says, 'God is love.' He who loves is a participant in the being of God. He who hates does not know God."[53]

Since love is at the center of the universe, so, necessarily, is the idea of community. Indeed, this concept is deeply rooted in the African American familial, religious, and cultural heritage. Personalism helped King to ground the concept philosophically.

King frequently expressed the idea of the interrelatedness of all life, as well as the conviction that persons are by nature social. He gave primacy to both the centrality of the person and the community. "All life is interrelated," he said. "All men are caught in an inescapable network of mutuality, tied in a single garment of destiny."[54] This led King to reason that what affects one person directly, affects all persons indirectly. An unjust civil law is not only an injustice to select individuals or groups, but to all persons—human and divine: "We are made to live together because of the interrelated structure of reality."[55] To treat even a single person unjustly, therefore, is an affront to *all* persons, including the Supreme Person. Unjust civil laws and political practices violate the dignity of all persons—human and divine.

Since King sought consistently to acknowlege the claims and values of both the autonomous individual and the community, we may characterize his personalism as "personal-communitarianism." Just as the individual owes duties to the community, so does the community owe duties to the individual. King generally concluded that the individual, not the community, has the right of way. The individual may selfishly seek his own interests at the expense of the community, but as repulsive as this may be, the dignity of the individual must not be disregarded. Even when a murderous criminal is caught, prosecuted, and incarcerated, he still possesses a fundamental and absolute dignity and therefore is to be treated accordingly. If in the end he is executed, it must be done as humanely as possible.[56] King was in this sense a true disciple of the Bowne type of personalism: "The individual who has no interest in the common good deserves all condemnation, but that view is equally selfish and odious which would sacrifice the individual to society."[57] It is always important to remember that the individual has rights against the community.[58]

In other words, for King, as for Bowne and other personalists, the individual is the basic moral unit.[59] Not only does value exist for, of, and in persons,[60] but everything else does as well. The community exists for all persons,[61] a point that King often expressed. It is not difficult to understand why the person had such prominence for King when it is remembered that, like Malcolm X, he championed the dignity of his people in a way and to an extent that most did not. This is but one of the concrete ways that King went beyond the personalism of his teachers, taking it to a much higher level.

Transcending the Personalism of His Teachers

Although a thoroughgoing personalist, King's personalism transcended that of his teachers in two other important respects. First, his personalism developed and matured in a hostile environment, and therefore against the odds. It developed in a social context that was not friendly to either his own humanity or that of his people. Although his family was well off in comparison to many other blacks, *all* were victims of racism. All of this affected the contours of King's personalism, giving it a qualitatively different flavor and look than that of his teachers. What King learned about human dignity, the need for self-love, cooperative endeavor, and the Beloved Community he learned from the Bible, from behavior modeled by his parents and grandparents, and from what he knew of the black struggle and contributions of black foreparents since the time of slavery. These things were not learned primarily through reading philosophy and theology books and listening to highly refined lectures. They were etched into King's soul and bones while he was struggling in the hot cauldron of racial oppression.

There is an important corollary to this. King's personalism grew up in an environment that was fused with social activism. Both his father and maternal grandfather were pastors who lived and modeled the conviction that the church is morally obligated to do all that it can to help people attain their full stature as persons. Ministry for them was not a nine-to-five job, but a vocation to which pastors are *called* by God, a conviction that King took as his own.[62] It requires that pastors be available to address the peoples' needs whenever they arise. This leads to the second important way that King's personalism differed from that of his personalist teachers.

While also a metaphysical personalist, King was fundamentally a *social-activist* personalist, inasmuch as he spent his entire ministerial vocation applying personalistic principles to practical solutions to the triple menaces of racism, economic exploitation, and militarism. The meaning of King's personalism was worked out in the scorching heat of the social struggle for dignity and justice, rather than in the relative comfort and safety of the classroom or in a cozy study. From the Montgomery, Alabama, bus boycott to the sanitation workers' strike in Memphis, Tennessee, King lived with and through the constant threat of death. This was the context in which he forged his personalism, and why his was undoubtedly the most vibrant and relevant of the varieties of personalisms in existence during his thirteen-year ministry. We now turn to a more explicit consideration of King's conviction that the universe hinges on moral foundations.

Objective Moral Order

Bowne argued for "an essential goodness at the heart and root of things."[63] This means that no matter how much evil is done in the world there is a presumption that good will win out in the end, for reality rests on moral grounds. One can act contrary to good, justice, righteousness, and love. However, she does so at a cost. The same applies to society itself. Bowne maintained that when "injustice, oppression, and iniquity are enacted by law, social earthquakes and volcanoes begin to rock society to its foundations. The elements melt with fervent heat, and the heavens pass away with a great noise."[64] One may disregard and even attack truth and justice, but when all is said and done, these values will stand: "No cunning, no power, can forever avail against the truth."[65] On this view, even when persons and societies work against truth and justice they invariably and unwittingly contribute in some strange way to God's truth and justice being done in the world:

> The one truth, it is said, which can be verified concerning the world-ground is that it makes for righteousness. Out of the clash of selfish interests a moral system emerges. Altruism is rooted deep in life itself, and glorifies even the animal impulses. Animalism and selfishness are made to contribute to moral progress, and thus, across the confusion of human development, we discern more and more clearly a moral factor immanent in the process.[66]

Out of the system of segregated buses and public facilities came the protests of Vernon Johns,[67] Claudette Colvin,[68] Mary Louise Smith,[69] Rosa Parks,[70] and the unprecedented leadership of Martin Luther King, Jr. No matter how demeaning social conditions are, God always intends that good be done. A select group of humans may intend that injustice be done, but God always intends that justice be done, and therefore works to create the conditions for that to happen.

Bowne was basically arguing for the existence of an objective moral order or the idea that there is an essential goodness at the heart of reality. This essentially means that one can't do wrong in the world and expect—in the deepest sense—to get by. This idea is expressed in an old church hymn that my mother used to sing as a reminder that no matter what persons and institutions do to demean other persons, the universe is so constructed by God that there will be severe consequences for such behavior. For the universe itself is on the side of morality, justice, and righteousness. The words of that song were simple: "You can't do wrong and get by, no matter how hard you may try."

An objective moral order is one that is relevant for all being. In this sense it is not relative (subjective) to the psyche of a single individual for whom value is not in the nature of things. To speak of an objective moral order is to refer to that which is universal, and therefore can be experienced by all. The assumption that there is an objective moral order says something significant about the structure of reality as well as the universe. It says something about the world and how persons ought to relate to and behave toward each other and the rest of creation. Accordingly, this view of reality is so structured that value is its key ingredient. Any person who thinks reasonably is capable of acknowledging and sharing objective values. But in addition, an objective value is valid not only for individuals and groups, but for the universe.[71] This means that the structure of the universe is grounded in moral values. More than a mere psychological fact in persons, moral law is "an expression of a Holy Will which can be neither defied nor mocked"[72] without penalty. At the end of the day moral law will reign supreme because it is established and maintained by God.

King came to the formal study of personalism with a deeply ingrained conviction that the structure of the universe is on the side of justice and righteousness; that there is a higher law than human law, and that persons violate it at great risk. This meant for King that civil law must always be judged in light of moral law.

King's earliest conviction that there are objective moral laws and that the universe is value-fused can be traced to a sermon that he gave at Morehouse College in his senior year. King "declared that 'there are moral laws of the universe that man can no more violate with impunity than he can violate its physical laws.'"[73] Because of this homespun personalistic conviction he could easily resonate to Brightman's philosophical doctrine of an objective moral order in the universe which persons ought to obey. Brightman maintained that the existence of such an order is as real to one's moral experience as the objective physical order is to one's sense experience.[74] Both the moral and physical orders are grounded in God. That persons have moral experience at all implies both that a moral order exists, and that it has a source. For the theist-creationist that source is God. Therefore, to violate moral law places one in jeopardy with God and the universe.[75] It would be equivalent to going against the grain of the universe, which is to disregard God's law. There can be nothing but grave consequences for violating moral law, just as if one violated a physical law, such as the law of gravity.

King's belief in the existence of an objective moral order can be seen in a number of his speeches and sermons. In one sermon he said, "God walks with us. He has placed within the very structure of this universe certain absolute moral laws. We can neither defy nor break them. If we disobey them, they will break us."[76] In other words, one cannot violate moral law without also having to contend with the consequences. Elsewhere King said, "There is a law in the moral world—a silent, invisible imperative, akin to the laws in the physical world—which reminds us that life will work only in a certain way."[77] This statement reflects the influence of Brightman's view of the existence of an objective moral order in the universe which requires that persons live together in ways that are consistent with moral laws. These laws require respect and love for persons both as individuals and as members of communities. If persons choose not to live in harmony with these laws, all efforts to achieve the highest good, both for self and for the common good, will be unnecessarily hampered. For both persons and the universe are so structured that fundamentally there is in them a *nisus* or an inherent urge toward harmonious and communal living based on mutual respect, love, and sharing. This point is of no small importance for King's Beloved Community ideal. Since he held that reality hinges on moral foundations, it follows that reality itself draws persons toward the Beloved Community. To disregard this is to severely jeopardize the quality of personal-communal living.

Violation of physical laws of the universe may lead to severe consequences. We can expect the same when there is violation of the moral law on which all reality is grounded. King's conviction was that moral law in the universe is as absolute and permanent as physical law. If one intentionally jumps off the Bank One Tower, one violates the law of gravity. Unless one is incredibly lucky, one will either be severely injured or mortally wounded. If one violates the law of gravity, one can generally count on suffering the consequences. So, too, are there consequences when one violates the moral law, which is also absolute and ingrained in the universe by God.

King maintained that because reality is value-fused, persons live in a moral universe, despite human and group behavior. In such a universe, God is on the side of justice and love.[78] There was no doubt in King's mind that in such a universe there are some things that are right, and some things that are wrong.[79] Because there is a law of love in this value-fused universe, hatred, for example—and anything else that is contrary to love—is absolutely wrong. One need not get into an intellectual debate over the matter. To disobey the law of love in a value-friendly universe means that one is out of step with the best in the universe and must face the consequences. And because love is a social category, there will be consequences for both the individual and the community. To hate an individual or a group has consequences not only for the hater and the hated, but for the entire community, inasmuch as the social nature of reality means that persons are interdependent. In addition, the logic of this means that to violate the law of love is to disobey God, since God is the author of both moral law and the law of love.

King frequently quoted a line from the nineteenth-century abolitionist preacher Theodore Parker:[80] "The arc of the moral universe is long, [but] it bends toward justice."[81] By this King expressed a fundamental conviction that no matter how much injustice exists in the world, no matter how badly one is treated by outside forces, there is something at the very center of the universe which sides with good and justice. The basis of this conviction was King's belief in the existence of an objective moral order created and sustained by God.

To say that reality is value-fused may be interpreted to mean that there is a fundamental goodness at the center of the universe such that all being has an essential goodness, notwithstanding the capacity of persons (because of freedom of will) to behave in ways that are contrary to, or that thwart, goodness. At any rate, King believed that the universe is friendly rather than unfriendly to values. This means that everything that persons do in the world has value implications. Therefore, there is no such thing as moral neutrality. No person or group is allowed to escape the moral hook. The conviction that reality hinges on moral foundations means that there are no moral holidays in the face of injustice, oppression, or other practices that undermine the humanity and dignity of persons. Persons are morally obligated to resist injustice and oppression, whether done to themselves or to others.

Because persons are created in freedom and thus are self-determining beings, they can choose to obey or disobey moral law. The rational awareness that reality is grounded on moral foundations is not in itself sufficient to guarantee that persons will always behave accordingly. God therefore creates persons with freedom of will. Persons are not only capable of knowing that the universe is friendly to values, but have the potential power to orchestrate and live their lives in ways that are consistent with such knowledge. In the area of morality there is no room on the fence. One stands for right, or for wrong. There is nothing else.

King's conviction that the universe hinges on moral foundations means that persons ought—at all times—to live and relate to each other in ways that exhibit respect for their own and each other's humanity and dignity. The invisible eternal moral laws are a reminder that there are some things that are right and some wrong, whether someone sees us or not.

In King's view, God instilled value in the universe. From this he concluded that the universe itself is on the side of all who endeavor to achieve and sustain the highest personal-communal values. "God has made the universe to be based on a moral law," said King. The progress of humanity is therefore dependent on its willingness to come to terms with, and abide by, the conviction that the universe is based on moral foundations, and that God is its author and sustainer.[82] This was King's way of theologically grounding his belief that reality is value-fused. This is why he was adamant about challenging unjust civil laws and political practices, for these contradicted his conviction that the universe is on the side of justice.

King's frequent statement that freedom fighters have cosmic companionship was an outgrowth of, and a further solidification of, his conviction that the grain of the universe is on the side of right and justice. Those who are outraged at injustice and oppression, *and* who fight and strive toward the establishment of justice, have the assurance of being in harmony with the moral law and with God's will. Because persons have constant cosmic companionship, they—and most especially the poor and the oppressed—need never be dissuaded from their struggle against the forces of evil and injustice. King possessed an unqualified trust in this cosmic companionship.

Moral Law and the Moral Law System

A moral law is a principle which is *universal* in application. It applies to all cases and is valid for all persons everywhere. Brightman developed a moral law system, which was later enhanced and/or enlarged by some of his disciples.[83] He intended that this system be relevant and meaningful in every culture. However, he rightly sensed that cultural differences may require certain adaptations of the respective laws.

Brightman distinguished moral law from civil, religious, natural, and logical law.[84] Moral law has two necessary conditions: (1) it must be a universal principle or norm, and (2) it must apply to the obligation of the will in choosing.[85] Because it is a universal norm it is a law. Because it requires the will to choose, it is moral. Accordingly, Brightman held that no act is moral merely because it conforms to a social code. Merely obeying a written civil law, for example, does not make one moral, for such a law might well be immoral or unjust. King applied this principle throughout his ministry. He concluded early in his career that an unjust law, for example, a segregation law, is no law at all since it demeans the humanity and dignity of select individuals or groups.[86] An act is moral only if it conforms to moral law.[87] Therefore, every civil law is subject to critique by moral law.

The moral law system is regulative, not prescriptive. That is, it does not tell us what specific moral choices to make. Instead, it is intended to guide us as we endeavor to make responsible moral choices. Because it is a "system" its use requires effort and intentionality on the part of those who use it. For in order to accomplish what Brightman intended, the moral law system must be seen in its totality. This means that one must be aware at all times of the place and role of each law, as well as their interrelationship with each other and the entire system.

There are three sets of laws in Brightman's moral law system: *Formal Laws* (Logical Law, Law of Autonomy); *Axiological Laws* (Axiological Law, Law of Consequences, Law of the Best Possible, Law of Specification, Law of the Most Inclusive End, Law of Ideal of Control); and *Personalistic Laws* (Law of Individualism, Law of Altruism, Law of the Ideal of Personality). Each category and the laws in them presuppose the law which came before and anticipate the law which follows in the line of progression toward the most concrete law in the system. Each law beyond the Logical Law (the first law in the system) includes more content than the one that precedes it. Brightman sums up the contribution of each set of laws to the system. "The Formal Laws deal solely with the will as a subjective fact. The Axiological Laws deal with the values which the will ought to choose. The Personalistic Laws are more comprehensive; they deal with the personality as a concrete whole."[88] In the Personalistic Laws, the emphasis is on the person and persons-in-relationship as the *subjects* of the preceding laws. The Law of the Ideal of Personality is, for Brightman, the summary law of the entire moral law system. It states: "All persons ought to judge and guide all of their acts by their ideal conception (in harmony with the other Laws) of what the whole personality ought to become both individually and socially."[89]

King and Moral Law

When King matriculated at Boston University in the Ph.D. program, he was a student of Brightman's for only a brief period, for he died less than two years after King began his work. Since King also studied under DeWolf (who became his major adviser when Brightman died), there is no question that he was familiar with Brightman's moral law system. During his first year of graduate study he wrote a paper in DeWolf's class on personalism entitled "The Personalism of J. M. E. McTaggart Under Criticism." At several points King contrasted Mc-Taggart and Brightman. In the discussion on the significance of freedom, King cited passages in Brightman's book *Moral Laws* to support his criticism of McTaggart's rejection of freedom. At one point he wrote, "As Brightman has cogently put it: 'If choice is not possible, the science of ethics is not possible. If rational, purposive choice is not effective in the [control] of life, goodness is not possible.'"[90] King believed that without freedom persons would be little more than automatons. And then in a passage reminiscent of Bowne's emphasis not only on the ethical, but the speculative significance of freedom,[91] King again quoted *Moral Laws* approvingly: "Without freedom, we are not free to think, for the power to think means that the individual can impose on himself the ideal of logic or scientific method and hold it through thick and thin."[92] This requires self-determination or power of will.

One who is familiar with the moral law system and has also studied King's writings can easily detect his appropriation of these laws in his writings and speeches. However, what one should not look for in King is explicit naming of the individual laws, although there is clear-cut evidence that his moral reasoning was influenced by the moral law system. Furthermore, unlike Brightman and other moral law theorists, King sought to apply and work out these laws in the context of his social justice work. So while he did not specifically name the laws, he often cited the basic principle of a particular moral law. For example, when he works through the practical application of the Logical Law he does not cite the Logical Law as such. Rather, we find him citing the principle involved, namely, "logical consistency." We see this, for example, when he discusses whether one can be "logically consistent" when advocating the need to obey some laws and disobey others.[93]

Both Walter Muelder and John Ansbro have addressed the subject of the moral laws in the work of King. Although Kenneth Smith and Ira Zepp, Jr., considered the influence of the existence of an objective moral law on King's thinking, they did not examine his appropriation of the moral law system as such.[94] However, Muelder and Ansbro have done an admirable job of this.[95]

Ansbro suggests that in several instances King appropriated the moral laws differently than Brightman. Consideration of two of these will suffice for our purpose. Although King appealed to both the Law of Individualism and the Law of Altruism, Ansbro suggests that he identified more with the latter law. This implies that there was in King's ethics a stronger other-regarding sentiment than we find in Brightman. The Law of Individualism points to the individual as the basic moral unit. The importance of self-love follows from this. It expresses what Bowne meant when he said that no person should ever be used as fuel to warm society.[96] King accepted the validity of the Law of Individualism, but seemed to place less emphasis on it than did Brightman. Instead, King focused more on regard for the other, or the ethics of agape. This ethic emphasizes the needs of the other, not of the self.[97]

According to King, agape "is the love of God working in the lives of men. When we love on the *agape* level, we love men not because we like them, not because their attitudes and ways appeal to us, but because God loves them."[98] It is this understanding of love which led King to the provocative conclusion that "unearned suffering is redemptive."[99] But he went further: "I pray that, *recognizing the necessity of suffering*, the Negro will make of it a virtue. To suffer in a righteous cause is to grow to our humanity's full stature."[100] (Emphasis added) As for the need to abide by the philosophy of nonviolence, King liked to speak of "a willingness to accept suffering without retaliation, to accept blows from the opponent without striking back." He quoted Gandhi approvingly in this regard: "Rivers of blood may have to flow before we gain our freedom, but it must be our blood."[101] There was no question in King's mind that "suffering . . . has tremendous educational and transforming possibilities."[102] This stance might be repulsive to some, but it is consistent with King's conviction that the universe is grounded on a moral foundation. For the logic of such a stance easily leads to an ethic of nonviolence and a willingness to accept blows without retaliating in kind. One is obligated to retaliate, but nonviolently. The implication is that one who shares King's conviction would not want to harm persons because each possesses innate dignity.

Ansbro contends that King "was convinced that *agape* may at times demand even the suspension of the law of self-preservation so that through our self-sacrifice we can help create the beloved community."[103] King did not believe that such self-sacrifice necessarily precludes self-respect and self-love, although one surely wonders about this when it is known that he frequently placed the moral onus on those who are actually suffering oppression and injustice. That is, more often than not King expected the oppressed to make sacrifices in order to love their oppressors. For example, in one place he said that "there will be no permanent solution to the race problem until oppressed men develop the capacity to love their enemies."[104] King believed that in the best interest of the redemption of others and the establishment of the Beloved Community, it is sometimes necessary for individuals to sacrifice all for such an end. Ansbro rightly concludes that, more than Brightman, King's application of the Law of Altruism was more open to self-sacrifice.[105]

This is an interesting point, since the philosophy of personalism maintains that the self is the basic moral unit. A necessary precondition of respect and regard for others, then, is that one respect and love self. According to Bowne,

> The condition of owing anything to others is to owe something to myself. The humanity which I respect in others, I must respect in myself. I am not permitted to act irrationally toward myself any more than toward others.[106]

In this regard, duties to self are not of secondary, but primary importance. Such duties "must take first rank in ethics." One is never more responsible for others than for self. It may be argued that this is important because of the social or communal implications. Bowne continues: "Every one must be a moral object for himself, and an object of supreme importance; for *he is not simply the particular person, A or B, he is also a bearer of the ideal of humanity*, and its realization depends preeminently upon himself."[107] (Emphasis added) This fundamentally Kantian stance means that one is more likely to respect the dignity of others if one first learns to acknowledge duties to oneself; to recognize that one is an end in oneself. If one acknowledges one's own worth or dignity one will more likely acknowledge that of others.[108]

Personalistic ethics condemns not self-interest, but selfishness. Since the time of Bowne this type of ethics has sought a balance between self-

and other-regarding interests. Just as the individual is not to disregard the needs and interests of society, society is not to unduly sacrifice the individual for its ends. Both the individual and society have values that each must respect.[109] And yet there is no question that in personalism the individual has the right of way, a stance that King took as his own.

As the basic moral unit, the individual always has rights against others and society. However, King seemed more likely to sacrifice this principle than did Brightman or Bowne. One wonders how it can be expected that a person can have proper regard for others if not first and continuously for self. If one has little or no regard for self, it is inconceivable that one will have a healthy regard for the neighbor, let alone for those who oppress and demean one's humanity. And while it may be conceded that it is difficult to maintain a good balance between the Law of Individualism and the Law of Altruism, I would say that for a period of time it behooves groups like young African American males to place more emphasis on healthy regard for self. This might heighten their regard for others as well. Because many have never been taught the importance and meaning of love of self, I understand perfectly why so many young African American males live only to be murdered or to commit murder in their community. The need for a much higher regard for self among them is absolutely crucial in light of the alarmingly high incidence of black-on-black violence and murder. Yet I want to be careful not to suggest that King was not aware of the need for self-love among young African American males. He most assuredly was aware of this deficit, as reflected in his comments on having met and talked with young gang members during the Chicago campaign in 1966.[110]

What now are some ethical implications of King's belief that the universe is friendly to value and therefore hinges on moral foundations? What is the ethical importance of his belief in the existence of objective moral laws? The last section of this chapter responds to these and related questions.

Ethical Implications for Today

As a personalist, King's most original and creative contribution was his determination to translate personalism into social action by applying it to major social problems such as racism, poverty/consumerism/ economic exploitation, and militarism.[111] By focusing on socioethical personalism, King was only following the precedence set by the African American John Wesley Edward Bowen (1855–1933), who studied under Bowne.[112] But more than any other personalist, King forged the concept of the dignity of the person in the fire of nonviolent demonstrations, which often pitted him and his followers against vicious and venomous racists, high-powered fire hoses, and vicious attack dogs. Therefore, the very texture of his personalism was different from that of his teachers.

That King was a member of a race of people who have been systematically discriminated against from the time of American slavery to this writing is reason in itself that he would have been the premier social-activist personalist in this country. It would not have been enough for him to merely study the philosophy and theology of personalism and write monographs on the subject to satisfy the intellectual curiosity of those who do not suffer under, *and* benefit from, the iron feet of oppression and injustice. It was never enough to simply know the truth of personalism.

King was from a long tradition of African Americans who believed that *to know* obligates one morally. That is, to know the truth necessarily means that one is obligated to do what it requires. To *have* the truth is to *do* the truth, a view that has not been popular in white Western civilization. For King the truth may be an end in itself only if to have access to it means also that one is required to do what possessing truth requires. He was not consoled by simply having the truth for the sake of having it. Therefore, King could not merely accept as truth the personalistic tenets that God is personal and loving, that persons are ends in themselves and thus possess infinite dignity, and that the universe rests on a moral foundation, without also applying these to the everyday affairs of concrete flesh-and-blood human beings.

But something else pushed and pulled King toward social-activist personalism, and would not let him be content with a theoretical or abstract personalism that did not address persons' everyday lives. We have seen that he believed there is something about the nature of reality itself that places on all persons a moral onus to act to eliminate injustice and oppression in whatever forms they manifest themselves. That is, King believed that the "stuff" of reality is of the nature of value or that which is moral. Reality is grounded on a moral, rather than an immoral or even amoral, foundation. This has important implications for individual and communal living in the world.

Indeed, not only does it have implications for personal-communal living, but for how persons relate to all aspects of God's creation. For the conviction that reality hinges on moral foundations must be applicable to the entire creation, not merely to that which pertains to persons and their communities. In other words, the faith that the universe is grounded on value means that any viable personalism must be ecopersonalism. That is, it must acknowledge not only the intrinsic worth of all life-forms—human and nonhuman—but must be concerned about how they interrelate and contribute to the well-being of other areas of creation. Ecopersonalism is concerned about how to ensure respect and appreciation for every life-form, including moral relations between persons and the natural world.

What does it mean for our personal-communal living when it is said that the universe is friendly to value, or that it hinges on moral foundations? We can be certain that when Martin Luther King, Jr., made this declaration he was saying something deep and profound about the fundamental nature of the universe and the way(s) that persons ought to be and live in the world. He was saying that the universe, indeed reality itself, is based on moral foundations. This, he believed, has everything to do with how persons should think and relate to themselves, other persons, and the rest of creation. Moreover, King's declaration means that every life-form—human and nonhuman—has intrinsic value, although not all life-forms have the same degree of worth. A person, for example, has more value than a dog (although this is not always evident in the way we humans treat each other). The point is that, although we may rank the worth of life-forms, all life-forms possess intrinsic value. This must be the conclusion that one comes to if he agrees with King that reality is founded on a moral foundation.

The claim that there is an objective moral order and that the universe is grounded on moral values also says something of significance about the nature of the Creator. King was both a theist and a creationist. He lived by the conviction that as Creator, God is personal. Minimally, any personal being has the capacity for rationality or intelligence and for self-determination. As Creator, then, God would be the supreme exemplification of both rationality and self-determination. In addition, the source of these traits in all created persons must be attributed to God.

If God is supremely intelligent and self-determining, it is reasonable to conclude that God thoughtfully and willingly established the universe on a moral foundation. This not only implies God's essential love and goodness, but tells us something about how God expects persons to treat each other in the world. It also reveals something about how God must expect persons to behave in the world, individually and collectively.

If one is really serious when one says that the universe is friendly to value, it must be the case that whatever else one may believe and do, one cannot intentionally violate one's own or the personhood of others. One cannot intentionally adhere to a racist, sexist, heterosexist, or classist lifestyle if one truly believes in the existence of an objective moral order whose source is the God of Martin Luther King, Jr. For this God requires that justice be done in the world, and that it be done in ways that both respect and enhance the dignity of persons. This God requires that persons live in communities where respect for the dignity of persons and love of persons is the rule rather than the exception.

The universe is created in such a way that everybody ought to be treated with dignity and respect just because they are. For the claim being made here is that the universe is charged with value, or that which is moral. Therefore, moral agents such as we humans are obligated to acknowledge, respect, and celebrate (not just tolerate!) the value of all life-forms. And now, more specifically, what does it mean for our personal-communal living when it is said that the universe is friendly to value, or that it hinges on moral foundations?

For one thing it means that every person, regardless of gender, race, class, health, sexual orientation, and age, is imbued with the image, fragrance, and voice of God. Because God is both rational and self-determining, we may say that God thoughtfully and willingly calls every person into existence. No person exists by accident. God calls every person into existence, and, as African Americans like to say, calls each person by name! Thus every person has absolute and infinite value, for every person belongs (in the best sense) to God. Martin Luther King was fond of saying that every person is somebody, because every person is a child of God.[113] Every person has infinite worth because every person is loved by God.[114] As such, we owe self and each other respect. Indeed, whenever and wherever any two or more persons meet in the world, they owe each other respect and goodwill.[115] In addition, no person or group should be easily sacrificed for the well-being of another, considering that each is equally imbued with the image of God. King put it poetically: "There are no gradations in the image of God. Every man from a treble white to a bass black is significant on God's keyboard, precisely because every man is made in the image of God."[116]

The conviction that the universe is grounded on a moral foundation also implies the obligation to exert a strong sense of self-determination in the face of dehumanizing and oppressive treatment. In such cases, persons are morally obligated to exert to the fullest their will to overcome injustice and other dehumanizing practices. Those who are oppressed must never submit to their oppressors and oppressive conditions, but must assert their entire being against them.

Although African Americans are not the cause of their oppression, King, not unlike Malcolm X and a host of African American ancestors, was convinced that they are responsible for how they respond to what has been (and is being) done to them. They are responsible for their liberation and empowerment. No matter how violently their personhood is assaulted by powerful and racist whites, for example, it is within African Americans' power as persons to accept such treatment or not, to fight to eradicate it or not. King did not excuse what racist whites did and were doing. His primary focus was on the recovery of his people and the conviction that they themselves possessed the key to their recovery and freedom. He was confident that because of the long history of the African American protest tradition, his people had in them what it takes to regain their sense of dignity and worth. Indeed, they are morally obligated to do this because the universe stands on a moral foundation.

King believed that there was no lack of human and other resources to solve the problems being created to undermine the humanity and dignity of blacks. What was lacking, he believed, was *the will* to make the effort to eliminate this problem. The basic deficit in ethics is the absence of the will to do the right thing.[117] King conceded that the mere possession of a good will would not in itself solve social problems. And yet such a will must be the basis of all ethics—a necessary prerequisite toward solving social maladies, a necessary element in the enhancement of human dignity. If one has the will to do the right thing, one can usually find a way to do it. But it requires effort. King himself held firm to the conviction that human progress never rolls in on the wheels of inevitability. It occurs when persons believe that the grain of the universe is on the side of right, justice, and righteousness, and when they work cooperatively with each other and with God to achieve that which is good for all.[118]

King was convinced that his people would regain neither their lost sense of dignity nor their freedom without a staunch determination and willingness to struggle to overcome and to stand up. He frequently told his people that a new sense of dignity would come about only through determined struggle and hard work. The awareness that there exists an objective moral order, that the universe hinges on moral foundations, is not sufficient in itself to guarantee that persons will behave in ways that are consistent with and honor such a conviction. But there is consolation in the faith that the universe itself is so constructed by God that persons will live and prosper on the highest plane only if they live in ways that encourage living together respectfully as sisters and brothers. God has infused the universe and all being with value. Therefore, when persons and groups intentionally strive to live according to the highest moral principles, they live in obedience to moral law.

Yet another implication of the claim that the universe is friendly to value is that persons and communities have to own responsibility for what happens or is allowed by them to happen. The conviction that the universe hinges on moral foundations does not undermine the existence in persons of moral agency. Persons are free within limits to make choices. This means that they must also own responsibility for the choices made. That the universe is grounded on moral foundations implies that persons are created with the capacity to do what is good, just, and noble. And although they also have the capacity to do the opposite, in the end they are responsible for whatever direction is chosen.

NOTES

1. Martin Luther King, Jr., *Strength to Love* (New York: Harper & Row, 1963), p. 105.

2. For a more extensive discussion on the meaning of personalism, see my book, *Personalism: A Critical Introduction* (St. Louis: Chalice Press,

1999), chapter 9. There is also a brief discussion on King and the moral laws. That text also discusses the impact of personalism on King, as well as his contributions to it. Portions of the discussion on moral law in the present chapter are found in my article "Martin Luther King, Jr., Personalism, and Moral Law," *The Asbury Theological Journal*, vol. 52, no. 2 (Fall 1997): pp. 32–39. In addition, a shorter, revised version of several areas of the present chapter appears in my article "Martin Luther King, Jr., and the Objective Moral Order: Some Ethical Implications," *Encounter*, vol. 61, no. 2 (Spring 2000): pp. 219–244.

3. See David Garrow, "The Intellectual Development of Martin Luther King, Jr.: Influences and Commentaries," in Garrow, ed., *Martin Luther King, Jr.: Civil Rights Leader, Theologian, Orator* (New York: Carlson Publishing, 1989), vol. 2, p. 451 n. 23.

4. See Martin Luther King, Jr., *Stride toward Freedom* (New York: Harper & Brothers, 1958), p. 100.

5. Quote taken with permission from a paper submitted by Susan Harlow in a class on the Theological Ethics of Martin Luther King, Jr., April 1997, Christian Theological Seminary.

6. See Rufus Burrow, Jr., "Personal-Communitarianism and the Beloved Community," *Encounter*, vol. 61, no. 1 (Winter 2000): pp. 23–43.

7. See the recently published anthology of Ransom's writings edited by Anthony B. Pinn, *Making the Gospel Plain: The Writings of Bishop Reverdy C. Ransom* (Harrisburg, Pa: Trinity Press International, 1999).

8. See Howard Thurman, *The Search for Common Ground: An Inquiry into the Basis of Man's Experience of Community* (New York: Harper & Row, 1971). This text comprises Thurman's most systematic and philosophical discussion on community.

9. See Lawrence N. Jones, "Black Christians in Antebellum America: In Quest of the Beloved Community," *Journal of Religious Thought*, vol. 38, no. 1 (Spring–Summer 1981): p. 12.

10. These include the Englishman John Grote and the Americans Walt Whitman and A. Bronson Alcott.

11. Borden P. Bowne, *The Philosophy of Herbert Spencer* (New York: Phillips & Hunt, 1874).

12. See Rufus Burrow, Jr., "Borden Parker Bowne's Doctrine of God," *Encounter*, vol. 53, no. 4 (Autumn 1992): pp. 381–400.

13. Albert C. Knudson, *The Philosophy of Personalism* (New York: Abingdon, 1927), pp. 85 and 433.

14. However, it should be noted that there was a similar movement afoot at the University of California under the leadership of George Holmes Howison (1836–1916). Unlike Bowne, who came to consider

himself "a Personalist, the first of the clan in any thoroughgoing sense," Howison named his philosophy Personal Idealism. There are several differences between their philosophies, the chief of which is that Howison was a noncreationist, believing that God is the Final, not the First, cause. Bowne, on the other hand, was a creationist. He insisted that God is the fundamental cause of all things. I discuss at length some similarities and dissimilarities between Bowne and Howison in my book *Personalism: A Critical Introduction* (St. Louis: Chalice Press, 1999).

15. King, *Stride toward Freedom*, pp. 19 and 20.

16. Martin Luther King, Sr., *Daddy King: An Autobiography*, with Clayton Riley (New York: William Morrow and Company, 1980), p. 82.

17. Cited in Leo Sandon, Jr., "Boston University Personalism and Southern Baptist Theology," *Foundations*, vol. 20 (April–June 1977): p. 105. King wrote about Brightman's influence in a 1957 publication in *Bostonia* (Spring 1957), p. 7. He also mentioned in his application to Boston University Graduate School the influence of Brightman's ideas on his thinking as a seminarian at Crozer Theological Seminary [See Clayborne Carson, ed., *The Papers of Martin Luther King, Jr.* (Berkeley: University of California Press, 1992), vol. 1, p. 390]. King noted Brightman's presence at Boston University as one of two reasons that institution appealed to him.

18. See King, "The Personalism of J. M. E. McTaggart under Criticism." This was a paper King did in Brightman's course on philosophy of religion in 1951, and is included in Clayborn Carson, ed., *The Papers of Martin Luther King, Jr.* (Berkeley: University of California Press, 1994), vol. 2, pp. 61–76.

19. See King, "A Comparison and Evaluation of the Philosophical Views Set Forth in J. M. E. McTaggart's *Some Dogmas of Religion* and William E. Hocking's *The Meaning of God in Human Experience* with Those Set Forth in Edgar S. Brightman's Course on 'Philosophy of Religion,'" in Carson, ed., *The Papers of Martin Luther King, Jr.*, vol. 2, pp. 76–92.

20. King, *The Autobiography of Martin Luther King, Jr.*, ed. Carson (New York: Warner Books), p. 32.

21. However, Jimmy L. Kirby and I argue that there are a number of openings for theistic finitism in King's writings. See our article "Conceptions of God in the Thinking of Martin Luther King, Jr. and Edgar S. Brightman," *Encounter*, vol. 60, no. 3 (Summer 1999): pp. 283–305.

22. See King's doctoral dissertation, "A Comparison of the Conceptions of God in the Thinking of Henry Nelson Wieman and Paul Tillich," Boston University, 1955. Here King opts for a doctrine of God similar to that of Bowne and DeWolf.

23. See David Garrow, ed., *Martin Luther King, Jr. and the Civil Rights Movement* (New York: Carlson Publishing, 1989), vol. 1, p. xiv. Garrow also argues that King often used the phrase "the dignity and worth of all human personality" in sermons and speeches because "it was the consonance between King's already-developed views and the principal theme of personalism that led King to adopt and give voice to that tenet so firmly and consistently" (Garrow, "The Intellectual Development of Martin Luther King, Jr.: Influences and Commentaries," in Garrow, ed., *Martin Luther King, Jr. and the Civil Rights Movement*, vol. 2, p. 445). In addition, Garrow complains in an endnote that King's teachers and mentors at Boston University "have badly overstated the formative influence their instruction and personalism had on King" (ibid., 451 n. 23). He then invites the reader to examine writings by DeWolf ("Martin Luther King, Jr., as Theologian," *Journal of the Interdenominational Theological Center*, vol. 4 [Spring 1977]: pp. 1–11) and Muelder ("Communitarian Christian Ethics: A Personal Statement and a Response," in Deats, ed., *Toward a Discipline of Social Ethics*, pp. 295–320, at 299 and 314; and "Martin Luther King, Jr.'s Ethics of Nonviolent Action," unpublished paper, 1985, King Center).

24. See Keith D. Miller, *Voice of Deliverance: The Language of Martin Luther King, Jr. and Its Sources* (New York: The Free Press, 1992), pp. 7 and 17.

25. See Peter J. Paris, *Black Religious Leaders: Conflict in Unity* (Louisville, Ky.: Westminster/John Knox Press, 1991), pp. 100–101.

26. Garrow, "The Intellectual Development of Martin Luther King, Jr.: Influences and Commentaries" in *Martin Luther King, Jr.: Civil Rights Leader, Theologian, Orator*, ed. Garrow (New York: Carlson Publishing, 1989), p. 5.

27. Taylor Branch, *Parting the Waters: America in the King Years 1954–63* (New York: Simon and Schuster, 1988), p. 918.

28. Garrow, "The Intellectual Development of Martin Luther King, Jr.: Influences and Commentaries" in *Martin Luther King, Jr.: Civil Rights Leader, Theologian, Orator*, p. 6.

29. Coretta Scott King, *My Life with Martin Luther King, Jr.* (New York: Holt Rinehart and Winston, 1969), p. 92.

30. Carson, ed., *The Papers of Martin Luther King, Jr.* (Berkeley: University of California Press, 1992), vol. 1, p. 390.

31. King, "A Comparison of the Conception of God in the Thinking of Henry Nelson Wieman and Paul Tillich," p. 270. The claim that complete and perfect personality inheres only in God was the view of Bowne's teacher, Hermann Lotze. In an early book, *Studies in Theism* (New York: Phillips & Hunt, 1879), p. 275, Bowne credited Lotze with this idea. Here he wrote that "we must say with Lotze that full personality is possible only

to the infinite. It alone is in full possession and knowledge of itself. . . . Full personality exists only where the nature is transparent to itself, and where all the powers are under absolute control. Such personality is not ours; it can belong only to the infinite, while ours is but its faint and imperfect image." God is perfect consciousness, selfhood, will, and wisdom.

32. King, "A Comparison of the Conception of God in the Thinking of Henry Nelson Wieman and Paul Tillich," p. 270. See also Bowne, *Personalism* (Boston: Houghton Mifflin, 1908), p. 266, where he characterizes essential person as selfhood, self-consciousness, self-control, and the power to know.

33. Cited in King, "A Comparison of the Conception of God in the Thinking of Henry Nelson Wieman and Paul Tillich," p. 268, taken from Albert C. Knudson, *The Doctrine of God* (Nashville, Tenn.: Abingdon Press, 1930), p. 300.

34. King, *The Trumpet of Conscience* (New York: Harper and Row, 1968), p. 72.

35. The types of personalisms include (but may not be limited to): Atheistic Personalism, Pantheistic Personalism, Absolutistic Personalism, Relativistic Personalism, Ethical Personalism, Theistic Personalism, Realistic Personalism, Political Personalism, Panpsychistic Personalism, Anthropormorphic Personalism, and Afrikan American Personalism. Included in my unpublished essay "Francis John McConnell and Personalistic Social Ethics."

36. King, "The Ethical Demands for Integration," in Washington, ed., *A Testament of Hope*, p. 122.

37. Ibid., p. 119.

38. See Bowne, *The Principles of Ethics* (New York: American Book Company, 1892), pp. 97, 203, 216–217.

39. Bowne, *Studies in Theism* (New York: Phillips & Hunt, 1879), pp. 411–412.

40. Bowne, *Studies in Theism*, p. 4.

41. King, "Pilgrimage to Nonviolence," in King, *Strength to Love* (New York: Harper & Row, 1963), p. 141.

42. King, "An Experiment in Love," in Washington, ed., *A Testament of Hope*, p. 20. I find it interesting that King did not characterize God's power as absolute or omnipotent, but as "matchless." This seems a subtle qualification of the classical view of divine omnipotence. Even Brightman, whose doctrine of God King both appreciated and criticized, would appreciate the idea of the "matchless" power of God. For it does not mean that God possesses absolute power in the classical sense, and thus has affinity with Brightman's idea of the finite-infinite God.

43. Here I follow the distinction that Paul W. Taylor makes between *moral subjects* and *moral agents*. Any conscious being is a moral subject, even if unable to make responsible moral choices. In any event they are beings to whom moral agents owe responsibilities. Moral agents, on the other hand, are moral subjects whose faculties are such that they are capable of making responsible moral choices, anticipating the consequences of those choices, willing to take responsibility for these, and able to assess the outcome and apply what is learned in new situations calling for moral choice. See Taylor, *Respect for Nature: A Theory of Environmental Ethics* (Princeton, N.J.: Princeton University Press, 1986), pp. 14–16.

44. King, "The Ethical Demands for Integration" in Washington, ed., *A Testament of Hope*, p. 120.

45. King, "The Personalism of J. M. E. McTaggart under Criticism," in Carson, ed., *The Papers of Martin Luther King, Jr.*, vol. 2, p. 73. This paper was presented to DeWolf on December 4, 1951, in his class on Personalism.

46. King, *Strength to Love*, p. 90.

47. Edgar S. Brightman, *Nature and Values* (New York: Abingdon Press, 1945), p. 117.

48. See Kwame Gyekye's excellent discussion on the relation between the individual and the community in *Tradition and Modernity: Philosophical Reflections on the African Experience* (New York: Oxford University Press, 1997), chapter 2.

49. Francis J. McConnell, *Personal Christianity* (New York: Fleming H. Revell Company, 1914), p. 48.

50. Walter G. Mueuelder, *Moral Law in Christian Social Ethics* (Richmond, Va.: John Knox Press, 1966), p. 124.

51. Brightman, *An Introduction to Philosophy,* 3rd ed., rev. by Robert N. Beck (New York: Holt Rinehart Winston, 1963), p. 353.

52. Knudson, *The Principles of Christian Ethics* (New York: Abingdon Press, 1943), p. 118.

53. See Lotte Hoskins, ed., *"I Have a Dream": The Quotations of Martin Luther King, Jr.* (New York: Grosset & Dunlap, 1968), p. 71.

54. King, "The Ethical Demands for Integration" in Washington, ed., *A Testament of Hope*, p. 122.

55. King, "A Christmas Sermon on Peace" in Washington, ed., *A Testament of Hope*, p. 254.

56. Bowne, *Principles of Ethics*, p. 276.

57. Ibid., p. 198.

58. Ibid., p. 199.

59. Ibid., p. 208.

60. Thomas Hill Green, *Prolegomena to Ethics* (Oxford: Clarendon Press, 1884), p. 193.

61. Bowne, *Principles of Ethics*, p. 253.

62. King, "Guidelines for a Constructive Church" in *A Knock at Midnight*, eds. Clayborne Carson and Peter Holloran (New York: Warner Books, 1998), pp. 110–111.

63. Bowne, *The Philosophy of Herbert Spencer*, p. 265.

64. Bowne, *Theism* (New York: American Book Company, 1902), p. 255.

65. Ibid., p. 255.

66. Ibid., p. 254.

67. Branch, *Parting the Waters*, p. 14.

68. Ibid., p. 120.

69. Ibid., p. 127.

70. Ibid., pp. 128–129.

71. See Edgar S. Brightman's enlightening discussion on the objectivity of value in *An Introduction to Philosophy*, 3rd ed., rev. by Robert N. Beck, chapter 7.

72. Bowne, *Principles of Ethics*, p. 201.

73. Quoted in Branch, *Parting the Waters*, p. 68.

74. Brightman, *Moral Laws* (Nashville, Tenn.: Abingdon Press, 1933), 286.

75. Bowne, *Principles of Ethics*, p. 201.

76. King, "Our God Is Able," in *Strength to Love*, p. 105.

77. Lotte Hoskins, comp. and ed., *"I Have a Dream": The Quotations of Martin Luther King, Jr.* (New York: Grosset & Dunlap, 1968), p. 79.

78. Bowne, *Principles of Ethics*, p. 201.

79. King, "Rediscovering Lost Values," in *A Knock at Midnight*, eds. Clayborne Carson and Peter Holloran (New York: Warner Books, 1998), p. 12.

80. Taylor Branch attributes this line to Parker. See *Parting the Waters*, p. 197.

81. Hoskins, ed., *"I Have A Dream,"* p. 63.

82. King, *The Autobiography of Martin Luther King, Jr.*, ed. Carson, p. 33.

83. These include: Peter A. Bertocci and Richard Millard, *Personality and the Good: Psychological and Ethical Perspectives* (New York: David McKay Company, 1963); Walter G. Muelder, *Moral Law and Christian Social Ethics* (Richmond, Va.: John Knox Press, 1966); L. Harold DeWolf, *Responsible Freedom: Guidelines for Christian Action* (New York: Harper & Row, 1971); Paul Deats, Jr., "Conflict and Reconciliation in Communitarian Social Ethics," in *The Boston Personalist Tradition in Philosophy, Social Ethics, and Theology*, eds. Deats and Carol Robb (Macon, Ga.: Mercer University Press, 1986), pp. 273–285; and J. Philip Wogaman, *Christian Moral Judgment* (Louisville, Ky.: Westminster/John Knox, 1989).

84. Brightman, *Moral Laws,* pp. 35–45.

85. Ibid., p. 45.

86. King, "Letter from Birmingham Jail," in *Why We Can't Wait,* p. 85.

87. Brightman, *Moral Laws,* p. 45.

88. Ibid., p. 204.

89. Ibid., p. 242.

90. King, "The Personalism of J. M. E. McTaggart under Criticism," in Carson, ed., *The Papers of Martin Luther King, Jr.,* vol. 2, p. 72.

91. See Bowne, *Theory of Thought and Knowledge* (New York: Harper & Brothers, 1897), p. 239.

92. Cited in Carson, ed., *The Papers of Martin Luther King, Jr.,* vol. 2, pp. 72–73. It should be noted that this quote is not exact. King both omitted and added words and phrases without alerting his reader. Brightman's exact words are: ". . . without it we are not even free to think, to say nothing of making other moral choices. The power to think means that the individual can impose on himself the ideal of logic or scientific method and hold it through thick and thin" (Brightman, *Moral Laws,* p. 282).

93. See King, "Love, Law, and Civil Disobedience," in Washington, ed., *A Testament of Hope,* p. 48.

94. See Kenneth Smith and Ira Zepp, Jr., *Search for the Beloved Community: The Thinking of Martin Luther King, Jr.* (Valley Forge, Pa.: Judson Press, 1974), pp. 110–113.

95. In 1983 Muelder addressed this topic in a paper read at Morehouse College on "Martin Luther King, Jr. and the Moral Laws."

96. Bowne, *The Principles of Ethics* (New York: American Book Company, 1892), p. 199.

97. King, "An Experiment in Love," in Washington, ed., *A Testament of Hope,* p. 19.

98. King, "Nonviolence and Racial Justice," in Washington, ed., *A Testament of Hope,* pp. 8–9.

99. Hoskins, ed., *"I Have a Dream,"* p. 138.

100. Hoskins, ed., "I Have a Dream," p. 139.

101. Cited in King, "An Experiment in Love," in Washington, ed., *A Testament of Hope,* p. 18.

102. King, "An Experiment in Love," in Washington, ed., *A Testament of Hope,* p. 18.

103. Ansbro, *Martin Luther King, Jr.: The Making of a Mind,* p. 85.

104. Hoskins, ed., *"I Have a Dream,"* p. 71.

105. Ansbro, *Martin Luther King, Jr.: The Making of a Mind,* p. 86.

106. See Bowne, *The Principles of Ethics,* p. 113.

107. Ibid., p. 209.

108. See Immanuel Kant's discussion of this subject in "Duties to Oneself," in *Lectures on Ethics* (New York: The Century Company, 1930), pp. 116–126.

109. Bowne, *The Principles of Ethics*, pp. 197–198.

110. King, "A Gift of Love," in Washington, ed., *A Testament of Hope*, pp. 62–63.

111. See King, "A New Sense of Direction," *Worldview* (April 1972): 11; and King, "Where Do We Go From Here?" in Washington, ed., *A Testament of Hope*, p. 250.

112. See my article "The Personalism of John Wesley Edward Bowen," *Journal of Negro History*, vol. 82, no. 2, (Spring 1997): pp. 244–254.

113. King, "A Christmas Sermon on Peace," in Washington, ed., *A Testament of Hope*, p. 255.

114. King, "The Ethical Demands for Integration" in Washington, ed., *A Testament of Hope*, p. 122.

115. Bowne, *The Principles of Ethics*, pp. 190–191.

116. King, "A Knock at Midnight" in *A Knock at Midnight*, eds. Clayborne Carson and Peter Holloran, p. 88.

117. Bowne, *Principles of Ethics*, p. 305.

118. King, "Letter from Birmingham City Jail," in *Why We Can't Wait* (New York: Harper, 1963), p. 89.

Beyond National Borders

King, the United Nations, and Global Politics

LEWIS V. BALDWIN

And I think that in our family we don't need bombs and guns, to destroy, to bring peace—just get together, love one another, bring that peace, that joy, that strength of presence of each other in the home. And we will be able to overcome all the evil that is in the world.

—Mother Teresa[1]

The United Nations was ten years old when Martin Luther King, Jr., assumed leadership in the Montgomery bus boycott. This international body was formally organized in San Francisco in October 1945, when China, France, the Soviet Union, the United Kingdom, the United States, and most of the other original forty-six member states convened and ratified its charter.[2] Variously referred to as "an organization of independent, sovereign nations," "an international peace authority," and "the central meeting ground of opposing power blocs," the U.N. emerged out of the ashes of World War II, rooted in the conviction that one nation alone could not solve the multitude of problems that afflicted the global community.[3] Its determination to promote peace, security, and social and economic development became enormously important to King as he envisioned and struggled for a world devoid of hatred, economic injustice, and violence and human destruction.[4]

Toward a Communitarian Ideal:
The Visions of the United Nations and King

The United Nations Charter set forth a vision of international community that anticipated King's on some levels. The framers of the charter vowed to "develop friendly relations among nations based on the principle of equal rights and self-determination of peoples," to promote "respect for human rights and fundamental freedoms," to "cooperate in solving international economic, social, cultural and humanitarian problems," and to "be a centre for harmonizing the actions of nations in attaining these common ends."[5] They also upheld the equality of all member states, agreed to repudiate bigotry and intolerance, and resolved to "settle their disputes with other nations by peaceful means."[6] These same principles, affirmed also in the U.N.'s Universal Declaration of Human Rights, which was adopted by the General Assembly on December 10, 1948, stood at the core of King's vision of "the world house" or "the worldwide neighborhood." King fully embraced the idea of the U.N. as "a family of nations," for it was profoundly symbolic of his conviction that humans everywhere constitute "a family unduly separated in ideas, culture and interest, who, because we can never again live apart, must learn somehow to live with each other in peace."[7]

This idea of a mutually dependent, even symbiotic, relationship between nations could not have been more vital in a world stunted by various forms of injustice and oppression. King accepted in principle the claim, made consistently in the 1950s and 1960s by so-called Third World representatives in the U.N., that the freedom of poor and oppressed nations from political and economic domination inevitably required the liberation of their wealthy counterparts from greed, fear, and ignorance. In other words, the nations of the world had to struggle together as a matter of necessity and self-interest, giving mutual obligation precedence over individual choice. This perspective flowed naturally out of King's belief in the interrelatedness and interdependence of all life, a conviction expressed at least tacitly during his time in the many debates, public statements, and documents of the U.N.[8]

The U.N. and King ultimately became essentially one in identifying racism, poverty, and war as major external barriers to human community.[9] But the U.N. was slow in translating its human rights principles into constructive measures to deal with these problems. The problem of racism surfaced very early among the member states, due mainly to the initiatives of representatives of color. The need for "a racial-equality declaration among nations" was actually raised by China in the fall of 1944, when the U.N. was still in its embryonic stage, but no significant action occurred.[10] Serious exchanges concerning racism resurfaced in 1952, when India, inspired by the Defiance Campaign led by Albert J. Luthuli, Manilal Gandhi, and others in South Africa, called upon the U.N. General Assembly "for an agenda item" addressing the problem.[11] But once again, the U.N., dominated by the United States, refused to take decisive action, despite support for India's proposal from Africans and Asians. By the time Martin Luther King, Jr., emerged to national and international prominence in 1956, the U.N. had become widely known for its failure to bridge the chasms between proclamation and action in the area of racial justice.

Discussions and debates concerning racism increased significantly in U.N. circles in the 1960s, due largely to the challenge presented by the civil rights movement in America and the antiapartheid struggle in South Africa. Aware of the activities of King in the United States, and of Luthuli, Manilal Gandhi, and other black and Indian reformers in South Africa, the General Assembly adopted the United Nations Declaration on the Elimination of All Forms of Racial Discrimination in 1963, affirming that "discrimination between human beings on the grounds of race, color or ethnic origin is an offence to human dignity, a denial of Charter principles, a violation of the rights proclaimed in the Universal Declaration of Human Rights, and an obstacle to friendly and peaceful relations among people."[12] This action was followed two years later by the U.N.'s adoption of the International Convention on the Elimination of All Forms of Racial Discrimination, which formed a committee of eighteen experts to achieve its goal.[13] King applauded these developments, but felt that the U.N., owing to the influence of South Africa, the United States, and other major Western powers which practiced organized and institutionalized racism, was not prepared to take the radical steps necessary to end racial oppression.[14]

The same could be said of the problems of poverty and economic exploitation. Although the U.N. had expressed the desire to eliminate these problems from its founding, little was done by the 1960s to combat hunger, malnutrition, disease, and homelessness in poor nations. United Nations food and agricultural programs, established as early as 1945, were highly deficient.[15] King addressed the problem forthrightly, noting that aid to the poverty-stricken peoples of the world should be motivated by a spirit of goodwill and compassion, not by political considerations, all the more because the developed countries had solidified their wealth and power by exploiting the underdeveloped ones:

> The first step in the worldwide war against poverty is passionate commitment. All the wealthy nations—America, Britain, Russia, Canada, Australia, and those of Western Europe—must see it as a moral obligation to provide capital and technical assistance to the underdeveloped areas. These rich nations have only scratched the surface in their commitment. There is a need now for a general strategy of support. Sketchy aid here and there will not suffice, nor will it sustain economic growth. There must be a sustained effort extending through many years. The wealthy nations of the world must promptly initiate a massive, sustained Marshall Plan for Asia, Africa and South America. If they would allocate just 2 percent of their gross national product for a period of ten or twenty years for the development of the underdeveloped nations, mankind would go a long way toward conquering the ancient enemy, poverty.[16]

King refused to attribute some of the blame for the U.N.'s weak record in the economic development sphere to the lack of proper pressure from poor nations within its ranks. He understood the extent to which the underdeveloped countries languished under the colonialism and neocolonialism of the rich and powerful nations. Even so, he must have known that as more and more new states joined the U.N., especially from the so-called Third World, they would be increasingly inclined to use their voices, their votes, and other forms of political pressure to achieve the full benefits of collective economic assistance. Such an outlook would have been inescapable for King, especially considering the fact that "the great masses of people everywhere," as he put it in March 1965, "are now rising up, determined to end the exploitation of their races and lands."[17] In any case, the conviction that stronger U.N. action was required to end poverty and economic exploitation was central to King's communitarian ethic.

Any serious effort to eliminate hunger and privation on a global scale, King thought, necessarily had to take into account the burden placed on human resources by "the enormous acceleration in the rate of growth of the world's population." Convinced that "birth control is now a necessity not only in our nation, but all over the world, particularly in the larger nations like China and India," King insisted that "more and more the United Nations will have to deal with this problem" through "planned structured methods" because "the population explosion is as great a threat to mankind as the problem of war." At the same time, King doubted the possibility of "a stabilization of the population without a prior stabilization of economic resources."[18]

The challenges confronting the U.N. concerning war and human destruction occupied a special place in King's thinking. This should not be surprising in view of his commitment to nonviolence as both a personal and social ethic, and as the only ethic consistent with claims for peace with justice in the world. As its charter stated, the U.N. had been established in part "to protect future generations against the scourge of war, which has twice in our lifetime brought untold suffering on mankind."[19] As a peacemaking and peacekeeping force, it had resolved from its origins to not only ensure that "military weapons will be used only in the common interest in the future," but also to

> take effective collective measures to prevent and to eliminate threats to peace, to suppress aggressive actions and other peace-breaking acts, and to settle and resolve international conflicts or situations leading to breaking the peace by peaceful means in accordance with the principles of fairness and international law.[20]

Such functions could not have been more important and necessary for King, who shared the U.N.'s claim that war, like racism and poverty, is a perennial threat to the survival and welfare of the human family. Furthermore, war undermines the concept of humans as social beings who find growth, fulfillment, and purpose through wholesome and harmonious relationships based on the love ethic. With this in mind, King and the U.N. used terms like "peaceful coexistence," "human rights," "peaceful change," "nonviolent action as a form of political protest," and "diplomatic reasonableness and restraint" in articulating their visions of a global community free of weapons of mass destruction and wars of aggression.[21]

But King went much further than the U.N. in that he declared that "war is obsolete." "There may have been a time when war served as a negative good by preventing the spread and growth of an evil force," he argued, "but the destructive power of modern weapons eliminates even the possibility that war may serve any good at all."[22] While he recognized the messianic trust that the United States and other nations placed in military might, King always found some basis for hope in the peacemaking and peacekeeping roles assumed by the U.N.:

> The United Nations is a gesture in the direction of nonviolence on a world scale. There, at least, states that oppose one another have sought to do so with words instead of with weapons. But true nonviolence is more than the absence of violence. It is the persistent and determined application of peaceable power to offenses against the community—in this case the world community. As the United Nations moves ahead with the giant tasks confronting it, I would hope that it would earnestly examine the uses of nonviolent direct action.[23]

The fact that many representatives in the U.N. extolled the virtues of "just war" or "limited war" remained a matter of deep concern for King. "A so-called limited war will leave little more than a calamitous legacy of human suffering, political turmoil and spiritual disillusionment," he observed.[24] He was equally disturbed with the Cold War brand of international relations, which framed peoples' understanding of the world in terms of threats and conflict. "The alternative to disarmament, the alternative to a greater suspension of nuclear tests, the alternative to strengthening the United Nations and thereby disarming the whole world may well be a civilization plunged into the abyss of annihilation," King wrote.[25] To those political conservatives in the U.S. who advocated war instead of establishing diplomatic ties with communist countries in the U.N., a forum which afforded excellent opportunities for healthy and informal exchanges between diplomats, King offered a direct rejoinder:

Communism will never be defeated by the use of atomic bombs or nuclear weapons. Let us not join those who shout war and who through their misguided passions urge the United States to relinquish its participation in the United Nations. These are days which demand wise restraint and calm reasonableness. We must not call everyone a Communist or an appeaser who advocates the seating of Red China in the United Nations, or who recognizes that hate and hysteria are not the final answers to the problems of these turbulent days. We must not engage in a negative anti-Communism, but rather in a positive thrust for democracy, realizing that our greatest defense against Communism is to take offensive action in behalf of justice.[26]

King was among those who wondered how the U.N. could raise the banner of peace and "expiate on the subject of the brotherhood of nations" while voting in 1962 to deny membership to the People's Republic of China, "which represented one of every four human faces in the world."[27] For King, diplomatic links with the People's Republic of China were absolutely essential and consistent with the common good. Moreover, he held that when confronted with a threat from some aggressive nation, the U.N. had more to gain from imposing economic sanctions than from severing diplomatic ties and offering a military response. The best avenue to the full realization of "the brotherhood of nations," he thought, was available only through unrestricted diplomatic relations, careful and good-faith negotiations, and an intellectual analysis and practical application of nonviolent means.[28]

Perhaps the greatest limitation of the politics of both the U.N. and King rested in their failure to treat sexism and religious intolerance as major problems connected with, and as evil as, racism, economic injustice, and war. When the U.N. Charter was signed in 1945, females could vote in national elections on equal terms with males in only thirty of the fifty-one original member states. The Commission on the Status of Women initiated action in 1952 which led to the General Assembly's adoption of the first legal instrument focusing exclusively on women's rights. The Convention on the Political Rights of Women reaffirmed women's right to vote "without any discrimination," and made them "eligible to hold public office, and to exercise all public functions established by national law, on equal terms with men." Most of the human rights documents of the U.N., including the Universal Declaration of Human Rights and the International Covenants, upheld the principle of gender equality. But despite such provisions, women were still discriminated against worldwide at the time of King's death in 1968.[29] Strangely enough, King himself never publicly challenged the U.N. around this issue, nor did he make it a critical component of his own crusade for freedom. But whatever the weaknesses in King's view of women, his struggle for the actualization of the Beloved Community ideal—an ideal extending beyond all human differences—was in some measure a compensating factor.

Interestingly enough, King believed that women had much to contribute to the U.N.'s quest for peace and justice in the world. In a speech in Philadelphia in October 1965, on the occasion of the fiftieth anniversary of the Women's International League for Peace and Freedom, he said as much and more to the many delegates present, declaring that "your endeavors constitute impressive milestones marking man's trek along the rugged roadway to peace" in "this chaotic world of ours."[30] Because King's globalism became more enlightened and explicit from that point up to the time of his death almost three years later, it is safe to say that he would not support those countries in the U.N. which seek to curb women's rights today. In June 2000, five years after a historic conference in Beijing "articulated what more than 180 nations agreed were universal rights of women," opponents sought "to reverse those gains," especially as they related to women's right to freely decide on "matters related to their sexuality."[31] In nations such as Iran, Libya, Sudan, and Algeria, and to some extent Israel and the Vatican, evidence of "a backlash" against the progress made at Beijing looms large in the minds of women.[32] Consequently, sexism remains as one of the greatest barriers to global peace and community.

The same holds true for the problem of religious bigotry and intolerance. The framers of the Universal Declaration of Human Rights and the earliest international covenants affirmed the "freedom of thought, conscience and religion," a principle King associated with the Declaration of Independence, the Constitution, and a range of other political traditions in the United States.[33] King's belief in religious freedom and tolerance was at least as strong as that of the most liberal U.N. representatives in his time. However, operating in a church establishment in which both blacks and whites typically viewed Christianity as the only route to salvation, the civil rights leader most likely felt that he had more to lose than to gain by making religious freedom and tolerance a major issue in his pursuit of human community. Be that as it may, it is worth noting that King, in his last book, stressed the need for Gentiles, Jews, Catholics, Protestants, Moslems, and Hindus to coexist peacefully without compromising their convictions and traditions.[34] As he ultimately realized, only in this manner could people from different nations be successfully drawn together in a fruitful convergence of ideas. Thus, King has much to say today to the people of India, China, Sudan, and other countries, where people are still persecuted because of their faiths.[35]

Despite its many shortcomings, King recognized the U.N. as one of the best hopes for world community—one whose significance perhaps transcended that of even the World Council of Churches. He attached a level of sacred significance to the U.N.'s Universal Declaration of Human Rights that recalls his high regard for the Declaration of Independence and the Constitution in his own country's heritage. By struggling for a world of shared values—built around the principles of mutual obligation, intergroup and interpersonal living, human rights, and power sharing—the U.N., King felt, was playing a vital role in keeping the world from blindly plunging into tragic self-destruction. Many in the U.N. viewed King in a similar fashion. U Thant, the U.N. Secretary General, echoed the feelings of so many of his colleagues when he, shortly after the assassination of the civil rights leader, committed these few words to paper: "Dr. King worked so unceasingly and by nonviolent methods for the cause of peace, international understanding and human rights."[36]

In the Spirit of Freedom:
The U.N. and the African American Struggle

The United Nations was confronted from its origins with questions about the relationship of its principles and mission to the African American freedom cause. In late 1944, when King was a freshman at Morehouse College in Atlanta, Georgia, W. E. B. DuBois and Paul Robeson, the two most visible African American leaders, raised the issue in appeals to the preliminary conference of the United Nations Organization at Dumbarton Oaks. Both called upon the United States to become a force in encouraging the United Nations organization to end all forms of political, social, and economic discrimination based on race or color.[37] Convinced that the plight of African Americans could not be separated from that of other peoples of color, a position King would articulate with piercing clarity, DuBois and Robeson insisted that the U.N. not become merely another structure for the preservation of white domination worldwide.[38] While they found some hope in the presence of colored nations in the U.N., they, as would be the case with King, wondered if peoples of color would receive direct and proper representation, especially since some of these nations, as DuBois put it, "are so under the economic domination of great powers that they will hardly be able to take an independent stand."[39]

The formal organization of the U.N. was welcomed by many African American leaders who felt that their people's struggle for civil rights in America would not succeed without world pressure. In 1947, the NAACP presented to the new international body "An Appeal to the World," a document subtitled "A Statement on the Denial of Human Rights to Minorities in the Case of Citizens of Negro Descent in the United States of America and an Appeal to the United Nations for Redress." This document denounced the treatment of African Americans as a clear violation of the Universal Declaration of Human Rights, and urged the U.N. not to separate the human rights claims of American blacks from those of colonized peoples throughout the world.[40] In 1951, three years later, William R. Patterson, Paul and Eslanda Goode Robeson, and others presented the petition "We Charge Genocide" to the U.N., a document which catalogued lynchings and other acts of violence against African Americans.[41] Interestingly enough, Martin Luther King, Jr., became keenly aware of these developments, but chose not to make appeals to the U.N. a significant part of his civil rights crusade. His failure at this level reflected a serious limitation in his strategy and methods.

The potential role of the U.N. in the African American freedom movement became one of the issues that separated Malcolm X and King in the 1960s, especially as they seriously considered those means most likely to win freedom. Convinced that America's race problem had to be redefined as a violation of basic human rights, Malcolm proposed in 1964 that his people seek African assistance in taking their case before the U.N. Encouraged by the fact that South African apartheid and the persecution of Soviet Jews had already emerged as test cases in the U.N., Malcolm, like DuBois and Robeson before him, insisted that the *internationalization* of the African American plight provided the best hope for genuine liberation.[42] While King supported the idea of oppressed peoples abroad having their cases heard in the U.N., he was not persuaded by the power of Malcolm's arguments, a situation difficult to understand since, as James Baldwin pointed out, each attempted, in his own way, to release the African American struggle "from the domestic context and relate it to the struggles of the poor and the nonwhite all over the world."[43] Furthermore, King knew that the civil rights movement had benefitted morally, spiritually, and politically from public sympathy and support from abroad, especially after media sources in various parts of the world showed southern racists using clubs, cattle prods, dogs, and guns against nonviolent demonstrators.[44]

There are several possible explanations for King's failure to actively pursue the question of African American rights through the U.N. First, he believed that his people had to take primary responsibility for their own liberation, a view that became more pronounced during the last three years of his life. He could hardly have expected less of African Americans, especially since he considered them morally and spiritually capable of assuming a vanguard role in transforming the world.[45] But *primary* responsibility need not have implied *only* responsibility, a point Malcolm X understood well. Moreover, the vanguard role King envisioned for his people need not have precluded U.N. intervention in the African American struggle. The decision not to seriously promote such intervention seemed uncharacteristic of King, influenced as he was by both the Hegelian and personalistic methods. The complexity of what confronted American blacks required multiple involvements and strategies. Theoretically, King knew this, and yet it is understandable that he wanted his people to be more self-determined in their bid for liberation and empowerment, all the more because they had so much to learn about assuming the responsibilities that come with freedom.[46]

Second, King sensed that U.S. influence in the U.N. was such that appeals to that body on behalf of African Americans were not likely to reap great benefits.[47] In fact, such a strategy was, perhaps in his esti-mation, more likely to embarrass and further alienate the American government from the civil rights cause. King had reason to believe this, but his feeling that international pressure would not have a sig-nificant, positive impact on America's approach to the race problem remains open to serious debate.

Finally, although King agreed in principle with Malcolm's call for the U.N. to condemn America's treatment of his people, the civil rights leader was more inclined to see liberation coming through the struggle in America. Such a position proved only natural in view of his faith in America's natural rights tradition and democratic heritage, a faith not shared by Malcolm X.[48] In short, King felt that freedom could be won within the jurisdiction of America by combining appeals to her democratic traditions with creative nonviolent dissent and protest. In this regard, King had a misplaced faith. In other words, he was somewhat naive in this case, while Malcolm X was the realist.[49]

King's ambivalence regarding the relevance of the U.N. to the civil rights movement in America never really faded. While he valued that body as a force in the continuing struggle for human rights and peace, he knew that its potential as a vehicle in overcoming racism was not likely to be fully realized as long as its structures and policies were con-trolled by nations from the white Western world. In other words, mean-ingful and lasting change would result only after the achievement of a balance of power in the U.N. along racial and ethnic lines. While King pointed with great pride to the U.N.'s Under-Secretary General Ralph J. Bunche, who "sits near the top in the ranks of world government," and to African "statesmen voting on vital issues in the United Nations," the civil rights leader felt that representatives of African descent needed stronger roles in the decision-making processes of the U.N.[50] King's feelings on this matter found some vindication, since very few blacks held high diplomatic positions and no black had been appointed as U.S. ambassador to the U.N. up to his time.[51]

Sources in the federal government probably played a greater role than previously imagined in discrediting the civil rights movement in the eyes of the U.N. The FBI is reported to have bombarded officials from the "United Nations . . . and even embassies overseas with nasty interpretations of King's sexual habits."[52] Rumors about King's "com-munist sympathies" and "inflammatory speeches," and about "the gross indecency and debauchery of his nonviolent demonstrators," reached various parts of the world, largely through the activities of government officials who had targeted the movement as a threat to national security.[53] While it is clear that large numbers of African Americans had difficulty grasping the ultimate significance of strong U.N. support for the civil rights cause, racist officials in the United States did not.

The African American freedom struggle presented a strong challenge to the United States' claim to moral leadership in the U.N. King raised this issue consistently, much to the disgust of parties in the federal government. In a speech delivered to a branch of the NAACP on September 25, 1960, he noted that his country was paying a high price in the U.N. for its failure to seriously address its race problem:

> My recent travels in Asia, Africa, the Middle East and South America have convinced me that America is at its lowest ebb in international prestige; and most of this loss of prestige is due to our failure to grapple with the problems of racial injustice. We must face the painful fact that we are losing out in the struggle to win the minds of the uncommitted peoples of the world. Just this week the most eloquent spokesman of the communist bloc, Nikita Khrushchev, suggested in his speech to the U.N., among other things, that the headquarters of this great organization be moved from the United States. The American press generally was very careful to conceal one of the reasons Mr. Khrushchev gave for suggesting this move. His direct words were: "Facts are known . . . of representatives of young African and Asian states being subjected to racial discrimination in the United States." While we are used to Mr. Khrushchev's intemperate and sometimes irresponsible words, we cannot dismiss these as totally false.[54]

In a speech given much later, King reiterated the point with intense feeling. Said he: "The matter of racial segregation in America has international implications. Either we must solve our human relations dilemma occasioned by race and color prejudice, and solve it soon, or we will lose our moral and political voice in the world community of nations."[55] Significantly, these comments remain relevant to any discussion of the U.S. role in the politics of the United Nations.

Crossing Oceans and Mountains:
King, the United Nations, and Troubled Spots Abroad

Martin Luther King, Jr., displayed much interest in the United Nations' involvements in human rights cases outside the United States. His interest in that regard owed much to his affiliation with organizations like the American Committee on Africa (ACOA) and the American Negro Leadership Conference on Africa (ANLCA). King joined the ACOA in 1957, five years after it had been organized in New York to support resistance to South African apartheid and the whole anticolonial struggle in Africa. George Houser, Donald Harrington, A. Philip Randolph, Norman Thomas, Roger N. Baldwin, Bayard Rustin, Conrad Lynn, and Charles Y. Trigg, the founders of this interracial organization, shared King's interest in the U.N. as a force for nonviolent change on a world scale.[56] The same could be said of Whitney M. Young, James Farmer, Dorothy Height, Roy Wilkins, and other black civil rights leaders, who joined King in the first major meeting of the ANLCA in New York in November 1962.[57]

Much of King's attention focused on the moral responsibility of the U.N. in relation to South African apartheid.[58] He was convinced that world pressure was essential to the liberation of black Africans, Asians, and other people of color in South Africa, especially since that country lacked the kind of democratic and natural rights traditions claimed by the United States.[59] In July 1957, King joined Eleanor Roosevelt and Bishop James A. Pike as initial sponsors, under the auspices of the ACOA, of the Declaration of Conscience, a document proclaiming December 10, 1957, the U.N.'s Human Rights Day, "as a Day of Protest against the organized inhumanity of the South African Government and its *apartheid* policies."[60] Eleanor Roosevelt served as international chairperson of the campaign, Pike as U.S. chairman, and King as U.S. vice chairman.[61] Noting that "we support the overwhelming majority of the South African people, non-white and white, in their determination to achieve the basic human rights that are the rightful heritage of all men," the sponsors of the declaration went on to explain, "in the spirit of the Universal Declaration of Human Rights adopted on December 10, 1948, by the General Assembly of the United Nations," how peoples of goodwill worldwide could best contribute to the crusade against apartheid:

We ask them to join us in calling on the Government of the Union of South Africa to honor its moral and legal obligations as a signatory to the United Nations Charter by honoring the Declaration of Human Rights. We call upon members of all free associations— churches, universities, trade unions, business and professional organizations, veterans and other groups—to petition their organizations and their governments to use their influence to bring about a peaceful, just, and democratic solution in South Africa. We call upon all men and women to mobilize the spiritual and moral forces of mankind on this day of Protest to demonstrate to the Government of the Union of South Africa that free men abhor its policies and will not tolerate the continued suppression of human freedom. We seek to persuade the South African government, before it reaches the point of no return, that only in democratic equality is there lasting peace and security.[62]

The Declaration of Conscience was supported by many representatives in the U.N., and it bore the signatures of 123 world leaders. Endorsements came from politicians such as Mayor Robert F. Wagner of New York City and Senator Wayne Morse of Oregon, but the U.S. and other world powers refused to use their influence in the U.N. to properly promote the declaration.[63] Martin Luther King, Jr., wondered how the U.S., Great Britain, and other powerful nations could justify supporting a stubbornly racist country like South Africa, one of the early member states of the U.N., while opposing, for political reasons, the seating of the People's Republic of China in that international body.

During the two years after the appearance of the Declaration of Conscience, King considered numerous options designed to increase U.N. involvement in the movement against the apartheid policies and practices of South Africa. Those options ranged from the exclusion of South Africa from world competition in the Olympic Games to the imposition of economic sanctions against that country. The timing could not have been better since the U.N. was considering "fast-breaking developments" concerning the South African treason trial and the oppressive situations in Algeria, the Trust Territories, and Portuguese Africa.[64] In 1959, King acknowledged that the U.N., the "legal successor" to the League of Nations, had blocked South Africa's move to annex South West Africa, but the international community, he asserted, had not "been able to prevent South Africa from treating the Africans in this territory with the same regime of oppression and segregation as it gives the nonwhites in its own territory."[65] In King's view, the silence of Christians on this matter compounded the problem. He wrote:

> While Christianity has been timid in too much of Africa, I am glad that Michael Scott—a clergyman for more than a decade—has represented the Herero people of South West Africa when South Africa refused to allow their representatives to appear before the U.N. Now two or three residents have managed to tell the U.N. their own story. It is not a pleasant story. At places, it has a night-marish effect and points up some of the most tragic expressions of man's inhumanity to man. It is the story of more than 450,000 people constantly being trampled over by the iron feet of injus-tice. This is the story the American people should know—one which their delegates at the U.N. should act upon. If for no other reason, we should know this story and act upon it because injus-tice anywhere is a threat to justice everywhere.[66]

As a political realist, King knew that the African and Asian delega-tions in the U.N. had to assume moral leadership to ensure any action at all on the part of that body against South African apartheid. Such a perspective was inescapable since virtually every U.N. proposal deal-ing with racism, up to the late 1950s, had been initiated by Asians, Africans, or African Americans, peoples who had long been victimized by white supremacist doctrines and structures.[67] Even so, King also knew that many representatives of color in the U.N. were not willing to initiate the kind of serious antiapartheid action that would have au-tomatically threatened their relations with the U.S. and other power-ful nations.

Questions about the role of the U.N. in eliminating apartheid sur-faced anew in March 1960, when South African police killed sixty-nine black peaceful protesters against Pass Laws at Sharpeville. King was among those who felt that U.N. action was necessary to avoid a race war in South Africa, a position difficult to dismiss casually since black organizations like the African National Congress (ANC) and the Pan-Africanist Congress (PAC) went underground, abandoned their nonviolent methods, and resolved that the era of armed struggle had begun. In April 1960, King's name appeared on an ACOA statement calling upon the international community to "protest the cruel, inhuman massacre in Sharpeville."[68] King and others in the ACOA also joined more than fifty leaders in Americans for Democratic Action (ADA) in urging that "the White House suspend United States buying of gold from South Africa and recall Philip K. Crowe, who has been President Eisenhower's Ambassador at Cape Town since February 1959." The ADA went on to declare that such measures have long been "sanctified by diplomatic usage, and are a form of language among nations," but the U.S. government refused to act in accordance with the group's recommendations.[69]

The Sharpeville massacre and the warnings of King and others did attract the attention of leaders in the U.N. Shortly after the tragedy, the Security Council met at the request of twenty-nine African and Asian member states to discuss "the situation arising out of the large-scale killings of unarmed and peaceful demonstrators" in South Africa. Convinced that the slaughter of blacks had "led to international friction and, if continued, might endanger international peace and security," the Security Council urged the South African government "to abandon its policy of apartheid."[70] But South Africa, still supported by the U.S., Great Britain, and other powers, simply ignored the Security Council, declared a state of emergency, and began a crackdown that resulted in the arrest of thousands and the passage of the Unlawful Organizations Act. King's contention that South Africa "is the most stubborn and rugged place in the world in the area of race relations" could not have been more accurate.[71]

In early 1962, as the situation in South Africa grew worse, King became involved with an Appeal for Action Against Apartheid. Initially sponsored by King and the South African leader Albert Luthuli, under the auspices of the ACOA, this appeal was "in the nature of a follow-up on our "Declaration of Conscience," which had been sponsored five years earlier by King, Eleanor Roosevelt, and James Pike. It admonished "U.N. delegations from every land to support a drive for sanctions at the United Nations." It also admonished persons and local communities to "write to your Mission to the United Nations urging adoption of a resolution calling for the isolation of South Africa," and to organize "public meetings, picket demonstrations, marches or silent vigils," choosing "an appropriate place so that" their protest "clearly relates to pressure on the United States, the United Nations, or the Government of South Africa."[72] King's involvement with the appeal vividly expressed what Charles R. Wilson calls his "blendings of localism and universalism," a tendency King displayed from the time of the Montgomery bus boycott.[73] In fact, this wedding of the *particular* and the *universal* reveals the depth of King's communitarian ethic. He warned against the perils of isolationism, declaring, in December 1962, that "the American Negro's growing awareness of his world citizenship is an earmark of his developing maturity."[74] This is all the more reason he should have been open to heavy U.N. involvement in the civil rights struggle.

The Appeal for Action Against Apartheid was well-received in many circles worldwide, a development not surprising since King was an internationally known civil rights leader and Luthuli a recent Nobel Prize recipient. It was signed by approximately 150 world leaders, aside from King and Luthuli. Signatories from the U.S. included Senator Clifford P. Chase of New Jersey, U.S. Congressman Adam Clayton Powell, Jr., of New York, and numerous civil rights activists, authors, professors, clergymen, and persons in other fields. The list of signatories and sponsors from abroad was long and quite impressive, including Prime Minister Ahmed Ben Bella of Algeria, President Barbara Castle of the Anti-Apartheid Movement in Great Britain, President Jomo Kenyatta of Kenya, Oliver Tambo of the African National Congress, Foreign Minister Julio Del Vayo of the Spanish Republic, and U.N. representatives from Algeria, Sierra Leone, the Congo, Ethiopia, Tunisia, Iraq, Guinea, the Republic of Chad, and India.[75] The appeal afforded further proof that King and Luthuli refused to separate the struggles in the United States and South Africa from the human rights mission of the U.N. Indeed, they were convinced that the moral obligation for eliminating apartheid rested with people everywhere.

King found much satisfaction in the U.N.'s decision to take strong measures against South Africa in the fall of 1962. In a strongly worded resolution, the U.N. chided the South African government for ignoring the repeated requests and demands of the General Assembly and the Security Council, and urged member states to sever "diplomatic relations with South Africa, to boycott South African goods, and to refrain from all exports to South Africa, including the export of armaments."[76] Passed on November 6, 1962, this was the first General Assembly resolution (Resolution 1761) calling for sanctions against South Africa.[77] The United States' refusal to endorse the resolution evoked a strong response from King:

> It is tragic that our foreign policy on Africa is so ambivalent; for example, on the one hand, we decry in some mild manner the apartheid policy of the Union of South Africa, but economically we continue "business as usual" in spite of the stringent racist policies being enforced and intensified. We do not support economic sanctions in the United Nations though we impose them ourselves.[78]

The ANLCA provided an organizational platform from which King and other civil rights leaders could seriously discuss problems throughout Africa while pressing their call for U.N. sanctions against the South African regime. Eighteen days after the passage of Resolution 1761, the ANLCA, at its first major meeting, held in New York, expressed regret for the United States' position on South African apartheid, insisting that "it is our hope that the American Negro Leadership Conference on Africa can play some meaningful role in shaping American foreign policy that will be consistent with our democratic posture."[79] King and others in the ANLCA issued the following statement as part of a resolution on South Africa:

> We deplore our government's opposition to the United Nations resolution calling for sanctions against South Africa. We urge the United States to support such action by the United Nations against South Africa and to seek its implementation through effective policing of the modes of entry.[80]

At the New York meeting, the ANLCA delegates declared that the time had come for America to assume more active and positive roles in U.N. policies toward Africa as a whole. While endorsing "the continued United States financial support of the United Nations operation in the Congo," which was designed to restore "territorial unity, integrity and unification of the Congo with Katanga," the ANLCA suggested that the American government had a moral obligation to also assist U.N. initiatives toward South West Africa, Portuguese Africa, and Southern Rhodesia. In a series of resolutions, King and other ANLCA members urged the U.S. to support the U.N. "in its attempt to win acceptance of its claim that South West Africa belongs under the trusteeship of the United Nations," and to assist the U.N. in its efforts to persuade "the Portuguese Government to enter into negotiations with African Nationalists for the purpose of implementing self-government" for Angola, Mozambique, and Portuguese Guinea. Moreover, the United States' earlier decision to abstain on a U.N. resolution concerning the oppression of Africans in Southern Rhodesia was strongly challenged.[81] The need for the U.S. to join other nations in condemning the racist practices of the Portuguese and South African governments throughout southern Africa could not have been more urgent for the ANLCA, especially since the American government hoped to gain the friendship and trust of the newly independent peoples of Africa and Asia.[82]

The ANLCA meeting in New York covered three days, ending on November 25, 1962. King, A. Philip Randolph, Whitney M. Young, James Farmer, Roy Wilkins, Dorothy Height, and Theodore E. Brown, the executive body of the ANLCA, met with President John F. Kennedy on December 17, less than a month later, to discuss the concerns raised in their resolutions. The U.N. resolutions dealing with South Africa and Angola were discussed, and the ANLCA recommended "a closer working relationship with the American mission to the United Nations." The group also reasserted the need for the U.S. to "support economic sanctions against South Africa on the grounds that apartheid threatens the peace of the world and is in conflict with our national interest," a concern raised in a letter to Kennedy.[83] King and the other ANLCA members maintained:

> We Americans are committed to the precepts of the United Nations' Human Rights Charter. Our government, however, has failed to play a role in the black Africans' fight for political freedom commensurate with that commitment. Our nation was founded upon this principle, imbedded immovably in the Declaration of Independence, in the Constitution, and in our national policy expressed in Supreme Court decisions, in executive orders, and in national, state and local Civil Rights Legislation.[84]

The ANLCA went on to state, with a profound sense of urgency and frustration:

> We were distressed to see that our country's delegation to the United Nations voted against a resolution calling upon member states not to supply arms or military assistance to Portugal as long as she persisted in her policies in Angola, Mozambique, and Portuguese Guinea. We urge that our government place an embargo on the sale of arms and munitions to Portugal unless an adequate inspection system is established to insure that these weapons are not used to continue the subjugation of Portugal's African territories.[85]

The meeting with President Kennedy was followed by a conference with Adlai Stevenson, the U.S. ambassador to the U.N., during which the aforementioned concerns were reiterated extensively.[86] Ambassador Stevenson suggested "a liaison with him on problems of mutual interest to the U.S. Mission to the United Nations and the American Negro Leadership Conference on Africa."[87] But despite the sympathetic interest generated by these historic meetings, and the constant urgings of King, no major shift occurred in U.S. policy toward Africa in the U.N. The Kennedy administration gave virtually no support to anticolonial struggles throughout the continent, and many in the federal government felt that Africans were not ready for independence. King saw this as further proof of America's arrogance, an attitude reinforced perhaps by her successful handling of the Cuban missile crisis in October 1962. Thus, he cautioned that "we must not allow the delicate balance that has been established in matters of foreign policy to be destroyed by our arrogance."[88]

The establishment of the U.N. Special Committee on the Policies of Apartheid, in April 1963, was a hopeful sign for King and other activists who believed that world pressure was the key to peaceful change in South Africa. At that time, ACOA Director George Houser to wrote King, noting that his appearance before that "committee to make a brief statement would have great impact around the world and certainly in South Africa."[89] In June 1963, such an invitation was formally extended to King by Leslie O. Harriman, the committee's chairman, Enuga S. Reddy, an Indian activist and the committee's principal secretary, and H. E. M. Diallo Telli, the U.N. representative from Guinea.[90] Reddy took care of the practical arrangements, scheduling King's possible appearance for July 16, and Collin Gonze of the ACOA prepared a statement for the civil rights leader to deliver on that occasion.[91] King seemed genuinely interested, but did not vigorously pursue the opportunity. "We felt that perhaps Dr. King was prevailed upon by the State Department not to speak before the U.N. Special Committee," wrote Reddy, an impression quite reasonable since this "was the first U.N. Committee boycotted by the Western powers."[92] But the fact is that King's commitments in the American South at that time, coupled with his involvement with plans for the March on Washington, made his appearance before the U.N. special committee impossible.[93]

In September 1963, soon after the March on Washington, King was approached again concerning the possibility of testifying before the U.N. Special Committee on Apartheid. The request came from George Houser, who repeated his conviction that King's testimony would make "a tremendous impact on the international level in the cause of racial justice." But once again, a convenient time for King's appearance could not be found.[94] King's unavailability did not amount to a declining interest in U.N. initiatives for African freedom. In November 1963, he was one of more than five thousand persons who signed an ACOA petition urging the U.S. "to support in the United Nations resolutions calling for boycotts and sanctions against South Africa."[95] Furthermore, King, mainly through his support for ACOA and ANLCA appeals, declarations, and petitions, continued to advocate U.N. involvement in the independence struggles in Central Africa, Nigeria, Kenya, Algeria, Southern Rhodesia, and other parts of the continent.

The Johnson administration's refusal to assume a different posture toward the U.N.'s pro-Africa policies virtually assured continued conflict with King and other activists who endorsed the agenda of the ANLCA and ACOA. In January 1964, the ANLCA drafted a letter to President Johnson, declaring:

> We believe our nation's foreign policy as expressed through our various Missions around the world and the United States Mission to the United Nations leaves much to be desired. As we see it,

the major concern of our foreign policy as far as sub-Sahara Africa is concerned seems to be tied to the interests of Great Britain and France. It seems to say in effect: "Leave it to the European metropolitan governments." It is this concept which we thoroughly reject. Such nations as Great Britain and France, while traditional allies of the United States, continue to maintain vestiges of colonialism and its by-products.[96]

The concerns expressed by the ANLCA elicited no significant response from Johnson. But when the ANLCA announced its annual conference for the fall of 1964, to be held in Washington, D.C., Johnson's closest aides asked to be kept informed of all developments relative to foreign policy issues.[97] King was involved in planning the conference, which took place on September 24–27, and its resolutions reflected his spirit and sentiments. The delegates criticized "the unwillingness of the United States to support any concrete proposals for economic, financial and related sanctions against the South African government," insisting that this "is a major obstacle to the efforts of the United Nations and independent African states to solve the South African problem."[98] The ANLCA, echoing concerns expressed also by the ACOA, went on to recommend U.S. support for the U.N.'s economic sanctions against South Africa, and for U.N. resolutions "calling for aid to families of political prisoners in South Africa and refugees from that country." South Africa's efforts to incorporate within its government the three High Commission Territories of Basutoland, Swaziland, and Bechuanaland were strongly denounced. The ANLCA also endorsed U.N. Resolution 1702, which demanded the evacuation of South Africa's military forces from South West Africa, and which defined that region as "a trust territory under the United Nations."[99]

Other resolutions were passed concerning Southern Rhodesia, the Portuguese Territories, and the Congo. In terms commonly used by King, the ANLCA urged the United States to support the release of political prisoners in Southern Rhodesia, and to strongly oppose, "through its votes at the United Nations," the independence of that country until its African majority "enjoys full participation in government based on the principle of 'one man, one vote.'" The need for the United States to work with the U.N. in ensuring that Portugal "promote massive educational and economic development in Portuguese Africa" was also highlighted. The civil conflict in the Congo was discussed at great length, with the ANLCA calling for the removal of all external military forces from that territory, and for the U.S. government to "support all reasonable initiatives by the Organization of African Unity, in cooperation with the United Nations, to stop the fighting."[100]

King personally addressed some of the challenges confronting the U.N. in Africa while en route to Norway to receive the Nobel Peace Prize in December 1964. Convinced that the U.S. and Great Britain were bolstering South African apartheid, the civil rights leader, in a speech delivered in London to a group of Americans, Africans, and Asians on December 7, resolved that "increasingly we intend to influence American policy in the U.N. and towards South Africa."[101] In a radio interview two days later, King spoke candidly of the civil strife in the Congo, taking essentially the same position set forth in a resolution by the ANLCA three months earlier. Said he: "I don't see a military solution to the problem in the Congo. The situation is not in the realm of violence. It is in the realm of negotiation, and I think one of the best channels would be the Organization of African States under the guidance and auspices of the United Nations."[102]

King received the Nobel Peace Prize in Oslo, Norway, on December 10, 1964, and promptly declared it a mandate to speak more consistently and forthrightly on issues and problems facing the international community.[103] Far more mindful of the role he could play in achieving world peace, King, in the four years that followed, increasingly turned his attention to international issues ranging from South African apartheid to the Vietnam War. Beginning in January 1965, he renewed and intensified his call for the U.S. to support the U.N.'s economic sanctions against the South African regime.[104] He constantly called for similar action toward Southern Rhodesia, asserting that this country "will become another South Africa and the world cannot stand another South Africa":

I think the U.N. should be the force that will stand behind the British government in not granting independence to Southern Rhodesia as it is presently seeking it. I'm all for independence, but it must be an independence with a one-man, one-vote idea behind it. And I think the British Government should stand firm and not grant this independence, and I think the U.N. should stand behind Britain.[105]

On December 10, 1965, as the U.N. celebrated Human Rights Day, King made his most important speech on racism in southern Africa before an audience of 3,500 in the Hunter College auditorium in New York City, vigorously attacking the major Western powers for refusing to engage in concerted economic action against South Africa:

> When it is realized that Great Britain, France and other demo-cratic powers also prop up the economy of South Africa, and when to all this is added the fact that the U.S.S.R. has indicated its willingness to participate in a boycott, it is proper to wonder how South Africa can so confidently defy the civilized world. The con-clusion is inescapable that it is less sure of its own power, but more sure that the great nations will not sacrifice trade and profit to ef-fectively oppose them. The shame of our nation is that it is objec-tively an ally of this monstrous government in its grim war with its own black people.[106]

King pressed his point further, arguing that positive and lasting change throughout southern Africa was possible only if the nations of the world were willing to engage in a serious experimentation with nonviolent means:

> Have we the power to be more than peevish with South Africa, but yet refrain from acts of war? To list the extensive economic re-lations of the great powers with South Africa is to suggest a potent nonviolent path. The international potential of nonviolence has never been employed. Nonviolence has been practiced within na-tional borders in India, the United States and in regions of Africa with spectacular success. The time has come fully to utilize non-violence through a massive international boycott which would involve the U.S.S.R., Great Britain, France, the United States, Ger-many and Japan. Millions of people can personally give expres-sion to their abhorrence of the world's worst racism through such

a far flung boycott. No nation professing a concern for man's dignity could avoid assuming its obligations if people of all states and races adopted a firm stand. Nor need we confine an international boycott to South Africa. Rhodesia has earned a place as a target, as has Portugal, colonial master of Angola and Mozambique. The time has come for an international alliance of peoples of all nations against racism.[107]

H. E. Achkar Marof of Guinea, the chairman of the U.N. Special Committee on Apartheid, heard King's speech and spoke himself. The U.N. Centre Against Apartheid, at the request of the special committee, published King's speech and the Appeal for Action Against Apartheid (1962) as a pamphlet. Although the speech, known by such titles as "Let My People Go" and "The South Africa Benefit Speech," evoked attention and interest worldwide, it did not persuade the major powers to change their actions toward South Africa. Their failure to assume moral leadership in U.N. policy toward South Africa further convinced King that they were on the wrong side of the world revolution.[108]

King knew that stronger U.N. provisions for the progressive advancement of Africa were the key to that continent's full participation in a system of global democracy and prosperity. But one wonders if King, who was known and respected universally, and who profoundly articulated a vision of world peace and community, could have done more to persuade the major Western powers of the urgent need for such provisions. Perhaps he could have taken the time, despite his extensive involvements in the U.S., to honor at least one of the many requests put to him to testify against South African apartheid in the U.N. in the 1960s. Such a move, over and beyond his support for the many ACOA and ANLCA appeals to the U.N., would have been in line with his view that African Americans had a leadership role to play in liberating the world from the structures of racist imperialism and economic exploitation.[109]

In the period from 1965 to 1968, the year of his death, King seemed increasingly frustrated with America's failure to adhere to U.N. standards of human rights in her actions toward Vietnam. In the fall of 1965, he told U.N. Ambassador Arthur Goldberg that the U.S. government's "efforts to seek peace" in Vietnam "by negotiations could be speeded by agreeing to negotiate directly with the National Liberation Front, by admitting Red China to the U.N., and by halting the bombing of North Vietnam."[110] Knowing that North Vietnam had long-standing reservations concerning the U.N., because she and Red China were denied admission, and because she regarded it as being dominated largely by the U.S., King understood clearly the problematics involved in getting the world community to lead in peacefully resolving the conflict. As he saw it, the war had "played havoc with the destiny of the entire world," had torn up "the Geneva Agreement," had "seriously impaired the United Nations," and had "exacerbated the hatreds between continents" and "races."[111] Moreover, he held that the United States had obviously "violated the charter of the United Nations by not submitting to the Security Council its charge of aggression against North Vietnam and by entering the civil war."[112]

While often distrustful of the politics that dominated the decisions and actions of the U.N., King never abandoned the belief that that international body has a critical role in actualizing the Beloved Community. Moreover, he maintained that there was a very obvious and almost facile link between the U.N.'s quest for world peace and the struggle he and others were leading in the U.S. To be sure, his communitarian ideal was irreducible in that fundamental sense. But one might conclude that King's efforts to translate that ethical ideal into practical reality were somewhat slighted by his failure to seriously explore more aggressive, creative, and practical ways of influencing U.N. involvement in both the civil rights movement and human rights struggles abroad. After all, it was he who constantly said that oppressed people everywhere were engaged in essentially the same struggle.[113]

An International Symbol of Community:
U.N. Recognition of King

King's challenge to the U.N. around the issues of human rights and peace did not end with his death. United Nations Secretary General U Thant said as much and more at the time of King's assassination. But reactions to King's death in the U.N. varied, from those who publicly expressed anger and grief to those who remained amazingly silent. Perhaps more important are the ways in which certain elements in the U.N. sought to keep King's memory and his vision of a new humanity alive.

A special session of the U.N. Special Committee Against Apartheid (UNSCAA) met at the King Center in Atlanta, Georgia, in January 1979 to pay an international tribute to King on his fiftieth birthday. Participants hailed from the United States and from nations in Europe, Africa, Asia, and Latin America.[114] This event was arranged in part by Enuga S. Reddy, the director of the U.N. Centre Against Apartheid (UNCAA), a longtime antiapartheid activist and admirer of Gandhi, and one of the U.N. representatives who sought King's testimony against South Africa in 1963.[115] The international tribute undoubtedly owed much to the influence of Andrew J. Young, the U.S. representative to the U.N. and a former aide to King.

Tributes from the American representatives set the tone and created the spirit of the occasion. Andrew Young spoke in profound terms of "the tradition of nonviolence" King represented, contending, with special reference to southern Africa, that "what we see happening across the world today is very much influenced by a nonviolent understanding of how change can occur." Mayor Maynard H. Jackson of Atlanta reminded those present of the significance of King's legacy for southern Africa, and, paraphrasing the civil rights leader, declared that "the oppression of any people anywhere is the oppression of all people everywhere."[116] Equally powerful were the brief remarks of Coretta Scott King, who insisted that "the teachings, the strategies and the social change" that her late husband "initiated" be extended to "the length and breadth of our nation and throughout the world." One of the most stirring tributes came from Governor George Busbee of Georgia, who, in opening comments, captured the meaning of King for those who continued to struggle for a just and peaceful world:

> An essential aspect of Dr. King's struggles for human rights was its nonviolence. Dr. King denounced using violent methods to further human rights, because he realized that it was a contradiction to destroy one group for the benefit of another group. Your Committee should take this important fact into account as you review the human rights struggles around the world. The most successful and beneficial change cannot come through guns and

violence but through negotiation. . . . As terrorism continues to instill fear in the hearts of all men, your Committee should make it a basic goal to work toward ending this method of social change. Dr. King's life was a testimony to this precept.[117]

Representatives from parts of Europe, the most ever to appear at a single event at the King Center, offered tributes that were just as moving and challenging. Kurt Waldheim, secretary general of the U.N., called King "one of those extraordinary personalities who embodied the vision and will to achieve a global order in which all people can walk in peace and dignity." Noting that King invoked "reason over force," Waldheim explained how the civil rights leader's "overriding belief in world community coincided with the steadfast position taken by the United Nations."[118] Prime Minister Olla Ullsten of Sweden echoed Waldheim's points, giving special attention to "the universality of" King's ideas. Kurt Frydenlund, Norway's minister of foreign affairs, described King as "a man who had both a vision and the strategy and strength to do something about it." The representative of the Holy See, Francis Norman, related Pope John Paul II's wish that "many will be inspired by the luminous example of Dr. King to work fearlessly and tenaciously" for the welfare and survival of humanity. Vladimir N. Martynenko, the representative of the Ukrainian Soviet Socialist Republic and chairman of the East European Group, asserted that the "best tribute" to King lies in "a growing unity of actions, of all people of goodwill, and the fight for the final elimination of racism, *apartheid*, and colonialism from our earth."[119]

Perhaps the most powerful tributes given by the European Group came from Hugo Scheltema, the representative from the Netherlands, and Yury E. Fokine, the representative of the Union of Soviet Socialist Republics. Scheltema noted how King's achievements transcended "the borders of his country, of the Western world," and "indeed of the world as a whole":

> Through his words and his actions, Dr. King has affected victims of discrimination, oppression, warfare and poverty all over the world by showing them that even in extremely difficult situations, changes for the better can be brought about. . . . This has been done first of all by putting his person in the service of every

human being in need of justice, peace and social progress, regardless of his race or nationality. By so doing, Martin Luther
King, Jr. has translated the principles that inspire the United Nations into action.[120]

Fokine reminded the representatives that they "should not
engage merely in laudatory speeches about" King's "great contribution to the triumph of justice and the victory of good over evil." "This
is not what Martin Luther King, Jr. would expect from his national as
well as the international community," he observed. Noting that "many
things which Dr. King opposed are still poisoning the world," Fokine
attacked the major Western powers which, despite "the appeals of the
Organization of African Unity and the United Nations and the world
public at large," continued "their collusion" with racist regimes in
southern Africa. A fitting footnote to the European tributes was added
in the brief statements of politicians and activists from Britain, Bel-
gium, and Germany, who were not present in Atlanta. These statements, which were read and included in a book of international
tributes to King, labeled the nonviolent advocate a champion of both
civil and human rights.[121]

Tributes from the so-called Third World were highly charged with
emotion and a sense of urgency about the need for the ongoing appropriation of King's ideas in the quest for world peace and community. This was especially true of the African Group, which felt a special
spiritual, moral, intellectual, and cultural bond with King. Insisting
that "love is the legacy" that King "has bequeathed to the world," Alex
Quaison-Sackey, the ambassador of Ghana to the U.S., suggested that
the international community could never be true to King's "noble
ideals" as long as it refused to break with South African apartheid,
"that terible crime against humanity." O. J. Jolaoso, the ambassador of
Nigeria to the U.S., read a statement from his government, declaring
that King's message "will forever remain a clarion call to all nations to
abhor violence, eschew injustice, and uphold human dignity and freedom." The Nigerian leader Leslie O. Harriman, who chaired the
Special Committee Against Apartheid, spoke in similar terms as he recalled King's work with Albert Luthuli in connection with the Appeal
for Action Against Apartheid (1962). Mohamed Osman, the Su-
danese representative, expressed a commitment to King's vision of "a

world free of racial injustice, poverty, and war," reminding fellow representatives that "large parts of our continent are still dominated by racist regimes, foremost among which is the *apartheid* regime in South Africa."[122] Abdirizak Haji Hussen, the U.N. representative from Somalia, pressed the point further, claiming that "we must see" in King's "life's work" a

> commitment to wider concerns, such as universal respect for human rights, the abolition of racial discrimination, the self-determination of peoples, the elimination of hunger, poverty, and disease, and the creation of harmonious relationships among peoples and nations of the world. These fundamentals championed by Dr. Martin Luther King, Jr. are also cornerstones of the Charter of the United Nations and of the Universal Declaration of Human Rights.[123]

Other statements made by Africans during the 1979 tribute to King added significantly to the drama and power of the occasion. Paul Bomani, the Tanzanian ambassador to the U.S., read comments from President Julius Nyerere, praising King as "an enlightening and inspiring example to the liberation struggle the world over." Ahmed Esmat Abdel Meguid, the Egyptian representative to the U.N., highlighted King's efforts for South African liberation, declaring that "he is regarded, until the present moment, by the freedom fighters in southern Africa, as their spiritual leader who guides and inspires them in their struggle for freedom, independence and dignity." Although Gabriel Seteloane of the African National Congress in South Africa, and Erett Radebe of the Pan-Africanist Congress of Azania, raised questions about the relevance of King's nonviolent methods for fighting apartheid, both insisted that the civil rights leader stands among the great heroes of the African continent.[124]

Tributes on behalf of Latin American countries in the U.N. were shared by Representatives Felix Pita Astudillo of Cuba and George A. Griffith of Grenada. Both recalled the tragic circumstances of King's death while affirming the vitality and durability of his spirit. Claiming that King's death was caused by the "retrogressive forces in the United States, which feared" his "example" and "the dissemination of his struggle," Astudillo suggested that the civil rights leader's life and work had much to teach the world about hope and the indomitability of the human spirit. Griffith spoke of King in a similar vein, reminding his hearers that, "like the rest of the world, Latin America was deeply saddened and shocked at the untimely and brutal 'obliteration' of such a personality," a "personality whose very outreach was universal and whose devotion" is still appreciated by "all the nations of Latin America."[125]

The tributes from the Asian Group could not have been more sobering, coming, as they did, at a time when the horror of Vietnam still loomed large in the world's collective memory. Although Pham Van Dong, the prime minister of the Socialist Republic of Vietnam, could not be present for the international tribute, he sent a statement which praised King for his "valiant struggle against racism," and which noted that "the Vietnamese people highly esteem him and are grateful to him for his support to our past patriotic struggle against United States imperialists' aggression." A similar message concerning King's crusade against all forms of discrimination came from President J. R. Jayewardene of the Democratic Socialist Republic of Sri Lanka.[126]

Those Asian representatives present in Atlanta addressed King's significance around the whole question of human values. After acknowledging that King's contributions "to the cause of human dignity" and "man's spiritual upliftment" are "too well-known to need recapitulation," Japan's U.N. Representative Rikhi Jaipal called the nonviolent leader "a disciple who proved the rightness of the master's teaching and in doing so became a master in his own right." Isao Abe, who also represented Japan in the U.N., described King as "one of the truly great champions of human freedom and dignity," and concluded that much of his greatness "lies in the fact that he recognized the need for" a "reworking of the world order, and realized that this could occur only if there was a revolution in the values of the people of the developed countries." Pakistan's Representative Tayyab Siddiqui echoed this conviction, and, in the spirit of King, reported that his people "are convinced that the international community should impose sanctions against South Africa for constantly violating the United Nations resolutions."[127]

An appropriate climax to the 1979 tribute to King came in the words of Herschell Challenor, who represented the United Nations Educational, Scientific and Cultural Organization (UNESCO) in Washington. Quoting King, she said:

Let us in the international community pledge ourselves to renew and fulfill Martin Luther King's dream of a time when the world would see itself as one great "family of nations" where "no man would be an island unto himself" and "where man would not be judged by the color of his skin but by the content of his character."[128]

This event was followed three years later by another international tribute to King. The U.N. Special Committee Against Apartheid sent a mission to Atlanta in January 1982 for the observance of King's birthday and the dedication of the King Center's Freedom Hall Complex.[129] The delegation consisted of Alhaji Yusuff Maitama-Sule of Nigeria, the chairman of the UNSCAA; Vladimir A. Kravets of the Ukraine, the vice chairman; Ibrahim Noor, the secretary; and the ambassadors of India, Somalia, Trinidad, and Tobago. King's contributions to the South African freedom cause were the focus of attention, as parties in the U.N. prepared to initiate "the International Year of Mobilization for Sanctions against South Africa." Seminars and other events were held, and the U.N. delegation laid a wreath at King's grave.[130]

The appearance of representatives of the UNSCAA in Atlanta connected well with the King Center's broadening sense of mission regarding South African liberation. In a letter to Enuga S. Reddy, the director of the UNSCAA, Coretta Scott King declared that "the presence of this distinguished delegation gave witness to the universality of Martin's work and Dream of a worldwide Beloved Community with peace and justice for all people." The widow of King went on to rededicate herself to the spreading of "Martin's message of love and nonviolence throughout the world," noting the pressing need to confront "nations and peoples in such a way that Martin's nonviolence will be universally embraced as our only viable alternative to world chaos."[131] Bernice A. King, the daughter of the late civil rights leader, echoed her mother's remarks, asserting that "my father's words and the challenge he laid before us are as relevant today as they were in 1965."[132]

On November 5, 1982, the U.N. General Assembly evoked King's memory during a special meeting "devoted to the International Year of Sanctions against South Africa." The event commemorated the twentieth anniversary of the first General Assembly resolution urging sanctions against South Africa (Resolution 1761 of 6 November

1962), a resolution fully supported by King and his colleagues in both the ACOA and the ANLCA. After reaffirming its "solidarity with the national liberation movement of South Africa," the U.N. General Assembly awarded gold medals to the late King and many other world leaders who had impacted the antiapartheid crusade since the middle of the century. The assembly recognized the irony of honoring King, who "shall always belong to that same United States whose government is responsible for collaboration with the *apartheid* regime."[133]

The spirit of the 1982 tributes to King matched those paid to him by world leaders in 1979. Indeed, such tributes afforded proof of King's continuing significance for the U.N., and also for the liberation struggles of the oppressed worldwide. But the real test of the civil rights leader's meaning for the U.N. would come in the years that followed, as that international body confronted issues ranging from health care to child labor to ethnic cleansing in Yugoslavia.

Toward a New World Order:
The U.N. and Human Rights since King

The United Nations consisted of 126 member states at the time of King's death in 1968.[134] In the decades that followed, that international body grew and underwent fundamental changes as it confronted many of the same crisis situations it struggled with during the King years, chief among which stood South African apartheid, the social and economic development of poor nations, and nuclear disarmament. Thus, King's communitarian ideal remained relevant to discussions and debates concerning the ways in which the U.N. could function more successfully as a forum for international cooperation, as a force in overcoming conflict between nations and peoples, and as a peacemaking and peacekeeping instrument.

The U.N.'s central mandate relative to human rights concerns remains essentially what it was in King's time; namely, "to ensure that the human dignity" of "the 'peoples' of the United Nations, in whose name the Charter was written, is fully respected." But the role and scope of U.N. activities in promoting and protecting human rights continue to expand.[135] Toward this end, the U.N. operates on several fronts, serving as researcher, as fact finder, as the global conscience, as lawmaker, as monitor, and as a forum of appeal. Those human rights pertaining to different racial and ethnic groups, women, children, prisoners and detainees, refugees, workers, and disabled persons are now "a major part of international law," and so are crimes such as torture and genocide.[136] Such a broad and inclusive approach to human rights concerns—one grounded in practical considerations and the collective approval of the highest standards of behavior—is what King had in mind when he spoke of the moral responsibility of the international community to wipe out all forms of discrimination.

The U.N. has resorted increasingly to diplomatic efforts and economic sanctions and embargoes as a nonviolent strategy in cases where human rights abuses are flagrant. This posture is obviously consistent with what King envisioned for that body.[137] Significantly, the Security Council made sanctions against South Africa's apartheid regime mandatory in 1977, emphasizing an arms embargo and specific trade bans, and the U.S. ultimately supported this action by favoring sanctions in 1986. The U.N. subsequently lifted the sanctions when South Africa moved toward nonracial democracy in 1994, thus fulfilling recommendations consistently made by King in the 1960s.[138] In recent years, sanctions have been imposed against Rwanda, Kosovo, and East Timor, where human rights violations have taken the form of ethnic cleansing. The U.N. tribunal's indictment in early 2001 of Yugoslavia's former president Slobodan Milosevic for "crimes against humanity" affords additional evidence of that international body's efforts to eliminate racism. The same could be said of the U.N.'s World Conference against Racism, Racial Discrimination, Xenophobia, and Related Forms of Intolerance in Durban, South Africa (fall 2001). Such a conference is clearly in the tradition of King, who consistently called for "an international alliance of peoples of all nations against racism."[139] Similar steps may be required on the part of the U.N. in the future to deal more specifically with the widespread, systematic, and officially sanctioned abuse of women in Afghanistan, Pakistan, and other parts of the world.[140] In any case, King's vision of a world order free of glaring human rights problems and abuses is possible only if representatives of the international community are willing to continuously indulge in some serious Utopian thinking.

The same applies with respect to the U.N.'s efforts in addressing the social and economic problems of what King termed "the poor" and "underdeveloped" nations in Africa, Asia, the Caribbean, and Latin America.[141] Although the U.N. has taken steps, through its Economic and Social Council, its world food programs, and other human rights agencies, to deal with grinding poverty, hunger, malnutrition, drug addiction, disease, and other problems worldwide, its efforts are often dominated more by politics and self-interest than by moral considerations. This helps explain why thirty of the forty-three poorest countries today are in Africa, and the remaining thirteen in Asia, Latin America, and the Caribbean. King spoke consistently of the danger of politically motivated foreign aid programs, and he maintained that such programs should never be used by rich nations as "a surreptitious means" to control poor countries.[142] King's views on this subject still present a serious challenge because definitions of the new world economic order have little, if anything at all, to do with the significant enhancement of poor nations and peoples.

The relevance and implications of King's ideas for addressing war, human destruction, and the proliferation of nuclear weapons are also still evident. More than three hundred small wars have resulted in the deaths of more than thirty million people since the U.N. was founded in 1945, and nuclear weapons have become more widespread, sophisticated, and destructive in terms of their potential. Moreover, the threat of biological and chemical warfare is far greater than was the case in King's lifetime. Over the past two decades, the U.N. has been called upon to address the threats posed by Iran, Libya, and Iraq, acts of terrorism, and internal political unrest and violence in Grenada, Central America, Afghanistan, the Middle East, and in various parts of Africa and Asia. In 1998 alone, the U.N. launched sixteen peacekeeping missions encompassing 14,500 civilian and military personnel from seventy-seven countries, with a specific focus on Latin America, Africa, the former Soviet Union, and the Middle East.[143] But such efforts, even if intensified in the future, will bear little fruit if the U.N. fails to develop more creative ways of encouraging peaceful coexistence. Unfortunately, King's call for the employment of nonviolent strategies and tactics to settle conflict between nations and peoples seems far more unrealistic today than it was in the 1960s, especially considering the enormity and the accessibility of weapons, the threat of global terrorism, and humanity's obsession with war and human destruction as avenues to survival and self-realization.[144]

In his challenge to the U.N., King maintained that genuine community in a global context is more than the absence of discrimination, poverty and economic injustice, and war and human destruction. It is also the affirmation and uplift of all human personality, the actualization of economic justice and equality of opportunity, and the triumph of peace and a spirit of toleration. In short, it is the recognition that human survival rests on the kind of "positive revolution of values" that "lifts neighborly concern beyond one's tribe, race, class and nation."[145]

NOTES

1. Irwin Abrams, ed., *The Words of Peace: Selections from the Speeches of the Winners of the Nobel Peace Prize* (New York: New Market Press, 1990), p. 60.

2. *Basic Facts about the United Nations* (New York: The United Nations Department of Public Information, 1998), p. 3; and *Everyone's United Nations: A Handbook on the Work of the United Nations* (New York: United Nations, 1986), p. 3.

3. *Everyone's United Nations*, p. 1; Wolfgang Huber, *Violence: The Unrelenting Assault on Human Dignity*, translated by Ruth C. L. Gritsch (Minneapolis: Fortress Press, 1996), p. 93; and Arthur P. Mendel, ed., *The Twentieth Century, 1914–1964* (New York: Free Press, 1965), p. 23.

4. Martin Luther King, Jr., *Where Do We Go from Here: Chaos or Community?* (Boston: Beacon Press, 1968), p. 184; and James M. Washington, ed., *A Testament of Hope: The Essential Writings of Martin Luther King, Jr.* (San Francisco: HarperCollins, 1986), pp. 276 and 628.

5. *Basic Facts about the United Nations* (1998), p. 5; *Everyone's United Nations*, pp. 3–4; and John Tessitore and Susan Woolfson, eds., *A Global Agenda: Issues before the 53rd General Assembly of the United Nations—An Annual Publication of the United Nations Association of the United States of America* (Lanham, Md.: Rowman & Littlefield, 1998), pp. 162–163. One scholar has noted that "the trend toward universality runs as a continuous thread through the history of the United Nations." See Inis L. Claude, Jr., *The Changing United Nations* (New York: Random House, 1967), pp. 106–107.

6. *Everyone's United Nations*, pp. 324–325.

7. King, *Where Do We Go from Here?*, pp. 167–168.

8. Martin Luther King, Jr., *The Trumpet of Conscience* (San Francisco: Harper & Row, 1989), pp. 69–70; and George M. Houser, *No One Can Stop*

the Rain: Glimpses of Africa's Liberation Struggle (New York: Pilgrim Press, 1989), pp. 16–17 and 348–349.

9. Tessitore and Woolfson, eds., *A Global Agenda*, pp. 59–84 and 159–167; *Basic Facts about the United Nations* (1998), pp. 80–81 and 224–235; *Everyone's United Nations*, pp. 37–327; and King, *Where Do We Go from Here?*, pp. 173–186. King was equally perceptive in addressing the *internal barriers* to human community, among which he included ignorance, fear, greed, and hatred. See Walter E. Fluker, *They Looked for a City: A Comparative Analysis of the Ideal of Community in the Thought of Howard Thurman and Martin Luther King, Jr.* (Lanham, Md.: University Press of America, 1989), pp. 129–152; Lewis V. Baldwin, *To Make the Wounded Whole: The Cultural Legacy of Martin Luther King, Jr.* (Minneapolis: Fortress Press, 1992), p. 262 n46; and Lewis V. Baldwin, *Toward the Beloved Community: Martin Luther King, Jr. and South Africa* (Cleveland: Pilgrim Press, 1995), pp. 16, 31, 39, 42–43, and 45.

10. See Philip S. Foner, ed., *W. E. B. DuBois Speaks: Speeches and Addresses, 1920–1963* (New York: Pathfinder Press, 1972), p. 151.

11. See Houser, *No One Can Stop the Rain*, pp. 16–17.

12. *Basic Facts about the United Nations* (New York: United Nations Department of Public Information, 1986), chapter 4, p. 4.

13. Ibid.

14. From E. S. Reddy to Lewis V. Baldwin (15 May 1994); From George M. Houser to Lewis V. Baldwin (9 October 1987), p. 1; Martin Luther King, Jr., "South Africa Benefit Speech," delivered at Hunter College, New York, New York (10 December 1965), Archives of the Martin Luther King, Jr., Center for Nonviolent Social Change, Atlanta, Georgia, pp. 1–5; and King, *Where Do We Go from Here?*, p. 173.

15. *Everyone's United Nations*, p. 9; and Claude, *The Changing United Nations*, pp. 115–118.

16. King, *Where Do We Go from Here?*, p. 178.

17. Ibid., pp. 169–170; and Baldwin, *To Make the Wounded Whole*, pp. 247 and 250.

18. King, *Where Do We Go from Here?*, pp. 177–179; and Hugh Downs's Interview with Martin Luther King, Jr., NBC "Today" Show (18 April 1966), King Center Archives, p. 4.

19. *Basic Facts about the United Nations* (1998), pp. 3–4; *Everybody's United Nations*, pp. 3–5; Huber, *Violence: The Unrelenting Assault*, pp. 103–104; and Joseph P. Baratta, *United Nations System*, vol. 10 (New Brunswick, N.J.: Transaction Publishers, 1995), pp. xi–xiii. Unlike the U.N., which operated mostly out of political considerations, King's commitment to nonviolence as an avenue to world peace was more theological and moral than political. King was a politician of sorts, but he was at

bottom a Baptist preacher, a minister of the Gospel of Jesus Christ, who saw these matters through powerful theological and ethical categories.

20. Huber, *Violence: The Unrelenting Assault*, pp. 103–104; and *Everyone's United Nations*, pp. 37–42 and 97–100.

21. King, *Where Do We Go from Here?*, pp. 181–191; King, *The Trumpet of Conscience*, pp. 21–34; Baldwin, *Toward the Beloved Community*, pp. 8–63; and Edmund Jan Osmanczyk, *The Encyclopedia of the United Nations and International Agreements/Relations* (New York: Taylor and Francis, 1990), pp. 390, 634, and 683.

22. King actually went through "a kind of intellectual pilgrimage on the whole question of war and the pacifist position." See King, *Where Do We Go from Here?*, p. 183; Martin Luther King, Jr., "Interview on World Peace," *Red Book Magazine* (November 1964): pp. 3–7; and Baldwin, *To Make the Wounded Whole*, pp. 269–270. One scholar convincingly claims that King, in denying that war could "serve any good at all," was essentially a unilateralist. Reinhold Niebuhr would have called King naive at this point, for the civil rights leader had rejected even just-war theory by this time. From Rufus Burrow, Jr. to Lewis V. Baldwin (22 September 1999), p. 8.

23. King, *Where Do We Go from Here?*, p. 184; and Washington, ed., *A Testament of Hope*, p. 628.

24. King, *Where Do We Go from Here?*, p. 184; and Baldwin, *To Make the Wounded Whole*, pp. 271–272.

25. Washington, ed., *A Testament of Hope*, p. 276.

26. King, *Where Do We Go from Here?*, p. 189; and Clayborne Carson, ed., *The Autobiography of Martin Luther King, Jr.* (New York: Warner Books, 1998), p. 237.

27. See Jim Bishop, *The Days of Martin Luther King, Jr.* (New York: G. P. Putnam's Sons, 1971), pp. 264 and 402; King, *Where Do We Go from Here?*, pp. 187 and 189; and Carson, ed., *The Autobiography of Martin Luther King, Jr.*, p. 334. Interestingly enough, African American leaders like W. E. B. DuBois and Paul Robeson prefigured King in calling for the seating of the People's Republic of China in the U.N. See Foner, ed., *W. E. B. DuBois Speaks*, p. 150–151; and Philip S. Foner, ed., *Paul Robeson Speaks: Writings, Speeches, Interviews, 1918–1974* (Secaucus, N.J.: Citadel Press, 1978), pp. 259, 267, 275, 281, 373, and 573.

28. King, *The Trumpet of Conscience*, pp. 63–64 and 68; and Baldwin, *To Make the Wounded Whole*, pp. 284–285 and 310–311.

29. *Everyone's United Nations*, pp. 312–313; *Basic Facts about the United Nations* (1998), pp. 235–236; and Tessitore and Woolfson, eds., *A Global Agenda*, pp. 159–177.

30. Martin Luther King, Jr., "An Address," delivered at the fiftieth anniversary of the Women's International League for Peace and Freedom,

Philadelphia, Pennsylvania (15 October 1965), King Center Archives, pp. 1–2.

31. "Push Renewed to Accelerate Women's Rights Worldwide: Global Conference of Women Has Formidable Roadblocks," *Tennessean,* 4 June 2000, p. 2A; "U.N. Delegates Struggle with Women's Rights," *Tennessean,* 10 June 2000, p. 4A; and "U.N. Conference Fends Off Efforts to Curb Women's Rights," *Tennessean,* 11 June 2000, p. 4A.

32. "Push Renewed to Accelerate Women's Rights," p. 2A; and "Jewish Women Pray Aloud at Wall, Defying Israeli Bill," *Tennessean,* 5 June 2000, p. 3A.

33. *Everybody's United Nations,* pp. 324–325.

34. King obviously experienced an intellectual struggle around the issues of religious pluralism and tolerance on a global scale. In 1958, he described Christianity as "an expression of the highest revelation of God"—as "the synthesis of the best in all religions." At times, however, his tendency to refer to the United States as "becoming a Christian nation" did not go unchallenged, experiences that led him, in 1961, to declare that "it is my sincere conviction that no religion has a monopoly on truth and that God has revealed Himself in all of the religions of mankind." See Martin Luther King, Jr., "Advice for Living," *Ebony,* vol. 13, no. 11 (September 1958): p. 68; and From Martin Luther King, Jr. to Bernard Resnikoff (17 September 1961), Martin Luther King, Jr. Papers, Special Collections, Mugar Memorial Library, Boston University, Boston, Massachusetts, pp. 1–2.

35. For a brief but interesting statement on the persecution of Christians in China, see Elaine Kurtenbach, "Religious Persecution in China on Rise, Christian Group Says," *Atlanta Journal-Constitution,* 20 May 2000, p. B4.

36. Quoted in Lerone Bennett, Jr., *What Manner of Man: A Biography of Martin Luther King, Jr.* (New York: Pocket Books, 1968), p. 146.

37. See Foner, ed., *W. E. B. DuBois Speaks,* pp. 150–160; and Foner, ed., *Paul Robeson Speaks,* pp. 158–160 and 164.

38. Foner, ed., *W. E. B. DuBois Speaks,* pp. 150–160; Foner, ed., *Paul Robeson Speaks,* pp. 158–160 and 164; Baldwin, *To Make the Wounded Whole,* pp. 163–244; and Baldwin, *Toward the Beloved Community,* pp. 1–63.

39. Foner, ed., *W. E. B. DuBois Speaks,* pp. 150–151; and Foner, ed., *Paul Robeson Speaks,* pp. 158–160 and 164.

40. This document was prepared under the editorial supervision of DuBois, with the assistance of black and white scholars. On October 23, 1947, at a public meeting of the U.N. in Lake Success, New York, Walter White, executive secretary of the NAACP, presented the contents of this document. See Foner, ed., *W. E. B. DuBois Speaks,* pp. 203–221; Foner, ed.,

Paul Robeson Speaks, p. 581; and Taylor Branch, *Parting the Waters: America in the King Years, 1954–63* (New York: Simon and Schuster, 1988), p. 293n.

41. Foner, ed., *Paul Robeson Speaks*, p. 581.

42. George Breitman, ed., *By Any Means Necessary: Speeches, Interviews and a Letter by Malcolm X* (New York: Pathfinder Press, 1970), pp. 19–20 and 27; George Breitman, ed., *Malcolm X Speaks: Selected Speeches and Statements* (New York: Merit Publishers, 1965), pp. 34–35 and 217; Steve Clark, ed., *February 1965: The Final Speeches—Malcolm X* (New York: Pathfinder Press, 1992), pp. 26–27 and 169–170; Foner, ed., *Paul Robeson Speaks*, p. 581; and Taylor Branch, *Pillar of Fire: America in the King Years, 1963–65* (New York: Simon & Schuster, 1998), pp. 314, 316, and 345.

43. James Baldwin, "Malcolm and Martin," *Esquire*, vol. 67 (April 1972): p. 201; and Baldwin, *To Make the Wounded Whole*, p. 43.

44. King, *The Trumpet of Conscience*, p. 5.

45. King, *Where Do We Go from Here?*, p. 57; King, *My Life with Martin Luther King, Jr.*, p. 239; and King, "Interview on World Peace," pp. 6–7. King's views on the transforming role of African Americans are treated in great depth in Lewis V. Baldwin, *There Is a Balm in Gilead: The Cultural Roots of Martin Luther King, Jr.* (Minneapolis: Fortress Press, 1991), pp. 229–268.

46. For these ideas, I am heavily indebted to Rufus Burrow, Jr. From Burrow to Baldwin (22 September 1999), p. 14.

47. Malcolm X did not share this position. He declared in 1964 that "there are enough independent nations in the UN from Africa and Asia who have become politically mature and also have enough independence to do what is necessary to see that some results are gotten from any plea, bona fide plea, that's made on the part of our people." See Breitman, ed., *By Any Means Necessary*, p. 27; and Breitman, ed., *Malcolm X Speaks*, pp. 35–36.

48. Breitman, ed., *Malcolm X Speaks*, pp. 34–37, 40, and 53–54; and Breitman, ed., *By Any Means Necessary*, pp. 19–20.

49. I am heavily indebted to Rufus Burrow, Jr., for these thoughts. From Burrow to Baldwin (22 September 1999), p. 15.

50. Martin Luther King, Jr., *Why We Can't Wait* (New York: New American Library, 1964), p. 22; Martin Luther King, Jr., "Civil Right No. 1—The Right to Vote," *New York Times Magazine*, section 6, part 1 (14 March 1965), p. 25; and Baldwin, *Toward the Beloved Community*, pp. 40 and 45.

51. The first African American to serve as U.S. ambassador to the U.N. was Andrew Young, a former associate of King who was appointed in the late 1970s by President Jimmy Carter. See Robert C. Smith, *We Have*

No Leaders: African Americans in the Post-Civil Rights Era (Albany: State University of New York Press, 1996), p. 148.

52. See Branch, *Pillar of Fire*, p. 518.

53. See Baldwin, *Toward the Beloved Community*, p. 59.

54. Martin Luther King, Jr., "The Negro and the American Dream," a speech at a public meeting of the Charlotte branch of the NAACP, Charlotte, North Carolina (25 September 1960), King Papers, Boston University, pp. 1–2.

55. Martin Luther King, Jr., "The Ben Bella Conversation" (October 1962), King Papers, Boston University, p. 2; and Martin Luther King, Jr., "My Talk with Ben Bella," *New York Amsterdam News*, 27 October 1962, p. 12.

56. Houser, *No One Can Stop the Rain*, pp. 12–20, 63, and 265; Houser to Baldwin (9 October 1987), p. 1; a private interview with George M. Houser, Pomona, New York (26 May 1993); From George M. Houser to Lewis V. Baldwin (14 May 1994), p. 1; and Baldwin, *Toward the Beloved Community*, pp. 14–21.

57. Houser, *No One Can Stop the Rain*, p. 266; and Baldwin, *Toward the Beloved Community*, pp. 38–39 and 206 n57.

58. One activist persuasively claims that "King gave most attention to the fight against apartheid in South Africa," mainly because "resistance to racism in South Africa most nearly paralleled the experience of combatting segregation in the United States." See George M. Houser, "Freedom's Struggle Crosses Oceans and Mountains: Martin Luther King, Jr., and the Liberation Struggles in Africa and America," in Peter J. Albert and Ronald Hoffman, eds., *We Shall Overcome: Martin Luther King, Jr. and the Black Freedom Struggle* (New York: Pantheon Books, 1990), p. 189.

59. This perspective grew out of King's readings concerning South Africa, his conversations with the Anglican priest Michael Scott in Ghana in 1957, his exchanges with Bishop Ambrose Reeves of Johannesburg and Archbishop Trevor Huddleston of Tanganyika, and his dialogue with parties in the ACOA. See From George M. Houser to Martin Luther King, Jr. (6 February 1962), ACOA Collection, Amistad Research Center, Tulane University, New Orleans, Louisiana, p. 1; and Baldwin, *Toward the Beloved Community*, pp. 7–63.

60. From Eleanor Roosevelt, James A. Pike, and Martin Luther King, Jr. to Friends and Supporters of the ACOA (July 1957), King Papers, Boston University, p. 1; From James A. Pike and Martin Luther King, Jr. to the Honorable Paul H. Douglas (4 November 1957), King Papers, Boston University, pp. 1–2; Houser, *No One Can Stop the Rain*, pp. 123–124; Houser, "Freedom's Struggle Crosses Oceans and Mountains," p. 189; and Baldwin, *Toward the Beloved Community*, p. 15.

61. From George M. Houser to Irwin Kern (13 August 1957), ACOA Collection, Amistad Center, Tulane University, p. 1; and From George M. Houser to Diarmuid O'Scannlian (22 August 1957), ACOA Collection, Amistad Center, Tulane University, p. 1.

62. *Declaration of Conscience: An Appeal to South Africa*, drafted by the American Committee on Africa (10 December 1957), King Papers, Boston University, pp. 1–5.

63. Houser, *No One Can Stop the Rain*, p. 124; From George M. Houser to Julius Mueller (18 September 1957), ACOA Collection, Amistad Center, Tulane University, p. 1; *The ACOA Reports on the Declaration of Conscience* (9 January 1958), King Papers, Boston University, pp. 1–3; From Wayne Morse to James A. Pike and Martin Luther King, Jr. (12 November 1957), ACOA Collection, Amistad Center, Tulane University, p. 1; From Margaret Chase Smith to Eleanor Roosevelt, James A. Pike, and Martin Luther King, Jr. (23 August 1957), ACOA Collection, Amistad Center, Tulane University, p. 1; From Michael Scott to Martin Luther King, Jr. (23 January 1958), King Papers, Boston University, pp. 1–2; and Baldwin, *Toward the Beloved Community*, pp. 17–19.

64. From Scott to King (23 January 1958), pp. 1–2; From Donald Harrington to Friends of the American Committee on Africa (18 September 1958), King Papers, Boston University, p. 1; and Baldwin, *Toward the Beloved Community*, pp. 15–19.

65. Martin Luther King, Jr., "Introduction," in *Southwest Africa: The U.N.'s Stepchild* (New York: American Committee on Africa, ca. 1959), King Papers, Boston University, p. 1.

66. Ibid. King met with Scott, the Anglican priest and antiapartheid activist, while in Ghana in 1957. See "Conversation in Ghana," *Christian Century*, vol. 74, no. 15 (10 April 1957): pp. 446–448; and Baldwin, *Toward the Beloved Community*, pp. 10, 17–18, and 38.

67. Interestingly enough, King once received a letter from a Jewish activist who complained that the Asian and African delegations to the U.N. were guilty of "a serious discriminatory act" in excluding the Israeli delegation from one of their receptions. See From Isidore W. Ruskin to Martin Luther King, Jr. (30 November 1959), King Papers, Boston University, pp. 1–2.

68. "Americans Protest South African Massacre," *Atlanta Daily World*, 24 March 1960, p. 1; From Hope R. Stevens to Friends and Supporters of Africa Freedom Day of the ACOA (April 1960), King Papers, Boston University, p. 1; and Baldwin, *Toward the Beloved Community*, pp. 33–34 and 202 n35.

69. "Liberals Urge Ambassador to South Africa Be Recalled for Consultation—Suspension of Gold Purchases," *Press Release: Americans for*

Democratic Action, Washington, D.C. (17 April 1960), King Papers, Boston University, pp. 1–2; "ADA Asks U.S. Protest on African Apartheid," *Sunday Star*, Washington, D.C., 17 April 1960, p. 1; and Paul W. Ward, "Liberals Bid U.S. Censure South Africa: A.D.A. Petition Urges Envoy's Recall, Halt in Gold-Buying," *Baltimore Sun*, 17 April 1960, p. 1.

70. *Basic Facts about the United Nations* (1986), chapter 2, p. 38; and From Stevens to Friends of Africa Freedom Day (April 1960), p. 1.

71. Martin Luther King, Jr., to Enoch Dumas (11 January 1960), King Papers, Boston University, p. 1.

72. From Houser to King (6 February 1962), p. 1; From Albert J. Luthuli to Friends of the American Committee on Africa (6 August 1962), ACOA Collection, Amistad Center, Tulane University, p. 1; From Donald S. Harrington to Friends of the American Committee on Africa (26 November 1962), King Papers, Boston University, pp. 1–2; *Appeal for Action Against Apartheid*, drafted by the American Committee on Africa (1962), King Center Archives, pp. 1–2; and Baldwin, *Toward the Beloved Community*, pp. 36–39 and 41.

73. See Charles Reagan Wilson, *Judgment and Grace in Dixie: Southern Faiths from Faulkner to Elvis* (Athens: University of Georgia Press, 1995), p. 36. A common view is that King's perspective did not become truly international until after he received the Nobel Peace Prize in 1964, a view clearly undermined by the content of this chapter. See Baldwin, *To Make the Wounded Whole*, pp. 165 and 247–250; and Baldwin, *Toward the Beloved Community*, pp. 3–42.

74. Martin Luther King, Jr., "The Negro Looks at Africa," unpublished manuscript (8 December 1962), King Center Archives, p. 1.

75. *Appeal for Action Against Apartheid*, pp. 1–4; and Baldwin, *Toward the Beloved Community*, pp. 37–38.

76. *Basic Facts about the United Nations* (1986), chapter 2, p. 38.

77. From E. S. Reddy to Lewis V. Baldwin (10 April 1994), p. 1.

78. Martin Luther King, Jr., "The Negro Looks at Africa," p. 3.

79. Ibid.; and Martin Luther King, Jr., "Statement at the American Negro Leadership Conference on Africa," Arden House, Harriman, New York (24 November 1962), King Papers, Boston University, pp. 1–2.

80. *American Negro Leadership Conference on Africa: Resolutions November 23–25* (New York: The American Negro Leadership Conference on Africa, 1962), ACOA Collection, Amistad Center, Tulane University, p. 2.

81. Ibid., pp. 2–3.

82. Ibid.

83. From George M. Houser to President John F. Kennedy (7 December 1962), ACOA Collection, Amistad Center, Tulane University,

pp. 1–3; From the American Negro Leadership Conference on Africa to President John F. Kennedy (17 December 1962), King Papers, Boston University, pp. 1–2; From George M. Houser to the American Committee on Africa (14 December 1962), ACOA Collection, Amistad Center, Tulane University, pp. 1–3; and Martin Luther King, Jr. to Theodore E. Brown (1 April 1963), King Papers, Boston University, pp. 1–2.

84. From the ANLCA to Kennedy (17 December 1962), pp. 1–2.

85. Ibid.

86. Houser, "Freedom's Struggle Crosses Oceans and Mountains," p. 186.

87. From Theodore E. Brown to all Participants in the American Negro Leadership Conference on Africa (8 February 1963), King Center Archives, pp. 1–2; "Negro Leaders Meet with Ambassador Stevenson on U.S.-U.N. Africa Policy," press release from the American Negro Leadership Conference on Africa (29 January 1963), King Center Archives, pp. 1–3; From Theodore E. Brown to Martin Luther King, Jr. (27 February 1963), King Center Archives, p. 1; and "Minutes of the Call Committee Meeting of the American Negro Leadership Conference on Africa," unpublished document (16 December 1963), King Center Archives, pp. 1–3.

88. Martin Luther King, Jr., "New Year Hopes," *New York Amsterdam News,* 5 January 1963, p. 1; and Baldwin, *To Make the Wounded Whole,* pp. 270–271.

89. Houser, *No One Can Stop the Rain,* pp. 348–349; Baldwin, *Toward the Beloved Community,* pp. 42–43; From E. S. Reddy to Lewis V. Baldwin (14 September 1993), pp. 1–2; and From George M. Houser to Martin Luther King, Jr. (9 January 1963), ACOA Collection, Amistad Center, Tulane University, p. 1. Houser told King in another letter that "there was never a time . . . when solidarity between African nationalist leaders and American civil rights leaders was more needed than at the present time." See From George M. Houser to Martin Luther King, Jr. (6 September 1963), ACOA Collection, Amistad Center, Tulane University, p. 1.

90. From E. S. Reddy to Martin Luther King, Jr. (28 June 1963), King Center Archives, p. 1; From Reddy to Baldwin (14 September 1993), pp. 1–2; and From E. S. Reddy to Lewis V. Baldwin (2 December 1994), p. 1.

91. From Reddy to Baldwin (2 December 1994), p. 1; From Wyatt Tee Walker to George M. Houser (10 July 1963), King Center Archives, p. 1; and From George M. Houser to Wyatt T. Walker (11 July 1963), King Center Archives, p. 1.

92. Reddy ultimately concluded that "I believe we were wrong" in assuming that pressure from the federal government prevented King from

appearing before the U.N. Special Committee on the Policies of Aparthied of the Government of the Republic of South Africa. But Reddy offers no other explanation for King's action. See From Walker to Houser (10 July 1963), p. 1; From Reddy to Baldwin (14 September 1993), p. 1; and "Request for a Hearing by Rev. Dr. Martin Luther King," *Report of the Sub-Committee*, unpublished U.N. document (27 June 1963), p. 2.

93. From Walker to Houser (10 July 1963), p. 1; and Baldwin, *Toward the Beloved Community*, p. 43.

94. From George M. Houser to Martin Luther King, Jr. (4 September 1963), King Center Archives, p. 1; and Baldwin, *Toward the Beloved Community*, p. 43.

95. From George M. Houser to Martin Luther King, Jr. (5 November 1963), King Center Archives, p. 1; From Miss Dora McDonald to George M. Houser (14 November 1963), King Center Archives, p. 1; and Baldwin, *Toward the Beloved Community*, p. 43.

96. From the American Negro Leadership Conference on Africa to President Lyndon B. Johnson (25 January 1964), King Center Archives, pp. 1–2.

97. M. S. Handler, "Negroes Ask Role in Foreign Policy: Leaders to Meet in Capital—White House Interested," *New York Times*, 9 July 1964, p. L-15.

98. *American Negro Leadership Conference on Africa: Resolutions* (New York: The American Negro Leadership Conference on Africa, 1964), p. 4.

99. Ibid.

100. Ibid., pp. 5–6.

101. Martin Luther King, Jr., "On South African Independence," speech delivered in London, England (7 December 1964), unpublished document, King Center Archives, p. 2; *Four Decades of Concern: Martin Luther King, Jr.* (Atlanta: Martin Luther King, Jr. Center for Nonviolent Social Change, 1986), p. 19; and "King Accuses U.S.A. and Britain of Bolstering Racial Segregation in South Africa," *Relay News in English* (8 December 1964), pp. 1 and 3.

102. "Radio Interview with Martin Luther King, Jr. regarding the Nobel Peace Prize," Oslo, Norway (9 December 1964), pp. 3–4. James Cone's claim that King "was strangely silent about the U.S. invasion of the Congo" must not be accepted uncritically. King addressed this issue in an interview in Norway, and also through his support for ACOA and ANLCA letters, petitions, and resolutions. See From James H. Cone to Lewis V. Baldwin (18 February 1987), p. 1; "International Pact on Congo Proposed," unpublished statement by the American Committee on Africa (29 November 1964), pp. 1–2; and *ANLCA: Resolutions* (1964), pp. 5–6.

103. Baldwin, *To Make the Wounded Whole*, p. 250.

104. "U.S. Negroes' Goal: To Set Africa Policy," *U.S. News and World Report*, vol. 58, no. 2 (11 January 1965): p. 61.

105. Martin Luther King, Jr., "A Lecture before the Federation Protestante de France Mutualite" (24 October 1965), unpublished document, King Center Archives, p. 18; and "On the World Taking a Stand on Rhodesia: An Interview with Martin Luther King, Jr." (25 October 1965), unpublished document, King Center Archives, p. 1.

106. *Four Decades of Concern*, p. 21; and Baldwin, *Toward the Beloved Community*, p. 21.

107. *Four Decades of Concern*, p. 21; Houser, *No One Can Stop the Rain*, p. 266; and Houser, "Freedom's Struggle Crosses Oceans and Mountains," p. 191.

108. "Human Rights Day Rally and Benefit for South African Victims of Apartheid," a program, Hunter College (10 December 1965), pp. 1–3; "Let My People Go," *South Africa Freedom News* (14 June 1966), issued by the African National Congress of South Africa, Dar Es Salaam, pp. 3–4; From Mary Louise Hooper to Martin Luther King, Jr. (12 October 1965), King Center Archives, pp. 1–2; From Reddy to Baldwin (14 September 1993), p. 1; and Baldwin, *Toward the Beloved Community*, pp. 47–49 and 211 n92.

109. King, *Where Do We Go from Here?*, p. 57; and King, *The Trumpet of Conscience*, p. 17.

110. Carson, ed., *The Autobiography of Martin Luther King, Jr.*, pp. 334 and 344; Hugh Downs's Interview with Martin Luther King, Jr., p. 3; and "Martin Luther King, Jr. and Ambassador Goldberg of the U.N.: War Statements," unpublished document (10 September 1965), King Center Archives, p. 3.

111. Carson, ed., *The Autobiography of Martin Luther King, Jr.*, p. 344; and Martin Luther King, Jr., "An Address," United Nations Plaza, New York, New York (15 April 1967), pp. 6–7, 10–12, and 26. Having a diminishing faith in the capacity of nations to peacefully resolve human conflict, King expressed the conviction that "in the near future the Church must find some way to direct her concern toward the question of world peace." He was disturbed by the fact that "Christians have lost the right to serve as reconciling agents in international disputes because of our inaction and cautious strategies in the midst of two past world conflicts." See Martin Luther King, Jr., "Closing Address at the European Baptist Assembly," Amsterdam, Holland (16 August 1964), King Center Archives, pp. 10–11.

112. John J. Ansbro, *Martin Luther King, Jr.: The Making of a Mind* (Maryknoll, N.Y.: Orbis Books, 1982), pp. 262 and 264.

113. King, *Why We Can't Wait*, p. 77.

114. *Four Decades of Concern*, p. 45; James H. Cone, "Martin Luther King, Jr., and the Third World," in Albert and Hoffman, eds., *We Shall Overcome*, p. 213; Baldwin, *Toward the Beloved Community*, pp. 85–92; and *International Tribute to Martin Luther King, Jr.* (New York: United Nations, 1979), pp. 1–65.

115. From Coretta Scott King to E. S. Reddy (28 March 1979), King Center Archives, p. 1; and Baldwin, *Toward the Beloved Community*, p. 85.

116. *International Tribute to Martin Luther King, Jr.*, pp. 3 and 37–38; and Baldwin, *Toward the Beloved Community*, pp. 85–86.

117. *International Tribute to Martin Luther King, Jr.*, p. 1.

118. Ibid., pp. 4–5; *Four Decades of Concern*, p. 45; and Baldwin, *Toward the Beloved Community*, p. 87.

119. *International Tribute to Martin Luther King, Jr.*, pp. 8, 13, 26 and 32–33.

120. Ibid., p. 36.

121. Ibid., pp. 39 and 58–59.

122. Ibid., pp. 16–17, 19, 22, and 53; and Baldwin, *Toward the Beloved Community*, pp. 89–90.

123. *International Tribute to Martin Luther King, Jr.*, p. 21.

124. Ibid., pp. 23–24, 27–28, and 48–52.

125. Ibid., pp. 15 and 34.

126. Ibid., pp. 56–57.

127. Ibid., pp. 18–19, 25–26, 28, and 30.

128. Ibid., p. 44.

129. From Reddy to Baldwin (10 April 1994), pp. 1–2; *Annual Report of the U.N. Special Committee Against Apartheid*, unpublished document (1982), p. 39; From Coretta Scott King to E. S. Reddy (4 February 1982), King Center Archives, pp. 1–2; *United Nations General Assembly, Thirty-Seventh Session: Official Records of the 56 Plenary Meeting*, New York, New York (5 November 1982), pp. 963–976; and Baldwin, *Toward the Beloved Community*, pp. 116–118.

130. *Annual Report of the U.N. Special Committee Against Apartheid*, p. 39; *United Nations General Assembly, Thirty-Seventh Session: Official Records*, pp. 963–976; Baldwin, *Toward the Beloved Community*, pp. 116–117; and *Four Decades of Concern*, p. 46.

131. King to Reddy (4 February 1982), pp. 1–2; and Baldwin, *Toward the Beloved Community*, p. 117.

132. *United Nations General Assembly, Thirty-Seventh Session: Official Records*, pp. 971–972.

133. Reddy to Baldwin (10 April 1994), pp. 1–2; *United Nations General Assembly, Thirty-Seventh Session: Official Records*, pp. 964–976; and Baldwin, *Toward the Beloved Community*, pp. 117–118.

134. *Basic Facts about the United Nations* (1986), appendices, p. 3.

135. *Basic Facts about the United Nations* (1998), pp. 227–228.

136. Ibid., pp. 227–235; Baratta, *United Nations System*, pp. 410–431; and *Everyone's United Nations*, pp. 303–323.

137. *Basic Facts about the United Nations* (1998), p. 76; King, *Where Do We Go from Here?*, p. 184.

138. *Basic Facts about the United Nations* (1998), p. 76; Houser, "Freedom's Struggle Crosses Oceans and Mountains," pp. 189–196; and Baldwin, *Toward the Beloved Community*, p. 128.

139. *Basic Facts about the United Nations* (1998), p. 76; Tessitore and Woolfson, eds., *A Global Agenda*, pp. 11–14; "U.N. to Return Albanians," *Tennessean*, 17 August 1999, p. 4A; "U.N. Is Only Law and Order across Kosovo," *Atlanta Journal-Constitution*, 4 July 1999, pp. A1–A8; "Serbs Pressing U. N. for Kosovo Havens," *Tennessean*, 26 August 1999, p. 5A; "U.N. War Crimes Tribunal Gets Milosevic," *Tennessean*, 29 June 2001, p. 3A; Lynn Huntley, "Combating Racism in the Global Era," *New Crisis*, vol. 108, no. 4 (July–August 2001): pp. 24–26; and Baldwin, *Toward the Beloved Community*, p. 49.

140. The U.N. is already expressing a deep concern for the abuse of women in Pakistan. See "Taliban Blasted for Abuse of Women," *The Tennessean*, 13 September 1999, p. 4A.

141. King, *Where Do We Go from Here?*, pp. 177–181.

142. Tessitore and Woolfson, eds., *A Global Agenda*, pp. 160–162; *Basic Facts about the United Nations* (1998), p. 11; *Everyone's United Nations*, pp. 18–20; and King, *Where Do We Go from Here?*, pp. 178–179.

143. Tessitore and Woolfson, eds., *A Global Agenda*, p. 1.

144. King, *Where Do We Go from Here?*, pp. 181–191; King, *The Trumpet of Conscience*, pp. 63–64 and 68; Baldwin, *To Make the Wounded Whole*, pp. 310–313; *Basic Facts about the United Nations* (1986), chapter 2, pp. 1–43; *Everyone's United Nations*, pp. 42–155; *Basic Facts about the United Nations* (1998), pp. 68–224; and Tessitore and Woolfson, eds., *A Global Agenda*, pp. 1–158.

145. King, *Where Do We Go from Here?*, pp. 186–190.

Epilogue

ROGER D. HATCH

A contemporary observer of American society might conclude that Martin Luther King, Jr.'s dream of a racially transformed America has largely been realized. African Americans are among the news anchors in major television markets. African American athletes star on sports teams at both southern and northern universities. Advertisements aimed at general—not just black—consumers often feature black models. A whole range of jobs has opened up to African Americans. Black elected officials have occupied seats at almost every level of government, and this is still the case. School curricula regularly include attention to such figures as Rosa Parks and King. And the third Monday in January is a national holiday honoring the birth of Martin Luther King, Jr.

But most of these changes are superficial. A more careful look suggests that in many key areas of life little has changed in the three decades since King's death, and that King and his ideas have been opposed, distorted, and trivialized. In effect, Americans have embraced Martin Luther King, Jr., as a personality, but have not taken seriously his ideas and his commitment to racial justice and political empowerment for all people.

This failure to properly honor and build on King's legacy is evident even at the highest levels of our nation's political life. It was reflected in President Richard M. Nixon's "benign neglect" toward racial matters, in President Gerald Ford's reluctance to seriously enforce existing civil rights laws, in President Jimmy Carter's mixed and multiple messages on race, in President Ronald Reagan's politics of racial backlash, in President George Bush's exploitation of white male fears regarding affirmative action, and in President Bill Clinton's abandonment of Jocelyn Elders, Lani Guinier, and other African Americans "who promised something more than the superficial."[1] And there is no reason to believe that President George W. Bush, with his conservative political agenda, will do any more than the previous six presidents to translate King's dream into practical reality.

In his final book, *Where Do We Go from Here: Chaos or Community?*, published in 1967, just a year before his death, King looked back at the recent gains of the civil rights movement. He noted especially the passage of the 1964 Civil Rights Act, which provided for nondiscrimination in public accommodations and in employment, and the 1965 Voting Rights Act, which extended the right to vote and hold public office to every qualified American citizen. King described the range of apparently ordinary citizens, black and white, who came together to support the civil rights movement. "These were the best of America," he wrote, but they were "not all of America. Elsewhere the commitment was shallow. . . . Justice at the deepest level had but few stalwart champions."[2]

It had been a very difficult, decade-long struggle, beginning with the Montgomery bus boycott in 1955–1956. There had been failures and setbacks, as well as progress. Some lost hope and many died. Yet King accurately predicted that what lay ahead was going to be even more difficult:

> The practical cost of change for the nation up to this point has been cheap. The limited reforms have been obtained at bargain rates. There are no expenses, and no taxes are required, for (black people) to share lunch counters, libraries, parks, hotels, and other facilities with whites. . . . Even the more significant changes involving voter registration required neither large monetary nor psychological sacrifice. . . . The real cost lies ahead. The stiffening of white resistance is recognition of that fact. The discount education given (black people) will in the future have to be purchased at full price if quality education is to be realized. Jobs are harder and costlier to create than voting rolls. The eradication of slums (that) house millions is complex far beyond integrating buses and lunch counters.[3]

So King foresaw a difficult struggle as the civil rights movement worked to complete its mission. He saw that achieving quality, desegregated education and providing good, integrated housing would be very difficult. What King had no way of foreseeing, however, was just how formidable the opposition would be. Nor could King have foreseen how his opponents in the struggle for racial justice would twist his own words until they were routinely used as a weapon *against* measures seeking more racial justice.

So today, partly as a result of opposition to, and distortion and trivialization of, Martin Luther King, Jr.'s vision and message, contemporary American life continues to demonstrate racial disparities in employment and unemployment, the justice system and the courts, health and health care, and family life and political representation.

Were he able to comment on these current racial disparities, Martin Luther King, Jr., might ask, as he did in 1967: "Why is equality so assiduously avoided? Why does white America delude itself, and how does it rationalize the evil it retains?"

The majority of white Americans consider themselves sincerely committed to justice for African Americans. They believe that American society is essentially hospitable to fair play and to steady growth toward a middle-class utopia embodying racial harmony. But unfortunately, this is a fantasy of self-deception and comfortable vanity. . . . America has been sincere and even ardent in welcoming some change. But too quickly, apathy and disinterest rise to the surface when the next logical steps are to be taken.

This book has explored in rich detail much of King's understanding of the ways that religion and morality must interact with law and politics if Americans are ever to create a more democratic and inclusive society and a more just and peaceful world. King understood that achieving the Beloved Community is a difficult task, and that the obstacles are many. It requires more than superficial changes and the sporadic commitments of well-meaning individuals. After reading this book, let us devote ourselves not only to understanding King and his ideas better, but, more important, to working together to achieve—in our day, and in the particular avenues available to us—some of the goals for which he fought and died.

NOTES

1. Kenneth O'Reilly, *Nixon's Piano: Presidents and Racial Politics from Washington to Clinton* (New York: Free Press, 1995), p. 417.

2. Martin Luther King, Jr., *Where Do We Go from Here: Chaos or Community?* (New York: Harper & Row, 1967), p. 10.

3. Ibid., p. 6.

Contributors

Lewis V. Baldwin is Professor in the Department of Religious Studies at Vanderbilt University and the author of numerous articles and books on religion and civil rights. His works include *There Is a Balm in Gilead: The Cultural Roots of Martin Luther King, Jr.* (1991), *To Make the Wounded Whole: The Cultural Legacy of Martin Luther King, Jr.* (1992), and *Toward the Beloved Community: Martin Luther King, Jr., and South Africa* (1995).

Rufus Burrow, Jr., is Professor of Theological Social Ethics at Christian Theological Seminary and the author of numerous articles on the theological and social dimensions of the African American experience. He is also the author of *James H. Cone and Black Liberation Theology* (1994) and *Personalism: A Critical Introduction* (1999).

Clayborne Carson is Professor of History at Stamford University and director and senior editor of the Martin Luther King, Jr., Papers Project, an anticipated fourteen-volume, chronologically arranged edition of the civil rights leader's speeches and writings. Dr. Carson is also the author of numerous books and essays on King and the civil rights movement, among them *In Struggle: SNCC and the Black Awakening of the 1960s* (1981).

Roger D. Hatch is Professor of Religion at Central Michigan University, where he teaches social ethics. His publications deal with the relationship between religion, race, and politics in America. He is the author of *Beyond Opportunity: Jesse Jackson's Vision of America* (1988).

BARBARA HOLMES is Professor in ethics and African American Religious Studies at Memphis Theological Seminary and holds doctoral degrees in both ethics and law. She writes and teaches on the intersection of law and religion and is the author of *A Private Woman in Public Spaces: Barbara Jordan's Speeches on Ethics, Public Religion, and Law* (2000).

SUSAN HOLMES WINFIELD holds a law degree and was appointed to the Superior Court bench in 1984 by President Ronald Reagan. Judge Winfield has served as an Adjunct Trial Practice Professor at George Washington University, Columbia School of Law, and the Harvard University Law School Advocacy Program.

Index